Trump Fights Back with Statements

Against the Lies of Joe Biden, Attacks from Dems, and the Bias of the Media, of Big Tech, and of the J6 Commission

By Gary F. Zeolla

Table of Contents

Chapters – 11

Appendixes ... 329

About the Author

The author has a B.S. in Nutrition Science (Penn State; 1983) and attended Denver Seminary from 1988-1990. Zeolla is the director, webmaster, and primary writer for his four websites:

Zeolla.org personal website (www.Zeolla.org)
Darkness to Light Christian Ministry (www.Zeolla.org/Christian)
Fitness for One and All (www.Zeolla.org/Fitness)
Biblical and Constitutional Politics (www.Zeolla.org/Politics)

Zeolla is the translator of the *Analytical-Literal Translation of the Bible* and the author of over 30 Christian, fitness, and politics books. He is also a powerlifter, holding fifteen all-time world records and over a 100 federation records.

A detailed autobiography is available on his personal website. Details on these writings are found in Appendixes Two and Three.

Format Comments

The propensity of the mainstream media (MSM) to take Trump's words out for context is one of the reasons for this book. It presents Trump's entire Statements, unedited, except to sometimes add paragraphing and to redact foul language. That way, readers can read what Trump wrote for themselves, without the MSM's spin on it. Foul words are replaced with "[expletive]."

The Bibliography in Appendix One of this book contains an extensive list of references documenting the claims I make in my comments. In digital versions of this book, those are clickable links. In that way, readers can finish reading this book then check out the linked to documentation of claims made.

Also, I often refer to my other books in this one. That is because, if I repeated all of the referenced information here, it would extend this book by many pages, probably to being a two-volume set.

Some of my comments are in the second person and refer to "you". These are my responses to Trump's Statements that I posted online and are directed towards him. Others are in the third person and refer to "Trump." These are the ones written just for this book.

Preface

President Donald J. Trump was banned from Twitter on January 8, 2021. But in mid-February 2021, now as a former President, he began to email Statements to the press under his "Save America" banner.

These Statements were often Trump fighting back against now President Joe Biden by exposing the disastrous nature of Biden's policies and Biden's attempts to blame Trump for the problems that Biden's policies were creating.

The Statements also reflect Trump fighting back against the ongoing bias of the mainstream media (MSM) and of Big Tech and against the Dem-controlled J6 Commission or better Select Committee (which Trump calls the "Unselect Committee") investigating the tragic events of January 6, 2021 (J6).

Trump also often endorses political candidates in his Statements and touts his record in his endorsed candidates' victories. Plus, he reminds readers of his accomplishments as President, as compared to the failures of President Biden.

This book reproduces those Statements from when Trump began to issue them in mid-February 2021 to the end of April 2022. It also includes comments by this author that were posted in response to Trump's Statements. I have added an occasional "Extended Comment" to provide further context and commentary to some of his Statements.

The End Date

The end date of April 30, 2022 is because the month before, in March 2022, Trump's own social media site "Truth Social" went online. But it was not until April 29 that Trump began to post "Truths" on it rather than issuing emailed Statements.

With that change, Trump began to post Truths much more often than he had been issuing Statements. However, his Truths were limited to the 500-character limit of Truth Social and most often were just links to news articles. As such, they would not be worth reproducing.

Therefore, ending this book with the end of his emailed Statements seemed fitting. But I will reproduce one class of his Truths for another book to be mentioned shortly.

But here, if you enjoyed reading Trump's Tweets on Twitter until January 8, 2021 or are enjoying his Truths on Truth Social since April 29, 2022, then you should enjoy this book, as it fills in the gap with all of his email Statements issued between those dates.

Related Books

This book is a follow-up to three prior books:

Alleged Corruption, Bias, and Fraud: Allegations of the Corruption of Joe Biden, Bias of the Media and Big Tech, and Fraud in the 2020 Election.

Trump's 2020 Election Tweets, Georgia Phone Call, and January 2021 Speeches: Did Trump's Claims of Election Fraud Lead to the Capital Building Uprising?

Tragic Ending to Donald J. Trump's Great Presidency: Capitol Building Uprising Leads to Impeachment 2.0, as Media and Big Tech Bias and Claims of Election Fraud Continues.

The *Corruption* book covers events surrounding the disputed 2020 presidential election up it the end of 2020.

The *Trump's Tweets* book presents all that Trump said about the election from Election Day 2020 through the end of his presidency on January 20, 2021.

The *Tragic Ending* book covers events to the end of Trump's presidency, plus the second impeachment and Senate trial that occurred in February 2021, plus additional later updates.

This *Fights Back* book picks up the story after the Senate trial in February 2021.

Also picking up the story about that time is my two-volume set *Joe Biden Tweets During the First Year of His Failing Presidency: Reversing Trump, while Dividing and Destroying America.*

These books together cover the transition period from the presidency of Donald J. Trump into the presidency of Joseph R. Biden Jr.

Add in my three-volume set *Dems Cannot Beat Trump, So They Impeach Trump* and my earlier book *Tearing the USA Apart: From Kavanaugh, to Incivility, to Caravans, to Violence, to the 2018 Midterm Elections, and Beyond*, along with my politics website (www.Zeolla.org/Politics), and you have a detailed record of the entirety of the presidency of Donald J. Trump on into the start of Biden's presidency.

A future book to note will be my book *The Biased J6 Committee: The Public Hearings Were Half a Trial; This Book Gives You the Other Half.* As with my *Tragic Ending* book, it will also cover the January 6th uprising but by way of responding to that very biased Committee.

Trump does that with his Statements recorded in this book and with Truths later, which I will reproduce in the *J6 Committee* book.

6

Definitions

This Introductory Page will define some terms that are important to understand in reading this book.

First, the name of this writer's politics website is "Biblical and Constitutional Politics." I describe it as, "Political news and commentary from a conservative Christian and politically conservative perspective."

To define these terms, "Conservative Christian" includes the belief that the Bible is God-breathed and fully reliable in all that it teaches and is the divine and final authority on all matters it addresses, including politics. Conversely, a "liberal Christian" would deny the divine inspiration, reliability, and ultimate authority of the Bible.

"Politically conservative" refers to the belief in limited government, separation of powers, traditional values, personal and national security, capitalism, freedom and liberty, and most of all, an adherence to the Constitution of the United States, following an originalist interpretation thereof.

The definition of "politically liberal" would be mostly opposite of all these aspects of politically conservative, beginning with "big federal government" instead of "limited government." That would then lead to an erosion of the rest of the points.

Conservatives are often said to be on the "right," while liberals are said to be on the "left."

Republicans generally claim to be conservatives, while Democrats are generally liberal, though some prefer the term "progressive." That word is seen in YourDictionary's definition of liberal. "Progressive is someone who advocates for reform and change."

The term "leftist" is often used interchangeable with liberal, though the two are not exactly the same. A leftist is defined as, "a person whose political position is of the left (noun), esp., a communist or socialist."

The difference is, a liberal will advocate for some socialist policies, such as universal government run health care, but is not fully a socialist, while a leftist will advocate for full socialism.

Also, the definition of liberal says, "tolerant of views differing from one's own." That is truer of conservatives than liberals, and not at all true of leftists. As a result, a leftist is more likely to engage in civil disobedience and even uncivil disobedience than a liberal.

States and areas are color coded as to how they tend to vote. A "red" state tends to vote Republican, while a "blue" state tends to vote Democrat. You can remember the difference by both "red" and "Republican" beginning with "re."

A swing state or area, which is to say, one that sometimes votes Republican and sometimes Democrat, is called a "purple" state. That of course comes from the fact that mixing blue and red produces purple.

By "Mainstream Media" (MSM) is meant traditional and generally liberal news outlets like ABC, CBS, NBC, CNN, MSNBC, The New York Times (NYT), and The Washington Post (WaPo).

Conservative news outlets are generally newer news agencies, like Fox News Channel (FNC), Fox Business Network (FBN), Breitbart, and The Daily Caller, plus The Wall Street Journal (WSJ).

By "Dems" is meant elected and non-elected Democrat officials in Washington D.C. Specifically, the Democrat members of the US House of Representatives and Democrat Senators in the Senate, along with their staff and other support personal, and all of the other non-elected Democrat bureaucrats in the nation's capital. It must be noted, the term "Dems" does *not* refer to the average registered Democrat US voter.

Similarly, by "Repubs" is meant the same, except to substitute "Republican" for "Democrat" in the preceding paragraph.

Abbreviations Used in this Book

These pages list the abbreviations used in this book.

AG – Attorney General
ALT – *Analytical Literal Translation of the Bible* (authors' translation). All Scripture quotes in this book are from the ALT.
Antifa – Anti-Fascist, though Antifa is in fact a fascist group, so "Protifa" would be a better nickname.
AOC – Alexandria Ocasio-Cortez (a NYC US House Representative)
BCP – Biblical and Constitutional Politics (author's politics website)
BLM – Black Lives Matter (the left-wing group, not the slogan)
CV – Coronavirus
Dem – Democrat, referring to government officials, not voters
DHS – Department of Homeland Security
DNC – Democratic National Committee/ Convention
DOJ – Department of Justice
DNI – Director of National Intelligence
ECA – Electoral Count Act of 1887
FBI – Federal Bureau of Investigation
FBN – Fox Business Network
FISA – Foreign Intelligence Surveillance Act
FLOTUS – First Lady of the United States
FNC – Fox News Channel
GOP – Grand Old Party (another name for the Republican Party)
HFAC – House Foreign Affairs Committee
HIC – House Intelligence Committee
HJC – House Judiciary Committee
HOC – House Oversight Committee
IC – Intelligence Community
IG – Inspector General
ISIS – Islamic State in Iraq and Syria
J6 – Capitol Building Uprising of January 6, 2021
MAGA – Make America Great Again
MSM – Mainstream Media (outlets like CNN, MSNBC, NYT, WaPo)
NAFTA – North American Free Trade Agreement (old trade deal)
NATO – North Atlantic Treaty Organization.
NDAA – National Defense Authorization Act
NSA – National Security Advisor
NSC – National Security Council
NYC – New York City
NYP – New York Post

NYT – New York Times

OIG – Office of the Inspector General

OLC – Office of Legal Counsel (for the Executive Branch)

POTUS – President of the United States

Rep – Representative in the US House, unless indicated as in a particular state House

Repub – Republican, referring to government officials, not voters

RNC – Republican National Committee/ Convention

SCOPA – Supreme Court of Pennsylvania

SCOTUS – Supreme Court of the United States

SFAC – Senate Foreign Affairs Committee

SHSC – Senate Homeland Security Committee

SIC – Senate Intelligence Committee

SJC – Senate Judiciary Committee

SOC – Senate Oversight Committee

SOTU – State of the Union (Address)

USMCA – United States, Mexico, Canada Agreement (new trade deal)

WaPo – Washington Post

WSJ – Wall Street Journal

Chapters

Chapter One
Trump's Statements
Background

Donald J. Trump was banned from Twitter and other social media sites in early January 2021. I cover his ban from Twitter in my book *Trump's 2020 Election Tweets, Georgia Phone Call, and January 2021 Speeches: Did Trump's Claims of Election Fraud Lead to the Capitol Building Uprising?*, hereafter referred to as my *Trump's Tweets* book.

My answer to the question posed by the subtitle is "No" for reasons explained in that book. That is why Trump was acquitted in the second Senate impeachment trial, in which he was charged with inciting the Capitol Building uprising.

That trial is covered in my book *Tragic Ending to Donald J. Trump's Great Presidency: Capitol Building Uprising Leads to Impeachment 2.0, as Media and Big Tech Bias and Claims of Election Fraud Continues*, hereafter referred to as my *Tragic Ending* book.

Despite that acquittal, Trump remained banned from Twitter and other social media sites. Therefore, starting in mid-February 2021, he began to issue Statement via email to various news outlets.

Meanwhile, alternative social media site Gab.com copied all of Trump's tweets before Twitter closed his account. Gab then set up an account for Trump on Gab and reprinted all of those tweets. They then began adding Trump's Statements as he issued them.

The "About" for the @RealDonaldTrump page initially read:
Reserved for the 45th President of the United States of America. This account is an uncensored Twitter archive and shares email statements sent by The Office of Donald J. Trump.

Later, that About was changed to:
Reserved for the 45th President of the United States of America. This account is an uncensored Twitter archive and shares email statements sent by The Office of Donald J. Trump.
Member since August 2016

That member line is not when Gab began to post Trump's Statements but when Trump first began to post on Twitter. But since Gab copied all of those tweets back to 2016, it uses that date.

Gab says Trump can take over this account any time he wants. But until then, Gab will continue to post his email Statements as they are issued. For this book, I have also reproduced Trump's email Statements, occasionally followed by comments by yours truly.

At first, Gab posted Trump's statements as an image, so I had to transcribe the text myself. Also at first, Trump did not issue many Statements. But eventually, he began to issue them more often. Gab then posted his statements as both an image and as text. I appreciated that change, as it made it much easier for me to copy his messages. Later, Gab only posted the Statements as text. In the initial image, each of these messages began with a graphic reading:

Save America
President Donald J. Trump

I will only quote that header the first two times to show the format. After that, I will distinguish my words from Trump's words by beginning Trump's Statements as Gab does with "Donald J Trump @RealDonaldTrump" and ending them with the date.

I will then begin my comments with "To comment." These comments for the most part were posted on Gab as I was copying Trump's Statements. Gab has a 2,000 character limit, so I generally did not expanded on my comment for inclusion here.

Longer comments by me are prefixed by "Extended Comment." Most of these were written just for this book to provide further context and commentary on a topic mentioned by Trump in a Statement.

I will go through the Statements chronologically. I will not put them into block quotes, as that would extend this book by many pages.

I have included the URL for articles and videos Trump refers to. These are clickable links in digital versions of this book.

Some of Trump's Statements were formatted as one long paragraph. I have broken them up into smaller paragraphs. Also, unfortunately, Trump occasionally uses foul language in his Statements, as he does in his speeches. As a Christian, that is one aspect of Trump's language that I take offense at, so foul words are replaced with "[expletive]." Otherwise, Trump's Statements are reprinted in full without editing.

Trump did not issue any Statements in January 2021, so my reprinting of his Statements begins with the next chapter with his February 13, 2021 Statement. Trump did not issue very many Statements initially, so there are a lot of skipped dates in that chapter. But in the following chapters, almost every date has at least one Statement.

Chapter Two
Trump's Statements
February 2021

This chapter begins the reproduction of Trump's Statements.

February 13, 2021

After his acquittal in the second Senate impeachment trial, Trump issued the following Statement that was posted as an image on Gab.

Statement by Donald J. Trump, 45th President of the United States of America. February 13, 2021

I want to first thank my team of dedicated lawyers and others for their tireless work upholding justice and defending truth.

My deepest thanks as well to all of the United States Senators and Members of Congress who stood proudly for the Constitution we all revere and for the sacred legal principles at the heart of our country.

Our cherished Constitutional Republic was founded on the impartial rule of law, the indispensable safeguard for our liberties, our rights and our freedoms.

It is a sad commentary on our times that one political party in America is given a free pass to denigrate the rule of law, defame law enforcement, cheer mobs, excuse rioters, and transform justice into a tool of political vengeance, and persecute, blacklist, cancel and suppress all people and viewpoints with whom or which they disagree. I always have, and always will, be a champion for the unwavering rule of law, the heroes of law enforcement, and the right of Americans to peacefully and honorably debate the issues of the day without malice and without hate.

This has been yet another phase of the greatest witch hunt in the history of our Country. No president has ever gone through anything like it, and it continues because our opponents cannot forget the almost 75 million people, the highest number ever for a sitting president, who voted for us just a few short months ago.

15

I also want to convey my gratitude to the millions of decent, hardworking, law-abiding, God-and-Country loving citizens who have bravely supported these important principles in these very difficult and challenging times.

Our historic, patriotic and beautiful movement to Make America Great Again has only just begun. In the months ahead I have much to share with you, and I look forward to continuing our incredible journey together to achieve American greatness for all of our people. There has never been anything like it!

We have so much work ahead of us, and soon we will emerge with a vision for a bright, radiant, and limitless American future. Together there is nothing we cannot accomplish.

We remain one People, one family, and one glorious nation under God, and it's our responsibility to preserve this magnificent inheritance for our children and for generations of Americans to come.

May God bless all of you, and may God forever bless the United States of America.

To comment. Trump is referring to his acquittal in the second Senate impeachment trial. I cover that trial and all that led up to it and its aftermath in my *Tragic Ending* book.

February 17, 2021

The Office of Donald J. Trump
February 17, 2021

Statement by Donald J. Trump, 45th President of the United States.

The great Rush Limbaugh has passed away to a better place, free from physical pain and hostility. His honor, courage, strength, and loyalty will never be replaced. Rush was a patriot, a defender of Liberty, and someone who believed in all the greatness our Country stand for. Rush was a friend to myself and millions of Americans—a guiding light with the ability to see the truth and to paint vivid pictures over the airwaves. Melania and I express our deepest condolences to his wonderful wife, Kathryn, his family, and all his dedicated fans. He will be greatly missed.

Trump Fights Back with Statements

To comment, Trump is referring to the death of the premier conservative commentator Rush Limbaugh on February 17, 2001.

Extended Comment
The Death and Legacy of Rush Limbaugh

I knew things were not looking good when Rush Limbaugh had not been behind the EIB microphone since January 22, 2021. Then when his wife Kathryn Limbaugh was introduced at the start of his show on February 17, I knew it was not good. She said she knew she was not the Limbaugh people were tuning in to hear. Then she announced the sad news that Rush had passed away that morning.

Conservatives everywhere will be mourning his passing. But I rejoice that I have been listening to Rush since my pastor told me about him back in the summer of 1991. Rush gave voice to my conservative views and helped to form them.

But most of all, I rejoice that Rush had mentioned in a show late last year that his faith in the LORD had deepened since his cancer diagnosis in January of last year (2020). It sounds like he had truly trusted in Jesus Christ as his Lord and Savior. Therefore, Kathryn was correct in saying he is now in heaven. He will be missed, but it blunts the loss knowing he is now in a better place. As Rush once stated:

> "I told the staff today that I have a deeply personal relationship with God that I do not proselytize about, but I do, and I have been working that relationship tremendously" (Newsmax. Rush).

What Paul the Apostle said about himself could be said about Rush:

> [7]I have fought the good fight; I have finished the course [or, race]; I have kept the faith. [8]Finally, [there] is laid up for me the victor's wreath [or, crown] of righteousness which the Lord, the Righteous Judge, will give to me in that Day, but not only to me, but also to all the ones having loved His appearing (2Timothy 4:7-8).

Media Bias Seen in Coverage of Rush's Death:

The reaction of the mainstream media (MSM) to Rush's death was predictable. A large headline about his passing was seen on the websites for Fox News and Newsmax, with a link to a glowing article about him. Those headlines were still prominent the next day.

The Fox News article begins:

Rush Limbaugh, the monumentally influential media icon who transformed talk radio and politics in his decades behind the microphone, helping shape the modern-day Republican Party, died Wednesday morning at the age of 70 after a battle with lung cancer, his family announced....

Limbaugh is considered one of the most influential media figures in American history and has played a consequential role in conservative politics since "The Rush Limbaugh Show" began in 1988. Perched behind his Golden EIB (Excellence in Broadcasting) Microphone, Limbaugh spent over three decades as arguably both the most beloved and polarizing person in American media (Fox News. Rush).

The Newsmax article states about Rush:

Conservative icon Rush Limbaugh, who single-handedly created the era of national political talk radio and had the most listened to program in U.S. history, died Wednesday of lung cancer a year after announcing his diagnosis with the disease. He was 70.

A cultural force with a cumulative weekly radio audience of more than 20 million at his peak, an author of seven books — two of which were New York Times best sellers, and the host of a nationally syndicated TV show, Limbaugh was hailed by Republicans and conservatives and derided by Democrats and liberals (Newsmax. Rush).

Both Fox News and Newsmax also had many accompanying articles paying tribute to Rush. And again, these accompanying articles were still prominent on their home pages the next day.

However, CNN had a much smaller headline that disappeared by the next day. The article it linked to was not so complimentary. It called Rush "a partisan force and polarizing figure in American politics" and said, "he often waded into conspiratorial waters and generated controversy for hateful commentary on gender and race" and had a "penchant for pushing conspiracy theories and peddling misinformation" and "divisive rhetoric and inflammatory comments." And that was it on CNN. There were no tribute articles.

Meanwhile, on TV, both Fox News and Newsmax spent much of the day talking about Rush, with his death being the top story on every show I watched. CNN and *CBS Evening News* both had reports about Rush, but they were near the end of the shows I saw.

18

Trump Fights Back with Statements

On CNN's Anderson Cooper, the piece about Rush declared without qualification that Rush, "promoted lies and conspiracy theories" and that he was "a racist and sexist." More on that "racist" charge in a moment. But here, at least the CBS segment was fair, except for Norah O'Donnell introducing it by saying Rush was "a deeply polarizing figure."

My local TV and radio new stations had quick mentions about Rush, but mostly to indicate he had gotten his start here in Pittsburgh. My local newspaper's website also focused on his local beginnings.

The headline read, "Before making it big, Rush Limbaugh got his start in Pittsburgh as 'Jeff Christie.'" The article then talks about him working for radio stations WIXZ and KQV. He got fired from both jobs, and was told by KQV general manager John Gibbs when he fired Rush, he, "would never make it as an on-air talent and that he should think about going into sales."

My local newspaper comments, "But it wouldn't be too many more years before Limbaugh would have the last laugh and make John Gibbs eat his words" (Trib Live. Before).

Newsmax also correctly pointed out Rush was, "a devout Pittsburgh Steelers fan from his time on radio in Western Pennsylvania."

In any case, by the next day, Newsmax was still leading with stories about Rush, while Fox and CNN were leading with stories about the power outages in Texas after a winter storm.

Checking the web the next day, I couldn't even find an article about Rush in the long list of articles on the home page of Yahoo! News. The same goes for the home pages of Reuters and the AP. But there was a reprint of an AP article on my local newspaper's website, though the link was buried way at the bottom of the home page. However, that article was mostly fair in its coverage. It begins:

> You didn't have to like or even listen to Rush Limbaugh to be affected by what he did.
> Conservative talk radio wasn't a genre before him. Without Limbaugh, it's hard to imagine a Fox News Channel, or a President Donald Trump, or a media landscape defined by shouters of all stripes that both reflect and influence a state of political gridlock.
> To his fans, Limbaugh's death Wednesday of lung cancer at the age of 70 was an occasion for deep mourning. For his foes, it was good riddance. Somewhere, Rush could surely appreciate it.
> He left a legacy.

The AP article also indicated the difference in coverage of Rush's death:

> The headline on HuffPost's obituary on Wednesday said Limbaugh "saturated America's airwaves with cruel bigotries, lies and conspiracy theories." The Root called him a "spouter of racist, hate-filled garbage."
>
> On Foxnews.com, Limbaugh's obituary's headline was "Greatest of All Time" (Trib/ AP. Even).

That difference could be seen in the coverage by the *New York Times* (NYT). Its website had two articles halfway down its home page. The main article was titled, "Rush Limbaugh Dies at 70; Turned Talk Radio Into a Right-Wing Attack Machine. It begins, "With a following of 15 million and a divisive style of mockery, grievance and denigrating language, he was a force in reshaping American conservatism." It then claims:

> He became a singular figure in the American media, fomenting mistrust, grievances and even hatred on the right for Americans who did not share their views, and he pushed baseless claims and toxic rumors long before Twitter and Reddit became havens for such disinformation.
>
> In politics, he was not only an ally of Mr. Trump but also a precursor, combining media fame, right-wing scare tactics and over-the-top showmanship to build an enormous fan base and mount attacks on truth and facts.

The NYT had an accompanying article titled, "Rush Limbaugh's Legacy of Venom: As Trump Rose, 'It All Sounded Familiar.'" It then claims:

> Weaponizing conspiracy theories and bigotry long before Donald Trump's ascent, the radio giant helped usher in the political style that came to dominate the Republican Party....
>
> Few media stars were as crucial in making disinformation, false rumors and fringe ideas the right's new reality....
>
> Mr. Limbaugh's recklessness with the truth and lack of any evident concern for the danger posed by feeding paranoia on the right served him well once Mr. Trump became the Republican nominee in 2016 and later the president.

Trump Fights Back with Statements

Such is how much the left first hated Rush Limbaugh and then hated Donald J. Trump. But worst is the NYT made it sound like Rush made up Bo Snerdly, his longtime producer and call screener:

> Unlike Howard Stern, Don Imus and other big names in shock radio, Mr. Limbaugh had no on-the-air sidekicks, though he had conversations with the unheard voice of someone he called "Bo Snerdly." Nor did he have writers, scripts or out-lines, just notes and clippings from newspapers he perused daily (NYT. Rush).

The reason for this doubt that Bo even existed is that Bo is a black man, so his longtime association with Rush would destroy the narrative of the MSM that Rush was a racist.

> Far from being a fiction of Limbaugh's apparently broad imagination, a quick Google search for "Bo Snerdly" brings up Bo Snerdley, the pseudonym of James Golden, Limbaugh's screener, producer, and engineer. Wikipedia states that Golden, aka Bo Snerdley, "has been a Producer/Executive for Premiere Networks, the largest radio syndication company in the United States" since 2001.
>
> Golden is, it should be noted, a black man – making this yet another instance of the "anti-racist" liberal media erasing a suc-cessful black man (Postmillennial. New).

I can attest to Bo being real, as he did speak on Rush's show once, back in early February 2020, shortly after Rush revealed about his can-cer diagnosis. After Rush's well-known intro music played, Bo came on the air, sounding very embarrassed. He said, "This has never happened before. Rush isn't here yet."

Yes, Rush was late for the start of his own show. But he had a good reason—he was speaking with POTUS. Apparently, Trump had called Rush shortly prior to noon and was inviting Rush to his State of the Union address (SOTU).

I discuss Rush receiving the Medal of Freedom at Trump's State of the Union Address in February 2020 in *Volume Three* of my three-vol-ume set *Dems Cannot Beat Trump, So They Impeach Trump*, hereafter referred to as my *Impeach* trilogy. But here was when Rush's appear-ance at the SOTU was being planned around his cancer treatments.

In any case, due to talking to President Trump about the arrange-ments, Rush was late, so Bo took over the EIB microphone and adlibbed for a few minutes, until Rush showed up. Given this situation, it was quite disingenuous for the NYT to insinuate Bo doesn't even exist and just plain wrong for them to say he was an "unheard voice." He was heard, at least on this one occasion.

Dems and Celebrities on Rush:
Additional Tributes to Rush:

In the References in Appendix One are listed article with quotes from Democrats and celebrities. Their bias against Rush is just as strong as that of the MSM. But also listed are additional glowing tributes to Rush from a wide variety of people, from Trump's VP Mike Pence to Israeli Prime Minister Benjamin Netanyahu. The difference in their take on Rush is as striking as that of the MSM versus conservative media.

Rush at CPAC:

The following excerpt from Rush's speech at CPAC back in 2009 will give the reader the tone of his ideas.

> While Limbaugh made his career on radio, a speech he delivered at the Conservative Political Action Conference (CPAC) in 2009 is widely considered one of the most important moments of his career -- an explanation of "who conservatives are" that caused the crowd to erupt with chants of "USA! USA!"
>
> "We love people. When we look out over the United States of America, when we are anywhere, when we see a group of people, such as this or anywhere, we see Americans. We see human beings. We don't see groups. We don't see victims. We don't see people we want to exploit. What we see -- what we see is potential. We do not look out across the country and see the average American, the person that makes this country work. We do not see that person with contempt. We don't think that person doesn't have what it takes. We believe that person can be the best he or she wants to be if certain things are just removed from their path like onerous taxes, regulations and too much government," Limbaugh told the crowd.
>
> "We want every American to be the best he or she chooses to be. We recognize that we are all individuals. We love and revere our founding documents, the Constitution and the Declaration of Independence," he continued. "We believe that the preamble to the Constitution contains an inarguable truth that we are all endowed by our creator with certain inalienable rights, among them life, liberty, Freedom and the pursuit of happiness" (Fox News. Rush)

Back to Trump and the rest of his Statements for February 2021.

February 24, 2021

Donald J Trump @RealDonaldTrump
Endorsement of Bob Paduchik
Bob Paduchik is running for Chair of the Republican Party of Ohio. He successfully led my campaign in both 2016 and 2020, having even more success the second time around. He is outstanding in every way, and I give him my full and complete endorsement. Bob loves our country and the Great State of Ohio. He will be an outstanding Chairman! President Donald J. Trump. February 24, 2021

Extended Comment
Trump's Endorsements

Breitbart reported about this first endorsement by Trump:
Former President Trump endorsed Bob Paduchik for Chair of the Republican Party of Ohio....

Trump's first endorsement comes as he begins screening 2022 midterm candidates who are eager to forward MAGA policies while ensuring every open Republican seat has a MAGA-approved contender vying for it.

Trump has received dozens of requests from prospective candidates who wish to earn his support, and he is fielding them as he sees fit. Trump has rejected meetings with former South Carolina governor and 2024 hopeful Nikki Haley and with some House and Senate GOP candidates vying for his ear (Breitbart. Trump Announces).

Therefore, Trump is going to be picky about whom he endorses. He will not be endorsing just anyone who asks, even former members of his administration like Nikki. She was his UN Ambassador, but she fell out of his favor over her comments about him in regard to the events of January 6, 2021, hereafter referred to as J6. I cover that day and its aftermath in my *Tragic Ending* book.

In any case, the AP reports about the rift between the two of them:
Former U.N. Ambassador Nikki Haley, often mentioned as a possible 2024 GOP presidential contender, is among the latest

from her party to denounce President Donald Trump's comments stoking supporters to mount a violent assault on the Capitol.

"He was badly wrong with his words," Haley said Thursday [1/7/21] during a speech at the Republican National Committee's winter meeting, according to excerpts obtained by The Associated Press. "His actions since Election Day will be judged harshly by history."

She called it "deeply disappointing" because of the effect it will have on the legacy of the Trump administration.

"It's a real shame, because I am one who believes our country made some truly extraordinary gains in the last four years," Haley said. She cited the withdrawal from the Iran nuclear pact and confirmation of three Supreme Court justices (AP. Haley).

February 26, 2021

Donald J Trump @RealDonaldTrump
Endorsement of Max Miller

Max Miller is a wonderful person who did a great job at the White House and will be a fantastic Congressman. He is a Marine Veteran, a son of Ohio, and a true PATRIOT. Current Rep. Anthony Gonzalez should not be representing the people of the 16th district because he does not represent their interest or their heart. Max Miller has my Complete and Total Endorsement! February 26, 2021

Donald J Trump @RealDonaldTrump
Endorsement of Senator Jerry Moran

Senator Jerry Moran is doing a terrific job for the wonderful people of Kansas. Strong on Military, Vets, the Border, and our Second Amendment, Jerry has my Complete and Total Endorsement for his re-election in 2022! February 26, 2021

These were the first three Trump endorsements, but many more would be forthcoming.

Chapter Three
Trump's Statements
March 2021

These Trump Statements are continued from Chapter Two.

March 2, 2021

Donald J Trump @RealDonaldTrump
Endorsement of Senator Tim Scott

It is my great honor to give Senator Tim Scott of South Carolina my Complete and Total Endorsement. He is both an outstanding Senator and person who works tirelessly for the people of his great state, and the USA. Strong on the Military, Law Enforcement, loves our Vets, protects our Second Amendment and our Borders. Tim will continue to do an OUTSTANDING job for our country! President Donald J. Trump. March 2, 2021

March 5, 2021

Donald J Trump @RealDonaldTrump

Statement by Donald J. Trump, 45th President of the United States of America

The Wall Street Journal editorial page continues, knowingly, to fight for globalist policies such as bad trade deals, open borders, and endless wars that favor other countries and sell out our great American workers, and they fight for RINOS that have so badly hurt the Republican Party. That's where they are and that's where they will always be. Fortunately, nobody cares much about The Wall Street Journal editorial anymore. They have lost great credibility.

To set the record straight, there were two reasons the Senate races were lost in Georgia. First, Republicans did not turn out to vote because they were so angry and disappointed with Georgia Republican leadership and Governor Kemp for failing to stand up to Stacey Abrams and the disastrous Consent Decree that virtually eliminated signature verification requirements across the state (and much worse), and was not approved by the State Legislature as required by the Constitution—having a major impact on the result, a rigged election. Second, Senator Mitch McConnell's refusal to go above $600 per person on the stimulus check payments when the two Democrat opponents were touting $2,000 per person in ad after ad. This latter point was used against our Senators and the $2,000 will be approved anyway by the Democrats who bought the Georgia election—and McConnell let them do it!

Even more stupidly, the National Republican Senatorial Committee spent millions of dollars on ineffective TV ads starring Mitch McConnell, the most unpopular politician in the country, who only won in Kentucky because President Trump endorsed him. He would have lost badly without this endorsement. March 5, 2021

To comment, I discuss the lack of signature verification in my book *Alleged Corruption, Bias, and Fraud: Allegations of the Corruption of Joe Biden, Bias of the Media and Big Tech, and Fraud in the 2020 Election*, hereafter referred to as my *Corruption* book.

I also discuss that issue and the $600 to $2,000 checks in my book *Trump's 2020 Election Tweets, Georgia Phone Call, and January 2021 Speeches: Did Trump's Claims of Election Fraud Lead to the Capitol Building Uprising?*, hereafter referred to as my *Trump's Tweets* book.

Donald J Trump @RealDonaldTrump
Endorsement of Senator John Kennedy

John Kennedy of the Great State of Louisiana is a spectacular Senator and person. He is a tireless advocate for the people of his State, and stands strongly with the forgotten men and women of our Country. Strong on Energy Independence, the Military, our great Vets and the Border, John has my Complete and Total Endorsement!
President Donald J. Trump March 5, 2021

To comment, Kennedy is my favorite Senator. He always makes his point with a humorous quip, like, "There are three things don't hang themselves: Christmas decorations, dry wall, and Jeffery Epstein."

Donald J Trump @RealDonaldTrump
Statement by Donald J. Trump, 45th President of the United States of America

Karl Rove has been losing for years, except for himself. He's a RINO of the highest order, who came to the Oval Office lobbying for 5G for him and a group. After a lengthy discussion with Rove and Chief of Staff Mark Meadows, I said no, they're not qualified. Our Nation can do much better!

On Election Evening, Nov. 3rd, at 10:30pm, Rove called to congratulate me on "a great win." I said thank you Karl, only to watch the rigged election take its final form.

26

Trump Fights Back with Statements

Karl Rove's voice on Fox is always negative for those who know how to win. He certainly hasn't helped Fox in the ratings department, has he?

Never had much of a feeling for Karl, in that I disagreed with so many of the things he says. He's a pompous fool with bad advice and always has an agenda. He ran the campaign for two Senators in Georgia, and did a rotten job with bad ads and concepts. Should have been an easy win, but he and his friend Mitch blew it with their $600 vs. $2,000 proposal. Karl would be much more at home at the disastrous Lincoln Project. I heard they have numerous openings!

If the Republican Party is going to be successful, they're going to have to stop dealing with the likes of Karl Rove and just let him float away, or retire, like Liddle' Bob Corker, Jeff "Flakey" Flake, and others like Toomey of Pennsylvania, who will soon follow. Let's see what happens to Liz Cheney of Wyoming.

If it weren't for me, the House would have lost 25 seats instead of gaining 15—it was a shock to everyone, and almost cost Pelosi her Speaker position. Likewise, 8-10 Senators would have lost their position, including Karl's friend Mitch, our wonderful leader who would rather spend his time fighting me than Pelosi, Schumer, and Sleepy Joe.

In last year's Congressional primaries, 120 of the 122 candidates I endorsed won - and the two that lost were beaten by people claiming to be more Trump than their opponent. In the Senate, I was undefeated in primary endorsements with a record of 21 and 0, and close to that in the general election.

31 million people listened to my CPAC speech online, and it had among the largest television audience of the week, even though it was on cable at 4pm on Sunday afternoon.

Karl Rove is all talk and no action! Next time Karl, save your Election night phone call and keep doing a great job for the Democrats. Fox should get rid of Karl Rove and his ridiculous "whiteboard" as soon as possible! March 5, 2021

To comment, Trump spoke at CPAC on Sunday evening, February 28, 2021. His speech was well received at the event. Conservative news outlets also lauded his speech. But liberal news outlets had a far different take. They declared it was "lie-filled" and vindictive.

In the Bibliography in Appendix One are listed news reports on his speech separated by liberal and conservative news outlets. That way, the reader can see how very different the reporting on his speech was based on the presumptions of the news agency.

Against Lies of Biden, Attacks from Dems, and Bias of Media

Donald J Trump @RealDonaldTrump

Statement by Donald J. Trump, 45th President of the United States of America

Our border is now totally out of control thanks to the disastrous leadership of Joe Biden. Our great Border Patrol and ICE agents have been disrespected, demeaned, and mocked by the Biden Administration. A mass incursion into the country by people who should not be here is happening on an hourly basis, getting worse by the minute. Many have criminal records, and many others have and are spreading covid. Interior enforcement has been shut down—criminals that were once promptly removed by our Administration are now being released back onto the street to commit heinous and violent crimes. ICE officers are desperate to remove these convicted criminals, but Biden won't let them.

The spiraling tsunami at the border is overwhelming local communities, depleting budgets, crowding hospitals, and taking jobs from legal American workers. When I left office, we had achieved the most secure border in our country's history. Under Biden, it will soon be worse, more dangerous, and more out of control than ever before. He has violated his oath of office to uphold our Constitution and enforce our laws.

There has never been a time on our southern border like what is happening now but more importantly, what is about to happen. Now that Biden has implemented nationwide Catch-and-Release, illegal immigrants from every corner of the Earth will descend upon our border and never be returned. You can never have a secure border unless people who cross illegally are promptly removed.

I had a great relationship with Mexico, and its wonderful president, but all of that has been dissipated by the gross incompetence and radicalism of the people currently in charge. The Remain in Mexico Policy was incredible, but immediately abandoned by Biden, probably because it worked so well. Likewise, our Safe Third Agreements in Central America were extraordinarily successful, so Biden foolishly ditched them too. We stopped payment of the hundreds of millions of dollars paid to them and then developed an excellent relationship that made our country and their countries more secure. We put in place powerful rules and procedures to stop the smuggling and trafficking, but the Biden Administration has abandoned these proven strategies and instead given the smugglers and traffickers effective control of our border.

Despite being delayed by years of litigation and politics by the democrats, the wall is almost finished and can be quickly completed. Doing so will save thousands of lives.

The Biden Administration must act immediately to end the border nightmare that they have unleashed onto our Nation. Keep illegal immigration, crime, and the China Virus out of our country! March 5, 2021

To comment, I discuss Biden's disastrous border polices and the crisis they created at our southern border in depth in my two-volume set *Joe Biden Tweets During the First Year of His Failing Presidency: Reversing Trump, while Dividing and Destroying America*, hereafter referred to as my *Biden Tweets* books.

But here, one aspect of that "Reversing Trump" part of the subtitle is Biden's reversal of Trump's border polices, starting with ending construction on the border wall and the "Remain in Mexico" policy. Those two decisions fueled the subsequent crisis that Trump correctly predicted would happen in this Statement.

March 9, 2021

Donald J Trump @RealDonaldTrump
Statement by Donald J. Trump, 45th President of the United States of America

I very much appreciate and respect the career of Senator Roy Blunt of Missouri. He was one of the first people who came to my defense against the Impeachment Hoax #2 (IH-2), and it was greatly appreciated by me. Congratulations to the entire Blunt family, and to Roy on a wonderful career! March 9, 2021

To comment, the occasion for this Statement is Roy Blunt announcing he would not seek reelection.

Missouri GOP Sen. Roy Blunt said Monday [3/8/21] that he won't seek 2022 reelection.

"After 14 General Election victories – three to county office, seven to the United States House of Representatives, and four statewide elections – I won't be a candidate for reelection to the United States Senate next year," Blunt said in a video (Just the News. Missouri).

Donald J Trump @RealDonaldTrump
Statement by Donald J. Trump, 45th President of the United States of America

When I was President, our Southern border was in great shape — stronger, safer, and more secure than ever before. We ended Catch-and-Release, shut down asylum fraud, and crippled the vicious smugglers, drug dealers, and human traffickers. The wall, despite horrendous Democrat delays, would have easily been finished by now, and is working magnificently. Our country is being destroyed at the Southern border, a terrible thing to see! March 9, 2021

March 12, 2021

Donald J Trump @RealDonaldTrump
Wouldn't it be fantastic if the legendary Herschel Walker ran for the United States Senate in Georgia? He would be unstoppable, just like he was when he played for the Georgia Bulldogs, and in the NFL. He is also a GREAT person. Run Herschel, run! March 12, 2021

To comment, later this in fact happened. Herschel threw his hat in the ring to challenge Raphael Warnock. The latter became Senator via the Georgia runoff races I discuss in my *Tragic Ending* book.

Donald J Trump @RealDonaldTrump
I hope everyone remembers when they're getting the COVID-19 (often referred to as the China Virus) Vaccine, that if I wasn't President, you wouldn't be getting that beautiful "shot" for 5 years, at best, and probably wouldn't be getting it at all. I hope everyone remembers! March 12, 2021

To comment, Trump indeed deserves the credit for the Covid vaccines. But sadly, only once did Biden ever give credit to Trump for their development. If Biden had been more gracious and reminded Trump supporters repeatedly that the Covid vaccines were indeed developed under Trump, maybe there would not have been so much vaccine hesitancy among Trump supporters.
I document the many missteps of Biden in regard to Covid in my *Biden Tweets* books. I will discuss the misinformation that led to vaccine hesitancy among conservatives and others in my forthcoming book *Coronavirus Fearmongering on the Left, Covid-19 Lies on the Right: What the Authorities Got Correct and Incorrect about SARS-CoV-2*, hereafter referred to as my *Coronavirus* book.

March 15, 2021

Donald J Trump @RealDonaldTrump
Statement by Donald J. Trump, 45th President of the United States of America
The Washington Post just issued a correction as to the contents of the incorrectly reported phone call I had with respect to voter fraud in

the Great State of Georgia. While I appreciate the Washington Post's correction, which immediately makes the Georgia Witch Hunt a non-story, the original story was a Hoax, right from the very beginning. I would further appreciate a strong investigation into Fulton County, Georgia, and the Stacey Abrams political machine which, I believe, would totally change the course of the presidential election in Georgia.

Fulton County has not been properly audited for vote or signature verification. They only looked at areas of the State where there most likely would be few problems, and even there they found large numbers of mistakes. We are seeking to find and reveal the large-scale election fraud which took place in Georgia. Many residents agree, and their anger caused them not to turn out and vote for two Republican Senators in the January election.

The Consent Decree signed between Raffensperger and Stacey Abrams was not approved by the Georgia State Legislature, and therefore should be deemed invalid, and the election result changed. Why the Governor and Raffensperger ever approved this Consent Decree is one of the great questions? We look forward to an answer.

You will notice that establishment media errors, omissions, mistakes, and outright lies always slant one way—against me and against Republicans. Meanwhile, stories that hurt Democrats or undermine their narratives are buried, ignored, or delayed until they can do the least harm—for example, after an election is over. Look no further than the negative coverage of the vaccine that preceded the election and the overdue celebration of the vaccine once the election had concluded. A strong democracy requires a fair and honest press. This latest media travesty underscores that legacy media outlets should be regarded as political entities—not journalistic enterprises. In any event, I thank the Washington Post for the correction. March 15, 2021

To comment, the correction Trump is referring to is WaPo misreporting what was said in Trump's phone call with Georgia Secretary of State Brad Raffensperger. I reprint that entire call in my *Trump's Tweets* book. That book also discusses the Consent Decree and details the fraud Trump believes happened.

I discuss the timing by Pfizer of the vaccine in my *Corruption* book. Basically, Pfizer waited until a week after the election to announce its Covid vaccine was ready. If it had been announced a week before the election, that might have made a difference, as many voted for Biden rather than Trump believing Biden would handle the pandemic better. But with a vaccine available, Covid might not have been the most pressing issue, and its quick development would show Trump was indeed serious about ending the pandemic.

31

Otherwise, a theme of my *Corruption* and *Tragic Ending* books is the bias of the MSM and how it could have affected the election results.

March 17, 2021

Donald J Trump @RealDonaldTrump
MEDIA ADVISORY

45th President Donald J. Trump will be interviewed tonight at 7pm EDT on "Fox News Primetime" with host Maria Bartiromo. Enjoy! March 17, 2021.

March 21, 2021

Donald J Trump @RealDonaldTrump

The New York Times did a story today saying that various Republican groups, many of them outstanding, are rallying on false claims that conservative activists are finding that the best way to raise money and keep voters engaged is to make Donald J. Trump's biggest fabrication, Election Fraud, their top priority.

Sadly, the Election was Rigged, and without even going into detail, of which there is much, totally game changing. Democrats could not get Republican Legislatures in Swing States to approve many of the voting changes which took place before the Election, which is mandated under the Constitution of the United States.

For that reason alone, we had an Illegitimate Election. The Supreme Court and other Courts were afraid to rule, they were "gutless," and will go down in history as such. No wonder so much money is being raised on this issue, and law-abiding people have every right to do so! March 21, 2021

To comment, Trump is referring to the change in election laws by entities other than state legislatures. He is also referring to the courts that refused to even hear the evidence for election fraud. Instead, tossing out cases based on lack of standing or some other such technicality.

I document both of these issues in my *Corruption* book and theorize in my *Tragic Ending* book that frustration over such led to the events of January 6, 2021 (J6), more so than anything Trump said, as Dems claim.

Donald J Trump @RealDonaldTrump

Congratulations to Julia Letlow on her BIG win in Louisiana! Despite running in a field with a dozen candidates, no runoff election is necessary because she received 65% of the vote—an incredible victory.

Trump Fights Back with Statements

I am thrilled for Julia and the entire Letlow family. Luke is looking down proudly from above. March 21, 2021

To comment, Julia ran to fill the seat left vacant by the death of her husband Luke from Covid-19.

Donald J Trump @RealDonaldTrump
We proudly handed the Biden Administration the most secure border in history. All they had to do was keep this smooth-running system on autopilot. Instead, in the span of a just few weeks, the Biden Administration has turned a national triumph into a national disaster. They are in way over their heads and taking on water fast.

The pathetic, clueless performance of Secretary Mayorkas on the Sunday Shows today was a national disgrace. His self-satisfied presentation—in the middle of the massive crisis he helped engineer—is yet more proof he is incapable of leading DHS. Even someone of Mayorkas' limited abilities should understand that if you provide Catch-and-Release to the world's illegal aliens then the whole world will come.

Furthermore, the Mayorkas Gag Order on our Nation's heroic border agents and ICE officers should be the subject of an immediate congressional investigation. But it's clear they are engaged in a huge cover-up to hide just how bad things truly are. The only way to end the Biden Border Crisis is for them to admit their total failure and adopt the profoundly effective, proven Trump policies.

They must immediately complete the wall, which can be done in a matter of weeks—they should never have stopped it. They are causing death and human tragedy. In addition to the obvious, drugs are pouring into our country at record levels from the Southern Border, not to mention human and sex trafficking. This Administration's reckless policies are enabling and encouraging crimes against humanity. Our Country is being destroyed! March 21, 2021

March 22, 2021

Donald J Trump @RealDonaldTrump
Lisa Boothe, who has been doing an outstanding job at Fox News, is starting her own podcast, which begins this morning. I have agreed to an interview where we talk about Election Fraud, Joe Biden's dangerously radical policies (2A and the Border!) and the future of the Republican Party.
https://podcasts.apple.com/us/podcast/the-truth-with-lisa-boothe/id1557742167

Donald J Trump @RealDonaldTrump
MEDIA ADVISORY
45th President Donald J. Trump will be interviewed by Greg Kelly on Newsmax at 7pm EDT. Enjoy! March 22, 2021

To comment, in Appendix One are news reports about this interview. The big news was YouTube removed the video of the interview due to Trump's continuing claims of election fraud. Big Tech will not even allow such to be discussed. Such censorship by Big Tech is another theme of my *Corruption* and *Tragic Ending* books and of this book.

March 26, 2021

Donald J Trump @RealDonaldTrump
Congratulations to Georgia and the Georgia State Legislature on changing their voter Rules and Regulations. They learned from the travesty of the 2020 Presidential Election, which can never be allowed to happen again. Too bad these changes could not have been done sooner! March 26, 2021

Extended Comment
Record Voter Turnout in Georgia

This election integrity law passed by Georgia was much vilified by Joe Biden and other Dems. Biden called it "Jim Crow 2.0," "Jim Crow on steroids," and "Jim Eagle," though no one had any idea what the latter meant. But basically, Biden and Dems claimed this law was intended to suppress election turnout, especially among people of color.

I expose all of the false claims being made by Biden and others in my *Biden Tweets* books. In the end, it was much ado about nothing, as Georgia experienced record voter turnout, including among people of color. But Biden and Dems never apologized for their lies about the law.

According to Axios, amidst the concerns from President Biden and other Democrats who called the state's new ballot restrictions a version of "Jim Crow 2.0," the Georgia Secretary of State reports "record early-voting turnout." In 2018, early primary in-person voter turnout was 299,347; in 2020, it was 326,351, and in 2022 the "total turnout" was 857,401, with 795,567 early in-person votes and 61,744 absentee votes (Newsmax. Early).

Emboldened Republicans plan to double down on a nationwide "election integrity" push after Georgia saw record early voting in today's primary.

Why it matters: President Biden and other Democrats had attacked the state's new ballot restrictions as "Jim Crow 2.0." But early voting came in at nearly triple Georgia's 2018 level.

What's happening: Republicans argue the results refute Democrats' claims that the 2021 election law signed by Gov. Brian Kemp (R) amounted to voter suppression (Axios. Republicans).

Georgians demonstrated their confidence in the state's election integrity and ease of voting by showing up in record numbers during three weeks of early voting for the 2022 primary.

Short lines, smooth easy ballot access, and confidence in ballot security brought out more than 850,000 to cast a ballot in person or return an absentee ballot. Compared early-voting turnout in recent primaries, this represented a 168 percent increase over the 2018, the last gubernatorial primary and a 212 percent jump above 2020, the last presidential primary year.

"The record early voting turnout is a testament to the security of the voting system and the hard work of our county election officials," said Georgia Secretary of State Raffensperger. "The incredible turnout we have seen demonstrates once and for all that Georgia's Election Integrity Act struck a good balance between the guardrails of access and security" (Georgia Secretary).

As I say in response to Biden's claims in my *Biden Tweets* books, Georgia's election integrity law made it easier to vote but harder to cheat. I was proven correct in that observation, while Biden was proven wrong in his fear mongering and divisive claims. Back to Trump.

Donald J Trump @RealDonaldTrump
Where's Durham? Is he a living, breathing human being? Will there ever be a Durham report? March 26, 2021

35

Extended Comment
Durham Investigation

Durham is John Durham, the special prosecutor appointed to investigate the origins of the Trump/ Russia collusion hoax. I report about his investigation in my *Impeach* trilogy. I thought his investigation would be competed before those books were finished, but that did not happen.

In the spring of 2022, one person was put on trial. He was acquitted, but it was established in that trial that the idea of Trump/ Russia collusion was indeed a hoax perpetrated and paid for by the Hillary Clinton campaign, with support by Hillary herself.

An extensive list of references in Appendix One document this trial and its results. Back to Trump.

March 30, 2021

Donald J Trump @RealDonaldTrump
Based on their interviews, I felt it was time to speak up about Dr. Fauci and Dr. Birx, two self-promoters trying to reinvent history to cover for their bad instincts and faulty recommendations, which I fortunately almost always overturned. They had bad policy decisions that would have left our country open to China and others, closed to reopening our economy, and years away from an approved vaccine—putting millions of lives at risk.

We developed American vaccines by an American President in record time, nine months, which is saving the entire world. We bought billions of dollars of these vaccines on a calculated bet that they would work, perhaps the most important bet in the history of the world. Dr. Fauci and Dr. Birx moved far too slowly, and if it were up to them we'd currently be locked in our basements as our country suffered through a financial depression. Families, and children in particular, would be suffering the mental strains of this disaster like never before.

In a fake interview last night on CNN, Dr. Fauci, who said he was an athlete in college but couldn't throw a baseball even close to home plate, it was a "roller," tried to take credit for the vaccine, when in fact he said it would take three to five years, and probably longer, to have it approved. Dr. Fauci was incapable of pressing the FDA to move it through faster. I was the one to get it done, and even the fake news media knows and reports this.

Dr. Fauci is also the king of "flip-flops" and moving the goalposts to make himself look as good as possible. He fought me so hard because he wanted to keep our country open to countries like China. I closed it against his strong recommendation, which saved many lives. Dr. Fauci also said we didn't need to wear masks, then a few months later he said we needed to wear masks, and now, two or three of them. Fauci spent U.S. money on the Wuhan lab in China—and we now know how that worked out. March 30, 2021

Donald J Trump @RealDonaldTrump

Dr. Birx is a proven liar with very little credibility left. Many of her recommendations were viewed as "pseudo-science," and Dr. Fauci would always talk negatively about her and, in fact, would ask not to be in the same room with her. The States who followed her lead, like California, had worse outcomes on Covid, and ruined the lives of countless children because they couldn't go to school, ruined many businesses, and an untold number of Americans who were killed by the lockdowns themselves. Dr. Birx was a terrible medical advisor, which is why I seldom followed her advice. Her motto should be "Do as I say, not as I do." Who can forget when Dr. Birx gave a huge mandate to the people of our Nation to not travel, and then traveled a great distance to see her family for Thanksgiving—only to have them call the police and turn her in? She then, embarrassingly for her, resigned.

Finally, Dr. Birx says she can't hear very well, but I can. There was no "very difficult" phone call, other than Dr. Birx's policies that would have led us directly into a COVID caused depression. She was a very negative voice who didn't have the right answers. Time has proven me correct. I only kept Dr. Fauci and Dr. Birx on because they worked for the U.S. government for so long—they are like a bad habit! March 30, 2021

To comment, Trump's comments here are very instructive. Fauci and Birx seemed reliable at first, but many of us quickly began to question their advice. It was they who first recommended the "15 days to slow the spread" which became 45 days, then would have lasted indefinitely if they were in charge.

But thank God, Trump realized as early as March 30, 2020 that the lockdowns were destructive and began to warn about their dangers. He correct predicted the lockdowns would cause emotional problems, drug and alcohol abuse to rise, and suicides to increase. Sadly, he was correct on all three, and we are still dealing with the ramifications to this day.

I will address all of these issues in my forthcoming *Coronavirus* book.

Against Lies of Biden, Attacks from Dems, and Bias of Media

Donald J Trump @RealDonaldTrump

President Donald J. Trump and Mrs. Melania Trump are pleased to announce the launch of http://45Office.com. The official website of the 45th President of the United States will allow individuals to submit correspondence, scheduling requests, and press inquiries for President and Mrs. Trump.

President and Mrs. Trump are continually strengthened by the enduring spirit of the American people, and they look forward to staying in touch. March 30, 2021

Chapter Four
Trump's Statements
April 2021

These Trump Statements are continued from Chapter Three.

April 1, 2021

Donald J Trump @RealDonaldTrump

Joe Biden's radical plan to implement the largest tax hike in American history is a massive giveaway to China, and many other countries, that will send thousands of factories, millions of jobs, and trillions of dollars to these competitive Nations. The Biden plan will crush American workers and decimate U.S. manufacturing, while giving special tax privileges to outsourcers, foreign and giant multinational corporations.

Biden promised to "build back better"—but the country he is building up, in particular, is China and other large segments of the world. Under the Biden Administration, America is once again losing the economic war with China—and Biden's ludicrous multi-trillion dollar tax hike is a strategy for total economic surrender. Sacrificing good paying American jobs is the last thing our citizens need as our country recovers from the effects of the Global Pandemic.

Biden's policy would break the back of the American Worker with among the highest business tax rates in the developed world. Under Biden's plan, if you create jobs in America, and hire American workers, you will pay MORE in taxes—but if you close down your factories in Ohio and Michigan, fire U.S. workers, and move all your production to Beijing and Shanghai, you will pay LESS. It is the exact OPPOSITE of putting America First—it is putting America LAST!

Companies that send American jobs to China should not be rewarded by Joe Biden's Tax Bill, they should be punished so that they keep those jobs right here in America, where they belong.

This legislation would be among the largest self-inflicted economic wounds in history. If this monstrosity is allowed to pass, the result will be more Americans out of work, more families shattered, more factories abandoned, more industries wrecked, and more Main Streets boarded up and closed down—just like it was before I took over the presidency 4 years ago. I then set record low unemployment, with 160 million people working.

This tax hike is a classic globalist betrayal by Joe Biden and his friends: the lobbyists will win, the special interests will win, China will win, the Washington politicians and government bureaucrats will win—but hardworking American families will lose.

Joe Biden's cruel and heartless attack on the American Dream must never be allowed to become Federal law. Just like our southern border went from best to worst, and is now in shambles, our economy will be destroyed! April 1, 2021

To comment, this Statement is in regard to Biden's plan to increase the corporate tax rate. Biden simply does not understand that corporations do not pay taxes. They pass the cost onto their customers in the form of higher taxes. This was one of Biden's many missteps that led to Bidenflation, as I document in my *Biden Tweets* books.

April 2, 2021

Donald J Trump @RealDonaldTrump

Why is it that every time the 2020 ELECTION FRAUD is discussed, the Fake News Media consistently states that such charges are baseless, unfounded, unwarranted, etc.? Sadly, there was massive fraud in the 2020 Presidential Election, and many very angry people understand that. With each passing day, and unfortunately for the Radical Left CRAZIES, more and more facts are coming out.

Other than that, Happy Easter! April 2, 2021

Extended Comment
Easter is Not a Time for Politics

Trump should not have coupled his election grievances with an Easter greeting. Easter is too precious of a holiday to be brought down to the level of politics. It is a celebration of the resurrection of our Lord and Savior Jesus Christ. Christ's resurrection was a demonstration that God the Father had accepted His sacrifice for our sins, so that all who trust in Jesus' death on the cross for their sins will be forgiven and saved from their sins.

[23]But it was not written on his account alone, *"it was accounted to him,"* [24]but also on account of us, to whom it is about to be accounted [or, imputed], to the ones believing on [or, trusting in] the One having raised up Jesus our Lord from [the] dead, [25]who was handed over because of our transgressions and was raised up because of our

justification [or, our [being] declared righteous]. [i.e., Jesus' resurrection was because of God's acceptance of Jesus' sacrifice for our sins, to show to us that the sacrifice had been accepted]....

⁹But you* are not in [the] flesh but in [the] Spirit, since [the] Spirit of God dwells in you*; but if anyone does not have [the] Spirit of Christ, this one is not His. ¹⁰But if Christ [is] in you*, on the one hand the body [is] dead because of sin, on the other hand the Spirit [is] life because of righteousness. ¹¹But if the Spirit of the One having raised up Jesus from [the] dead dwells in you*, the One having raised up Christ from [the] dead will also give life to your* mortal bodies through His Spirit indwelling in you*.

⁸But what does it say? *"The word is near you, in your mouth and in your heart"* [Deut 30:14]—that is, the word of the faith which we are preaching, ⁹that if you confess with your mouth [the] Lord Jesus [or, [that] Jesus [is] Lord], and believe in your heart that God raised Him from [the] dead, you will be saved! [cp. 1Cor 12:3] ¹⁰For with the heart it is believed to righteousness, and with the mouth it is confessed to salvation.

¹¹For the Scripture says, *"Everyone believing on* [or, *trusting in*] *Him will not put to shame."* [Isaiah 28:16, LXX] ¹²For there is no difference [or, distinction] [between] both Jew and Greek, for the same [Lord is] Lord of all, being rich [fig., giving generously] to all the ones calling on Him. ¹³For every[one], *"who himself shall call on the name of [the] LORD will be saved!"* [Joel 2:32] (Romans 4:23-25; 8:9-11; 10:8-13). Back to Trump.

Donald J Trump @RealDonaldTrump

Baseball is already losing tremendous numbers of fans, and now they leave Atlanta with their All-Star Game because they are afraid of the Radical Left Democrats who do not want voter I.D., which is desperately needed, to have anything to do with our elections. Boycott baseball and all of the woke companies that are interfering with Free and Fair Elections. Are you listening Coke, Delta, and all! April 2, 2021

April 4, 2021

Donald J Trump @RealDonaldTrump

For years the Radical Left Democrats have played dirty by boycotting products when anything from that company is done or stated in any way that offends them. Now they are going big time with WOKE CANCEL CULTURE and our sacred elections. It is finally time for Republicans and Conservatives to fight back—we have more people than they do—by far! Boycott Major League Baseball, Coca-Cola, Delta Airlines, JPMorgan Chase, ViacomCBS, Citigroup, Cisco, UPS, and Merck. Don't go back to their products until they relent.

We can play the game better than them. They didn't even get approval of State Legislatures, which is mandated under the U.S. Constitution. They rigged and stole our 2020 Presidential Election, which we won by a landslide, and then, on top of that, boycott and scare companies into submission. Never submit, never give up! The Radical Left will destroy our Country if we let them. We will not become a Socialist Nation. Happy Easter! April 4, 2021

Extended Comment
Emails to MLB

My MLB app had not been working, so I sent the following email to tech support:

———————

I tried all of the steps you have suggested, and nothing has worked. I have wasted enough time on this app, so please refund my money and cancel my subscription.

And besides, now that the MLB is boycotting Georgia for securing their elections, I am boycotting the MLB. I will not be watching, listening to, or attending any games this year.

Stop with playing politics and stick with playing baseball. Until then, REFUND MY MONEY AND CANCEL MY SUBSCRIPTION.

———————

I'm still fighting the MLB, trying to get them to refund my money for the MLB app, as it has not worked all season. I want my subscription canceled. With the MLB going woke, I will not be following it.

After a question as to how I paid for the app, a week later, I sent the following email.

———————

I paid via PayPal. I paid for this season. I want that money refunded, as I have not been able to listen to games all season. I also want my subscription canceled, now that the MLB has gone woke. I want nothing to do with you.

The Georgia voter law is NOT racist. It is securing elections. Denver's voting law is even more restrictive. Do your research before making an illogical woke move. Moreover, you are the racists, moving

---

the All-Star Game out of a city with 51% blacks to a city with 9% blacks. You hurt black businesses with this move. That's racist.

As a result of such nonsense, I will not be following the MLB anymore. Again, refund my money for this season and cancel my subscription for future seasons. Back to Trump.

Donald J Trump @RealDonaldTrump
Happy Easter to ALL, including the Radical Left CRAZIES who rigged our Presidential Election, and want to destroy our Country! April 4, 2021

Donald J Trump @RealDonaldTrump
Happy Easter! April 4, 2021

To comment, again, Trump should not couple an Easter greeting with a political comment. It is to bring Easter, which is for all peoples, down to the divisive level of politics.

April 7, 2021

Donald J Trump @RealDonaldTrump
In yet another highly partisan story, the failing New York Times wrote a completely misleading, one-sided attack piece this weekend that tried to disparage our record-setting grassroots fundraising operation during the 2020 campaign. Except for massive voter fraud, this was a campaign that was easily won by your favorite Republican President, me!

Our support in 2020 was so big—never before seen (received more votes than any sitting President in history, by far), that it has become a major threat to the Democrat Party, which explains why the New York Times immediately rushed to defend their Radical Left allies. Before our two campaigns, 2016 and 2020, Republicans would always lose small dollar donations. Now we win, or do very well, because we are the Party of Working Americans, and we beat the Democrats at their own game. We learned from liberal ActBlue—and now we're better than they are! In fact, many people were so enthusiastic that they gave over and over, and in certain cases where they would give too much, we would promptly refund their contributions. Our overall dispute rate was less than 1% of total online donations, a very low number. This is done by Dems also.

The New York Times knew this but buried these details in their story—they didn't talk about, however, how the CHEATING Democrats circumvented State Legislatures (approval is required by the U.S. Constitution) in Swing States to rig the 2020 Presidential Election, or how Democrats paid for votes in many Urban Centers, in a little thing called "walking around money," how Democrats threatened Union Members with the loss of their jobs if they didn't vote Democrat, massive Fake Mail-In Ballots, illegal immigrants and dead people who voted (for Dems), and much more. Our fundraising efforts, working together with the Republican party, were all done legally, and all with the goal of ensuring that my Administration could continue to Make America Great Again. The Election on the other hand, was massively rigged and stolen—and now look what is happening to our Country, and in particular at our southern border.

If you are one of the record-setting 75 million Americans who voted for me, donated or volunteered, THANK YOU! The best is yet to come! April 7, 2011

To comment, I did not see the NYT article Trump is referring to, but he is correct about the problem with entities other than state legislatures changing election laws. I document that point in my *Corruption* book. But his other claims of election fraud are on less stable ground, as I explain in that book and in my *Trump's Tweets* book.

Donald J Trump @RealDonaldTrump

Too bad the desperately needed election reforms in Georgia didn't go further, as their originally approved Bill did, but the Governor and Lt. Governor would not go for it. The watered-down version, that was just passed and signed by Governor Kemp, while better than before, doesn't have Signature Matching and many other safety measures, which were sadly left out. This Bill should have been passed before the 2020 Presidential Election, not after.

It is now reported that chain of custody records for over 400,000 Absentee Ballots are missing or not being shown. I wonder why? Show them now! The Democrats in Georgia really push the Republicans around, like the so-called Consent Decree, which was illegally signed by the Secretary of State without Legislative Approval—a Democrat DREAM. Boycott all of the woke companies that don't want Voter I.D. and Free and Fair Elections. April 7, 2011

Donald J Trump @RealDonaldTrump

ICYMI: Trump Isn't Getting the Proper Credit for Role in Vaccines Wow, so nice!

Trump Fights Back with Statements

"And while former President Trump and his administration were moving heaven and earth to rapidly deliver vaccine[s] to the American people, the media were parading expert after expert saying the goal was impossible, and VP Harris and President Biden never gave Trump any credit for the vaccine, despite both being fully vaccinated before taking office."

https://www.45office.com/images/uploads/trump_email_vaccine.pdf
April 7, 2011

To comment, I have been saying this over and over again on Biden's Twitter feed, now reprinted in my *Biden Tweets* books. Biden is trying to take credit for the vaccines that were developed under the Trump administration. The Trump administration also preplanned for the distribution of up to 250 million doses by April 30, according to former officials on Trump's Coronavirus Task Force. All that Biden can claim is he is not screwing up what Trump put into place.

Donald J Trump @RealDonaldTrump
"I think other people are making most of the decisions, but I may be wrong about that. To be honest with you, someone is making the decisions. This is Bernie Sanders on steroids." [1:21 video of Trump on Newsmax.] April 7, 2011

To comment, Trump is repeating the theory of many on the right that Biden is not really in charge at the White House. Many think it is really Jill Biden, Obama, the deep state, or others. Whether that is true or not is hard to say. But Biden does seem too frail and suffering with cognitive difficulties to really be in charge.

April 8, 2021

Donald J Trump @RealDonaldTrump
Georgia's election reform law is far too weak and soft to ensure real ballot integrity! Election Day is supposed to be Election Day, not Election Week or Election Month. Far too many days are given to vote. Too much "mischief" can happen during this very long period of time. You saw that in the 2020 Presidential Election. How's R___ F____ doing?
Governor Brian Kemp and Georgia Secretary of State should have eliminated no-excuse, widespread mass Mail-In Voting, gotten rid of the dangerous and unsecure Drop-Boxes, and should have kept and EXPANDED Signature Verification to do matches against the historical voter file, among other things! Hope the RINOs are happy.

Kemp also caved to the radical left-wing woke mob who threatened to call him racist if he got rid of weekend voting. Well, he kept it, and they still call him racist! April 8, 2011

Extended Comment
Georgia Election Integrity Law

In my *Trump's Tweets* book, I discuss the lack of signature verification and explain the "consent decree" in detail, along with other potential election problems in Georgia. These questions were never answered. But this law is an admission there were problems that were not resolved then.

Moreover, Georgia officials must have read an advance copy of my book, as the election integrity law they passed incorporates the very suggestions I make in my book. Note: The preceding was written days after that book was published.

As for "RF", she is mentioned in Trump's call with Brad Raffensperger that I record in that book, but I redacted her name there and here, as I am not sure if she is guilty of what Trump is alleging of her.

However, her name will come up again in the J6 Commission public hearings in June of 2022. I will be covering those hearings in my forthcoming book *The Biased J6 Commission: The Public Hearings Were Half a Trial; This Book Gives You the Other Half*, hereafter referred to as my *J6 Commission* book. Back to Trump.

Donald J Trump @RealDonaldTrump
Congressman Matt Gaetz has never asked me for a pardon. It must also be remembered that he has totally denied the accusations against him. April 8, 2011

To comment, the J6 Commission already at this time and more so later during the public hearings will claim several Trump administration officials began to ask for pardons from Trump after J6 but before he left office. The implication will be that they knew they did something wrong and wanted protection from prosecution.

However, most of them will deny they asked for a pardon. And even if they did, it is not an admission of some kind of guilt. It is just a recognition that Dems would use J6 for another witch hunt. That proved to be the case, as I demonstrated in my *Tragic Ending* and will do more so in my *J6 Commission* book.

Donald J Trump @RealDonaldTrump
Voter fraud in Georgia for the Presidential Election was rampant!

Trump Fights Back with Statements

Michael Goodwin—New York Post:

Reader Matt Conley calls voter fraud identity theft, and tells a story. He writes: "My youngest sibling lives in Missouri and found that a vote was cast under his name in Georgia. He asked the Georgia Secretary of State's Office if that vote could be removed and not included in the presidential recount. He was told no.

After the Senate runoffs, my brother wanted to know if a vote was cast in his name again. The Secretary's office told him that they took down the fake online account but would not say if votes were cast. Problem solved in their mind." April 8, 2011

April 9, 2021

Donald J Trump @RealDonaldTrump

Even though he has not yet announced that he is running, and I certainly hope he does, I am giving my Complete and Total Endorsement to Senator Ron Johnson of Wisconsin. He is brave, he is bold, he loves our Country, our Military, and our Vets. He will protect our Second Amendment, and everything else we stand for. It is the kind of courage we need in the U.S. Senate. He has no idea how popular he is. Run, Ron, Run! April 9, 2011.

To comment, Senator Johnson played an important role in the first impeachment. I devote an entire chapter to his letter about his conversation with Trump about the Ukraine pressure hoax in *Volume One* of my *Impeach* trilogy. Since then, I keep noticing Johnson's name and the good he is doing. Yes, he needs to run again.

Donald J Trump @RealDonaldTrump

Asa Hutchinson, the lightweight RINO Governor of Arkansas, just vetoed a Bill that banned the CHEMICAL CASTRATION OF CHILDREN. "Bye-bye Asa," that's the end of him! Fortunately for the Great State of Arkansas, Sarah Huckabee Sanders will do a fantastic job as your next Governor! April 9, 2011

To comment, to allow a child to make a life-changing decision makes no logical sense. That is especially the case in this situation, as most children out-grow their gender dysphoria. I document such in my two-volume set *God's Sex Plan*. See Appendix Two for details.

Against Lies of Biden, Attacks from Dems, and Bias of Media

Donald J Trump @RealDonaldTrump

Rand Paul has done a fantastic job for our Country, and for the incredible people of Kentucky. He fights against the Swamp in Washington, the Radical Left Liberals, and especially the destructive RINOS, of which there are far too many, in Congress. Rand will continue to stand up for our great AMERICA FIRST policies because he believes in stopping wasteful spending, defending our Second Amendment rights, and taking care of our Military and our Vets. I am proud to be working with Rand in our battle to Make America Great Again. He has my Complete and Total Endorsement for another term in the U.S. Senate. The Commonwealth of Kentucky has a true champion in Rand Paul. April 9, 2011.

To comment, Rand is a great Senator. Ditto that endorsement.

Donald J Trump @RealDonaldTrump

The world mourns the passing of Prince Philip, a man who embodied the noble soul and proud spirit of the United Kingdom and the Commonwealth.

Melania and I send our deepest and most profound condolences to Her Majesty Queen Elizabeth II, and to the entire Royal Family. We send our most heartfelt sympathies to the British people. This is an irreplaceable loss for Great Britain, and for all who hold dear our civilization.

Prince Philip defined British dignity and grace. He personified the quiet reserve, stern fortitude, and unbending integrity of the United Kingdom.

As a young man, he served Britain honorably and courageously as a naval officer in the Second World War. Aboard battleships in the Mediterranean, he saw combat at sea. He then participated in the pivotal Allied invasion of Sicily in 1943. Like so many of his generation, in Britain's darkest hour, he put his life on the line for God, country, and the values of freedom and self-government that forever unite America and the United Kingdom.

For seven decades, Prince Philip brought the same sense of duty and purpose to his role as consort and husband to the Queen. He was admired by his fellow citizens, and respected by everyone around the world. His exceptional example of service, constancy, and patriotism will be his greatest legacy.

Over the past few years, Melania and I were honored to have the opportunity to visit the United Kingdom. We saw firsthand how the Monarchy epitomizes and carries on the virtues of the British People—and no one did so more than Prince Philip.

Trump Fights Back with Statements

As we grieve his loss, we celebrate his memory and rededicate ourselves to the values to which he devoted his extraordinary life. He will be greatly missed. April 9, 2011

To comment, I for one have never understood the American fascination with the British royal family. We fought a war to get out from under their yoke. I have chided Biden in his twitter feed for using honorific titles for foreign leaders like "Her Majesty," so to be consistent, I will do the same for Trump here. Our Constitution specifically denies the use of such terms for our leaders, so we shouldn't use them for the leader of other countries. Although, in this case, the Queen of England is not a real leader. She is just a figure head.

April 13, 2021

Donald J Trump @RealDonaldTrump

Wouldn't it be ironic if the Supreme Court of the United States, after showing that they didn't have the courage to do what they should have done on the Great Presidential Election Fraud of 2020, was PACKED by the same people, the Radical Left Democrats (who they are so afraid of!), that they so pathetically defended in not hearing the Election Fraud case. Now there is a very good chance they will be diluted (and moved throughout the court system so that they can see how the lower courts work), with many new Justices added to the Court, far more than has been reported. There is also a good chance that they will be term-limited.

We had 19 states go before the Supreme Court who were, shockingly, not allowed to be heard. Believe it or not, the President of the United States was not allowed to be heard based on "no standing," not based on the FACTS. The Court wouldn't rule on the merits of the great Election Fraud, including the fact that local politicians and judges, not State Legislatures, made major changes to the Election—which is in total violation of the United States Constitution.

Our politically correct Supreme Court will get what they deserve—an unconstitutionally elected group of Radical Left Democrats who are destroying our Country. With leaders like Mitch McConnell, they are helpless to fight. He didn't fight for the Presidency, and he won't fight for the Court. If and when this happens, I hope the Justices remember the day they didn't have courage to do what they should have done for America. April 13, 2021

To comment, Trump is correct on all points here. SCOTUS' inaction on the election cases could very well come back to bite them and reduce their influence. And the issue of entities other than state legislatures making or changing election laws was the worse aspect of the many irregularities in the 2020 election. Only SCOTUS had the power to put a stop to such practices, but they failed to act. Truly sad.

Donald J Trump @RealDonaldTrump

Fake News CNN, relying on all anonymous sources, meaning they probably made the whole thing up, wrote a very dishonest story claiming Congressman Matt Gaetz asked for a meeting with me at Mar-a-Lago, in Palm Beach, Florida, and was denied. This is completely false.

Why doesn't CNN investigate and write about lightweight Democrat Congressman Eric Swalwell, who had a torrid and physical relationship with the Chinese spy Fang-Fang, but is somehow on the once-prestigious House Intelligence Committee. Swalwell, who ran for President and dropped out with a record-setting 0% in the polls, has been compromised and is a national security threat to the United States—he should be removed from the Committee immediately! April 13, 2021

To comment, I haven't mentioned the Matt Gaetz scandal, as it was outside the purview of this series of books. But I did mention the Swalwell scandal. And Trump is correct it is far more of an issue, but the MSM has mostly ignored it.

Donald J Trump @RealDonaldTrump

The Biden Administration did a terrible disservice to people throughout the world by allowing the FDA and CDC to call a "pause" in the use of the Johnson & Johnson COVID-19 vaccine. The results of this vaccine have been extraordinary but now it's reputation will be permanently challenged. The people who have already taken the vaccine will be up in arms, and perhaps all of this was done for politics or perhaps it's the FDA's love for Pfizer.

The FDA, especially with long time bureaucrats within, has to be controlled. They should not be able to do such damage for possibly political reasons, or maybe because their friends at Pfizer have suggested it. They'll do things like this to make themselves look important.

Remember, it was the FDA working with Pfizer, who announced the vaccine approval two days after the 2020 Presidential Election. They didn't like me very much because I pushed them extremely hard. But if I didn't, you wouldn't have a vaccine for 3-5 years, or maybe not at all. It takes them years to act!

Do your testing, clean up the record, and get the Johnson & Johnson vaccine back online quickly. The only way we defeat the China Virus is with our great vaccines! April 13, 2021

Extended Comment
The J&J Vaccine Pause

Trump is correct on every point he raises. This was a draconian overreach by the CDC. I was scheduled to receive the J&J vaccine tomorrow, April 15, 2021. I specifically wanted the one-dose J&J vaccine. Due to my unique health situation, I am very likely to have significant side effects from the second dose of the Pfizer vaccine. But now, I have no choice but to get the first Pfizer dose tomorrow, then the second doses in three weeks, and I will be fretting that entire time, rather than being one and done. Or, of course, I could just skip getting the vaccine altogether. That will probably be the reaction to this "pause" by many people. I am not sure yet what I will do, get the Pfizer, wait for the J&J to be reapproved, or just skip it altogether.

This has been the problem throughout this pandemic—governmental authorities treating we the people like children who cannot make our own risk/ benefit analyses. Just give us accurate information, then let we the people decide based on our own unique personal situations how to proceed. Wear a mask. Don't wear a mask. Attend a social gathering. Don't attend a social gathering. Get a vaccine. Don't get a vaccine. Just tell us the risks, and let us decide for ourselves what course of action to pursue.

April 14, 2021

Donald J Trump @RealDonaldTrump

Great news for the Republican Party! Senator Lisa Murkowski said she is "still weighing whether she will run again" for the Senate in Alaska. In other words, there is a chance that she won't run! Wouldn't that be great? And so many people are looking to run against Crazy Liz Cheney—but we only want one. She is so far down in Wyoming polls that the only way she can win is numerous candidates running against her and splitting the vote. Hopefully, that won't happen. I'll make an Endorsement soon! April 14, 2021

April 17, 2021

Donald J Trump @RealDonaldTrump

ICYMI: Europe's vax disaster shows Trump, UK's BoJo got biggest COVID challenge right

"Biden gets some credit for distributing the shots, but Trump is responsible for producing vaccines in record time and guaranteeing that America had first dibs on the supply. The current president claims he inherited a mess. In fact, he inherited a miracle—Trump's Operation Warp Speed." ...

"Trump insisted he would have vaccines ready by the end of 2020, a goal naysayers like government virus guru Anthony Fauci said was impossible. Thousands of column inches and many more tweets mocked Trump's optimism. Before the novel-coronavirus vaccines, the fastest ever vaccine development—for mumps in the 1960s—took four years." https://nypost.com/2021/04/12/europes-vax-disaster-shows-trump-uks-bojo-got-biggest-covid-challenge-right/ April 17, 2021

Donald J Trump @RealDonaldTrump
ICYMI: Team Biden halts J&J vaccine—and a return to normal

"The federal pause on the J&J shot makes no sense. Why is the Biden White House letting insanely risk-averse bureaucrats run the show?"

Just six people out of the nearly 7 million who've gotten the Johnson & Johnson vaccine reported blood clots. The condition is more common in the general population, and every vaccine—indeed, every medication—carries some risk, including the Moderna and Pfizer jabs. With COVID cases still rising nationwide, it's sheer lunacy to delay millions of vaccinations and feed fears among the vax-resistant.

Indeed, this moronic move is a gift to the anti-vax movement: The science bureaucrats are fueling that deranged pseudo-science." https://nypost.com/2021/04/13/team-biden-halts-jj-vaccine-and-a-return-to-normal/ April 17, 2021

To comment, very correct observations from these articles Trump quotes. I will have much more to say about all of this in my forthcoming *Coronavirus* book.

April 19, 2021

Donald J Trump @RealDonaldTrump
I wish Joe Biden wouldn't use September 11th as the date to withdraw our troops from Afghanistan, for two reasons.

First, we can and should get out earlier. Nineteen years is enough, in fact, far too much and way too long. I made early withdraw possible by already pulling much of our billions of dollars of equipment out and, more importantly, reducing our military presence to less than 2,000 troops from the 16,000 level that was there (likewise in Iraq, and zero troops in Syria except for the area where we KEPT THE OIL).

Secondly, September 11th represents a very sad event and period for our Country and should remain a day of reflection and remembrance honoring those great souls we lost. Getting out of Afghanistan is a wonderful and positive thing to do. I planned to withdraw on May 1st, and we should keep as close to that schedule as possible. April 19, 2021

To comment, do not miss this very prescient warning by Trump. Biden's Afghanistan withdrawal will be a disaster, as will be discussed later in this book and in my *Biden Tweets* books.

April 21, 2021

Donald J Trump @RealDonaldTrump
Statement from Highly Respected Pollster, John McLaughlin

"President Trump is the strongest endorsement I have ever witnessed in politics. Polling continually shows that when President Trump endorses, it almost always clears the field and puts his America First candidate on the path to victory. That's why everybody is coming to Mar-a-Lago for his support.

"Nationally, polling continually shows that 69% of all Republican primary voters want President Trump to run again in 2024—including 76% of Trump voters and 70% of Republicans. If President Trump runs again, Republican primary voters will support him 82% to 15%—including 89% among Trump voters and 83% among Republicans.

"John Bolton's failed warmonger views are completely out of touch with today's Republican Party and the majority of Americans. President Trump's successful America First policies kept us safe. This is a big reason why Republicans want him to run again." April 21, 2021

April 24, 2021

Donald J Trump @RealDonaldTrump
So many people would like to thank the brave and patriotic Republican State Senators from Arizona for the incredible job they are doing in exposing the large scale Voter Fraud which took place in the 2020 Presidential Election. Their tireless efforts have led to a massive recount, ballot examination, and full forensic audit, undertaken by experts retained by the State Senate, with results to be announced within six

weeks. The Democrats, upon hearing the news of the Court Order, have sent 73 lawyers to Arizona in an effort to stop this recount and full transparency because THEY KNOW WHAT THEY DID!

The Democrats are desperate for the FRAUD to remain concealed because, when revealed, the Great States of Wisconsin, Michigan, Georgia, New Hampshire, and the Great Commonwealth of Pennsylvania, would be forced to complete the work already started. The Arizona recount and examination will be on live TV (OAN) for all to watch. April 24, 2021

To comment, notice that Trump got it correct in calling PA a Commonwealth, in contrast to the rest being states. Trump did his homework before his rallies and knows the difference.

Donald J Trump @RealDonaldTrump

Why are the Democrats so desperate to stop this Election Fraud from being revealed? That answer is obvious! The Governor of Arizona, Doug Ducey, has been shockingly of zero help to the State Senate. He wants to "pretend" the election was free and fair. What are he and the Maricopa County Commissioners trying to hide? Our country needs the truth of the scam 2020 Election to be exposed. If it is not, just as if we have "no borders," we cannot be a Great Nation. Honest elections are America's Heart and Soul. We must never allow this to happen to our Great Country again. Thank you State Senators and others in Arizona for commencing this full forensic audit. I predict the results will be startling! April 24, 2021

Donald J Trump @RealDonaldTrump

Kim Jong-un of North Korea, who I have gotten to know (and like) under the most trying of circumstances, never respected the current President of South Korea, Moon Jae-in. I was always the one who stopped the aggression toward the South, but unfortunately for them, I am no longer there.

President Moon was weak as a leader and as a negotiator, except when it came to the continued, long term military ripoff of the USA (as is the case with many other countries we protect!). We were treated like fools for decades, however, I got them to pay billions of dollars more for the military protection and services we render. The Biden Administration is not even going to ask for the additional billions South Korea agreed to pay us.

All the USA now wants is a simple cost of living increase of 1% on the money I raised from them. The South Koreans are laughing all the way to the bank. Fortunately, before leaving office, I was able to make a new and FAR BETTER Trade Deal than what was in place. The deal will lead to billions of dollars in profits for the Great Farmers and Manufacturers of our Country! April 24, 2021

Donald J Trump @RealDonaldTrump
The Democrats are "swarming" the Great State of Arizona trying to get the Forensic Election Audit stopped, because only they know exactly what they've done, and they understand Voter Fraud far better than anyone. This could be Voter Fraud at the highest level. Don't think that Arizona is the only State. Much more to come! April 24, 2021

Donald J Trump @RealDonaldTrump
The Republican Party is demanding that Governor Ducey of Arizona immediately provide large-scale security for the brave American Patriots doing the Forensic Audit of the 2020 Presidential Election. Governor Ducey will be held fully responsible for the safety of those involved. State police or National Guard must be immediately sent out for protection. The Democrats do not want to have this information revealed, and they will do anything to stop it. Governor Ducey must finally act! April 24, 2021

Donald J Trump @RealDonaldTrump
Democrats are doing everything they can to stop the great Patriots of Arizona from doing a Forensic Audit of the 2020 Presidential Election Scam. If you want to watch these Patriots in action, go to: http://azaudit.org. April 24, 2021

April 26, 2021

Donald J Trump @RealDonaldTrump
Governor Doug Ducey of Arizona, one of the worst Governors in America, and the second worst Republican Governor in America, is refusing to provide security for the American Patriots who are hand counting the Rigged 2020 Arizona Election Ballots. April 26, 2021
Incredible organization and integrity taking place in Arizona with respect to the Fraudulent 2020 Presidential Election. These are Great American Patriots, but watch, the Radical Left Democrats "demean and destroy campaign" will start very soon. They will say anything they can to take away the integrity, validity, and credibility of what these incredible Patriots are doing—but the people of Arizona won't stand for it. They were among the earliest to see that this was a Rigged Election! April 26, 2021

To comment, there were several legal battels over this audit. Dems tried to stop it with legal maneuvers, and judges went back and forth as to whether it should continue or not. In the end, the results of this audit were debated. The MSM claimed it showed there was no fraud, while conservative news outlets claimed it did find fraud. See Appendix One for references on these legal battles and debates.

April 27, 2021

Donald J Trump @RealDonaldTrump

What used to be called The Academy Awards, and now is called the "Oscars"—a far less important and elegant name—had the lowest Television Ratings in recorded history, even much lower than last year, which set another record low. If they keep with the current ridiculous formula, it will only get worse—if that's possible. Go back 15 years, look at the formula they then used, change the name back to THE ACADEMY AWARDS, don't be so politically correct and boring, and do it right. ALSO, BRING BACK A GREAT HOST. These television people spend all their time thinking about how to promote the Democrat Party, which is destroying our Country, and cancel Conservatives and Republicans. That formula certainly hasn't worked very well for The Academy! April 27, 2021

April 28, 2021

Donald J Trump @RealDonaldTrump

The Radical Left Democrat Party has gone absolutely INSANE in fighting the Forensic Audit of the 2020 Presidential Election Scam, right now taking place in the Great State of Arizona. They sent a team of over 100 lawyers to try and stop it because they know what the result of the Arizona Senate sponsored audit will be—and it won't be good for the Dems. The audit is independently run, with no advantage to either side, but the Democrats don't want to hear anything about it because they know that they lost Arizona, and other scam election States, in a LANDSLIDE. They also know that the Arizona State Legislature approved virtually none of their many election requests, which is totally UNCONSTITUTIONAL. The people of Arizona are very angry, as are the people of our Country. If we can't have free and fair elections, we don't have a Country. The audit must continue. America deserves the TRUTH! April 28, 2021

Trump Fights Back with Statements

Donald J Trump @RealDonaldTrump

Liz Cheney is polling sooo low in Wyoming, and has sooo little support, even from the Wyoming Republican Party, that she is looking for a way out of her Congressional race. Based on all polling, there is no way she can win. She'll either be yet another lobbyist or maybe embarrass her family by running for President, in order to save face. This warmongering fool wants to stay in the Middle East and Afghanistan for another 19 years, but doesn't consider the big picture—Russia and China! April 28, 2021

April 29, 2021

Donald J Trump @RealDonaldTrump

BIG victory today in Arizona. A highly respected Judge has just ruled that the Forensic Audit being done by the Arizona State Senate can and will continue. Over 100 Democrat lawyers were sent to fight against this audit. The results will be very interesting for the USA and the World to see! Why are the Democrats fighting so hard to hide the facts? I know why, and so does everyone else! April 29, 2021

April 30, 2021

Donald J Trump @RealDonaldTrump

Congratulations to One America News OANN on their great ratings surge. Also, for their love of the United States of America! April 30, 2021

Donald J Trump @RealDonaldTrump

Twitter stock "plunged" as results are no longer cutting it for investors. Shares are off 15% today. Bad forecasts are hurting the outlook but more importantly, in my opinion, it has become totally BORING as people flock to leave the site. Michael Nathanson stated, "the math doesn't make sense" as he lowered his price target. I guess that's what happens when you go against FREEDOM OF SPEECH! It will happen to others also. April 30, 2021

To comment, I document Trump's fight with Twitter in my *Trump's Tweets* book. But later, he will launch his own social media site Truth Social. I am on both sites, with the handle GZeolla. See Appendix Three for further details.

Chapter Five
Trump's Statements
May 2021

These Trump Statements are continued from Chapter Four.

May 1, 2021

Donald J Trump @RealDonaldTrump

Today is Election Day in Texas, go out and vote for Susan Wright. She will be strong on the Border, Crime, Pro-Life, our brave Military and Vets, and will ALWAYS protect your Second Amendment. She will never let you down. VOTE TODAY! May 1, 2021

May 2, 2021

Donald J Trump @RealDonaldTrump

Congratulations to Susan Wright on her great surge yesterday which made her NUMBER ONE and assures her participation in the TX-06 runoff against another Republican. The Democrats have just conceded the race. Susan surged after I gave her an endorsement last week. Her wonderful husband is looking down, and is very proud of her! May 2, 2021

May 3, 2021

Donald J Trump @RealDonaldTrump

The Fraudulent Presidential Election of 2020 will be, from this day forth, known as THE BIG LIE! May 3, 2021

To comment, this post is important, as Dems and the MSM have labeled the idea that there was widespread fraud in the 2020 election as "The Big Lie." Trump is now trying to get that label placed on the election itself and the idea that Biden won the election.

Donald J Trump @RealDonaldTrump

Please explain to the Democrats and RINOs that the reason Texas-06 completely shut out Democrats in Saturday's Jungle Primary is because of my Endorsement of Susan Wright, who surged last week after receiving it. The Democrats were shut out and now it will be a contest between two Republicans, a very big win. It would be nice, however, if the pundits and Fake News Media would state the real reason for this unprecedented (Democrats have never been shut out before) victory! May 3, 2021

Donald J Trump @RealDonaldTrump

So nice to see RINO Mitt Romney booed off the stage at the Utah Republican State Convention. They are among the earliest to have figured this guy out, a stone cold loser! May 3, 2021

Donald J Trump @RealDonaldTrump

Heartwarming to read new polls on big-shot warmonger Liz Cheney of the great State of Wyoming. She is so low that her only chance would be if vast numbers of people run against her which, hopefully, won't happen. They never liked her much, but I say she'll never run in a Wyoming election again! May 3, 2021

May 4, 2021

Donald J Trump @RealDonaldTrump

In a time of silence and lies, a beacon of freedom arises, a place to speak freely and safely, straight from the desk of Donald J. Trump: https://donaldjtrump.com/desk https://media.gab.com/system/media_attach-ments/files/073/300/775/original/b153cfddb32be2d8.mp4 [0:29 video about these Statements] May 4, 2021

May 5, 2021

Donald J Trump @RealDonaldTrump

Warmonger Liz Cheney, who has virtually no support left in the Great State of Wyoming, continues to unknowingly and foolishly say that there was no Election Fraud in the 2020 Presidential Election when in fact, the evidence, including no Legislative approvals as demanded by the U.S. Constitution, shows the exact opposite.

Had Mike Pence referred the information on six states (only need two) back to State Legislatures, and had gutless and clueless

60

MINORITY Leader Mitch McConnell (he blew two seats in Georgia that should have never been lost) fought to expose all of the corruption that was presented at the time, with more found since, we would have had a far different Presidential result, and our Country would not be turning into a socialist nightmare! Never give up! May 5, 2021

Donald J Trump @RealDonaldTrump
What Facebook, Twitter, and Google have done is a total disgrace and an embarrassment to our Country. Free Speech has been taken away from the President of the United States because the Radical Left Lunatics are afraid of the truth, but the truth will come out anyway, bigger and stronger than ever before. The People of our Country will not stand for it! These corrupt social media companies must pay a political price, and must never again be allowed to destroy and decimate our Electoral Process. May 5, 2021

To comment, this post was in response to Facebook's new review board voting to keep Trump off of Facebook, at least for now.

Donald J Trump @RealDonaldTrump
Liz Cheney is a warmongering fool who has no business in Republican Party Leadership. We want leaders who believe in the Make America Great Again movement, and prioritize the values of America First. Elise Stefanik is a far superior choice, and she has my COMPLETE and TOTAL endorsement for GOP Conference Chair. Elise is a tough and smart communicator! May 5, 2021

Donald J Trump @RealDonaldTrump
[Graphic reading: "President Trump endorses Rep., Elise Stefanick for House GOP Chair!"] May 5, 2021

May 6, 2021

Donald J Trump @RealDonaldTrump
Congratulations to the great Patriots of Windham, New Hampshire for their incredible fight to seek out the truth on the massive Election Fraud which took place in New Hampshire and the 2020 Presidential Election. The spirit for transparency and justice is being displayed all over the Country by media outlets which do not represent Fake News. People are watching in droves as these Patriots work tirelessly to reveal

the real facts of the most tainted and corrupt Election in American history. Congratulations Windham—look forward to seeing the results. May 6, 2021

Donald J Trump @RealDonaldTrump

The Fake News Media, working in close conjunction with Big Tech and the Radical Left Democrats, is doing everything they can to perpetuate the term "The Big Lie" when speaking of 2020 Presidential Election Fraud. They are right in that the 2020 Presidential Election was a Big Lie, but not in the way they mean. The 2020 Election, which didn't even have Legislative approvals from many States (which is required under the U.S. Constitution), and was also otherwise corrupt, was indeed The Big Lie. So when they try to sell the American people the term The Big Lie, which they do in unison and coordination, think of it instead as the greatest Fraud in the history of our Country! An even greater Hoax than Russia, Russia, Russia, Mueller, Mueller, Mueller, Impeachment Hoax #1, Impeachment Hoax #2, or any of the other many scams the Democrats pulled! May 6, 2021

To comment, Trump is astute to point out the word games being used by the media and Big Tech. He is even more astute in comparing this coordination to what occurred in the various witch hunts perpetrated against him. I address "Impeachment Hoax #1" in my *Impeach* trilogy. I address "Impeachment Hoax #2" in my *Tragic Ending* book. I address the "Russia, Russia, Russia, Mueller, Mueller, Mueller" hoax in various articles on my politics website.

May 7, 2021

Donald J Trump @RealDonaldTrump

The Federal Election Commission in Washington, D.C., has totally dropped the phony case against me concerning payments to women relative to the 2016 Presidential Election. It was a case built on lies from Michael Cohen, a corrupt and convicted lawyer, a lawyer in fact who was so corrupt he was sentenced to three years in jail for lying to Congress and many other things having nothing to do with me. I thank the Commission for their decision, ending this chapter of Fake News. Between two sleazebag lawyers, Michael Avenatti and Michael Cohen, we were all able to witness law and justice in our Country at its lowest! May 7, 2021

Trump Fights Back with Statements

To comment, I address claims about Trump and women in my *God's Sex Plan* books. As for Avenatti, he was a darling of the left at one time when they thought he would bring down Trump. But now, he is serving a multi-year prison sentence for defrauding the very woman (Stormy Daniels) he was trying to use to bring down Trump and for other crimes.

Donald J Trump @RealDonaldTrump

At 6:31 in the morning on November 4th, a dump of 149,772 votes came in to the State of Michigan. Biden received 96% of those votes and the State miraculously went to him. Has the Michigan State Senate started their review of the Fraudulent Presidential Election of 2020 yet, or are they about to start? If not, they should be run out of office.

Likewise, at 3:42 in the morning, a dump of 143,379 votes came in to the state of Wisconsin, also miraculously, given to Biden. Where did these "votes" come from? Both were State Election changing events, and that is on top of the other corruption without even including the fact that neither state got Legislative approval, which is required under the United States Constitution. May 7, 2021

To comment, these "dumps" were probably the counts of the mail-in ballots being recorded. It was known before Election Day that far more Democrats than Republicans voted via mail-in ballots. Trump and Republicans in general made the mistake of discouraging Republicans from voting early, telling them to only vote on Election Day. That had the effect of spotting Biden and other Dems two touchdowns, and it cost Trump and many other Republicans dearly.

Here in PA, Doug Mastriano, a Republican candidate for governor, embraced mail-in ballots during the primary, while his Republican opponents continued to disparage them. As a result, Doug won the Republican nomination.

Republicans need to take a tip from Doug in the general election and embrace mail-in ballots if their state allows them. Yes, they are fraught with potential fraud and should not be allowed except for those who will be absent on election day from their precincts or who have difficulties getting to the polls. But they are here to stay for most states.

Donald J Trump @RealDonaldTrump

Josh Hawley, our fantastic Senator from the beautiful and great State of Missouri, has a fantastic new book, just out this week, about the terrible Big Tech companies and their attempt to ruin our Country. It's called *The Tyranny of Big Tech*—it has my Full and Complete Endorsement. Buy it now! May 7, 2021

To comment, I so wish I could get Trump to endorse this or one of my other books about him. I keep sending him copies, but I doubt he has ever seen them.

May 9, 2021

Donald J Trump @RealDonaldTrump
Happy Mother's Day to all. It will all come back BIGGER and BETTER and STRONGER than ever before. Do not worry! May 9, 2021

Donald J Trump @RealDonaldTrump
So now even our Kentucky Derby winner, Medina Spirit, is a junky. This is emblematic of what is happening to our Country. The whole world is laughing at us as we go to hell on our Borders, our fake Presidential Election, and everywhere else! May 9, 2021

May 10, 2021

Donald J Trump @RealDonaldTrump
The House GOP has a massive opportunity to upgrade this week from warmonger Liz Cheney to gifted communicator Elise Stefanik. Elise has intelligence, an endorsement from American Patriot Brandon Judd and the National Border Patrol Council, she has an A+ from the NRA, and she loves our Veterans. We need someone in Leadership who has experience flipping districts from Blue to Red as we approach the important 2022 midterms, and that's Elise! She knows how to win, which is what we need! May 10, 2021

Donald J Trump @RealDonaldTrump
Lieutenant Governor Dan Patrick is a great fighter for the people of Texas. He has stood up for up for Life, Liberty, the Second Amendment, Border Security, our Military and our Vets, and our God-given Freedoms. He has governed by conservative principles of LOW TAXES and careful spending, always doing what is best for his great State and for America. Texans should re-elect him! He is outstanding and has my Complete and Total Endorsement! May 10, 2021

Donald J Trump @RealDonaldTrump
After being loudly booed at the Utah Republican Party Convention, Utah's Weber County censured RINO Mitt Romney in the strongest of

terms. Washington County Republicans also censured Romney in April. He is BAD NEWS for our Country! May 10, 2021

To comment, I address the censuring of Romney and other Repubs who voted to impeach or convict Trump in the second impeachment in my *Tragic Ending* book.

Donald J Trump @RealDonaldTrump
The major Michigan Election Fraud case has just filed a bombshell pleading claiming votes were intentionally switched from President Trump to Joe Biden. The number of votes is MASSIVE and determinative. This will prove true in numerous other States. All Republicans must UNIFY and not let this happen. If a thief robs a jewelry store of all of its diamonds (the 2020 Presidential Election), the diamonds must be returned. The Fake News media refuses to cover the greatest Election Fraud in the history of our Country. They have lost all credibility, but ultimately, they will have no choice! May 10, 2021

May 11, 2021

Donald J Trump @RealDonaldTrump
Congratulations to Glenn Youngkin for winning the Republican nomination for Governor of Virginia. Glenn is pro-Business, pro-Second Amendment, pro-Veterans, pro-America, he knows how to make Virginia's economy rip-roaring, and he has my Complete and Total Endorsement! Glenn is running against Bill Clinton's longtime enabler, Terry McAuliffe. Terry McAuliffe was the Clintons' bagman in more ways than one, from the cover-ups to the get-rich-quick schemes, and his deals with Communist China look suspicious. He was responsible for many of the problems Virginia currently has. Virginia doesn't need the Clintons or the Communist Chinese running the state, so say no to Terry McAuliffe, and yes to Patriot Glenn Youngkin!
[graphic reading: "May 11, 2021. President Trump endorses Glenn Youngkin for Governor of Virginia!"] May 11, 2021

Donald J Trump @RealDonaldTrump
When I was in office we were known as the Peace Presidency, because Israel's adversaries knew that the United States stood strongly with Israel and there would be swift retribution if Israel was attacked. Under Biden, the world is getting more violent and more unstable because Biden's weakness and lack of support for Israel is leading to new attacks on our allies. America must always stand with Israel and make

clear that the Palestinians must end the violence, terror, and rocket attacks, and make clear that the U.S. will always strongly support Israel's right to defend itself. Unbelievably, Democrats also continue to stand by crazed anti-American Rep. Ilhan Omar, and others, who savagely attack Israel while they are under terrorist assault. May 11, 2021

To comment, Obama had weakened our relationship with Israel when then Israeli Prime Minister Benjamin Netanyahu came to Washington to address Congress but Obama refused to meet with him. Trump fixed that relationship with Beebe and Israel. But now Biden is weakening it once again. That was seen when Hamas attacked Israel, Israel responded in kind, but Biden made it sound like both sides were equally responsible for the hostilities, ignoring Israel's right to defend itself.

Trump also made headlines with his Abraham accords, peace treaties between Israel and four of its neighbors. If Trump had stayed in office, probably more such peace deals with additional neighbors would have been forthcoming. But under Biden, no more such treaties have been signed.

Donald J Trump @RealDonaldTrump

Wilton Simpson has done an outstanding job as President of the Florida State Senate, and I hope he runs for Florida Agriculture Commissioner in 2022—he will have my Complete and Total Endorsement! Wilton has been a great supporter and worked hard to get many good Conservatives elected in Florida. He helped us grow our Republican majority in the Florida State Senate, and gave us a historic win in Florida in the 2020 Presidential Election. Wilton will never let the great people of Florida down! May 11, 2021

Donald J Trump @RealDonaldTrump

The Government of the United Kingdom is proposing that anyone who wants to vote in a British election should show photo ID to eliminate any corruption and fraud and "ensure the integrity of elections." This is exactly what we should do in the United States, unlike the Democrats who want to abolish Voter ID laws with passing their horrible HR 1 Bill. All States should pass Voter ID laws along with many other fair and comprehensive election reforms, like eliminating mass mail-in voting and ballot harvesting, so we never again have an election rigged and stolen from us. The people are demanding real reform! May 11, 2021

Donald J Trump @RealDonaldTrump

Congratulations to Martha's Vineyard in Massachusetts for the privilege they will have in looking at massive windmills that have been

66

approved by the Biden Administration and are being built, in China of course, as part of an extraordinarily large wind farm. Wind is an incredibly expensive form of energy that kills birds, affects the sea, ruins the landscape, and creates disasters for navigation. Liberals love it, but they can't explain why. In any event, Martha's Vineyard, an absolutely wonderful place, will never be the same. Good Luck! May 11, 2021

May 12, 2021

Donald J Trump @RealDonaldTrump

The Republicans in the House of Representatives have a great opportunity today to rid themselves of a poor leader, a major Democrat talking point, a warmonger, and a person with absolutely no personality or heart. As a representative of the Great State of Wyoming, Liz Cheney is bad for our Country and bad for herself. Almost everyone in the Republican Party, including 90% of Wyoming, looks forward to her ouster—and that includes me! May 12, 2021

To comment, this Statement was a prelude to Cheney being ousted as the GOP conference chair.

House Republicans ousted Rep. Liz Cheney from her leadership position Wednesday [5/12/21], a rare move that highlights the power that former President Donald Trump still holds in the party.

Cheney — daughter of former Vice President Dick Cheney and one of Trump's most vocal critics — served as the House Republican Conference chairwoman, a position that entails leading the chamber's messaging efforts (NYP. Liz Cheney).

Donald J Trump @RealDonaldTrump

Liz Cheney is a bitter, horrible human being. I watched her yesterday and realized how bad she is for the Republican Party. She has no personality or anything good having to do with politics or our Country. She is a talking point for Democrats, whether that means the Border, the gas lines, inflation, or destroying our economy. She is a warmonger whose family stupidly pushed us into the never-ending Middle East Disaster, draining our wealth and depleting our Great Military, the worst decision in our Country's history. I look forward to soon watching her as a Paid Contributor on CNN or MSDNC! May 12, 2021

Against Lies of Biden, Attacks from Dems, and Bias of Media

To comment, Trump's disdain for Cheney will only increase when she is named the second chair on the J6 Commission. She will be joined by Adam Kinzinger, who also voted to impeach Trump in the second impeachment. Adam has already announced he is not seeking reelection, while at this writing, Cheney is down 30 percentage points to a Trump-endorsed challenger in the Republican primary. Most all of the other Repubs who voted to impeach Trump have either announced they are not seeking reelection or already lost their reelection bids.

Donald J Trump @RealDonaldTrump

I see that everybody is comparing Joe Biden to Jimmy Carter. It would seem to me that is very unfair to Jimmy Carter. Jimmy mishandled crisis after crisis, but Biden has CREATED crisis after crisis. First there was the Biden Border Crisis (that he refuses to call a Crisis), then the Biden Economic Crisis, then the Biden Israel Crisis, and now the Biden Gas Crisis. Joe Biden has had the worst start of any president in United States history, and someday, they will compare future disasters to the Biden Administration—but no, Jimmy was better! May 12, 2021

Donald J Trump @RealDonaldTrump

If there were long and horrible gas lines like this under President Trump, the Fake News would make it a national outrage! Did Joe Biden put Hunter in charge of our energy, with all of his Burisma experience? Even Energy Secretary Jennifer Granholm is lost! May 12, 2021

Donald J Trump @RealDonaldTrump

A guy named Miles Taylor, who I have no idea who he is, don't remember ever meeting him or having a conversation with, gets more publicity pretending he was in the inner circle of our Administration when he was definitely not. Some people refer to him as "absolutely nothing." I hear he is on CNN and MSDNC all the time, but he had nothing to do with any of my decisions, and I wouldn't even know what he looks like. He is the guy who fraudulently wrote a make-believe book and statement to the failing New York Times calling himself "Anonymous." That's right, he, a lowlife that I didn't know, was Anonymous.

Now he's putting together a group of RINOs and Losers who are coming out to protest President Trump despite our creating the greatest economy ever, getting us out of endless wars, rebuilding our Great Military, reducing taxes and regulations by historic levels, creating Space Force, appointing almost 300 Judges, and much, much more!

He is a phony who will probably be sued over his fake book and fake "Anonymous" editorial, which caused so much treasonous stir. Miles Taylor and his fellow RINO losers like Tom Ridge, Christine

Trump Fights Back with Statements

Todd Whitman, and Crazy Barbara Comstock voted for Biden, and now look what they have—a socialist regime with collapsing borders, massive tax and regulation hikes, unrest in the Middle East, and long gas lines. He is even giving us men setting new records playing women's sports. What a disaster for our Country it has been! May 12, 2021

To comment, I discuss the "Anonymous" editorial and book in my *Impeach* trilogy. Despite all of the speculations about him being a high-level official in the Trump administration, he turned out to be a lowling, a nobody.

Otherwise, what Trump does here in promoting his record as President is what he needs to do more of, and less of complaints about the election. That would set him up much better for a 2024 White House run.

Finally, the issue of men pretending to be women competing in women's sports is becoming more of an issue, as those fake women push records to levels that real women can never hope to reach and steal championships and scholarships from real women. If left unchecked, this trend has the potential to completely destroy women's sports. I address this issue in *God's Sex Plan: Volume Two*.

Donald J Trump @RealDonaldTrump
Sean Hannity statement: https://media.gab.com/system/media_attachments/files/073/965/389/original/33abacd75b5b4b2e.jpg
May 12, 2021

May 13, 2021

Donald J Trump @RealDonaldTrump
A devastating letter written by Arizona Senate President Karen Fann on voting irregularities, and probably fraud, in Maricopa County during the 2020 Presidential Election. Even the database was illegally deleted after the subpoena to produce the information. Senate President Fann has invited Maricopa County officials to a public hearing on May 18 to allow them the opportunity to try to explain what happened to the missing databases, ballots, and other significant issues.

The Fake News and Lamestream Media is doing everything they can not to cover this major story. They just refuse to talk or report about it. They don't want the United States or World to see what is going on with our corrupt, third world election.

Read the full letter here https://cdn.donaldjtrump.com/djtweb/general/5-12-21_Letter_to_Maricopa_County_Board.pdf May 13, 2021

Donald J Trump @RealDonaldTrump

Can't imagine Republican House Members would go with Chip Roy—he has not done a great job, and will probably be successfully primaried in his own district. I support Elise, by far, over Chip! May 13, 2021

To comment, Chip was a last-minute challenger to Elise Stefanik to replace Liz Cheney as GOP conference chair.

Congressman Chip Roy is slated to challenge Rep. Elise Stefanik in the race to replace Rep. Liz Cheney, who was ousted from her role on Wednesday as House Republican Conference chair, the No. 3 GOP leadership position in the lower chamber (NYP. Chip).

May 14, 2021

Donald J Trump @RealDonaldTrump

Isn't it incredible that because of the vaccines, which I and my Administration came up with years ahead of schedule (despite the fact that everybody, including Fauci, said would never happen), that we no longer need masks, and yet our names are not even mentioned in what everybody is calling the modern day miracle of the vaccines?

Without the vaccines, this world would have been in for another 1917 Spanish Flu, where up to 100 million people died. Because of the vaccines we pushed and developed in record time, nothing like that will be even close to happening. Just a mention please! The Biden Administration had zero to do with it. All they did was continue our plan of distribution, which was working well right from the beginning! May 14, 2021

To comment, all very true. And you would think this would make Trump supporters be the first in line for the vaccines. But sadly, Trump supporters will be in the forefront of pushing lies about the vaccines and creating vaccine hesitancy. That will result in far more Republicans than Democrats dying from Covid. That will blunt the "red wave" people were already predicting for 2022. Dead Republican don't vote, though dead Democrats might.

Trump Fights Back with Statements

Donald J Trump @RealDonaldTrump

Congratulations to Elise Stefanik for her Big and Overwhelming victory! The House GOP is united and the Make America Great Again movement is Strong! May 14, 2021

To comment, Trump is referring to Elise Stefanik replacing Liz Cheney as GOP conference chair.

House Republicans approved Rep. Elise Stefanik to their No. 3 leadership position Friday [5/14/21] — officially voting her into the post after Rep. Liz Cheney was forced out this week. The 134-46 tally for Stefanik (R-NY) was nearly guaranteed before the vote took place, given that she went into the meeting with former President Donald Trump's endorsement and without a serious challenger (NYP. Rep. Elise).

Donald J Trump @RealDonaldTrump

Good luck to Drew McKissick who is up for a big re-election vote tomorrow (Saturday) for Chairman of the South Carolina Republican Party. Drew and I have done nothing but WIN together, and that will continue into the future. He is strong on Voter Fraud, Crime, the Border, the Second Amendment, and our great Military and Vets. Drew has my Complete and Total Endorsement for re-election! May 14, 2021

May 15, 2021

Donald J Trump @RealDonaldTrump

As our Country is being destroyed, both inside and out, the Presidential Election of 2020 will go down as THE CRIME OF THE CENTURY! May 15, 2021

Donald J Trump @RealDonaldTrump

Wall Street Journal has reported (they finally got something right), that 2020 was the "Worst Presidential Poll Miss in 40 Years." The public opinion surveys ahead of the 2020 Presidential Election were the most inaccurate ever, according to a major polling panel. This was done purposely. The polls were a joke. I won States in a landslide that I was predicted to lose days before the election. Other states had me purposely so far down that it would force people, even fans, to say "Let's stay home Darling. We love our President, but he can't win." And then I would win those states or at least come very close.

Against Lies of Biden, Attacks from Dems, and Bias of Media

In one state that I actually won, but the results were rigged, ABC and the Washington Post had me down by 17 points. Even the rigged final result was extremely close. It's called SUPPRESSION POLLING and it should be illegal.

These are crooked, disgusting, and very dishonest media outlets and they know exactly what they are doing. The 2020 Presidential Election was, by far, the greatest Election Fraud in the history of our Country. The good news is, the American people get it and the truth is rapidly coming out!

Had Mike Pence had the courage to send the Electoral College vote back to states for recertification, and had Mitch McConnell fought for us instead of being the weak and pathetic leader he is, we would right now have a Republican President who would be VETOING the horrific Socialistic Bills that are rapidly going through Congress, including Open Borders, High Taxes, Massive Regulations, and so much else! May 15, 2021

Donald J Trump @RealDonaldTrump

The entire Database of Maricopa County in Arizona has been DELETED! This is illegal and the Arizona State Senate, who is leading the Forensic Audit, is up in arms. Additionally, seals were broken on the boxes that hold the votes, ballots are missing, and worse. Mark Brnovich, the Attorney General of Arizona, will now be forced to look into this unbelievable Election crime.

Many Radical Left Democrats and weak Republicans are very worried about the fact that this has been exposed. The DELETION of an entire Database and critical Election files of Maricopa County is unprecedented. Many other States to follow.

The Mainstream Media and Radical Left Democrats want to stay as far away as possible from the Presidential Election Fraud, which should be one of the biggest stories of our time. Fox News is afraid to cover it—there is rarely a mention. Likewise, Newsmax has been virtually silent on this subject because they are intimidated by threats of lawsuits. One America News (OAN), one of the fastest growing networks on television, and the "hottest", is doing a magnificent job of exposing the massive fraud that took place. The story is only getting bigger and at some point it will be impossible for the weak and/or corrupt media not to cover. Thank you to OAN and other brave American Patriots. It is all happening quickly! May 15, 2021

Donald J Trump @RealDonaldTrump

Congratulations to Drew McKissick on a great win today in his re-elect as Chairman of the Republican Party of South Carolina. It was a great win against a strong and talented opponent. The Republican Party of South Carolina is in good hands and we will continue to go on to victory as we have had in the past two Presidential Elections! May 15, 2021

May 16, 2021

Donald J Trump @RealDonaldTrump
Breaking News! New polling by CBS News on the state of the Republican Party (which is very strong!). "President Trump has a strong hold on the GOP." 80% of Republicans agree with the removal of Liz Cheney from GOP Leadership and only 20% disagree. The poll also showed that 67% of Republicans said that they do not consider Sleepy Joe Biden to be the legitimate winner of the 2020 Presidential Election. I agree with them 100%, just look at the facts and the data—there is no way he won the 2020 Presidential Election! May 16, 2021

May 18, 2021

Donald J Trump @RealDonaldTrump
Congratulations to Frank Eathorne for being reelected as Chairman of the Republican Party of Wyoming. It was my honor to work with you so that your great achievements can be continued. The people of Wyoming are special, and so are you! May 18, 2021

Donald J Trump @RealDonaldTrump
Republicans in the House and Senate should not approve the Democrat trap of the January 6 Commission. It is just more partisan unfairness and unless the murders, riots, and fire bombings in Portland, Minneapolis, Seattle, Chicago, and New York are also going to be studied, this discussion should be ended immediately. Republicans must get much tougher and much smarter, and stop being used by the Radical Left. Hopefully, Mitch McConnell and Kevin McCarthy are listening! May 18, 2021

To comment, Trump will have much more to say about the J6 Commission, as will I. I will be covering the public hearings of June to July 2022 in my *J6 Commission* book.

But here, Trump was prescient once again in realizing the Commons would consist of "partisan unfairness." He is also correct that the much more damaging and deadly BLM/ Antifa riots should be the target of such a commission. But Dems ignored and downplayed those riots

73

when they happened, saying they were "mostly peaceful" protests, while overemphasizing the seriousness of J6, calling it a "deadly insurrection." I refute both notions in my *Tragic Ending* book.

May 19, 2021

Donald J Trump @RealDonaldTrump
Breitbart News:

"President Donald Trump directly confronting radical Islamic terrorism made the United States and the world a much safer place, paving the path for historic peace deals like the Abraham Accords." — Secretary Pompeo. May 19, 2021

To comment, Trump never got the credit he deserved for defeating the radical Islamic caliphate and for the historic Abraham Accords. But under Biden, we are seeing ISIS and Al-Qaeda reconstituted and no progress on peace in the Middle East.

Donald J Trump @RealDonaldTrump

I have just learned, through leaks in the mainstream media, that after being under investigation from the time I came down the escalator 5 ½ years ago, including the fake Russia Russia Russia Hoax, the 2 year, $ 48M, No Collusion Mueller Witch Hunt, Impeachment Hoax #1, Impeachment Hoax #2, and others, that the Democrat New York Attorney General has "informed" my organization that their "investigation" is no longer just a civil matter but also potentially a "criminal" investigation working with the Manhattan District Attorney's Office.

There is nothing more corrupt than an investigation that is in desperate search of a crime. But, make no mistake, that is exactly what is happening here.

The Attorney General of New York literally campaigned on prosecuting Donald Trump even before she knew anything about me. She said that if elected, she would use her office to look into "every aspect" of my real estate dealings. She swore that she would "definitely sue" me. She boasted on video that she would be, and I quote, "a real pain in the ass." She declared, "just wait until I'm in the Attorney General's office," and, "I've got my eyes on Trump Tower." She also promised that, if elected, she would "join with law enforcement and other Attorney Generals across this nation in removing this President from office," and, "It's important that everyone understand that the days of Donald Trump are coming to an end."

Trump Fights Back with Statements

The Attorney General made each of these statements, not after having had an opportunity to actually look at the facts, but BEFORE she was even elected, BEFORE she had seen even a shred of evidence. This is something that happens in failed third world countries, not the United States. If you can run for a prosecutor's office pledging to take out your enemies, and be elected to that job by partisan voters who wish to enact political retribution, then we are no longer a free constitutional democracy.

Likewise, the District Attorney's office has been going after me for years based on a lying, discredited low life, who was not listened to or given credibility by other prosecutorial offices, and sentenced to 3 years in prison for lying and other events unrelated to me.

These investigations have also been going on for years with members and associates of the Trump Organization being viciously attacked, harassed, and threatened, in order to say anything bad about the 45th President of the United States. This would include having to make up false stories. Numerous documents, all prepared by large and prestigious law and accounting firms, have been examined, and many hours of testimony have been taken from many people, some of whom I have not seen in years. May 19, 2021

To comment, to put all of this another way, normally, you start with a crime, then law enforcement investigates to figure out whodunit. But in the case of Trump, they started with whodunit (Trump), then they did investigation after investigation to figure out a crime to pin on him. It is all so backwards and a breakdown of our entire criminal justice system. Trump is correct to be irate about it.

Donald J Trump @RealDonaldTrump

These Democrat offices are consumed with this political and partisan Witch Hunt at a time when crime is up big in New York City, shootings are up 97%, murders are up 45%, a rate not seen in 40 years, drugs and criminals are pouring into our Country in record numbers from our now unprotected Southern Border, and people are fleeing New York for other much safer locations to live. But the District Attorney and Attorney General are possessed, at an unprecedented level, with destroying the political fortunes of President Donald J. Trump and the almost 75 million people who voted for him, by far the highest number ever received by a sitting President.

That is what these investigations are all about—a continuation of the greatest political Witch Hunt in the history of the United States. Working in conjunction with Washington, these Democrats want to silence and cancel millions of voters because they don't want "Trump" to run again. As people are being killed on the sidewalks of New York at an unprecedented rate, as drugs and crime of all kinds are flowing through New York City at record levels, with absolutely nothing being done about it, all they care about is taking down Trump.

Our movement, which started with the Great Election Win of 2016, is perhaps the biggest and most powerful in the history of our Country. But the Democrats want to cancel the Make America Great Again movement, not by Making America First, but by Making America Last. No President has been treated the way I have. With all of the crime and corruption you read about with others, nothing happens, they only go after Donald Trump.

After prosecutorial efforts the likes of which nobody has ever seen before, they failed to stop me in Washington, so they turned it over to New York to do their dirty work. This is what I have been going through for years. It's a very sad and dangerous tale for our Country, but it is what it is, and we will overcome together.

I have built a great company, employed thousands of people, and all I do is get unfairly attacked and abused by a corrupt political system. It would be so wonderful if the effort used against President Donald J. Trump, who lowered taxes and regulations, rebuilt our military, took care of our Veterans, created Space Force, fixed our border, produced our vaccine in record-setting time (years ahead of what was anticipated), and made our Country great and respected again, and so much more, would be focused on the ever more dangerous sidewalks and streets of New York.

If these prosecutors focused on real issues, crime would be obliterated, and New York would be great and free again! May 19, 2021

To comment, Trump is so correct in this rant. NYC is in a mess as a result of defunding the police to the tune of $1 billion. Crime is rampant, and people are leaving in droves. But their new DA is focused on Trump rather than tracking down and prosecuting violent law-breakers.

Donald J Trump @RealDonaldTrump

Stick with Kirstie Alley! She is a great actress, loved by so many people, and a true original. She is also strong and smart. Many millions of people greatly appreciate her support of our Country. Thank you Kirstie, you are truly appreciated! May 19, 2021

To comment, Kirstie Alley is the former *Cheers* star and later was Saavik in *Star Trek II: The Wrath of Khan*. Most recently, she has been a spokeswoman for the Jenny Craig weight loss plan. But I am not sure what promoted mention of her by Trump.

Trump Fights Back with Statements

Donald J Trump @RealDonaldTrump
A loan of $1.2 billion has closed on the asset known as the Bank of America Building (555 California Street) in San Francisco, CA. The interest rate is approximately 2%. Thank you! May 19, 2021

To comment, no idea what this Statement is about.

May 21, 2021

Donald J Trump @RealDonaldTrump
Many people have asked about the beautiful Boeing 757 that became so iconic during the Trump rallies. It was effectively kept in storage in Upstate New York in that I was not allowed to use it during my presidency. It is now being fully restored and updated and will be put back into service sometime prior to the end of the year. It will soon be brought to a Louisiana service facility for the completion of work, inspection and updating of Rolls-Royce engines, and a brand new paint job. When completed, it will be better than ever, and again used at upcoming rallies! May 21, 2021

To comment, Trump of course used Air Force One during his time as President. But I would bet his own plane is even nicer.

May 23, 2021

Donald J Trump @RealDonaldTrump
The lackluster Attorney General of Arizona, Mark Brnovich, has to get on the ball and catch up with the great Republican Patriots in the Arizona State Senate. As massive crime in the 2020 Election is becoming more and more evident and obvious, Brnovich is nowhere to be found. He is always on television promoting himself, but never mentions the Crime of the Century, that took place during the 2020 Presidential Election, which was Rigged and Stolen. Arizona was a big part and Brnovich must put himself in gear, or no Arizona Republican will vote for him in the upcoming elections. They will never forget, and neither will the great Patriots of our Nation! May 23, 2021

Donald J Trump @RealDonaldTrump
Where's Durham—what ever happened to the Durham Report? May 23, 2021

May 25, 2021

Donald J Trump @RealDonaldTrump

Highly respected pollster John McLaughlin says 73% of all Republicans want Trump to run again in 2024 and Republican primary voters would support him 82%-13%. Even the Washington Post has just reported "All Republican Roads Lead to Mar-a-Lago."

What WaPo and other members of the Fake News Media don't report is that Joe Biden is of no interest to anybody—21 million less people watched his Joint Address to Congress than watched mine.

Also, Biden's ratings have killed the Radical Left Fake News Cable Channels. MSNBC and CNN have plummeted in the ratings. MSNBC doesn't have a show in the top 10 of all cable news programs, and CNN doesn't even have a show in the top 100. They should have embraced and endorsed "Trump"—their ratings would have been at new highs!

I have been doing very limited media so the American public could see just how big of a disaster the Biden Administration has been, and I was right. Inflation, the Border Crisis, our forgotten Military, war in the Middle East, all as a result of Biden's mistakes. Our Country is being destroyed. Watch, it's only going to get worse!

The Washington Post also incorrectly reported about my http://DonaldJTrump.com website viewership. We have not yet launched our own social media "platform," but even the very basic site we have to post our statements has received 36.7 million views over the past month alone, and we're getting more traffic to our website now than in 2020, an Election year! This number would be even greater if we were still on Twitter and Facebook, but since Big Tech has illegally banned me, tens of millions of our supporters have stopped using these platforms because they've become "boring" and nasty.

My website is a place where everyone can see my statements, issued in real time, and engage with the MAGA Movement. This is meant to be a temporary way of getting my thoughts and ideas out to the public without the Fake News spin, but the website is not a "platform." It is merely a way of communicating until I decide on what the future will be for the choice or establishment of a platform. It will happen soon. Stay tuned!

Save America Over the past four years, Donald J. Trump's administration delivered for Americans of all backgrounds like never before. Save America is about building on those... http://donaldjtrump.com/ May 25, 2021

Trump Fights Back with Statements

To comment, Trump is correct about Biden's failing presidency. I document all that Trump says and more in my *Biden Tweets* books.

On Trump's website, it did not last long. But it was replaced by Truth Social. More on that later.

Donald J Trump @RealDonaldTrump

New Hampshire's Election Audit has revealed that large-scale voting machines appear to count NON-EXISTING VOTES. State and local communities are seeking confirmation. It's probably true, but we'll soon know. Why aren't Minority Leader Mitch McConnell and Republicans doing anything about what went on in the 2020 Election? How can the Democrats be allowed to get away with this? It will go down as the Crime of the Century! Other States like Arizona, Georgia (where a Judge just granted a motion to unseal and inspect ballots from the 2020 Election), Michigan, Pennsylvania, and more to follow. May 25, 2021

Donald J Trump @RealDonaldTrump

Crazy Joe Scarborough and his blood-curdling, psycho wife (?), Mika, are going crazy because their ratings have absolutely TANKED. They are wrong too often and always predictable. They were right about me in 2016, but I did better in the 2020 Election with 12 million more votes. Stay tuned! May 25, 2021

Donald J Trump @RealDonaldTrump

Arizona Republican State Senators are engendering such tremendous respect, even adoration, for the great job they are doing on the Forensic Audit of the 2020 Presidential Election Scam. Our Country is watching as early public reports are indicating a disaster, far greater than anyone had thought possible, for Arizona voters. May 25, 2021

Donald J Trump @RealDonaldTrump

New United States COVID cases, because of the record-breaking development of the vaccine and its early purchase and distribution by the Trump Administration, has hit its lowest level in more than one year, and falling fast. I want to thank all within the Trump Administration who pushed so hard for a vaccine and got it done in less than nine months when everybody was saying it would take at least 3-5 years, and probably not happen. Without the vaccine the world would be a much different place right now.

Thank you also to the U.S. Military for its incredible distribution and logistical planning. Operation Warp Speed and our decision to purchase billions of dollars of vaccine before it was even approved, has been "One of the greatest miracles of the ages," according to many. Thank you! May 25, 2021

To comment, all very true. And if Biden would give Trump credit for all of this, rather than dishonestly trying to take credit himself, maybe there would not be so much vaccine hesitancy among conservatives, saving many lives and preventing much needless suffering.

May 26, 2021

Donald J Trump @RealDonaldTrump

Now everybody is agreeing that I was right when I very early on called Wuhan as the source of COVID-19, sometimes referred to as the China Virus. To me it was obvious from the beginning but I was badly criticized, as usual. Now they are all saying "He was right." Thank you! May 26, 2021

To comment, it never made sense that a virus just happened to originate in a city with a virology lab, but that lab had nothing to do with it.

As some late-night comedian put it (I forget which one), if you were in Hershey, PA and there was "chocolatey goodness" flowing down the street, you could come up with some weird theory it was created by a garbage truck slamming into a fire hydrant. But a more logical thesis would be it is coming from the chocolate factory down the street.

Donald J Trump @RealDonaldTrump

Thank you to the Washington Examiner newspaper for covering the Forensic Audits for the 2020 Presidential Election, the most corrupt Election in the history of our Country. Read and study it carefully—it's not Fake News! May 26, 2021

Donald J Trump @RealDonaldTrump

This is a continuation of the greatest Witch Hunt in American history. It began the day I came down the escalator in Trump Tower, and it's never stopped. They wasted two years and $48 million in taxpayer dollars on Mueller and Russia Russia Russia, Impeachment Hoax #1, Impeachment Hoax #2, and it continues to this day, with illegally leaked confidential information.

No other President in history has had to put up with what I have had to, and on top of all that, I have done a great job for our Country, whether it's taxes, regulations, our Military, Veterans, Space Force, our Borders, speedy creation of a great vaccine (said to be a miracle!), and protecting the Second Amendment.

This is purely political, and an affront to the almost 75 million voters who supported me in the Presidential Election, and it's being driven by highly partisan Democrat prosecutors.

New York City and State are suffering the highest crime rates in their history, and instead of going after murderers, drug dealers, human traffickers, and others, they come after Donald Trump.

Interesting that today a poll came out indicating I'm far in the lead for the Republican Presidential Primary and the General Election in 2024.

Our Country is broken, our elections are rigged, corrupt, and stolen, our prosecutors are politicized, and I will just have to keep on fighting like I have been for the last five years! May 26, 2021

To comment, this Statement is in response to the Southern District of New York announcing it has opened a criminal investigation into the Trump organization and formed a grand jury.

May 27, 2021

Donald J Trump @RealDonaldTrump

Trump Exclusive: Tuesday May 25th 2021 Steve Cortes.

Trump on McConnell, Biden and Fauci, what he'd do in a possible 2nd term | Newsmax EXCLUSIVE Newsmax TV.
https://tv.gab.com/me-dia/60adb8905cf6c5d8a9afc1ee?viewKey=df522e70-fff8-45d5-a596-40ed8bfe0acf&r=1080p May 27, 2021

May 28, 2021

Donald J Trump @RealDonaldTrump

With Memorial Day Weekend coming up, tomorrow people start driving in the biggest automobile days of the year. I'm sorry to say the gasoline prices that you will be confronted with are far higher than they were just a short number of months ago where we had gasoline under $2 a gallon.

Remember as you're watching the meter tick, and your dollars pile up, how great of a job Donald Trump did as President. Soon Russia and the Middle East will be making a fortune on oil, and you will be saying how good it was to have me as your President. Wasn't it great to be energy independent, but we are energy independent no more. Shame,

shame, shame. Other than that, have a great Memorial Day Weekend! May 28, 2021

To comment, do not miss that this Statement about rising gasoline prices is from the end of May 2021. Biden will later try to blame rising gasoline prices on Putin's invasion of Ukraine. But that will not happen for another nine months, the end of February 2022.

Donald J Trump @RealDonaldTrump
Breaking News! Massive numbers of dead people "voted" in the 2020 Presidential Election, far greater than anyone has known or seen before. Some of these "dead people" even applied for an application to vote. This is just one of the many fraudulent aspects of the 2020 Presidential Election. People are just now beginning to understand! May 28, 2021

Donald J Trump @RealDonaldTrump
CNN Loses Nearly 70% Of Its Viewers Since Trump Left Office
Recently released ratings from Neilson Media Research show that CNN has lost 67% of its total viewers since January.
https://dailycaller.com/2021/05/25/cnn-lost-viewers-since-january-msnbc-fox-cable-news/ May 28, 2021

Chapter Six
Trump's Statements
June 2021

These Trump Statements are continued from Chapter Five.

June 1, 2021

Donald J Trump @RealDonaldTrump
"BREAKING: Alarm Went Off at Secure Building in Fulton County Georgia Where Ballots Are Kept – Building Found Wide Open"

Great work is being done in Georgia revealing the Election Fraud of the 2020 Presidential Election. But, we must not allow ANYONE to compromise these ballots by leaving the building unsecured, which was done late Friday. Republicans and Patriots must protect this site and the Absentee Ballots. The Left talks about election security but they do not practice what they preach because they are afraid of what might be found. Fulton County Leadership—do the right thing and protect these ballots. Our Country is at stake! June 1, 2021

Donald J Trump @RealDonaldTrump
Wow! I hear they have thousands and thousands of boats parading in Jupiter [Florida], despite the fact that they tried to cancel us. Everyone is having an incredible time. On this day, we especially appreciate everyone who served and fought for our great Country. I love you all! June 1, 2021

June 2, 2021

Donald J Trump @RealDonaldTrump
Greg Abbott is a fighter and a Great Governor for the incredible people of Texas. No Governor has done more to secure the Border and keep our communities safe than Governor Abbott. Greg is a staunch defender of the Second Amendment and has made Texas a Second Amendment Sanctuary State.   Texas has become a job-creating machine, and our partnership helped restore America's economic power and success. Greg is also very tough on crime, fully supports the brave men and women of Law Enforcement, and is all in on Election Integrity.

Governor Greg Abbott will continue to be a great leader for the Lone Star State, and has my Complete and Total Endorsement for re-election. He will never let you down! June 2, 2021

June 3, 2021

Donald J Trump @RealDonaldTrump

Incredible to see that RINO Governor Doug Ducey of Arizona just vetoed a bill that would have outlawed Critical Race Theory training for State employees, and another that would have banned the mailing of ballots to citizens who never requested them. He did this under the guise of passing a budget. For those of you who think Doug Ducey is good for Arizona, you are wrong. Our Country needs Attorney General Mark Brnovich, who has done little so far on Voter Integrity and the 2020 Presidential Election Scam, to step it up—but patriotic Republicans in the State Senate are making up for unelectable RINOs. June 3, 2021

Donald J Trump @RealDonaldTrump

Remain in Mexico, also known as MPP (Migrant Protection Protocols), was not only a historic foreign policy triumph but one of the most successful border security programs anyone has ever put into effect anywhere. Along with our Central America Safe Third agreements, asylum reforms, and expedited removal procedures we drove border numbers to record lows and we ENDED the horrendous practice known as Catch-and-Release.

No American President had ever done more to defend the border and safeguard the whole immigration system.

The Biden Administration inherited the most secure border in history, and they turned it into the greatest border disaster in history. Our border is now run by cartels, criminals, and coyotes. Illegal immigrants, gang members, and lethal drugs are pouring across like never before. Not only are illegal immigrants being caught and released, they are be June 3, 2021ing put up in hotels at taxpayer expense.

Our country is being destroyed before our very eyes.

The Biden Administration's disastrous decision to formally end the Remain in Mexico policy is proof that their objective is to eliminate the U.S. border entirely and flood the country with so many illegal aliens that every community is overwhelmed.

Joe Biden is the first American President who doesn't want America to be a nation at all. June 3, 2021

Trump Fights Back with Statements

Donald J Trump @RealDonaldTrump

After seeing the emails, our Country is fortunate I didn't do what Dr. Fauci wanted me to do. For instance, I closed our Borders to China very early despite his not wanting them closed. The Democrats and the Fake News Media even called me a "xenophobe." In the end, we saw this was a life-saving decision, and likewise with closing our borders to Europe, specifically to certain heavily infected countries.

I was later given credit, even by "Tony," for saving hundreds of thousands of lives. Dr. Fauci also didn't put an emphasis on speed of vaccine production because he thought it would take 3, 4, or maybe even 5 years to create. I got it done in less than 9 months with Operation Warp Speed. In retrospect, the vaccine is saving the world. Then, I placed the greatest bet in history. We ordered billions of dollars' worth of vaccines before we knew it even worked. Had that not been done, our wonderful vaccines would not have been administered until October of this year. No one would've had the shot that has now saved the world and millions of lives!

Also, Dr. Fauci was totally against masks when even I thought they would at least be helpful. He then changed his mind completely and became a radical masker!

There are a lot of questions that must be answered by Dr. Fauci. The funding of Wuhan by the U.S. was foolishly started by the Obama Administration in 2014 but ended under the Trump Administration. When I heard about it, I said "no way." What did Dr. Fauci know about "gain of function" research, and when did he know it? June 3, 2021

To comment, Trump made a mistake early in listening to Fauci, and Birx and their advice to shut down the country via the "15 days to slow the spread." Trump quickly realized the disastrous nature of that policy. But sadly, Fauci and Dem governors and mayors continued to use lockdowns, much to the detriment of their states and cities and the country in general. We are still paying for those ill-decisions via inflation, supply chain shortages, increased mental health problems, and drug addictions and deaths. The latter are made worse by Biden's open border policies, as Trump mentions in the previous Statement.

Donald J Trump @RealDonaldTrump

Now everyone, even the so-called "enemy," are beginning to say that President Trump was right about the China Virus coming from the Wuhan Lab. The correspondence between Dr. Fauci and China speaks too loudly for anyone to ignore. China should pay Ten Trillion Dollars to America, and the World, for the death and destruction they have caused! June 3, 2021

To comment, these Statements are in regard to the Fauci emails that were released at this time. They show Fauci knew back in January 2020 the virus originated in a lab not in a wet market. As such, he lied under oath when he testified to the contrary to Congress. See Appendix One for references for "Fauci Emails and the Origins of Covid."

June 4, 2021

Donald J Trump @RealDonaldTrump
Great patriots led by State Senator Doug Mastriano, Senator Cris Dush, and State Representative Rob Kauffman went to Maricopa County, Arizona, to learn the best practices for conducting a full Forensic Audit of the 2020 General Election. Now the Pennsylvania Senate needs to act. Senate President Jake Corman needs to fulfill his promise to his constituents to conduct a full Forensic Audit. Senator Dave Argall, Chairman of the State Government Committee, has to authorize the subpoenas, if necessary. The people of Pennsylvania and America deserve to know the truth. If the Pennsylvania Senate leadership doesn't act, there is no way they will ever get re-elected! June 4. 2021

To comment, the GOP attempted to have such an audit here in PA, but it never came to full fruition.

Donald J Trump @RealDonaldTrump
A great honor to be speaking at the North Carolina GOP convention tomorrow night. I understand the place will be packed, all records broken! North Carolina produced a big victory for us, without a fraudulent outcome—missing ballots, illegal voting, dead people voting, and all of the other Democrat tricks. Before my Election in 2016, everybody said North Carolina was going "Blue," now they are saying that the Great State of North Carolina is surging big for Republicans. Look at the results we have produced. Thank you to Michael Whatley and the state party. See you tomorrow night! June 4. 2021

Donald J Trump @RealDonaldTrump
Facebook's ruling is an insult to the record-setting 75M people, plus many others, who voted for us in the 2020 Rigged Presidential Election. They shouldn't be allowed to get away with this censoring and silencing, and ultimately, we will win. Our Country can't take this abuse anymore! June 4. 2021

Trump Fights Back with Statements

Donald J Trump @RealDonaldTrump

Next time I'm in the White House there will be no more dinners, at his request, with Mark Zuckerberg and his wife. It will be all business! June 4. 2021

To comment, these Statements are in regard to Facebook's new advisory book rejecting allowing Trump back onto Facebook. Initially, it was to be a two-year ban. That would have taken it to January 2023, after the midterm elections. But later it became a permanent ban.

Trump threatened to sue in response. But nothing came of his lawsuit, as far as I know. Then when Trump started his Truth Social, it because a moot point. See Appendix One for references for "Trump and Facebook."

June 7, 2021

Donald J Trump @RealDonaldTrump

[0:40 video of Trump being interviewed on FBN. https://media.gab.com/system/media_attachments/files/076/126/494/original/79f1bc57e2f7a541.mp4]

June 7. 2021

June 8, 2021

Donald J Trump @RealDonaldTrump

Senator Lisa Murkowski has cost the great people of Alaska billions and billions of dollars by voting for Radical Left Biden appointees, which in turn led to the revocation of ANWR drilling, which Alaskans have been fighting to see happen for six decades. Not only did Murkowski kill the biggest economic stimulant for the State, but also one of the biggest energy producing sites in the world. Nobody thought ANWR could be opened. We got it done, and she allowed it to be killed. She's the best friend Washington Democrats ever had—and Alaska's reward for that betrayal is an empowered Left coming after their wealth and jobs. I think she will be met very harshly by the Alaska voters in 15 months, and I will be there to campaign against her! June 8. 2021

Donald J Trump @RealDonaldTrump

Why does Fox News keep Chris Wallace? His ratings are terrible, he's "almost" Radical Left, he was acknowledged to have failed badly as a Presidential debate moderator (except for Biden who he totally protected!), and so much else. Usually, these are not the qualities of a long-term stay! June 8. 2021

To comment, Chris' bias in the presidential debate he moderated was obvious and despicable. I cover that debate in my *Corruption* book. Chris interview of GOP candidates for the Georgia senatorial runoff was just as bad. I cover that in my *Tragic Ending* book. Later, Chris left FNC to be a part of CNN's new streaming service. But that service lasted all of three weeks! At this writing (August 2022), Chris is still out of a job.

June 9, 2021

Donald J Trump @RealDonaldTrump
Congratulations to the country of Nigeria, who just banned Twitter because they banned their President. More COUNTRIES should ban Twitter and Facebook for not allowing free and open speech—all voices should be heard. In the meantime, competitors will emerge and take hold. Who are they to dictate good and evil if they themselves are evil? Perhaps I should have done it while I was President. But Zuckerberg kept calling me and coming to the White House for dinner telling me how great I was. 2024? June 9. 2021

Donald J Trump @RealDonaldTrump
Thank you to the Department of the Interior Inspector General for Completely and Totally exonerating me in the clearing of Lafayette Park! [in Washington DC]
As we have said all along, and it was backed up in today's highly detailed and professionally written report, our fine Park Police made the decision to clear the park to allow a contractor to safely install antiscale fencing to protect from Antifa rioters, radical BLM protestors, and other violent demonstrators who are causing chaos and death to our cities.
In this instance, they tried burning down the church the day before the clearing. Fortunately, we were there to stop the fire from spreading beyond the basement—and it was our great honor and privilege to do so. Again, thank you to the Inspector General! June 9. 2021

Extended Comment
Trump and Lafayette Park

The background to this Statement is the following:

Trump Fights Back with Statements

A federal judge has dismissed a majority of the claims filed by activists and civil liberties groups who accused the Trump administration of violating the civil rights of protesters who were forcefully removed by police using chemical agents from a park near the White House before then-President Donald Trump walked to a nearby church to take a photo...

The lawsuit stemmed from one of the most high-profile moments of the Trump presidency, when federal and local law enforcement officials aggressively forced a group of largely peaceful protesters back from Lafayette Square outside of the White House, firing smoke bombs and pepper balls into the crowd to disperse the group. Officers were seen shoving protesters and journalists as they pushed the crowd back.

[AG William] Barr has said he met with other law enforcement officials earlier that day to review a plan to extend the security perimeter around the White House to protect federal agents after days of unrest in Washington following the death of George Floyd at the hands of police officers in Minneapolis.

After the crowd was forcefully dispersed, Trump, followed by an entourage of his most senior aides — including Barr — along with Secret Service agents and reporters, walked over to St. John's Church, a landmark building where every president has prayed, which had been damaged a day earlier in a protest fire. (AP. Judge tosses).

Critics accused Trump of using federal law enforcement to violently disperse protesters in the square in front of the White House so that he could cross through for a photo-op at a nearby church.

The Interior Department inspector general's report found that federal law enforcement had "begun implementing the operational plan" to clear the park "several hours before they knew of a potential Presidential visit to the park." The IG's investigation "did not support a finding that the [U.S. Park Police] cleared the park on June 1, 2020, so that then President Trump could enter the park" (Just the News. 'Proven).

The misreporting about this incident can still be seen in the AP's first paragraph. But then they bury the truth. Just the News reports the false claim then the truth of the matter. Back to Trump.

Donald J Trump @RealDonaldTrump

Our recently secured Southern Border is now worse than ever before. At no time in our Country's history has anything so outrageous taken place. The Biden Administration stopped construction of the small remaining openings in areas of the almost 500 mile long wall, have taken away all authority from our great Border Patrol, and have ended such long fought for policies including Remain in Mexico, Safe Third Agreements, and our hugely-successful program that completely stopped Catch-and-Release. June 9. 2021

Donald J Trump @RealDonaldTrump

Millions of people are pouring through our Border, including many criminals being released from jails, for such crimes as murder, drug smuggling, and human trafficking. In the history of our Country, it has never been more dangerous or worse. They do not have long to act as our Country is being destroyed! June 9. 2021

June 10, 2021

Donald J Trump @RealDonaldTrump

Now that I have been totally exonerated on the Mueller Witch Hunt with a charge of No Collusion, I have often wondered, if a fake investigation is illegally started based on information provided and paid for by the DNC and the Clinton campaign, shouldn't they be held accountable? Not to mention, wasting tens of millions of taxpayer dollars and interfering with years of a presidential administration? I fought the made-up Hoax strongly and effectively, and I won.

Then they fabricated, out of thin air, the fake allegation that I obstructed justice, and I won that too. Think of it, how can you obstruct justice when you were fighting a false and illegally submitted narrative?

This week I have been totally exonerated by the Inspector General in the clearing of Lafayette Park, despite earlier reports that it was done for political purposes.

And I have also been totally exonerated in Congress by the testimony of former White House lawyer Don McGahn. It came, it went, and it was a big "nothingburger."

But fear not, the Radical Left, country destroying, illegal Witch Hunts continue, and I will win those too! June 10. 2021

To comment, if there were a nonbiased investigation, you would also be exonerated on the J6 hoax, but what we are getting from the J6

Commission is anything but unbiased. That is why my book on it will have the word "Biased" in the title.

Donald J Trump @RealDonaldTrump

Biden just said that he was told by the Joint Chiefs of Staff that Climate Change is our greatest threat. If that is the case, and they actually said this, he ought to immediately fire the Joint Chiefs of Staff for being incompetent! June 10. 2021

Donald J Trump @RealDonaldTrump

It is now unanimous, and I have been proven right (once again) that the initial World Health Organization Report on the Wuhan Lab was flawed and must be redone, this time by a truly transparent investigation. We were right about the China Virus from the beginning, and now the entire world sees it. This is why the Chinese Communist Party should pay $10 Trillion in global reparations for what they allowed to happen, the worst event in world history.

Even here in the United States, the so-called experts like Dr. Fauci were wrong about the Wuhan Lab and China's role the entire time. Just think how bad things would have gotten if I followed Dr. Fauci's advice and never closed down travel from China (and other things)? Dr. Fauci likes to say that he is "science," when in fact he is merely science fiction! June 10. 2021

Donald J Trump @RealDonaldTrump

As President, I had a great and very productive meeting in Helsinki, Finland, with President Putin of Russia. Despite the belated Fake News portrayal of the meeting, the United States won much, including the respect of President Putin and Russia.

Because of the phony Russia, Russia, Russia Hoax, made-up and paid for by the Democrats and Crooked Hillary Clinton, the United States was put at a disadvantage—a disadvantage that was nevertheless overcome by me. As to who do I trust, they asked, Russia or our "Intelligence" from the Obama era, meaning people like Comey, McCabe, the two lovers, Brennan, Clapper, and numerous other sleezebags, or Russia, the answer, after all that has been found out and written, should be obvious. Our government has rarely had such lowlifes as these working for it.

Good luck to Biden in dealing with President Putin—don't fall asleep during the meeting, and please give him my warmest regards! June 10. 2021

Against Lies of Biden, Attacks from Dems, and Bias of Media

To comment, sadly, Biden had no luck with Putin. That was seen when Putin invaded Ukraine on February 24, 2022. That is something that would not have happened if Trump were still in office. How do I know that? Because it didn't happen while Trump was in office.

June 11, 2021

Donald J Trump @RealDonaldTrump
The union representing the great workers building the Keystone XL Pipeline endorsed Biden. Now their workers have no jobs and the pipeline, which was well under construction (like the Southern Border Wall), has been shut down, with thousands of jobs lost and the company announcing yesterday that they are "permanently pulling out." You should vote those people out of office immediately, and stop paying your union dues. A total waste of money. And I said it was going to happen before the 2020 Presidential Election Hoax! June 11, 2021

To comment, worse will be the effect that shutdown will have on oil prices, not only from the loss of oil from that pipeline but from the depression of oil exploration and development. Oil companies are not going to start million-dollar projects, knowing they could be shut down and all of that investment lost by a pen stroke by Biden.

Donald J Trump @RealDonaldTrump
I turned down two book deals, from the most unlikely of publishers, in that I do not want to do such a deal right now. I'm writing like crazy anyway, however, and when the time comes, you'll see the book of all books. Actually, I've been working on a much more important project right now! June 11, 2021

To comment, that project was probably Truth Social.

June 13, 2021

Donald J Trump @RealDonaldTrump
Have you noticed that they are now admitting I was right about everything they lied about before the election?

Hydroxychloroquine works
The Virus came from a Chinese lab
Hunter Biden's laptop was real
Lafayette Square was not cleared for a photo op

Trump Fights Back with Statements

The "Russian Bounties" story was fake
We did produce vaccines before the end of 2020, in record time
Blue state lockdowns didn't work
Schools should be opened
Critical Race Theory is a disaster for our schools and our Country
Our Southern Border security program was unprecedentedly successful. June 13, 2021

To comment, Trump is correct he has been proven correct on all of these points. I will document the Covid ones in my *Coronavirus* book.

Donald J Trump @RealDonaldTrump
The Department of Justice (DOJ) is adding more people onto its roles in order to fight against efforts to limit voting and, I assume, other illegal voting acts. Based on that it would seem the DOJ has no choice but to look at the massive voter fraud which took place in certain Swing States, and I assume elsewhere, during the 2020 Presidential Election Scam. Whether it be voting machines, underaged people, dead people, illegal aliens, ballot drops, ballot cheating, absentee ballots, post office delivery (or lack thereof!), lock boxes, people being paid to vote, or other things, the 2020 Presidential Election is, in my mind, the Crime of the Century.

Just look at what has happened to our Country, our Borders, our Economy, Inflation, and more in the last five months, and it will only get worse. If there is going to be honor and greatness for America, the voting irregularities and fraud of that election must be brought to light, immediately. Otherwise, we have no Country, certainly not a great one! This should not be an attempt by the Biden Administration to suppress the accountability of a dishonest election. That cannot be allowed to happen, nor can the events of the Presidential Election.

They want to cancel anything having to do with the result of that election because they know what was done. States cannot allow that to happen and should not be intimidated or suppressed by a government that wants nothing further to do with what took place during that period of time. They want it over with because they seem to know what will be found, and that would be a disaster for them. There has never been a time like this in our Country—hopefully courage will prevail! June 13, 2021

Donald J Trump @RealDonaldTrump
June 12, 2021 - President Trump at FrankSpeech MAGA Rally Part 1

https://tv.gab.com/me-dia/60c517037de7531ae270ebf3?viewKey=9c7f3c1f-483e-401d-bdaa-f4a21b041b1f&r=1080p [8:52 video] June 13, 2021

Donald J Trump @RealDonaldTrump
June 12, 2021 - President Trump at FrankSpeech MAGA Rally Part 2
https://tv.gab.com/me-dia/60c517bce1a65a1c15929ec2?viewKey=170bcbef-f392-4713-b14f-8030b3b316f9&r=1080p [6:59 video] June 13, 2021

Donald J Trump @RealDonaldTrump
"…I think it's great to have a US President part of the club and very willing to cooperate," said French President Emmanuel Macron.

This was a quote by the President of France. He and many other Leaders before him, in France and throughout Europe, were ripping off the United States like never before. We were treated very unfairly with horrible trade deals, and paying for a large portion of their defense.

They were taking advantage of the United States and therefore, of course, they like Biden because now they will be allowed to return to their old ways of ripping off our Country. If I were a leader of these countries, I too would like Biden far better than President Trump. They will now get very rich off the United States just like they have in the past until a change is made. I am for AMERICA FIRST! June 13, 2021

June 15, 2021

Donald J Trump @RealDonaldTrump
So much USA money has been given away to the "Club," as President Macron of France likes to call it, and to NATO, despite the fact that those countries have taken economic advantage of the United States for many years—until I came along. Not fair to America, or the American taxpayer! June 15, 2021

June 16, 2021

Donald J Trump @RealDonaldTrump
Donald J. Trump is pleased to announce Liz Harrington, a strong Republican conservative voice for America and who has represented conservative policies so well over the years, as our new spokesperson for Save America and Donald J. Trump, 45th President of the United States of America. Liz will be taking the place of Jason Miller, who will

be leaving to enter the private sector. "I greatly thank Jason for his service—he is outstanding!" said President Donald J. Trump.

"Liz Harrington is a fighter," said President Trump. "She was an important part of our receiving more votes than any incumbent President in U.S. history, far more than we received the first time we won."

"It is an honor of a lifetime to represent President Trump and to stand for the truth," said Harrington. "At such a critical time for our country, President Trump's fighting spirit is needed now more than ever. We will not stand idly by and let America fall to the Radical Left-Wing Mob."

Harrington is the former national spokesperson for the Republican National Committee, editor-in-chief of http://WarRoom.org, and senior writer for the Washington Free Beacon. She has long been a staunch supporter of President Trump. June 16, 2021

Donald J Trump @RealDonaldTrump

I have accepted the invitation of Texas Governor Greg Abbott to join him on an official visit to our Nation's decimated Southern Border on Wednesday, June 30, 2021.

The Biden Administration inherited from me the strongest, safest, and most secure border in U.S history and in mere weeks they turned it into the single worst border crisis in U.S history. It's an unmitigated disaster zone.

We went from detain-and-remove to catch-and-release. We went from having border security that was the envy of the world to a lawless border that is now pitied around the world. Biden and Harris have handed control of our border over to cartels, criminals, and coyotes. Drug dealers, MS-13 gang members, human smugglers, sex traffickers, and the criminal elements of the world now have free reign. Hospitals and schools are getting crushed and public health is being sacrificed all in service of a radical left anti-borders agenda. Our brave border agents and courageous ICE officers have been illegally stopped from doing their jobs. Our Nation is now one giant sanctuary city where even dangerous criminals are being cut loose and set free inside the U.S interior on a daily basis.

If this weren't bad enough, Biden and Harris won't even tour the scenes of the wreckage they created, or come down and visit with the Border Patrol and ICE heroes risking their lives to defend our Nation at a time when the White House is doing everything it can to make their job totally impossible.

What Biden and Harris have done, and are continuing to do on our border, is a grave and willful dereliction of duty.

My visit will hopefully shine a spotlight on these crimes against our Nation—and show the incredible people of ICE and Border Patrol that they have our unshakeable support. June 16, 2021

Extended Comment
Trump, Harris, and the Border

Two days after Trump announced this border visit, VP Harris announced she would visit the border. But unlike Trump who went to a hot spot, Kamala missed it by 800 miles. Then while there, Harris would blame Trump for the emerging border crisis, when in fact it was Biden's reversals of Trump policies that caused the crisis.

I document this latter point in my *Biden Tweets* books. In Appendix One is additional documentation of all of these points and salient quotes about this whole situation. Back to Trump.

June 17, 2021

Donald J Trump @RealDonaldTrump
President Donald J. Trump, 45th President of the United States of America, will hold a major rally in Wellington, Ohio on Saturday, June 26, 2021 at 7:00PM EDT.

This Save America rally marks President Trump's first of many appearances in support of candidates and causes that further the MAGA agenda and accomplishments of President Trump's administration. The rally is to support Max Miller, who President Trump has endorsed for election in Ohio's 16th Congressional District.

Saturday, June 26, 2021, at 7:00PM EDT
President Donald J. Trump, 45th President of the United States of America, Delivers Remarks
Venue:
Lorain County Fairgrounds
23000 Fairgrounds Rd.
Wellington, OH 44090
Doors open at 2:00PM EDT
All requests for media credentials must be submitted by Thursday, June 24, 2021 at 7:00PM EDT. June 17, 2021

To comment, as Trump indicates, this would be the first of many post-presidential Trump rallies. But only Newsmax will air them. They will be completely ignored by the MSM and even by Fox News, despite every event drawing 10,000s of rally-goers.

June 18, 2021

Donald J Trump @RealDonaldTrump

Thank you and congratulations to Laura Baigert of the Georgia Star News on the incredible reporting you have done. Keep going! The scam is all unraveling fast. June 18, 2021

Donald J Trump @RealDonaldTrump

This is very big news. People are starting to see the light. Great for America! [picture of tweet from Brad Raffensperger, Georgia Secretary of State, saying Fulton County is unable to produce all ballot drop box documents] June 18, 2021

Donald J Trump @RealDonaldTrump

Can anybody believe this? No wonder our Country is going to hell! [picture of Biden's anti-Trump paper notes for his NATO press conference] June 18, 2021

Donald J Trump @RealDonaldTrump

When Biden tries to claim credit for vaccine distribution, a distribution system that was set up by the Trump Administration, he should remember that if I didn't purchase, very early on, billions of dollars worth of the vaccine, bottles, needles, and everything else that goes with it, he and his administration would not have been giving vaccinations until October or November of this year. So let them go on and on with their Fake Campaign and Fake Election results and Fake Media, but without the Trump Administration's Operation Warp Speed, millions of people would be dying all over the World that will now be saved. June 18, 2021

To comment, Biden keeps trying to claim credit. But I won't let him get away with it, as my comments on his twitter feed reproduced in my *Biden Tweets* books show.

June 20, 2021

Donald J Trump @RealDonaldTrump

Happy Father's Day to all, including the Radical Left, RINOs, and other Losers of the world. Hopefully, eventually, everyone will come together! June 20, 2021

97

To comment, as with Trump's Easter message, this message was out of line. Just wish all fathers a Happy Father's Day, and leave it at that. I don't know why Trump does not realized how divisive it is to combine that with a dig at his political opponents.

June 22, 2021

Donald J Trump @RealDonaldTrump
Full Trump Interview on Real America News
https://tv.gab.com/channel/araisinghell/view/full-trump-interview-on-real-america-60d0ec6fe1a65a1c15969c89
June 22, 2021

June 23, 2021

Donald J Trump @RealDonaldTrump
Georgia now plans to remove over 100,000 "obsolete and outdated" names off their voter rolls. Doing this, they say, will ensure voting files are up to date, while at the same time ensuring voter integrity in future elections. BUT WHAT ABOUT THE LAST ELECTION? WHY WASN'T THIS DONE PRIOR TO THE NOVEMBER 3RD PRESIDENTIAL ELECTION, where they had us losing by a very small number of votes, many times less than the 101,789 figure? This means we (you!) won the Presidential Election in Georgia. But don't fret, much other information will soon be revealed about Georgia—and other States as well. It is coming out FAST and FURIOUS. The 2020 Presidential Election was rigged! June 23, 2021

To comment, this is just one of many election integrity steps, which through good, were too late. This purging of the roles should have been done before the 2020 election, not months later.

Donald J Trump @RealDonaldTrump
Big crowds in the Great State of Ohio this weekend for the Trump rally. See you on Saturday night. MAKE AMERICA GREAT AGAIN, AGAIN! June 23, 2021

Donald J Trump @RealDonaldTrump
The story that I asked the Department of Justice to go after ratings-challenged (without Trump!) Saturday Night Live, and other late-night Losers, is total Fake News. It was fabricated, there were no sources, and yet the Lamestream Media goes with it. I did say, however, that Alec

Trump Fights Back with Statements

Baldwin has no talent, certainly when it comes to imitating me. The one who had what it took was Darrell Hammond. With all of that being said, however, I do believe that the 100% one-sided shows should be considered an illegal campaign contribution from the Democrat Party, hard to believe I got 75 million votes (the most of any sitting President) despite all of that, together with a very Fraudulent Election. 2024 or before! June 23, 2021

June 24, 2021

Donald J Trump @RealDonaldTrump

After months of ignoring the crisis at the Southern Border, it is great that we got Kamala Harris to finally go and see the tremendous destruction and death that they've created—a direct result of Biden ending my very tough but fair Border policies.

Harris and Biden were given the strongest Border in American history. And now, it is by far the worst in American history.

If Governor Abbott and I weren't going there next week, she would have never gone! June 24, 2021

To comment, I already covered this prompting of Harris by Trump to go to the border. But Trump's comment here is spot on, as always.

Donald J Trump @RealDonaldTrump

There has never been, in our Country's history, a Border catastrophe like what is currently taking place at our Southern Border. All Biden had to do is leave it the way it was, by far the strongest Southern Border our Country has ever had. Millions of people will now be streaming into our Country unchecked, unvetted, and unknown. Other countries are emptying their prisons with their worst criminals flowing into our Country. Drugs, gangs, and fugitives are pouring in every day. Hospitals, schools, communities, and police are overwhelmed. This is far more than a crisis—our Country is being destroyed! June 24, 2021

To comment, do not miss that drugs part. The border crisis is fueling the opioid/ fentanyl crisis. But the MSM never makes that connection.

Donald J Trump @RealDonaldTrump

Good news! RINO Governor Doug Ducey of Arizona has restated the fact that he is not running for the United States Senate. It would not matter, however, because he could not get the nomination after failing to perform on the Voter Fraud in Arizona. Also, there is no way he would get my endorsement, which means, his aspirations would be permanently put to rest anyway. Again, thank you to our brave Republicans in the Arizona State Senate for their bravery in putting forward the Forensic Audit. Everybody is anxiously awaiting the result! June 24, 2021

June 25, 2021

Donald J Trump @RealDonaldTrump

Michigan State Senators Mike Shirkey and Ed McBroom are doing everything possible to stop Voter Audits in order to hide the truth about November 3rd. The Senate "investigation" of the election is a cover up, and a method of getting out of a Forensic Audit for the examination of the Presidential contest.

Corrupt (?) politicians falsely claim there was no Voter Fraud in Michigan (has anyone looked at what is considered the most corrupt election city in the U.S., DETROIT?), however, they admit to "problems with the numbers" that rigged 7,048 votes to illegally give a very conservative county to Joe Biden, which raised big signals, only to then find that it was actually President Trump that won the county by 3,788 votes, not Biden.

The report mentions that Detroit engaged in "illegal actions" by blocking our poll workers, and concludes mailing of unsolicited ballot applications "demonstrates a clear vulnerability for fraud", and then goes on to say that no one should question this election?

Instead of doing a Forensic Audit, they want to investigate the Patriots who have fought for the truth and who are exposing a very possibly Rigged Election. The truth will come out and RINO's will pay at the polls, especially with primary voters and expected challenges. Our Country was based on Free and Fair Elections, and that's what we must have!

Call those two Senators now and get them to do the right thing, or vote them the hell out of office! June 25, 2021

Donald J Trump @RealDonaldTrump

My thoughts and prayers are with all of those impacted by the building collapse in Surfside, Florida. Thank you to the incredible First Responders and Law Enforcement for arriving so quickly on the job, as always. We wish Governor Ron DeSantis, and all of those representing the Great State of Florida concerning this tragic event, Good Luck and God Speed. I am with you all the way! June 25, 2021

To comment, this was a tragic event. Prayers to all of those affected.

Trump Fights Back with Statements

Donald J Trump @RealDonaldTrump

Can you believe that New York wants to strip Rudy Giuliani, a great American Patriot, of his law license because he has been fighting what has already been proven to be a Fraudulent Election? The greatest Mayor in the history of New York City, the Eliot Ness of his generation, one of the greatest crime fighters our Country has ever known, and this is what the Radical Left does to him. All of New York is out of control, crime is at an all-time high—it's nothing but a Witch Hunt, and they should be ashamed of themselves. TAKE BACK AMERICA! June 25, 2021

To comment, Rudy did in fact have his law license revoked. A sad turn of events in the life of the man termed "America's Mayor" after 9/11.

Donald J Trump @RealDonaldTrump

Biden's Department of Justice just announced that they are suing the Great State of Georgia over its Election Integrity Act. Actually, it should be the other way around! The PEOPLE of Georgia should SUE the State, and their elected officials, for running a CORRUPT AND RIGGED 2020 PRESIDENTIAL ELECTION—and for trying to suppress the VOTE of the AMERICAN PEOPLE in Georgia. If we don't address these issues from the 2020 Election head on, and we allow the Radical Left Democrats to continue to politicize the DOJ and Law Enforcement, we will lose our Country. SAVE AMERICA! June 25, 2021

To comment, after Biden calling Georgia's election integrity law "Jim Crow 2.0" and other such silly names, with him, Dems, and the MSM claiming it would suppress voter turnout, the following primary saw record turnout. But not a word of apology was heard from any of the naysayers.

Donald J Trump @RealDonaldTrump

Wisconsin Republican leaders Robin Vos, Chris Kapenga, and Devin LeMahieu, are working hard to cover up election corruption, in Wisconsin. They are actively trying to prevent a Forensic Audit of the election results, especially those which took place in Milwaukee, one of the most corrupt election locales in the country. Don't fall for their lies! These REPUBLICAN "leaders" need to step up and support the people who elected them by providing them a full forensic investigation. If they don't, I have little doubt that they will be primaried and quickly run out of office. June 25, 2021

Donald J Trump @RealDonaldTrump

The greatest Witch Hunt in US history continues! June 25, 2021

June 26, 2021

Donald J Trump @RealDonaldTrump

Thank you to the people in Wellington, OH last night for an unbelievable evening of very serious talk but also, fun. In many ways with what was said, and the reaction to it, it was legendary. June 26, 2021

Donald J Trump @RealDonaldTrump

Great crowd in Ohio, thank you! [picture of crowd at the Ohio rally] June 26, 2021

June 28, 2021

Donald J Trump @RealDonaldTrump

RINO former Attorney General Bill Barr failed to investigate election fraud, and really let down the American people. Even the scam that took place in Georgia of ballot stuffing on camera, he couldn't see what was wrong with it. Just like he failed to understand the Horowitz report and let everyone down with respect to getting a timely investigation (where's Durham?) on all of the corruption of the Obama-Biden Administration.

It's people in authority like Bill Barr that allow the crazed Radical Left to succeed. He and other RINOs in the Republican Party are being used in order to try to convince people that the election was legitimate when so many incredible facts have now come out to show conclusively that it wasn't.

He came in with a semi-bang and went out with a whimper. Earlier in his term Bill Barr went ballistic on CNN with Wolf Blitzer warning Democrats were changing election rules to flood the system with mail-in ballots that "as a matter of logic" are "very open to fraud." They are, and Bill Barr did nothing about it.

If there was no fraud, why are Arizona, Georgia, Wisconsin, Pennsylvania, and other States spending so much time and effort on exposing the fraud? We already know that:

101,789 "obsolete" voters on the rolls in Georgia, including 18,486 dead people

Ballot batches off by up to 17.5 percent in Maricopa County, Arizona

Trump Fights Back with Statements

"Massive" chain of custody problems with drop boxes in Georgia, missing hundreds of thousands of records for months after the election

Thousands of ballots "wheeled in through the back door" in Fulton County days after the election

"Double feeding" ballots in Fulton County, Georgia

Nearly 200,000 illegal "indefinitely confined" votes in Wisconsin that violated Voter ID law

"Cash for votes" scheme in Nevada

Illegal alien votes

Election law changes were not authorized by the State Legislatures, which is mandated by the U.S. Constitution

And much more!

If he felt this way, why did Barr say he was "greatly honored" and "proud to have played a role in the many successes and unprecedented achievements you have delivered for the American people" in the final letter he wrote to me? He said, "Few could have weathered these attacks, much less forge ahead with a positive program for the country."

Now it was revealed that Barr was being pushed to tell lies about the election by Mitch McConnell, another beauty, who was worried about damaging the Republicans chances in the Georgia runoff. What really damaged the Senate Republicans was allowing their races to be rigged and stolen, and worse, the American people to no longer believe their vote matters because spineless RINOs like Bill Barr and Mitch McConnell did nothing. June 28, 2021

Extended Comment
Wisconsin Supreme Court and Drop Boxes

Some of Trump claims are debatable, but his final one is not, the one about election laws being changed by entities other than state legislatures. The Wisconsin Supreme Court confirmed this point when it ruled in July 2022 that the use of drop boxes was illegal.

To explain, election laws passed by the Wisconsin state legislature do not allow for drop boxes, but the Wisconsin election board allotted for them. That decision was challenged after the 2020 election back in November 2020. But it took 20 months for the Wisconsin Supreme Court to rule on the case. And their ruling was that indeed those drop boxes are illegal.

Since that is the case, then all ballots cast in those boxes should be voided. If that were done, then most likely Trump would have won Wisconsin, as far more Democrats than Republican voted via mail-in ballots retuned via drop boxes. Back to Trump.

June 29, 2021

Donald J Trump @RealDonaldTrump

Had Mitch McConnell fought for the Presidency like he should have, there would right now be Presidential Vetoes on all of the phased Legislation that he has proven to be incapable of stopping. Not to mention, he lost two Senatorial seats in Georgia, making the Republicans the Minority in the Senate. He never fought for the White House and blew it for the Country. Too bad I backed him in Kentucky, he would have been primaried and lost! Based on press reports, he convinced his buddy, Bill Barr, to get the corrupt (based on massive amounts of evidence that the Fake News refuses to mention!) election done, over with, and sealed for Biden, ASAP! June 29, 2021

Donald J Trump @RealDonaldTrump

Radical Left New York City and State Prosecutors, who have let murderers, rapists, drug dealers, and all other forms of crime skyrocket to record levels, and who have just announced that they will be releasing hundreds of people involved in violent crime back onto the streets without retribution of any kind, are rude, nasty, and totally biased in the way they are treating lawyers, representatives, and some of the wonderful long-term employees and people within the Trump Organization. After hundreds of subpoenas, over 3 million pages of documents, 4 years of searching, dozens and dozens of interviews, and millions of dollars of taxpayer funds wasted, they continue to be "in search of a crime" and will do anything to frighten people into making up the stories or lies that they want, but have been totally unable to get. In an unprecedented move, they retained an outside "Never Trumper" lawyer from a Trump-hating law firm to work on the case. It is a continuation of the greatest Witch Hunt of all time.

Now they are issuing ultimatums, working in close conjunction with the Washington, D.C. hacks who have been investigating me from the day I came down the escalator in Trump Tower, but who have failed. In fact, the guilty parties were these prosecutors' partners in crime, the Radical Left Democrats and friends. They will do anything to stop the MAGA movement (and me), even if it involves prosecutorial misconduct and harassment of a political opponent, which they are using at levels rarely seen before. They leak, they lie, and they campaign based on information that has already been gone through in other of the many investigations I have put up with.

Trump Fights Back with Statements

Now they just leaked that we were given one day, today, to make our case about things that are standard practice throughout the U.S. business community, and in no way a crime. They also know that no matter how strong our case, they will work hard to embarrass us and the Republican Party.

Having politically motivated prosecutors, people who actually got elected because they will "get Donald Trump," is a very dangerous thing for our Country. In the end, people will not stand for it. Remember, if they can do this to me, they can do it to anyone! Why would anyone bring their company to New York, or even stay in New York, knowing these Radical Left Democrats would willingly target their company if viewed as a political opponent? It is devastating for New York!

These Witch Hunters are relentlessly seeking to destroy a reputation of a President who has done a great job for this Country, including tax and regulation cuts, Border control, rebuilding the Military, and developing the vaccine in record time—thereby saving our Country, and far beyond. Washington, D.C. and ultimately, the U.S. Supreme Court, should finally stop these vicious, angry, and highly partisan prosecutors. They are a disgrace to our Nation! June 29, 2021

Donald J Trump @RealDonaldTrump

Jonathan Karl's story on Slow Moving Bill Barr is made-up beyond any level imaginable. It is, in other words, Fake News! I lost confidence in Bill Barr long before the 2020 Presidential Election Scam. It was when he dismissed and didn't act on the very powerful Horowitz Report, and instead gave everything over to John Durham, who has seemingly disappeared from the planet. Can you even believe a report coming out during the Biden Administration? We caught them but unfortunately didn't have an Attorney General who was capable of acting and wouldn't go against his friends in Washington, D.C.

Barr was a "swamp creature" who was devastated when the Radical Left wanted to impeach him. He, and other RINOs (you see it all the time!), always fold. If he becomes "less" for President Trump, maybe they will leave him alone. It takes a very strong and special person to go against the "mob". Bill Barr was not that person. Despite evidence of tremendous Election Fraud, he just didn't want to go there. He was afraid, weak, and frankly, now that I see what he is saying, pathetic. The facts are rapidly coming out in States and Courts about the 2020 Presidential Election Scam, and let's see if Bill Barr, a man who was unable to handle the pressure, was correct? The answer will be a resounding, NO! June 29, 2021

To comment, I thought I coined the term "swamp creature" for my *Impeach* trilogy. But here Trump is using it. But then, maybe he read my books, since I sent them to him, and picked up this term from them!

Donald J Trump @RealDonaldTrump

CNN ratings are down 70%. MSDNC is also way down. Actually, they are ALL way down. They say the news is "boring" since I left D.C. Morning Joe, Joy Reid (whoever that is?), Nicole Wallace, Jake Tapper, and even Chris Wallace, at Fox, in free fall. A wonderful thing to see! June 29, 2021

To comment, meanwhile, the ratings for Newsmax are improving, especially on nights they air Trump's rallies. On those nights, Newsmax beats both CNN and MSNBC.

Donald J Trump @RealDonaldTrump

The New York City Election, even though an embarrassment and total mess, is far better and more accurate than my 2020 Presidential Election—so what are people complaining about! June 29, 2021

June 30, 2021

Donald J Trump @RealDonaldTrump

Just like in the 2020 Presidential Election, it was announced overnight in New York City that vast irregularities and mistakes were made and that Eric Adams, despite an almost insurmountable lead, may not win the race. The fact is, based on what has happened, nobody will ever know who really won. The Presidential Race was a Scam and a Hoax with numbers and results being found that are massive, shocking, and determinative. Watch the mess you are about to see in New York City, it will go on forever. They should close the books and do it all over again, the old-fashioned way, when we had results that were accurate and meaningful. June 30, 2021

To comment, Eric Adams became mayor of NYC, despite the election irregularities, just like with Joe Biden. Both are proving to be failures, with crime skyrocketing in NYC.

Chapter Seven
Trump's Statements
July 2021

These Trump Statements are continued from Chapter Six.

July 1, 2021

Donald J Trump @RealDonaldTrump
Who shot Ashli Babbitt? July 1, 2021

To comment, great question! Millions of us would love to know the answer. For those who don't know, Ashli was an unarmed white Trump-supporter who was killed by a black Capitol Building police officer on January 6, 2021 (J6). She was in fact the only person killed on that day, despite deceptive media reports that make it sound otherwise

Later, her killer will be identified as Michael J. Byrd. He will be left off Scot-free, despite never even being interviewed by the FBI. I document all of this in my *Tragic Ending* book.

Donald J Trump @RealDonaldTrump
Heading to the Southern Border, which has never, in our Country's long history, been worse. We had the most successful Border policy in American history—and now we have, by far, the least successful policy. People are coming in by the millions. They are destroying our Country! See you soon. July 1, 2021

To comment, Trump, the former-President, doing the current President's job. Even Kamala couldn't seem to find the border, going 800 miles away from where the real problem is and never actually making it to the border. But don't expect the MSM to give the Trump administration credit and to criticize the current administration.

Donald J Trump @RealDonaldTrump
Gen. Mark Milley's greatest fear is upsetting the woke mob. July 1, 2021

To comment, Milley was chairman of the Joint Chiefs of Staff under Trump and remains so under Biden. But he and Trump had a falling out after Milley apologized for the Lafayette Park incident. As noted previously, Trump was cleared of any wrongdoing in that situation, so Milley's misgivings were unwarranted.

Donald J Trump @RealDonaldTrump
When Black Lives Matter rioters were threatening to destroy Washington, D.C., he practically begged me not to send in the military to stop the riots.

Milley later issued an embarrassing and groveling apology for walking at my side to St. John's Church, which far-left rioters almost burned to the ground the day before. Instead of denouncing the rioters, he denounced himself—a humiliation for our Military. A year later even the Fake News had to admit that their Lafayette Square narrative was a giant lie. Milley, once again, looked like a fool.

Now, in yet another desperate ploy to impress the Radical Left and keep his job, Milley made-up a false story that he yelled at me in the Situation Room. This is totally Fake News. If he had displayed such disrespect for his Commander-in-Chief I would have fired him immediately.

To further ingratiate himself with Biden, progressive Media, and the Radical Left, Milley went to Congress and actually defended Critical Race Theory being shoved down the throats of our soldiers. This Marxist, racist anti-American propaganda has no place in our Military—I banned these training programs, now Biden and the Pentagon have resumed them. As soon as possible, Congress must defund this racist indoctrination.

Gen. Milley ought to resign, and be replaced with someone who is actually willing to defend our Military from the Leftist Radicals who hate our Country and our Flag. July 1, 2021

To comment, the teaching of Critical Race Theory (CRT) in our schools and now military is a major problem. As conservative commentator Dan Bongino says, it should be Critical Racism Teaching, as that is what it does, it teaches our kids and now soldiers to be racists.

Donald J Trump @RealDonaldTrump
Do people see the Radical Left prosecutors, and what they are trying to do to 75M+++ Voters and Patriots, for what it is? July 1, 2021

Donald J Trump @RealDonaldTrump
The political Witch Hunt by the Radical Left Democrats, with New York now taking over the assignment, continues. It is dividing our Country like never before! July 1, 2021

Donald J Trump @RealDonaldTrump
Look forward to the big Sarasota, Florida rally tomorrow night at 8PM! Can be seen on OAN and Newsmax! July 2, 2021

July 2, 2021

Donald J Trump @RealDonaldTrump
The Democrats are WEAPONIZING Radical Left prosecutors against the Republican Party in order to STEAL ELECTIONS. We cannot let them get away with this. They are destroying our Country! July 2, 2021

Donald J Trump @RealDonaldTrump
Look what's going on in New York with their Fake Election. The same thing just happened with the 2020 Presidential Election Hoax. America is no longer a Country of Free and Fair Elections! July 2, 2021

July 3, 2021

Donald J Trump @RealDonaldTrump
Heading to Florida now. See you soon! July 3, 2021

Donald J Trump @RealDonaldTrump
See you later, Florida. Will be a big rally and a big day! July 3, 2021

July 4, 2021
Independence Day

Donald J Trump @RealDonaldTrump
Great crowd and energy (like you wouldn't believe!) in Florida last night. Thank you! [picture of crowd] July 4, 2021

Donald J Trump @RealDonaldTrump
Happy 4th of July to all! July 4, 2021

To comment, finally, Trump gives a holiday greeting without an attack on his political opponents. But I do miss Trump on this day, as he always had the best Independence Day celebrations. Joe Biden tweets and that is about it, while Trump held a military-honoring parade.

July 6, 2021

Donald J Trump @RealDonaldTrump

Seeing the record crowds of over 45,000 people in Ohio and Florida, waiting for days, standing in the pouring rain, they come from near and far. All they want is HOPE for their Great Country again. Their arms are outstretched, they cry over the Rigged Election—and the RINOs have no idea what this movement is all about. In fact, they are perhaps our biggest problem. We will never save our Country or be great again unless Republicans get TOUGH and get SMART! July 6, 2021

To comment, these were great rallies. The crowds in attendance and high ratings for Newsmax, the only station to carry the rallies, shows that millions of us still support Trump and his agenda.

July 7, 2021

Donald J Trump @RealDonaldTrump

Congratulations to Vito Fossella on winning the Republican Primary for Borough President of Staten Island. Now onto victory against a Radical Left Democrat. Vito will be representing the greatest people on Earth, and he will never let you down. I love Staten Island! July 7, 2021

Donald J Trump @RealDonaldTrump

Election Reform must happen in Swing States like Pennsylvania, Michigan, Georgia, Wisconsin, and Arizona where voters have lost confidence in their electoral process. The Secretary of State in Pennsylvania allowed 21,000 deceased registrants (dead people) to remain on the voter rolls for the 2020 Presidential Election—a total disgrace! Republicans in State Legislatures must be smart, get tough, and pass real Election Reform in order to fight back against these Radical Left Democrats. If they don't, they'll steal it again in 2022 and 2024, and further DESTROY our Country! July 7, 2021

To comment, there is no record those "21,000 deceased registrants" voted in our election. However, it is true voter rolls should be cleared up before election day each year. But for some reason, it took until after the 2020 election for several states to do so.

July 8, 2021

Donald J Trump @RealDonaldTrump
The Fake News and Big Tech (and Dems!) coordinated attack on the millions of people in our Country, who call the 2020 Presidential Election disgraceful and corrupt, is failing. More and more people are calling it RIGGED and STOLEN. July 8, 2021

To comment, my *Corruption* book documents the irregularities and should wake up more people to the problems with the 2020 election.

Donald J Trump @RealDonaldTrump
Major press conference at 11:00AM EDT! July 8, 2021

To comment, great press conference. You are doing what many of us want to do but don't have the resources. As always, you're fighting for us, the little guys.

Donald J Trump @RealDonaldTrump
Endorsement of Ryan Zinke
Under Ryan Zinke's leadership at the Department of the Interior, the U.S. achieved Energy Dominance, increased federal energy revenues, and responsibly opened federal acreage for energy production. He was instrumental in expanding public access to public lands for recreation and rebuilding our National Parks and Forests infrastructure.
As Montana's Congressman for the new 2nd District, Ryan will fight against the Radical Left Democrats who continually block the America First policies we put in place. He will be a strong leader for the great Patriots of Montana. Ryan has my Complete and Total Endorsement for Congress! July 8, 2021

Donald J Trump @RealDonaldTrump
Why I'm Suing Big Tech
Opinion | Donald J. Trump: Why I'm Suing Big Tech
If Facebook, Twitter and YouTube can censor me, they can censor you—and believe me, they are.
https://www.wsj.com/articles/donald-j-trump-why-im-suing-big-tech-11625761897 July 8, 2021

To comment, great move! I was overjoyed to watch your press conference and hear about your lawsuit. And this article in the WSJ is great. I love the following excerpt:

No longer are Big Tech giants simply removing specific threats of violence. They are manipulating and controlling the political debate itself....

In the weeks before a presidential election, the platforms banned the New York Post—America's oldest newspaper—for publishing a story critical of Joe Biden's family, a story the Biden campaign did not even dispute.

Perhaps most egregious, in the weeks after the election, Big Tech blocked the social-media accounts of the sitting president. If they can do it to me, they can do it to you—and believe me, they are.

To comment, all of this is exactly what I assert about Big Tech in my *Corruption* book.

July 9, 2021

Donald J Trump @RealDonaldTrump

Wow, the numbers are really looking good for Glenn Youngkin in his race against Terry McAuliffe for Governor of Virginia. Glenn has been an incredible success and will truly Make Virginia Great Again. Rarely have I seen such enthusiasm. Virginia has so much potential but has been badly hurt by awful economic policy, terrible crime, and the worst education system promoting Critical Race Theory, etc. But, Glenn will fix this immediately. He is a highly respected person, not just a figurehead like Virginia's current and recent past Governors. Terry McAuliffe was a failed and unpopular Governor, whose only claim to fame was his relationship with Crooked Hillary Clinton—how did that work out? I knew McAuliffe well. He accepted large campaign contributions from me, said only great things and would do whatever I wanted, until I ran for office. He was a political HACK! If Virginia wants to open up and take advantage of its great and virtually unprecedented opportunity, Glenn Youngkin is the very successful businessman that will get them there! July 9, 2021

Donald J Trump @RealDonaldTrump

The story written by third-rate reporter Michael Bender, that Mike Pence and I had a big fight over Corey Lewandowski, is totally false. No such fight ever happened, it is fiction as are so many others stories written in the vast number of books coming out about me. July 9, 2021

Trump Fights Back with Statements

Donald J Trump @RealDonaldTrump

Very important that Senate Republicans not allow our hard-earned tax reductions to be terminated or amended in an upward trajectory in any way, shape, or form. They should not be making deals on increasing taxes for the fake infrastructure proposals being put forward by Democrats, almost all of which goes to the ridiculous Green New Deal Marxist agenda. Keep the Trump Administrations tax cuts just where they are. Do not allow tax increases. Thinking about it, I have never seen anything so easy to win politically. Also, RINO Republicans should stop negotiating the infrastructure deal—you are just being played by the Radical Left Democrats—they will give you nothing! July 9, 2021

Donald J Trump @RealDonaldTrump

It seems to me that meeting with authors of the ridiculous number of books being written about my very successful Administration, or me, is a total waste of time. They write whatever they want to write anyway without sources, fact-checking, or asking whether or not an event is true or false. Frankly, so many stories are made-up, or pure fiction. These writers are often bad people who write whatever comes to their mind or fits their agenda. It has nothing to do with facts or reality. So when reading the garbage that the Fake News Media puts out, please remember this and take everything with a "grain of salt." July 9, 2021

Donald J Trump @RealDonaldTrump

Very important that Senate Republicans not allow our hard-earned tax reductions to be terminated or amended in an upward trajectory in any way, shape, or form. They should not be making deals on increasing taxes for the fake infrastructure proposals being put forward by Democrats, almost all of which goes to the ridiculous Green New Deal Marxist agenda. Keep the Trump Administrations tax cuts just where they are. Do not allow tax increases. Thinking about it, I have never seen anything so easy to win politically. Also, RINO Republicans should stop negotiating the infrastructure deal—you are just being played by the Radical Left Democrats—they will give you nothing! July 9, 2021

July 10, 2021

Donald J Trump @RealDonaldTrump

Very interesting, funny, yet sad, that every time I read or hear a story in the Lamestream Media about the 2020 Presidential Election

Scam, it always is preceded by the fact that, "while no evidence of voter fraud is available," or statements to that effect, this could not be more incorrect or "fake." Massive evidence has been accumulated which shows voter fraud at a level that is virtually beyond comprehension. The Radical left writers say this nonsense over and over again, and so does the Fake News Media. What is true, is that as evidence comes out, they don't write about it or bring it forward in any way, shape, or form. Nevertheless, and fortunately, it gets out through the internet and other methods, and the feeling of a Fake Election is stronger now than ever before.

Check out the recent story of 35,000 votes in the great State of Georgia, and watch what is happening in Arizona, New Hampshire, Pennsylvania, and other States. The only reason Detroit, Michigan, is not yet under investigation is because the Republicans in the State Senate are a bunch of weak RINOs that are afraid to act. Detroit is one of the most corrupt places on Earth, and the information is coming out, and fast. In any event, Mainstream Media should stop saying that, "while all the allegations are false," when they know the exact opposite is true. People and facts are coming out at a level which can only be called "fast and furious." July 10, 2021

July 11, 2021

Donald J Trump @RealDonaldTrump

Very proud of the campaign that Susan Wright is waging in Texas's 6th Congressional District runoff. She is working very hard, has already defeated the Democrat, and has a substantial lead to close it out on July 27, 2021. Her great late husband, Congressman Ron Wright, would be very proud of the job that Susan is doing. They had tremendous love and respect for each other. In any event, Susan Wright has my Complete and Total Endorsement. She will represent her district, and our Country, very well! July 11, 2021

Donald J Trump @RealDonaldTrump

I see that the RINO Senator from Alabama, close friend of Old Crow Mitch McConnell, Richard Shelby, is pushing hard to have his "assistant" fight the great Mo Brooks for his Senate seat. She is not in any way qualified and is certainly not what our Country needs or not what Alabama wants. For Mitch McConnell to be wasting money on her campaign is absolutely outrageous. Vote for Mo Brooks! He stands for America First, and everything Alabama wants. He also has my Complete and Total Endorsement. July 11, 2021

July 12, 2021

Donald J Trump @RealDonaldTrump

The Fake News Media continuously likes stating that I lost the "sub-urbs." How would this be possible when I was the one that stopped the low-income housing agenda of Obama/Biden, already enacted, from happening there. The suburbs would have been destroyed—but they continuously fail to mention that I got 12 million more votes than I did in 2016, a record for a sitting President along with the 75 million votes, also a record. So how did that happen and how come I "lost"? This is just more Fake News. And remember, they can say all of this, including the suburbs nonsense, because we had a Rigged Election! July 12, 2021

Donald J Trump @RealDonaldTrump

Remember when the Fake News Media would blast me about how well Seoul, South Korea was doing with the pandemic? Well now, sadly, Seoul is riddled with the China Virus almost beyond what other countries had to go through. They are having a terrible time of it. The Media also used India as another country doing really well—we all know how that ended. They talked about these two countries in order to demean my Administration, which has now been proven to have done an incredible job. I only bring this up to show how dishonest and corrupt the Fake News Media is! July 12, 2021

Donald J Trump @RealDonaldTrump

For all of those finally realizing what a great job we did with respect to the pandemic, including rapidly filling the cupboards that were left "bare" by the previous administration, in both the Federal Government and States, please also remember that it was the Trump Administration that produced the vaccine in less than 9 months—many years ahead of anticipated schedule. Biden and his group just used our plan of distribution, which had started long before he took office. Without the vaccine, the entire World would have ended up like it was in 1917, the Spanish Flu, where as many as 100 million people died. While we get no credit for this from the Fake News Media, the people know—that's why I got 75 million votes! July 12, 2021

To comment, I will refute the many disparagements about Trump in regard to Covid in my forthcoming *Coronavirus* book. I will also compare the response to Covid of Trump to that of Biden. I also discuss Biden's many failures in this regard in my *Biden Tweets* books.

Donald J Trump @RealDonaldTrump

Met with many of the most important "influencers" last night in Las Vegas. Lots of topics discussed, including the Fake News Media and how to go around dishonest journalists. Some really good ideas emerging. July 12, 2021

Donald J Trump @RealDonaldTrump

I am proud to inform you that the Lamestream Media has hit the lowest approval ratings ever recorded. I think it would be fair to assume that I had something to do with that. They are not only dishonest and corrupt, they are truly, according to a recent poll, the enemy of the people. In a similar category, CNN's ratings are down a whopping, and record-setting, 79% and likewise, horrible numbers at MSDNC (Joe Scarborough and his lovely wife, Mika, are at record lows). These developments are great news for the American People! July 12, 2021

Donald J Trump @RealDonaldTrump

President Trump: There's More Than Enough Dead Voters in Georgia to Overturn the Election Results
https://tv.gab.com/channel/davidkirkland/view/president-trump-theres-more-than-enough-60eb3fe5d66bc9cad3fa4e4a
[less than two minute video clip of Trump calling into Maria Bartiroma's FNC show] July 12, 2021

Donald J Trump @RealDonaldTrump

President Trump: We're Going to Take Back The House, The Senate and, that Glorious White House...
https://tv.gab.com/channel/davidkirkland/view/president-trump-were-going-to-take-60eb84c96c64949f9c2d95b1 [2:12 video clip of Trump at CPAC] July 11, 2021

Donald J Trump @RealDonaldTrump

Breaking: Donald Trump Scolds the SCOTUS "They Should Be Ashamed of Themselves" for Allowing Biden to Steal the 2020 Election
https://tv.gab.com/channel/davidkirkland/view/breaking-donald-trump-scolds-the-scotus-60eb4315b81f6c9e4f4801eb
[less than two minute video clip of Trump calling into Maria Bartiroma's FNC show] July 12, 2021

Donald J Trump @RealDonaldTrump

98% approval rating at CPAC, the highest ever, by far. A new record! July 12, 2021

Trump Fights Back with Statements

Donald J Trump @RealDonaldTrump
    1776, not 1619! July 12, 2021

To comment, this Statement is in regard to Biden replacing the teaching of our country being founded with the Declaration of Independence on July 4, 1776 to it being the day in 1619 when African slaves were first brought to Jamestown, VA. The latter idea comes from the NYT's 1619 Project. Included in it is the idea that slavery is central to the founding of America.

It would require an entire book or at least chapter to address the relevant issues in-depth. Suffice it to say, placing our founding on the former generates love and respect for America and patriotism. The latter generates hatred and disrespect for America and a lack of patriotism.

Donald J Trump @RealDonaldTrump

The drug cartels are making hundreds of millions of dollars under Joe Biden and the Biden Administration. They cannot believe their luck—they struck gold. Under Trump, they were just about in the process of almost giving up, it was a hard way to make a dollar! July 12, 2021

Donald J Trump @RealDonaldTrump

Big demonstrations are breaking out in Cuba and Miami in protest of the Communist Cuban Government (although, today there are zero protesters in Cuba—you know what that means!). Don't forget that Biden and the Democrats campaigned on reversing my very tough stance on Cuba. Remember when Obama attended baseball games with Castros while they imprisoned, beat, and killed the Cuban people.

I stand with the Cuban people 100% in their fight for freedom. The Government must let them speak and be free! Joe Biden MUST stand up to the Communist regime or—history will remember. The Cuban people deserve freedom and human rights! THEY ARE NOT AFRAID! July 12, 2021

Donald J Trump @RealDonaldTrump

Hopefully, American Republican Patriots will primary the RINO State Senators in Michigan who refuse to properly look into the election irregularities and fraud, which took place in Detroit and much of the rest of Wayne County, in the 2020 Presidential Election. The challengers will have great and powerful MAGA support. They are now seeing the extent of what took place in the 2020 Presidential Election Scam. Watch Arizona, Georgia, Pennsylvania, Wisconsin, and more! July 12, 2021

Donald J Trump @RealDonaldTrump

Four years ago, a man named Ed Gillespie ran for Governor of Virginia without "embracing" MAGA, or the America First movement. He tried to skirt the issue by wanting my endorsement, yet walking on both sides of the fence. The Trump base is very large in Virginia, they understood his game, and they didn't come out for Gillespie, nor did I do anything to help or hurt. He got creamed!

Now a great candidate, Glenn Youngkin, is running against political hack and unpopular former Governor of Virginia, Terry McAuliffe. Glenn has a very good chance of winning—but watch the "vote counters" in Virginia. As the 2020 Presidential Election Scam has proven, they can be far more important than the candidate! July 12, 2021

Donald J Trump @RealDonaldTrump

U.S. Attorney from the Eastern District of Pennsylvania was precluded from investigating election fraud allegations. Outrageous! https://cdn.donaldjtrump.com/djtweb/general/Letter_to_President_Trump.pdf July 12, 2021

Donald J Trump @RealDonaldTrump

President Donald J. Trump CPAC 2021 Speech Dallas, TX (7/11/21). https://tv.gab.com/channel/emerson_chris/view/president-donald-j-trump-cpac-2021-60ecb0d58daee8a2edc45c39 [1:32 video] July 12, 2021

July 13, 2021

Donald J Trump @RealDonaldTrump

Republicans in the U.S. Senate must not in any way, shape, or form increase taxes that were won in the TRUMP TAX CUT, the largest in the history of our Country. It's what made our economy grow and great. Democrats want major tax increases to pay for their fake infrastructure bill, where over 90% of the money goes to the ridiculous Green New Deal nonsense, which will destroy our economy.

The tax cuts were a great achievement of the Trump Administration and the Republican Party. More importantly, they were a great victory for our Nation. Do not increase them one penny. Republicans must learn to fight these vicious, Radical Left Democrats who are destroying lives and destroying our Country! July 13, 2021

Trump Fights Back with Statements

Donald J Trump @RealDonaldTrump

Joe Biden is going to Pennsylvania today in a rush in order to stop the Forensic Audit that the Pennsylvania Republican Senate is in the process of doing. Philadelphia was a cesspool of corruption, which will soon be revealed by the audit. Why are they so concerned that a President, who never goes anywhere, would hop onto beautiful Air Force One and head to Philadelphia if it were an honest election? Why not let the audit go forward and make everybody, on both sides, happy?

The results will be the results. But they know it was not an honest election, Philadelphia was one of the most corrupt cities in the Country—and so is Detroit, and so is Milwaukee, and so is Atlanta, and Pittsburgh, and Oakland, and Baltimore. Corruption has gone on for years, but in the 2020 Presidential Election Scam, with the mail-in ballots and the use of Covid to cheat, corruption reached new levels.

Remember the poll watchers being thrown out, the windows being sealed so nobody could look in, the ballot drops, and all of the other events that took place that changed so rapidly the Big Trump Win on election night.

Joe should say go forward with this, with all of these audits. His visit is a joke. He doesn't need to visit, all he needs to do is let them do an audit and find out what happened. Who knows, maybe they'll say the election was on the up and up, but many people would be shocked. Let the audit go forward like it is in Arizona, despite 107 Democrat lawyers trying to stop it and failing.

Let the Forensic Audit go, Joe. Don't fight it. Show them how honest it was. July 13, 2021

July 14, 2021

Donald J Trump @RealDonaldTrump

The news coming out of Georgia is beyond incredible. The hand recount in Fulton County was a total fraud! They stuffed the ballot box—and got caught. We will lose our Country if this is allowed to stand.

According to the just released report from Garland Favorito and the highly respected Voter GA, in Fulton County the hand recount was wrong by 60%; 100,000 tally sheets for ballots were missing; they duplicated thousands of extra votes for Joe Biden; and fabricated vote counts of 100–0 for Biden, many times! Ballot batch sheets fraudulently showed multiple unanimous 100–0 counts for Biden, as well as 150–0, and 200–0. Are we now in a Third World country? What else will they find once the full Forensic Audit takes place?

This means Brad Raffensperger certified the 2020 Presidential Election Scam despite it being "riddled with massive errors and provable fraud." This proves what Suzi Voyles, who worked Fulton elections for decades, suspected, that fraudulent photocopied ballots were counted for Biden. This is on top of the 35,000 illegal votes recently found in Georgia, and the over 100,000 obsolete voter registrations, plus thousands of dead people, deleted AFTER the election.

Will the Attorney General of Georgia Chris Carr finally act? How has Governor Brian Kemp allowed this to happen?

This is corruption at the highest level. Our Nation is at stake!

Read the report here.

https://voterga.org/wp-content/uploads/2021/07/Press-Release-New-Evidence-Reveals-Georgia-Audit-Fraud-and-Massive-Errors.pdf

Read the Federalist article here.

https://thefederalist.com/2021/07/09/new-evidence-indicates-enough-illegal-votes-in-georgia-to-tip-2020-results/

Watch the video of duplicate ballots here.

https://twitter.com/TalkMullins/status/1414997696021209096

July 14, 2021

Donald J Trump @RealDonaldTrump

Congratulations to Mark Levin on the release of his great new book, *American Marxism*, now available and doing really well. Mark is an American Patriot who loves his Country. In *American Marxism*, Levin explains how the core elements of Marxist ideology are now pervasive in American society and culture—from our schools, the press, and corporations, to Hollywood, the Democratic Party, and the Biden presidency—and how it is often cloaked in deceptive labels like "progressivism," "democratic socialism," "social activism," and more. Get your copy today—Save America! July 14, 2021

Donald J Trump @RealDonaldTrump

The press is corrupt in this Country. They refuse to report on the many cases of election irregularities and outright fraud. They are an embarrassment to our Country! July 14, 2021

Donald J Trump @RealDonaldTrump

Biden just said 150 people voted in the 2020 Presidential Election (Scam!). On the assumption that he meant 150 million people, and based on the fact that I got 75 million+++, that would mean that Biden got 75 million votes, which is 6 million votes less than what they said they got.

So what is that all about? Are they already conceding 6 million votes? July 14, 2021

Donald J Trump @RealDonaldTrump
Great new book out by Jesse Watters, *How I Saved the World.* Interspersed are his thoughtful suggestions for overcoming left-wing radicalism, maintaining American democracy, moving beyond aging hippies (like his long-suffering, loving parents), saving the world from social justice warriors and the deep state—all while smirking his way through life in only the nicest way. Get your copy today, congratulations Jesse! July 14, 2021

Donald J Trump @RealDonaldTrump
Quote from Bill O'Reilly on the History Tour
"Without any marketing at all, the Trump O'Reilly History Tour has already grossed more than $7 million. In some venues, the VIP tickets are almost sold out. This tour will be one of the most lucrative of all time." – Bill O'Reilly July 14, 2021

Donald J Trump @RealDonaldTrump
I will not be supporting or endorsing Senator Butch Miller, running for Lieutenant Governor of Georgia, because of his refusal to work with other Republican Senators on voter fraud and irregularities in the State. Hopefully there will be strong and effective primary challengers for the very important Lieutenant Governor position! July 14, 2021

Donald J Trump @RealDonaldTrump
ICYMI: "New Evidence Reveals GA Audit Fraud and Massive Errors"
Wow. Results of the VoterGA. [photocopy of report] July 14, 2021

July 15, 2021

Donald J Trump @RealDonaldTrump
Arizona Senate hearings on the Maricopa County Election Audit is devastating news to the Radical Left Democrats and the Biden Administration. While this, according to the Senate, is preliminary, with results being announced at a later date, it seems that 74,243 Mail-In Ballots were counted with "no clear record of them being sent." There were 18,000 voters who were scrubbed from the voter rolls AFTER the election. They also revealed that the voting system was breached or hacked

(by who?). Very big printer and ballot problems with different paper used, etc., and MUCH MORE.

The irregularities revealed at the hearing today amount to hundreds of thousands of votes or, many times what is necessary for us to have won. Despite these massive numbers, this is the State that Fox News called early for a Biden victory. There was no victory here, or in any other of the Swing States either.

Maricopa County refuses to work together with the Senate and others who are merely looking for honesty, integrity, and transparency. Why do the Commissioners not want to look into this corrupted election? What are they trying to hide? The highly respected State Senator Wendy Rogers said in a tweet the hearing today means we must decertify the election. In any event, the Senate patriots are moving forward with final results to be announced in the not-too-distant future, but based on today's hearing, why even wait? July 15, 2021

Donald J Trump @RealDonaldTrump

The proud people of Cuba are desperate to be free from the iron boot heel of the Island's wicked Communist Regime. These incredible warriors for freedom risk everything to take to the streets in their quest for freedom. I stand in total solidarity with the freedom fighters in Cuba and the brave Cuban Americans who have watched their families suffer in the motherland at the hands of this heartless and brutal regime.

The Biden Administration's refusal to forcefully condemn Communism and the Cuban Communist Regime is a national travesty. The Biden Administration's ludicrous suggestion that the Cubans are protesting government mismanagement—not brutal Communist oppression—is an insult to every Cuban patriot who has suffered, been imprisoned, or died in pursuit of freedom.

Today's Democrat Party is so far left they can't even take a stand against violent Communism. Many are Communists themselves!

As President, I advanced a strategic vision in which the people of Cuba, Venezuela, and Nicaragua would be free, and that the Western Hemisphere would be the first fully free hemisphere in all of human history. The Biden Administration is squandering a historic opportunity to stand for freedom and human rights in our home region. The Biden Administration is betraying the freedom-loving people of Cuba. I fought for Cuba, they didn't. July 15, 2021

Donald J Trump @RealDonaldTrump

Nobody had ever heard of some of these people that worked for me in D.C. All of a sudden, the Fake News starts calling them. Some of them—by no means all—feel emboldened, brave, and for the first time in their lives, they feel like "something special," not the losers that they are—and they talk, talk, talk!

Many say I am the greatest star-maker of all time. But some of the stars I produced are actually made of garbage. July 15, 2021

To comment, I believe this Statement is in regard to people who are testifying before the J6 Commission. That biased commission is digging deep into the Trump administration to find someone who will say something negative about him.

One such person will be Cassidy Hutchinson, an ex-aid to Trump's Chief of Staff Mark Meadows. She will testify publicly on June 28, 2022. But there will be five aspects of her testimony that will be called into question, and Trump will respond that he barely knew her. I will overview her testimony and that of other former minor White House aids in my *J6 Commission* book.

Donald J Trump @RealDonaldTrump
Big hearing in Arizona on the Forensic Audit at 1:00PM EDT. Watch on OAN! July 15, 2021

Donald J Trump @RealDonaldTrump
Despite massive Voter Fraud and Irregularities during the 2020 Presidential Election Scam, that we are now seeing play out in very big and important States, I never threatened, or spoke about, to anyone, a coup of our Government. So ridiculous! Sorry to inform you, but an Election is my form of "coup," and if I was going to do a coup, one of the last people I would want to do it with is General Mark Milley. He got his job only because the world's most overrated general, James Mattis, could not stand him, had no respect for him, and would not recommend him. To me the fact that Mattis didn't like him, just like Obama didn't like him and actually fired Milley, was a good thing, not a bad thing. I often act counter to people's advice who I don't respect.

In any event, I lost respect for Milley when we walked together to St. John's Church (which was still smoldering from a Radical Left fire set the day before), side by side, a walk that has now been proven to be totally appropriate—and the following day Milley choked like a dog in front of the Fake News when they told him they thought he should not have been walking with the President, which turned out to be incorrect. He apologized profusely, making it a big story, instead of saying I am proud to walk with and protect the President of the United States. Had he said that, it would have all been over, no big deal, but I saw at that moment he had no courage or skill, certainly not the type of person I would be talking "coup" with. I'm not into coups!

In fact, around the same time Milley, in a conversation, was an advocate of changing all of the names of our Military Forts and Bases. I realized then, also, he was a much different person than I had hoped. I said to him, "spend more time thinking about China and Russia, and less time on being politically correct."

But never during my Administration did Milley display what he is showing now. He was not "woke." Actually, I don't believe he ever was, but the way I look at Milley, he's just a better politician than a general, trying to curry favor with the Radical Left and the absolute crazy people espousing a philosophy which will destroy our Country! July 15, 2021

To comment, this tweet is in response to Milley testifying before the J6 Commission and claiming Trump had attempted a coup. That is a twist on J6 being called an insurrection. But both terms are false, as I explain in my *Tragic Ending* and *Trump Tweets* books.

Donald J Trump @RealDonaldTrump
Kevin McCarthy will be meeting with me this afternoon at Trump National in Bedminster, N.J. Much to discuss! July 15, 2021

Donald J Trump @RealDonaldTrump
Nancy Pelosi is a known nut job. Her enraged quotes that she was afraid that I would use nuclear weapons is just more of the same. In fact, I was the one that got us out of wars, not into wars. And I was the one who got respect for our Country again, not like now when the leaders of the entire World are laughing at us. They didn't laugh when I was there! July 15, 2021

July 16, 2021

Donald J Trump @RealDonaldTrump
Fox News and other media outlets incorrectly side with the outdated and terrible Maricopa County Election Board to report no fraud found in the Presidential Election. They spew the gross misinformation purposefully put out by the county and the Associated Press, and IGNORE the very important Arizona Senate's hearing yesterday, which showed 168,000 fraudulent ballots printed on illegal paper (unofficial ballots), 74,000 mail in ballots received that were never mailed (magically appearing ballots), 11,000 voters were added to the voter rolls AFTER the election and still voted, all the access logs to the machines were wiped, and the election server was hacked during the election. They sided with

124

the County and not the brave Arizona Senate who is fighting for the people of Arizona.

The same anchor at the desk the night Fox called Arizona for Joe Biden now wants you to believe there was no fraud. The anchor was Bret Baier. Thankfully, Arizona has strong State Senators willing to fight for the truth. Senator Wendy Rogers says "I have heard enough. It's time to decertify this election." Senator Kelly Townsend said the fraud was so bad "I want to see indictments." Senator Sonny Borrelli says "I've seen enough evidence to challenge the validity of the certification of the Maricopa County Election results." Arizona shows Fraud and Voting Irregularities many times more than would be needed to change the outcome of the Election. July 16, 2021

Donald J Trump @RealDonaldTrump

AP and other media outlets are doing major disinformation to try and discredit the massive number of voter irregularities and fraud found in both Arizona and Georgia. When the real numbers are released people will be shocked, but this is a concerted effort of the Fake News Media to discredit and demean. There has never been anything like it. Numbers will be released shortly, and they are extraordinarily big and highly determinative! July 16, 2021

Donald J Trump @RealDonaldTrump

As an answer to the many people asking, I am not on any social media platform in any way, shape, or form, including Parler, GETTR, Gab, etc. When I decide to choose a platform, or build or complete my own, it will be announced. Thank you! July 16, 2021

To comment, as mentioned at the beginning of this book, Gab has a page set up for Trump that they are holding for him to start using at any time. But he never took them up on the offer.

Donald J Trump @RealDonaldTrump

The Governor of Georgia, Brian Kemp, together with Brad Raffensperger, allowed this Election in Georgia to be Rigged and Stolen. Why they ever agreed to Stacey Abram's Consent Decree nobody will ever know. Thank you to Senator Burt Jones and all of the other Patriots for continuing the fight. Brian Kemp and Brad Raffensperger have done an absolutely terrible job of watching over Voter Integrity in Georgia. They must be held accountable! July 16, 2021

To comment, I discuss the Consent Decree Trump is referring to in my *Trump's Tweets* book, in the chapter on his phone call with Brad.

Donald J Trump @RealDonaldTrump

Despite the fact that the 2020 Presidential Election was Rigged and Stolen, and while numerous people, including the outside public, were saying we should bring in the Military, I never even gave it a thought. The writings within these third-rate books are Fake News, and "General" Milley (who Mattis wanted to send to Europe in order to get rid of him), if he said what was reported, perhaps should be impeached, or court-martialed and tried. Never once did I have a discussion with him about bringing in the Military, or a "coup," which makes sense, because I lost total confidence in him and the way he handled himself on our little walk to the church.

He tries to be a tough guy, which he is not, but he choked beyond belief as soon as a microphone was stuffed in front of his face or, at the mere sight of the Fake News Media. So, there was no talk of a coup, there was no coup, it all never happened, and it's just a waste of words by fake writers and a General who didn't have a clue. What there was, was a Rigged and Stolen election, and those facts have come out, and are coming out, loud and clear. Because of the Rigged Election, our Country will suffer like perhaps never before with open Borders, Crime, and Inflation, which will eat everyone alive! July 16, 2021

To comment, Trump was once again prescient here, as the three things he mentions, "open Borders, Crime, and Inflation," were bad at this time, but they will all become even greater problems as the failing Biden presidency continues.

Donald J Trump @RealDonaldTrump

Despite what is being reported in one of the many fake books that are coming onto the market, Bill Barr never once told me he thought I was going to lose the election. In fact, it was quite the opposite, he told me that I should win. In retrospect, had the election not been Rigged and Stolen, I would have won easily, and our Country would not be in the horrible position it is now with open Borders, Inflation, massive jumps in Crime, and cities that have no chance of ever recovering under Democrat leadership. July 16, 2021

July 18, 2021

Donald J Trump @RealDonaldTrump

Congratulations to Doug Collins on his new book, *The Clock and the Calendar: A Front-Row Look at the Democrats' Obsession with*

Trump Fights Back with Statements

Donald Trump. A great look from behind the scenes of someone who was there fighting the good fight—in Impeachment Hoax #1. Thank you Doug, for always being there—and supporting the MAGA Movement! July 18, 2021

July 19, 2021

Donald J Trump @RealDonaldTrump

Joe Biden kept talking about how good of a job he's doing on the distribution of the Vaccine that was developed by Operation Warp Speed or, quite simply, the Trump Administration. He's not doing well at all. He's way behind schedule, and people are refusing to take the Vaccine because they don't trust his Administration, they don't trust the Election results, and they certainly don't trust the Fake News, which is refusing to tell the Truth. July 19, 2021

Donald J Trump @RealDonaldTrump

Crime in our Country is escalating at a pace we've never seen before. At the same time, people are pouring through our Borders totally unchecked. Jails in other countries are being emptied out into the United States. This is far worse than anyone thought during the Fake Election! July 19, 2021

July 21, 2021

Donald J Trump @RealDonaldTrump

Big election coming up on Tuesday, July 27, in Texas. Go out and vote for Susan Wright! Susan is outstanding, and her late husband, Congressman Ron Wright, is looking down and is very proud of her. She will serve the people of the Great State of Texas in the 6th Congressional District very well. Susan is for Strong Borders, Pro-Life, Pro-Second Amendment, Great Education, and will fight to bring back Free and Fair elections. Susan has my Complete and Total Endorsement. She will make our Country proud. Vote on Tuesday! July 21, 2021

Donald J Trump @RealDonaldTrump

True now more than ever before!

Read the full article by Ben Weingarten with the American Mind here. https://americanmind.org/features/get-ready-for-a-fight/trumps-greatest-achievement/

Trump's Greatest Achievement

The president has exposed the rot and corruption of our ruling class. [picture of Trump at a podium] July 21, 2021

Donald J Trump @RealDonaldTrump

Republicans must take seriously the effort by Democrats to completely change America through the Reconciliation Process. Democrats are now suggesting that budget reconciliation can be used to pass Mail-In Ballot legislation as well as trying to include Amnesty in their infrastructure package. The infrastructure package has little to do with infrastructure as we know it, bridges, roads, tunnels, etc., but is a dramatic expansion of Government that will cost much more than the $3.5 trillion being discussed. Don't let this happen!

If Amnesty is included in the infrastructure package, there will be a run on our Southern Border the likes of which we have never seen before. It will be a signal that says "come to America now, because you will soon be a citizen." Providing Amnesty to illegal aliens, in the history of what already is considered the greatest Border catastrophe, will result in disaster beyond our gravest nightmares. No country can pay this price. Will lead to ruination!

Any effort to dictate national Mail-In Voting will be a disaster for our Country and for conservatism. There will never be a Republican elected to high office again. I urge every Republican to fight this and deny Democrats a quorum if that is what it takes to make sure that the Democrats can't use reconciliation.

Republicans must push back for the sake of our Country and, far less importantly, the sake of the Republican Party! July 21, 2021

To comment, I discuss Biden's infrastructure plan in-depth in my *Biden Tweets* books.

July 22, 2021

Donald J Trump @RealDonaldTrump

Great show!

Read Natalie Harp's opening monologue and interview with Garland Favorito from The Real Story on OAN here.

https://cdn.donaldjtrump.com/djtweb/general/Transcript_07-20.pdf

July 22, 2021

Donald J Trump @RealDonaldTrump

I am looking forward to speaking at Turning Point Action on Saturday afternoon, in the Great State of Arizona, at the Arizona Federal

Theatre. We will be broadcasting at approximately 6:00PM EST. Big crowd, see you there! July 22, 2021

Donald J Trump @RealDonaldTrump
  Republican Arizona State Senator Paul Boyer, a RINO if there ever was one, is doing everything in his power to hold up the damning Forensic Audit of Maricopa County which has been taking place over the last 90 days. The people of Arizona are demanding it. Boyer has been nothing but trouble, and nobody knows why. All we demand is Voter Integrity! He is being primaried by a strong and highly respected challenger, former Arizona State Representative Anthony Kern. July 22, 2021

July 23, 2021

Donald J Trump @RealDonaldTrump
  Can anybody believe that the Cleveland Indians, a storied and cherished baseball franchise since taking the name in 1915, are changing their name to the Guardians? Such a disgrace, and I guarantee that the people who are most angry about it are the many Indians of our Country. Wouldn't it be an honor to have a team named the Cleveland Indians, and wouldn't it be disrespectful to rip that name and logo off of those jerseys? The people of Cleveland cannot be thrilled and I, as a FORMER baseball fan, cannot believe things such as this are happening. A small group of people, with absolutely crazy ideas and policies, is forcing these changes to destroy our culture and heritage. At some point, the people will not take it anymore! July 23, 2021

  To comment, I find it interesting Trump describes himself as "a FORMER baseball fan." I use the same phraseology when talking about the Pittsburgh Pirates, Steelers, and Penguins. I used to be a huge fan of all three, but wokism in them caused me to lose interest in all three Pittsburgh teams and in professional sports in general.
  The final straws were when the Pirates played a video honoring Black Live Matter (better known as Building large Mansions) before their home opener in 2021, then the Steelers putting the names of criminals, like Antwon Rose, on their helmets.
  Meanwhile, both the Pirates and Penguins have special nights each year honoring the LGBTQ movement. I just cannot support organizations that promote sin and thugs who resist arrest, getting themselves killed.

July 25, 2021

Donald J Trump @RealDonaldTrump
Heading to Arizona for a speech. Will be aired on Newsmax, OAN, Right Side Broadcasting Network, and others at 6:00PM EDT. Enjoy! July 25, 2021

July 26, 2021

Donald J Trump @RealDonaldTrump
Senate Republicans are being absolutely savaged by Democrats on the so-called "bipartisan" infrastructure bill. Mitch McConnell and his small group of RINOs wants nothing more than to get a deal done at any cost to prove that he can work with the Radical Left Democrats. It is so important to him that he is agreeing to almost anything. Don't do the infrastructure deal, wait until after we get proper election results in 2022 or otherwise, and regain a strong negotiating stance. Republicans, don't let the Radical Left play you for weak fools and losers! July 26, 2021

July 27, 2021

Donald J Trump @RealDonaldTrump
Who are these RINO Republicans that are so dedicated to giving the Radical Left Democrats a big and beautiful win on Infrastructure? Republican voters will never forget their name, nor will the people of our Country! July 27, 2021

Donald J Trump @RealDonaldTrump
Big election tomorrow in the Great State of Texas! Susan Wright supports America First policies, our Military and our Veterans, is strong on Borders, tough on Crime, Pro-Life, and will always protect our Second Amendment. She will serve the people in the 6th Congressional District of Texas, and our Country, very well. Susan has my Complete and Total Endorsement. She will never let you down! Go out and vote for Susan Wright. July 27, 2021

Donald J Trump @RealDonaldTrump
Nancy Pelosi is spending a great deal of time, effort, and money on the formulation of a Fake and highly partisan January 6 Committee to ask, "what happened?"
Will Nancy investigate herself and those on Capitol Hill who didn't want additional protection, including more police and National Guard,

therefore being unprepared despite the large crowd of people that everyone knew was coming?

Will Nancy and her Committee study the massive Voter Fraud that took place during the 2020 Presidential Election, particularly in swing states, that was the reason hundreds of thousands of people came pouring into Washington and, therefore, must be a big factor in the final Committee Report? Now would be a very good time to study the large scale Voter Fraud in our Presidential Election.

Will Nancy release the thousands of hours of tapes so we can see the extent to which ANTIFA and Black Lives Matter played a role, while also revealing "who killed Ashli Babbitt?" A real and thorough investigation of this must be done—and what about all of the violence, murders, riots, and fires that took place in Democrat run cities throughout the United States by ANTIFA and Black Lives Matter, with virtually no consequence for this death and destruction?

Will Nancy look into the vicious partisan investigations of Conservatives and Republicans that are taking place by prosecutors all over the Country? The five-year investigation of me, and all that so many have been through, including the fake Russia Russia Russia charge, and including the local Democrat-controlled New York prosecutors who work around the clock to get President Donald Trump, while murderers, drug dealers, and human traffickers go free! July 27, 2021

To comment, Trump raises very valid concerns about the J6 Commission. I will cover each of these points in my forthcoming book on that subject.

July 28, 2021

Donald J Trump @RealDonaldTrump

Former California Senator Barbara Boxer was savagely assaulted and robbed yesterday in Oakland, where they defunded the police. Our once great cities, like New York, Detroit, San Francisco, and so many others, have become a paradise for criminals because of Democrats. We must give power back to police or America will never be safe. We cannot let Communist Democrats destroy our great cities. If we don't stop them, our communities and our Country will be lost forever. July 28, 2021

Donald J Trump @RealDonaldTrump

The fraudulent nightly network newscasts have devoted ZERO minutes to crime recently, even though crime is eating away at our cities and our Country. They don't want to talk about it because it will hurt the political narrative of the Communist Democrats. Just think, six months ago we had the most secure Border in our history. Today, it is the least secure in our history with criminals illegally flooding into our Country—many spreading COVID into our communities—and other Countries' prisons being emptied into our neighborhoods. America needs law and order, not defunding the police. We need our police back. America should and can be safe! July 28, 2021

To comment, Trump is indeed correct that the open border was allowing illegals to spread Covid. I will theorize in my forthcoming *Coronavirus* book that the "fourth wave" of Covid was fueled by illegals being spread around the country by Joe Biden.

Donald J Trump @RealDonaldTrump
My deepest condolences to the family and many friends of former Senator Mike Enzi. He was a fine man who always put America first. He will be missed! July 28, 2021

July 29, 2021

Donald J Trump @RealDonaldTrump
We won't go back. We won't mask our children. Joe Biden and his Administration learned nothing from the last year. Brave Americans learned how to safely and responsibly live and fight back. Don't surrender to COVID. Don't go back! Why do Democrats distrust the science? Don't let this happen to our children or our Country. July 29, 2021

To comment, Trump is correct that children should not and never should have been forced to wear masks. Children are at little risk form Covid, and the mask have hindered their development.

Donald J Trump @RealDonaldTrump
Numerous candidates in the Great State of Ohio, running in Congressional District 15, are saying that I am supporting them, when in actuality, I don't know them, and don't even know who they are. But I do know who Mike Carey is—I know a lot about him, and it is all good. Mike Carey is the only one who has my Endorsement and he's the one I feel will do the best job for Ohio, and for the United States. Please vote for Mike Carey next Tuesday, and let there be no further doubt who I have Endorsed! July 29, 2021

Trump Fights Back with Statements

Donald J Trump @RealDonaldTrump

Under the weak leadership of Mitch McConnell, Senate Republicans continue to lose. He lost Arizona, he lost Georgia, he ignored Election Fraud and he doesn't fight. Now he's giving Democrats everything they want and getting nothing in return. No deal is better than a bad deal. Fight for America, not for special interests and Radical Democrats. RINOs are ruining America, right alongside Communist Democrats. July 29, 2021

Donald J Trump @RealDonaldTrump

Hard to believe our Senate Republicans are dealing with the Radical Left Democrats in making a so-called bipartisan bill on "infrastructure," with our negotiators headed up by SUPER RINO Mitt Romney. This will be a victory for the Biden Administration and Democrats, and will be heavily used in the 2022 election. It is a loser for the USA, a terrible deal, and makes the Republicans look weak, foolish, and dumb.

It shouldn't be done. It sets an easy glidepath for Dems to then get beyond what anyone thought was possible in future legislation. It will be a continued destruction of our Country. Our Borders are horrible, crime is at an all time high, taxes and inflation are going way up, the economy is going way down, and now this. Don't do it Republicans— Patriots will never forget! If this deal happens, lots of primaries will be coming your way! July 29, 2021

July 30, 2021

Donald J Trump @RealDonaldTrump

The RINOs in the Senate are delivering a big win by caving to the Radical Democrats on infrastructure. Once they pass this bill out of the Senate, it will sit in the House until they get steamrolled by the biggest government expansion in a generation. Tax increases on everyone, government run health care, more government run schools, amnesty for illegal immigrants, MASKS, and many more terrible socialist programs. Nancy Pelosi has said NO INFRASTRUCTURE until they get everything else. Infrastructure is just a "carrot" for a massive socialist expansion.

Why are RINOs so desperate to push bad, Radical Leftist policies? And at the same time give a big win to the Democrats. They will be forced to give up some of the incredible tax cuts gotten during the Trump Administration, one of its many hallmarks. This is bad legislation and politically irresponsible. The Democrats will use it to show they can get anything they want from the Republicans. July 30, 2021

To comment, House Dems were trying to tie the infrastructure bill to Biden's much larger Build Back Better plan. I document this finagling in my *Biden Tweets* books.

Donald J Trump @RealDonaldTrump
Voters in the Great State of Wyoming want clear majority winners in elections, and the only mechanism that accomplishes majority victors is a Run-Off Election, pitting the top two candidates against each other. Conservative Republicans in the Wyoming State Legislature like Senator Bo Biteman and Representative Chip Nieman led this effort.
Unfortunately and sadly for Wyoming voters, RINO State Legislators stood in the way, defeating the Run-Off Election bills. The easiest way to defeat Deplorable Liz Cheney is by having only ONE Conservative candidate run and WIN! Wyoming Patriots will no longer stand for Nancy Pelosi and her new lapdog RINO Liz Cheney! July 30, 2021

To comment, there are four Repubs running against Cheney, Thus, Trump is correct that they could split the anti-Cheney vote, allowing Cheney to squeak in as the nominee. But if there were a two-person run-off, that would ensure she would not win, as the anti-Cheney vote is far larger than the pro-Cheney vote.

Donald J Trump @RealDonaldTrump
Thank you, Arizona! [graphic showing Trump's high approval rating sin Arizona] July 30, 2021

Chapter Eight
Trump's Statements
August 2021

These Trump Statements are continued from Chapter Seven.

August 1, 2021

Donald J Trump @RealDonaldTrump

The corrupt and highly partisan House Democrats who run the House Oversight Committee yesterday released documents—including court filings dealing with the rigged election of 2020—that they dishonestly described as attempting to overturn the election.

In fact, it is just the opposite. The documents were meant to uphold the integrity and honesty of elections and the sanctity of our vote. The American People want, and demand, that the President of the United States, its chief law enforcement officer in the country, stand with them to fight for Election Integrity and to investigate attempts to undermine our nation. Our country has just suffered an incredibly corrupt Presidential Election, and it is time for Congress and others to investigate how such corruption was allowed to take place rather than investigating those that are exposing this massive fraud on the American People. August 1, 2021

To comment, Trump is correct to expose the word games being played in regard to the 2020 election. The MSM and Dems always word Trump's actions as efforts to "overturn the election." However, what Trump and others are trying to do is to get to the correct results, the results that would have occurred were it not for the fraud and irregularities in the 2020 election.

August 3, 2021

Donald J Trump @RealDonaldTrump

In addition to the RECORD BREAKING money raised over the last 6 months to my political affiliates, I am pleased to see the entire party benefit from "Trump." By using my name and likeness through many of their efforts, the Republican National Committee raised $84 million, the National Republican Senatorial Committee raised $51.2 million, and

135

the National Republican Congressional Committee raised $79.2 million. Nearly $296.4 million in support of Trump! The Republican Party is unified behind Trump and the patriots continue to fuel this movement. Thank you, America! August 3, 2021

Donald J Trump @RealDonaldTrump
If I were President right now, with COVID raging back, people being shot and killed in record numbers all over our cities, and the Border totally open with criminals and heavily infected COVID people pouring through our Southern Border and into our communities, the Fake News Media would be having an absolute field day.

When I left office, law enforcement was supported like never before, the Border was strong, safe, and secure (the best ever!), and I got a highly effective vaccine developed in less than 9 months (when it was supposed to take 5 years, or more!). Hopefully, people will NEVER FORGET! August 3, 2021

To comment, though exposing the fraud in the 2020 election is important, Statements like this one are what Trump should focus on going forward, touting his many accomplishments while in office, as contrasted with the failures of Biden and his administration. But, as will be seen, Trump will never be able to let go of his many complaints about the 2020 election.

August 4, 2021

Donald J Trump @RealDonaldTrump
Great Republican win for Mike Carey. Big numbers! Thank you to Ohio and all of our wonderful American patriots. Congratulations to Mike and his family. He will never let you down! August 4, 2021

Donald J Trump @RealDonaldTrump
Highly respected Army intelligence captain, Seth Keshel, has just released his Report on National Fraud Numbers with respect to the 2020 Presidential Election. I don't personally know Captain Keshel, but these numbers are overwhelming, election-changing, and according to Keshel, could be even bigger in that they do not account for cyber-flipping of votes. They show I won the election—by A LOT!

Now watch the Democrats coalesce, defame, threaten, investigate, jail people, and do whatever they have to do to keep the truth from surfacing, and let the Biden Administration continue to get away with destroying our Country. The irregularities and outright fraud of this election are an open wound to the United States of America. Something must be done—immediately! August 4, 2021

To comment, yes, something must be done, and red state legislatures are doing just that. They are making it easier to vote but harder to cheat. Of course, Dems do not like the latter, as it is the only way they can win, so they lie and say the laws are racist, with faux-President Biden leading the way in the lies.

However, I document the fraud that occurred and ways to correct it in my *Corruption* book. The red state legislatures must have read my book, as they are instituting many of my recommendations.

Donald J Trump @RealDonaldTrump

One of the biggest stories in the Lamestream Media yesterday was the very important Congressional race in Ohio and whether or not Trump-backed candidate, Mike Carey, would lose against a large and outstanding field of other candidates. The mainstream was chomping at the bit to report a loss for a Trump endorsed candidate—they couldn't wait. In fact the Washington Post still hasn't corrected their very old story.

But lo and behold, instead of a loss, there was a landslide victory for Mike—a win far larger than even the most optimistic of polls. It was a great day for Ohio, but the story of this victory has been barely reported by the Fake News. If my endorsed candidate would have lost, it would have been nothing but front page. Such a double standard, but congratulations to Mike, he will never let Ohio down. August 4, 2021

Donald J Trump @RealDonaldTrump

Three months ago, two wonderful Republican candidates in Texas defeated ALL Democrats, so the Congressional election last week was between two Republicans. My endorsed candidate won in the Primary, but the other outstanding candidate won the General Election because virtually 100% of Democrats, approximately 17% of the total vote, supported the candidate I did not endorse.

I won because we ended up with a great Republican candidate—the Democrats never had a chance. Unfortunately, the Fake News never wrote that Democrats were in the race, obviously voting against me. It was a big Trump victory, a great Republican victory, and a great victory for American Patriot Congressman Jake Ellzey. Would really be nice if the Fake News would become real news! August 4, 2021

August 5, 2021

Donald J Trump @RealDonaldTrump

It's good to see that the Atlantic Magazine is losing large numbers of readers and a fortune of money. Only a widow of Steve Jobs and her boyfriend, I am sure Steve is thrilled, would keep it going. People think it will close soon, but who knows.

It is amazing what's happening to the discredited media like CNN, MSDNC, New York Times, and Washington Post. Their businesses have dropped off a cliff, which is actually a very good thing for the American people, because they are Fake News (likewise the networks, ABC, NBC, CBS). August 5, 2021

Donald J Trump @RealDonaldTrump

If our soccer team, headed by a radical group of Leftist Maniacs, wasn't woke, they would have won the Gold Medal instead of the Bronze. Woke means you lose, everything that is woke goes bad, and our soccer team certainly has.

There were, however, a few Patriots standing. Unfortunately, they need more than that respecting our Country and National Anthem. They should replace the wokesters with Patriots and start winning again. The woman with the purple hair played terribly and spends too much time thinking about Radical Left politics and not doing her job! August 5, 2021

Extended Comment
Lowest Rated Olympics

Except for a bit of weightlifting, I am not watching any of the 2020/21 Olympics because of these wokesters. Apparently, I am not alone. Newsmax reported that 8 of the first 9 nights of this Olympics were the lowest rated this century.

The Tokyo Olympics have been a ratings disaster for NBC, which on Wednesday [8/4/21] suffered the second-lowest numbers of the Games....

Through Tuesday, NBC's ratings averaged 16.8 million viewers nightly — a significant drop from the 29 million who tuned in through the same day of the Rio de Janeiro Olympics in 2016, The New York Times reported (Newsmax. NBC's).

Trump Fights Back with Statements

However, in that NYT article, they blame the low ratings on the pandemic, the style of coverage, and the plethora of alternative media options. There is not a word about wokeness contributing to the low ratings. Yet, that is *the* reason I am not watching, as I am sure it is for many other patriotic Americans. Back to Trump.

August 6, 2021

Donald J Trump @RealDonaldTrump

Do you think Rand Paul will apologize for spending nearly $1 Million on another candidate in Ohio's 15th District congressional race after I had already endorsed Mike Carey? In any event, Mike went on to an unprecedented victory, more than doubling the second placed finisher and Rand's candidate came in a distant third out of eleven. Rand is a different kind of guy, but I like him a lot anyway, and I'm proud to have endorsed him when when [sic] he ran. Do you think he learned his lesson? August 6, 2021

Donald J Trump @RealDonaldTrump

Thank you to Winged Foot Golf Club for honoring me last night. There was true love and spirit in the room. It is a great and well-run place! [picture of Trump golfing] August 6, 2021

Donald J Trump @RealDonaldTrump

The biggest election in a long time is the one that took place in Ohio's 15th district with the winner Mike Carey. All of the Radical Left were talking about it because they thought that my endorsed candidate would not win, but he won in a landslide. It would have been headline news for days. Instead, there is virtually no story written about Mike's win. Rather they cover another Democrat race that nobody even talked about before where a progressive went down in flames. Practically nothing is written about the big Mike Carey win. Nobody but OAN covered it. August 6, 2021

To comment, Newsmax did as well, on its crawl and website.

August 7, 2021

Donald J Trump @RealDonaldTrump

Joe Biden's infrastructure bill is a disgrace. If Mitch McConnell was smart, which we've seen no evidence of, he would use the debt ceiling card to negotiate a good infrastructure package.

This is a 2,700 page bill that no one could have possibly read—they would have needed to take speed reading courses. It is a gift to the Democrat Party, compliments of Mitch McConnell and some RINOs, who have no idea what they are doing. There is very little on infrastructure in all of those pages. Instead, they track your driving so they can tax you. It is Joe Biden's form of a gas tax but far bigger, far higher and, mark my words, far worse. They want to track you everywhere you go and watch everything you do!

Joe Biden's infrastructure bill will be used against the Republican Party in the upcoming elections in 2022 and 2024. It will be very hard for me to endorse anyone foolish enough to vote in favor of this deal.

The good news is that the progressive wing in the Democrat Party will lose all credibility with this approval. Additionally, Kevin McCarthy and Republican House members seem to be against the bill. If it can't be killed in the Senate, maybe it dies in the House!

Nancy Pelosi and the Democrats understand that this is the way to get the horrendous $3.5 trillion, actually $5 trillion, Green New Deal bill done in the House. Mitch is playing right into Nancy's hands, not to mention the fact Chuck Schumer is already going around saying this is a big victory for the Democrats.

Whether it's the House or the Senate, think twice before you approve this terrible deal. Republicans should wait until after the Midterms when they will gain all the strength they'll need to make a good deal, but remember, you already have the card, it's called the debt ceiling, which the Democrats threatened us with constantly. August 7, 2021

To comment, coupling these two very different bills is a disgrace on the part of the Democrats. The first, on real infrastructure, contains necessary spending, but also unnecessary pork, while the latter ("Human infrastructure?") is pure leftist pork.

And Trump is correct—lawmakers should actually read the bill before they vote on it, but they rarely do.

Donald J Trump @RealDonaldTrump

Wisconsin has just canceled 205,000 voter registrations because they say they could not find the voters. Why did they wait until AFTER the election? Would this mean that we would have won Wisconsin? Congratulations! August 7, 2021

<u>Trump Fights Back with Statements</u>

To comment, it seems obvious to most of us that election safeguards should be engaged before an election, not afterwards. But this past election was purposely left unsecure, as Dems knew it was the only way they could win.

August 8, 2021

Donald J Trump @RealDonaldTrump

On Purple Heart Day we pay solemn tribute to our Wounded Warriors and Fallen Heroes. These immortal patriots shed their blood, and many gave their lives, to defend our flag, families, and freedom. May we honor their sacred memory by protecting all that they sacrificed to secure. God bless our men and women in uniform, the greatest heroes in all the world. August 8, 2021

To comment, amen!

Donald J Trump @RealDonaldTrump

Thank you to Sean Hannity for your Patriotism and Wisdom! August 8, 2021

To comment, Sean is great. I listen to him all the time, have for many years.

August 9, 2021

Donald J Trump @RealDonaldTrump

This is not an infrastructure bill, this is the beginning of the Green New Deal. The bill I proposed, which Mitch McConnell couldn't do anything with, was pure infrastructure. I want what is best for America, not what's best for the Communist Democrat Party. This will be a big victory for the Democrats and will be used against Republicans in the upcoming elections. Schumer is using the threat of "we can do it the hard way or do it the easy way" and keeping people in town. McConnell never did that on a real infrastructure bill. Hopefully the House will be much stronger than the Senate.

Congratulations to Senator Bill Hagerty in remaining true to "AMERICA FIRST!" August 9, 2021

To comment, updating our infrastructure is a good idea, as Trump indicates. But infrastructure is just that, physical structures that last at least ten years and that are used by us all. But Biden and the radical Dems have made the term mean anything on their leftist wish list.

In my *Biden Tweets* books, I detail all that is in this bill. Only about half is about real infrastructure. I could never find out what was in the other half, except what Trump mentioned previously, that of putting trackers in cars. That is purportedly so those driving EVs can be taxed for their mileage, since it will not be possible to collect gasoline taxes from them. But those of us who believe in privacy have great concerns those trackers will track much more than just the amount of mileage but where we drive to as well.

August 10, 2021

Donald J Trump @RealDonaldTrump

Does everybody remember when we caught the Democrats, red-handed, SPYING ON MY CAMPAIGN? Where's Durham? August 10, 2021

To comment, when I finished my *Impeach* trilogy a year ago, I thought I would include an update about the Durham report at least in the last volume. But I, and the country, are still waiting. I've published two books since then, but still no Durham report to report about. Maybe by my next book?

"Books and eBooks by the Director of Biblical and Constitutional Politics" - https://www.zeolla.org/politics/subject/books.html

Donald J Trump @RealDonaldTrump

Just reported that over 20% of the people coming across our Southern Border have Coronavirus (sometimes referred to as the China Virus), many of them being immediately released into our communities—and then our "Government" tells you how to mask up, use three if possible, and how to otherwise act as highly infected people pour into our Country. Finish the wall in one month, stop paying contractors billions of dollars for NOT building the wall, and stop allowing some of the worst prisoners and criminals anywhere in the world into our Country—jails of other countries are being emptied into ours. Such a thing has never happened to any nation before. This is what a Rigged and Corrupt Presidential Election gets you! August 10, 2021

To comment, all very true. Biden should be impeached for seeding this fourth Covid wave through his disastrous border policies.

August 11, 2021

Donald J Trump @RealDonaldTrump
   Nobody will ever understand why Mitch McConnell allowed this non-infrastructure bill to be passed. He has given up all of his leverage for the big whopper of a bill that will follow. I have quietly said for years that Mitch McConnell is the most overrated man in politics—now I don't have to be quiet anymore. He is working so hard to give Biden a victory, now they'll go for the big one, including the biggest tax increases in the history of our Country. August 11, 2021

August 12, 2021

Donald J Trump @RealDonaldTrump
   BULLIES NEVER FIGHT! August 12, 2021

   To comment, I am not sure what precipitated this Statement.

Donald J Trump @RealDonaldTrump
   Good morning, America! While you were all sleeping, the Radical Democrats advanced a plan that will be known as the $3.5 trillion Communist Plan to Destroy America. This legislation is an assault on our Nation, on our communities, and on the American Dream.
   It destroys our Borders and the rule of law by granting dangerous amnesty that will flood America's beautiful cities. It will overwhelm our schools, and make our Nation less safe. It raises taxes like we have never seen, while also making many things you buy everyday more expensive (gas, groceries, and much more). And don't forget the crazy Green New Deal. America, you are being robbed in the dark of night. It's time to wake up! August 12, 2021

   To comment, I predict #Bidenflation will reach double digits by the end of next year. That will ensure a Republican landslide in 2022.

Donald J Trump @RealDonaldTrump
   Fox doesn't understand that it is missing a rating bonanza by not covering the 2020 Election Fraud, the Crime of the Century, which is being exposed throughout many states on a daily basis. They are also doing a disservice to our Country. People have turned them off! August 12, 2021

To comment, I tuned out of Fox and onto Newsmax after Fox's disastrous early calling of Arizona. Fox seems to have ignored all of the already known and more being revealed fraud that took place. I chronicle what was known back then in my *Corruption* book. I update some of the items in my *Tragic Ending* book for a year later.

Donald J Trump @RealDonaldTrump

I spoke to the wonderful mother and devoted husband of Ashli Babbitt, who was murdered at the hands of someone who should never have pulled the trigger of his gun. We know who he is. If that happened to the "other side," there would be riots all over America and yet, there are far more people represented by Ashli, who truly loved America, than there are on the other side. The Radical Left haters cannot be allowed to get away with this. There must be justice! August 12, 2021

To comment, Ashlie Babbitt is the lone person who was killed on J6. Do not believe the MSM and Dem lie of five people being killed. Ashli was an unarmed white female veteran, who was killed by the black Capitol Police officer Michael Byrd. He was not charged with her killing. It was said to be justified. But he was never interviewed. How they came to that concussion without interviewing him is beyond me.

But I am sure, if the skin shades had been reversed, and it was a white police officer killing an unarmed black woman, the MSM would have been all over it. As it is, her death has been ignored by the MSM.

Donald J Trump @RealDonaldTrump

Wow, the Governor of Georgia, Brian Kemp, was booed off the stage Saturday at a Georgia Republican Party event. They wouldn't let him speak. It is amazing how the people get what happened in Georgia, and elsewhere! The election was rigged, and everybody knows it. Kemp refused to call a Special Session of the Legislature, and did absolutely nothing. Now our Country is going to hell! August 12, 2021

To comment, I address the situation in Georgia in regard to the 2020 election in my *Trump Tweets* book. I follow that up with a chapter on the Georgian Senatorial run-off races in my *Tragic Ending* books.

Donald J Trump @RealDonaldTrump

RNC is meeting in the wonderful city of Nashville, Tennessee this week. I look forward to working with them to win in 2022 and beyond. The RNC members, Ronna and Tommy, are doing a great job! August 12, 2021

144

Trump Fights Back with Statements

Donald J Trump @RealDonaldTrump

Congratulations to Governor Mike Parson of Missouri for having the courage to give Mr. and Mrs. Mark McCloskey a full pardon. They were defending their property and if they had not done what they did, their property would have been completely destroyed and they would have been badly beaten, or dead—great going Mike! August 12, 2021

To comment, this is the couple who stood in front of their homes armed with a semi-automatic rifle and a pistol when a mob of BLM/Antifa types broke the barrier to their gated community. They were rightly afraid for their lives and property and had every right to defend themselves. But the woke Missouri DA said otherwise and charged them and confiscated their guns. But, as Trump says, the Governor did right in pardoning them.

August 13, 2021

Donald J Trump @RealDonaldTrump

Why are RINOs standing in the way of a full Forensic Audit in Michigan? The voters are demanding it because they have no confidence in their elections after the Rigged 2020 Presidential Election Scam. Michigan's Republican State Legislators should be ashamed of themselves for allowing this horrible situation to happen.

In particular, the incompetent RINO Majority Leader, Mike Shirkey, and Senator Ed McBroom. Maybe McBroom is really a Democrat who could not otherwise get elected in Northern Michigan. Our great Michigan voters will not stand for Republican Senators not to act on the Crime of the Century! August 13, 2021

Donald J Trump @RealDonaldTrump

Had our 2020 Presidential Election not been rigged, and if I were now President, the world would find that our withdrawal from Afghanistan would be a conditions-based withdrawal. I personally had discussions with top Taliban leaders whereby they understood what they are doing now would not have been acceptable. It would have been a much different and much more successful withdrawal, and the Taliban understood that better than anyone. What is going on now is not acceptable. It should have been done much better. August 13, 2021

To comment, very true. Trump's ex-generals have been on Newsmax explaining his plan and why it would have worked. But Biden abandoned it, simply because Trump designed it. Thus, Biden's hatred for Trump is leading to the Fall of Saigon 2.0 and much suffering in Afghanistan.

Donald J Trump @RealDonaldTrump
Tragic mess in Afghanistan, a completely open and broken Border, Crime at record levels, oil prices through the roof, inflation rising, and taken advantage of by the entire world—DO YOU MISS ME YET? August 13, 2021

To comment, great post! And all very true. The first seven months of the Biden administration has been a complete disaster. So very different from the start of Trump's administration, as I detail in two articles on my politics website:

100 Days of Productive Leadership (Never Mind What the Mainstream Media Tells You):
https://www.zeolla.org/politics/articles/2017/100-days.htm

One Year of Productive Leadership (What the Mainstream Media is Not Telling You):
https://www.zeolla.org/politics/articles/2018/one-year.htm

August 15, 2021

Donald J Trump @RealDonaldTrump
Joe Biden gets it wrong every time on foreign policy, and many other issues. Everyone knew he couldn't handle the pressure. Even Obama's Secretary of Defense, Robert Gates, said as much. He ran out of Afghanistan instead of following the plan our Administration left for him—a plan that protected our people and our property, and ensured the Taliban would never dream of taking our Embassy or providing a base for new attacks against America. The withdrawal would be guided by facts on the ground.

After I took out ISIS, I established a credible deterrent. That deterrent is now gone. The Taliban no longer has fear or respect for America, or America's power. What a disgrace it will be when the Taliban raises their flag over America's Embassy in Kabul. This is complete failure through weakness, incompetence, and total strategic incoherence. August 15, 2021

Extended Comment
Botched Afghanistan Withdrawal

What Trump understood that Biden doesn't is there is no real loyalty to the Afghan government among Afghans. Their loyalties are more to their local tribes and war lords. Trump had negotiated a shared power plan between all of these tribal war lords, the Taliban, and the Afghan government. But Biden abandon that plan.

As a result, those 300,000 Afghan troops that Biden bragged about back on July 8 were not really loyal to the Afghan government, but Biden never understood that. Rather than bravely standing against the Taliban, as Biden thought, as the Taliban surged across the country, those troops either turned tail and fled or joined the Taliban.

Trump also had a plan to get all US civilians and our Afghan allies out before removing our troops, and he had a plan for removing our military hardware. But again, Biden nixed all of those sound plans for the simple reason they were Trump's plans.

It is the same approach Biden used on the southern border. He reversed all of Trump's policies but now is trying to blame Trump for the disaster at the southern border.

But try as he might, both the Afghanistan debacle and the southern border disaster are on Biden. It is his polices that led to these messes, not Trump's policies, as again, Biden reversed Trump's policies for both, hence the phrase "Reversing Trump" in the subtitle of my *Biden Tweets* books. Back to Trump.

August 16, 2021

Donald J Trump @RealDonaldTrump

It is time for Joe Biden to resign in disgrace for what he has allowed to happen to Afghanistan, along with the tremendous surge in COVID, the Border catastrophe, the destruction of energy independence, and our crippled economy. It shouldn't be a big deal, because he wasn't elected legitimately in the first place! August 16, 2021

To comment, even the corrupt MSM is now having a hard time covering for Biden's incompetency.

Donald J Trump @RealDonaldTrump

What Joe Biden has done with Afghanistan is legendary. It will go down as one of the greatest defeats in American history! August 16, 2021

August 17, 2021

Donald J Trump @RealDonaldTrump

Afghanistan is the most embarrassing military outcome in the history of the United States. It didn't have to be that way! August 17, 2021

Donald J Trump @RealDonaldTrump

Can anyone even imagine taking out our Military before evacuating civilians and others who have been good to our Country and who should be allowed to seek refuge? In addition, these people left topflight and highly sophisticated equipment. Who can believe such incompetence? Under my Administration, all civilians and equipment would have been removed. August 17, 2021

Donald J Trump @RealDonaldTrump

First Joe Biden surrendered to COVID and it has come roaring back. Then he surrendered to the Taliban, who has quickly overtaken Afghanistan and destroyed confidence in American power and influence. The outcome in Afghanistan, including the withdrawal, would have been totally different if the Trump Administration had been in charge. Who or what will Joe Biden surrender to next? Someone should ask him, if they can find him. August 17, 2021

To comment, I have been saying for the past decade that Obama was the worst President of my lifetime, displacing Jimmy Carter for that dishonor. But in just over 200 days, Biden has now displaced Obama as the worst President of my lifetime. A disaster at our southern border and now a debacle in Afghanistan, all Biden's fault, and we still have 3-/12 years left of this incompetence. May God help us.

Donald J Trump @RealDonaldTrump

What took place yesterday in Afghanistan made our withdrawal from Vietnam look like child's play. Perhaps in World history, there has never been a withdrawal operation that has been handled so disastrously. A President who has been illegitimately elected has brought great shame, in many ways, to our Country! August 17, 2021

To comment, I titled my article about the withdraw, "Worst Foreign Policy Debacle in USA History." It details that Biden's incompetence led to the debacle we are now seeing in Afghanistan.
https://www.zeolla.org/politics/articles/2021/worst.htm

Trump Fights Back with Statements

Donald J Trump @RealDonaldTrump

It's not that we left Afghanistan. It's the grossly incompetent way we left! August 17, 2021

To comment, absolutely correct. Biden's speech was a joke. Biden did not address any of the issues I discussed in my article. He instead engaged in the red herring of talking about WHETHER we should withdrawal from Afghanistan, which all sides agree upon, rather than HOW that withdrawal was conducted, which he totally bungled.

He said the buck stopped with him, but then proceeded to blame everyone except himself for the chaos we all saw on TV, which he virtually ignored in his speech.

Bottom line is, people died, ISIS and/ or Al Qaeda will now be reconstituted, with them and the Taliban now armed with our military hardware, Afghanistan is in chaos, Afghans, especially Afghan women, will now see a restricted life, with few rights, and after 20 years, we are right back where we started, all due to Biden's incompetency. #Afghanistan #AfghanDebacle #BidenIncompetence

Donald J Trump @RealDonaldTrump

The corrupt Presidential Election of 2020 got us here. Never would have happened if I were President! August 17, 2021

To comment, elections have consequences, especially when that election is fraught with fraud and irregularities.

August 18, 2021

Donald J Trump @RealDonaldTrump

This plane should have been full of Americans. America First! [picture of US plane packed with hundreds of Afghans] https://media.gab.com/system/media_attachments/files/082/402/694/original/f323035d912daebc.png August 18, 2021

August 19, 2021

Donald J Trump @RealDonaldTrump

Biden did this to celebrate on September 11th when in actuality the celebration is our enemies and the fact that we already have the Taliban flag flying over our Obama-Biden built $1 Billion U.S. Embassy in Kabul. August 19, 2021

To comment, the USA losing in Afghanistan will cast a dark cloud on that already dreadful date.

Donald J Trump @RealDonaldTrump
Fake Elections have consequences, just look at the horror of Afghanistan coupled with the massive incompetence at our Southern Border! August 19, 2021

Donald J Trump @RealDonaldTrump
This could be—Afghanistan—another Dunkirk situation! August 19, 2021

August 20, 2021

Donald J Trump @RealDonaldTrump
First you bring out all of the American citizens. Then you bring out ALL equipment. Then you bomb the bases into smithereens—AND THEN YOU BRING OUT THE MILITARY. You don't do it in reverse order like Biden and our woke Generals did.
No chaos, no death—they wouldn't even know we left!
Leaving Americans behind for death is an unforgivable dereliction of duty, which will go down in infamy. August 20, 2021

To comment, Americans left behind. I never thought I'd see in it my lifetime, but here were are, thanks to Biden's incompetence.

Donald J Trump @RealDonaldTrump
Fmr. Google employee reveals company changed news algorithm to target President Trump
https://www.oann.com/fmr-google-employee-reveals-company-changed-news-algorithm-to-target-president-trump/
A Big Tech whistleblower has spoken out on Google's latest attempts to censor conservative speech.
Wow! August 20, 2021

August 21, 2021

Donald J Trump @RealDonaldTrump
Afghanistan under Biden was not a withdrawal, it was a surrender. Will he apologize for the greatest tactical mistake in history, pulling the Military out before our citizens? August 21, 2021

Trump Fights Back with Statements

Donald J Trump @RealDonaldTrump
This Afghanistan Disaster wouldn't have happened with Trump. The Taliban knew I would rain down fire and fury if any American personnel or interests were harmed, the likes of which have never been seen. This is a catastrophe of historic proportions. August 21, 2021

Donald J Trump @RealDonaldTrump
Joe Biden must apologize to America for allowing the Military to leave before civilians and for allowing $85 Billion dollars worth of sophisticated Military equipment to be handed over to the Taliban (and Russia and China so they can copy it) rather than bringing it back to the United States! August 21, 2021

To comment, I hadn't thought of China and Russia reverse engineering our sophisticated military hardware. But that is one more reason leaving it behind was absolute idiocy.

Donald J Trump @RealDonaldTrump
Trending on Twitter today, "TRUMP WAS RIGHT!" August 21, 2021

To comment, on so many things, not just Afghanistan.

August 22, 2021

Donald J Trump @RealDonaldTrump
I look forward to seeing you in Alabama tonight at 7:00PM CDT. Huge crowd and tremendous enthusiasm—people are already lined up! So much to discuss, mostly having to do with bringing our Country back. Will be broadcast live on OAN, Newsmax, Right Side Broadcasting, and Real America's Voice, among others. August 22, 2021

Donald J Trump @RealDonaldTrump
Donald Trump holds save America rally in Alabama. [0:21 video] https://media.gab.com/system/media_attachments/files/082/732/044/original/67916fbb45fe0910.mp4 August 22, 2021

August 23, 2021

Donald J Trump @RealDonaldTrump

Joe Biden gave our enemies all around the World a great and lasting victory when he unexpectedly and inexplicably removed our great soldiers from Afghanistan before taking out our U.S. citizens and allies, along with abandoning many billions of dollars of highest-grade Military equipment. Leaving our Military till the end was such a simple decision that anyone with intelligence and common sense would have made, but he called it wrong and instantly created perhaps the greatest embarrassment for our Country in its history—and it is far from over! August 23, 2021

To comment, none of this last-minute scrambling would have been necessary if Biden had planned correctly from the start.

1. Remove all American civilians.
2. Remove Afghan allies.
3. Retrieve or destroy American military hardware.
4. Remove American troops.

How hard is that to plan for? But Biden did it backwards, making all points harder and #3 impossible, arming the Taliban with our advanced weaponry.

August 24, 2021

Donald J Trump @RealDonaldTrump

Biden's biggest mistake was not understanding that the Military has to be last out the door, not first out the door. Civilians and equipment go first and then, when everyone and everything is out, the Military goes. So simple, and yet it wasn't done. Tragic! August 24, 202

To comment, such simplicity is lost on the cognitively struggling Biden.

August 25, 2021

Donald J Trump @RealDonaldTrump

How dare Biden force our Military to run off the battlefield in Afghanistan and desert what now have become many thousands of American hostages. We had Afghanistan and Kabul in perfect control with just 2,500 soldiers and he destroyed it when it was demanded that they flee! August 25, 2021

Trump Fights Back with Statements

Donald J Trump @RealDonaldTrump

Biden surrendered Afghanistan to terrorists and left thousands of Americans for dead by pulling out the Military before our citizens. Now we are learning that out of the 26,000 people who have been evacuated, only 4,000 are Americans. You can be sure the Taliban, who are now in complete control, didn't allow the best and brightest to board these evacuation flights. Instead, we can only imagine how many thousands of terrorists have been airlifted out of Afghanistan and into neighborhoods around the world. What a terrible failure. NO VETTING. How many terrorists will Joe Biden bring to America? We don't know! August 25, 2021

August 26, 2021

Donald J Trump @RealDonaldTrump

Our Country has never been so diminished. It has reached an all-time low! August 26, 2021

Donald J Trump @RealDonaldTrump

Biden is destroying America. His policies have created a living national nightmare: he's surrendered our energy independence, sabotaged the economy, surged violent crime, caved to China, crushed our citizens instead of the virus, created the single greatest humiliation in our history in Afghanistan, stranded thousands of our citizens overseas at the whim of Islamic extremists, and left a wide-open border to deadly drugs, vicious crime, and unlimited illegal immigration at home!

I created the most secure border in history. Biden has created the single most catastrophic border disaster in history—by far. Texas Attorney General Ken Paxton, whom I strongly endorsed for reelection, has just won a major Supreme Court victory against the Biden Open Borders agenda. I congratulate him on this win. Biden was found to have broken the law in terminating the Migrant Protection Protocols, or Remain in Mexico. Now, Biden must reinstate Remain in Mexico, one of my most successful and important programs in securing the border. Other State Attorneys General should follow suit and go after every one of Biden's unlawful border and immigration policies. August 26, 2021

To comment, Biden's goal to reverse everything you accomplished is truly having tragic consequences. I address some of his mess in my article, "Worst Foreign Policy Debacle in USA History" – https://www.zeolla.org/politics/articles/2021/worst.htm

I address many more of his failures in my *Biden Tweets* books.

Donald J Trump @RealDonaldTrump

The Leftist "select committee" has further exposed itself as a partisan sham and waste of taxpayer dollars with a request that's timed to distract Americans from historic and global catastrophes brought on by the failures of Joe Biden and the Democrats. Unfortunately, this partisan exercise is being performed at the expense of long-standing legal principles of privilege.

Executive privilege will be defended, not just on behalf of my Administration and the Patriots who worked beside me, but on behalf of the Office of the President of the United States and the future of our Nation. These Democrats only have one tired trick—political theater— and their latest request only reinforces that pathetic reality. August 26, 2021

August 27, 2021

Donald J Trump @RealDonaldTrump

Melania and I send our deepest condolences to the families of our brilliant and brave Service Members whose duty to the U.S.A. meant so much to them. Our thoughts are also with the families of the innocent civilians who died today in the savage Kabul attack.

This tragedy should never have been allowed to happen, which makes our grief even deeper and more difficult to understand.

May God Bless the U.S.A. August 27, 2021

To comment, this Statement is in regard to the deaths of 13 brave American soldiers and dozens of Afghans outside of the Kabul airport due to an ISIS-K terrorist attack. That tragedy only added to the debacle of the Biden Afghan withdrawal.

I added about this tragedy to my growing article, "Worst Foreign Policy Debacle in USA History."

https://www.zeolla.org/politics/articles/2021/worst.htm

I also address it and many more of Biden's failures in my *Biden Tweets* books.

Donald J Trump @RealDonaldTrump

"The FDA is virtually controlled by Pfizer. Pfizer has control, not Johnson and Johnson, not Moderna, but Pfizer has control over the FDA." [0:57 video about Covid vaccine booster shots]

Trump Fights Back with Statements
https://media.gab.com/system/media_attach-ments/files/083/197/876/original/dff9758402421bb1.mp4 August 27, 2021

Donald J Trump @RealDonaldTrump
Hannity exclusive: Former President Trump releases video reacting to deadly terror attack in Kabul. [2:13 video]
https://media.gab.com/system/media_attach-ments/files/083/227/204/original/dde86f1895e76e4d.mp4 August 27, 2021

August 31, 2021

Donald J Trump @RealDonaldTrump
If the Democrats could fight wars as well as they execute Election Fraud, we would have obliterated all of our many enemies throughout the World, and would have nothing to worry about! August 28, 2021

Donald J Trump @RealDonaldTrump
Never in history has a withdrawal from war been handled so badly or incompetently as the Biden Administration's withdrawal from Afghanistan. In addition to the obvious, ALL EQUIPMENT should be demanded to be immediately returned to the United States, and that includes every penny of the $85 billion dollars in cost. If it is not handed back, we should either go in with unequivocal Military force and get it, or at least bomb the hell out of it. Nobody ever thought such stupidity, as this feeble-brained withdrawal, was possible! August 31, 2021

Donald J Trump @RealDonaldTrump
MAKE AMERICA GREAT AGAIN! August 31, 2021

Chapter Nine
Trump's Statements
September 2021

These Trump Statements are continued from Chapter Eight.

September 1, 2021

Donald J Trump @RealDonaldTrump
Shana, you are 100% correct. If I were President, your wonderful and beautiful son Kareem would be with you now, and so would the sons and daughters of others, including all of those who died in the vicious Kabul airport attack. Civilians should have been brought out first, along with our $85 billion of equipment, with the Military coming out very safely after all was clear. I love you, and I love Kareem. September 1, 2021

To comment, this Statement is in response to an angry message from a gold-star mother to Biden, who lost her son due to Biden's ineptitude in the Kabul attack.

September 2, 2021

Donald J Trump @RealDonaldTrump
A heartbreaking loss for the United States and it's great Military. We must have hostages released and our Military equipment returned, NOW! [1:08 video with clips of Biden's statements, interspersed with images of the horrors occurring in Afghanistan and the words of even CNN newscasters criticizing Biden]
https://media.gab.com/system/media_attach-ments/files/083/794/041/original/4dc3ce253f078b47.mp4
September 2, 2021

September 3, 2021

Donald J Trump @RealDonaldTrump
Record low morale for our American troops! Who can blame them? September 3, 2021

September 4, 2021

Donald J Trump @RealDonaldTrump

Who are all of the people coming into our Country? In addition to the Southern Border, with millions of unvetted people pouring in, we now have tens of thousands of totally unvetted Afghans, who many say are not the ones that should have come in. How many terrorists are among them? How much money is this costing? With all of these developments, our Country is more unsafe now than ever before—and many Americans are still left behind! September 4, 2021

Donald J Trump @RealDonaldTrump

FIX 2020 FIRST! September 4, 2021

September 5, 2021

Donald J Trump @RealDonaldTrump

Why is it that nobody talks about the horrible job being done by the Biden Administration on COVID-19, often referred to as the China Virus? Are they using the same coverup methods that they are using on the greatest embarrassment in the history of our Country, the incompetent withdrawal from Afghanistan—leaving dead warriors, hostages, and $85 billion worth of the highest-grade Military equipment behind? No Military event in our Country has ever been so poorly handled. We could've left with dignity, honor, success, nobody killed, and our equipment. But we didn't! September 5, 2021

To comment, Biden is failing on Covid, because his vaccine plan is failing, due to him and Kamala dissing the vaccines before they came out and not giving credit to Trump for the vaccines. The former misstep increased vaccine hesitancy among Democrats, while the latter increased it among Republicans.

September 8, 2021

Donald J Trump @RealDonaldTrump

The only reason Senator "Gloomy" Pat Toomey is not running for the Senate in Pennsylvania is that I would not give him an endorsement—I feel he has been a terrible representative for both Pennsylvania and the United States, as a whole. His views on Tariffs and so-called

Trump Fights Back with Statements

Free Trade (where other nations take total advantage of the United States), are archaic. He ran with me in 2016 and wasn't expected to win, but because of my victory he did. He still doesn't realize what happened, and why—not the sharpest tool in the shed.

Fortunately for Pennsylvania, we have a great Senate candidate, Sean Parnell, who I have just given my Complete and Total Endorsement. He will do all of the things that Toomey is incapable of doing. Sean Parnell will represent the Commonwealth of Pennsylvania the way it should be represented—and it's about time! September 8, 2021

To comment, unfortunately, Parnell lost twice for the congressional seat here in western PA to Connor Lamb, who is also now running for Senator. I'm not confident Parnell will beat Lamb in a statewide election. But maybe Trump's endorsement will push him over the top.

As a later update, neither Parnell nor Lamb ended up being the nominees. Parnell dropped out due to personal scandals. Trump then switched his support to Mehmet Oz, the TV doctor, and he won the Repub nomination. Our Lt. Gov. John Fetterman won the Democratic nomination. John is leading in the polls at this writing (August 2022).

Donald J Trump @RealDonaldTrump

Thank you, Kathy. America feels your loss and fully understands your pain. Rylee will never be forgotten.

Message from Kathy McCollum, Mother of Lance Cpl. Rylee McCollum, USMC:

"Thank you. Just want the family to know I support them. We need the corrupt pseudo president gone. President Trump has to run. My son should not be gone. President Trump would never [have] allowed this to happen. We need him back in office to save this country. Just like he said years ago on Oprah. He would run when our country needed him. We need him. I can't live with knowing my son's life was taken for nothing. So Biden could repay his debt to China. They will now have full control of Afghanistan and my son will be a sacrificial lamb.

"My son was murdered for Biden optics. I will become more vocal soon. Grieving and not sure I can control my mouth. But watched Biden disrespect my son while I was standing across from him and he was checking his watch, and then Pelosi denying my son recognition and turning her back. Just as she tore up Donald's speech. We cannot give up our country. So even if no one gets back with me. I will always fight for the Trump administration just as my son did." September 8, 2021

To comment, Kathy is referring to Biden's disrespect during the "dignified transfer" of the bodies of the brave soldiers who were killed due to his incompetence. He checked his watch between each unloading of their bodies from the transport plane. I document this incomprehensible act of disregard in my *Biden Tweets* books.

Donald J Trump @RealDonaldTrump
Just watched as a massive crane took down the magnificent and very famous statue of "Robert E. Lee On His Horse" in Richmond, Virginia. It has long been recognized as a beautiful piece of bronze sculpture. To add insult to injury, those who support this "taking" now plan to cut it into three pieces, and throw this work of art into storage prior to its complete desecration.

Robert E. Lee is considered by many Generals to be the greatest strategist of them all. President Lincoln wanted him to command the North, in which case the war would have been over in one day. Robert E. Lee instead chose the other side because of his great love of Virginia, and except for Gettysburg, would have won the war. He should be remembered as perhaps the greatest unifying force after the war was over, ardent in his resolve to bring the North and South together through many means of reconciliation and imploring his soldiers to do their duty in becoming good citizens of this Country.

Our culture is being destroyed and our history and heritage, both good and bad, are being extinguished by the Radical Left, and we can't let that happen! If only we had Robert E. Lee to command our troops in Afghanistan, that disaster would have ended in a complete and total victory many years ago. What an embarrassment we are suffering because we don't have the genius of a Robert E. Lee! [collage of 3 pictures of the statue being taken down] September 8, 2021

September 11, 2021
20th Anniversary of 9/11

Donald J Trump @RealDonaldTrump
Congratulations to Rudy Giuliani (for the 20th time!), the greatest Mayor in the history of New York City, for having shown such leadership and doing such an incredible job during and after the attack on our Nation! September 11, 2021

Donald J Trump @RealDonaldTrump
For the great people of our Country, this is very a sad day. September 11th represents great sorrow for our Country. Many things were displayed that day, including most importantly the bravery of our police,

fire, and first responders of every kind. The job they did was truly unbelievable. We love them, and we thank them.

It is also a sad time for the way our war on those that did such harm to our Country ended last week. The loss of 13 great warriors and the many more who were wounded should never have happened. Overall, 250 people were killed in Afghanistan last week and so many more were seriously injured. We had $85 billion of the finest and most sophisticated military equipment taken from us without even a shot being fired.

The leader of our Country was made to look like a fool and that can never be allowed to happen. It was caused by bad planning, incredible weakness, and leaders who truly didn't understand what was happening. This is the 20th year of this war and should have been a year of victory, honor, and strength. Instead, Joe Biden and his inept administration surrendered in defeat.

We will live on, but sadly our Country will be wounded for a long period of time. We will struggle to recover from the embarrassment this incompetence has caused. Do not fear, however. America will be made great again! September 11, 2021

Donald J Trump @RealDonaldTrump
They did this strike quickly, in order to show they are tough. Instead, they killed a USAID worker and many children. This is what happens when you have grossly incompetent people at the helm. The Afghanistan tragedy will further mark what should have been an honorable and dignified September 11th. The Administration's surrender will go down in infamy. September 11, 2021

To comment, Trump's message includes a picture of a NYP article titled, "Biden droned the wrong guy, innocent aid worker killed in Kabul strike: NYT" -
https://nypost.com/2021/09/10/kabul-strike-killed-us-aid-worker-and-family-not-isis-bombers/]

The article states:
A US airstrike in Kabul against a supposed Islamic State bomber actually killed an innocent man who worked for a US aid group and his family, according to newly published testimony and footage — raising the specter that the Pentagon lied to the public about the strike.

The reported case of mistaken identity also further tars President Biden for his chaotic pullout of US troops from Afghanistan, which left behind hundreds of US citizens and thousands of at-risk Afghans.

Zemari Ahmadi and nine members of his family, including seven children, were killed in the airstrike on Aug. 29, one day before the final US evacuation flights from Kabul, his brother Romal Ahmadi told the New York Times.

Donald J Trump @RealDonaldTrump

Has anybody noticed that the Biden Administration, working in close conjunction with the Fake News Media, has promoted mandates very hard in order to get people to stop talking about the most incompetent withdrawal from a war site in history?

They will talk about anything, other than the Rigged 2020 Presidential Election results, in order to get people's minds off of the horror show that has just taken place in Afghanistan! September 11, 2021

September 13, 2021

Donald J Trump @RealDonaldTrump

Our Country is far more susceptible to attack by outside terrorist groups than ever before. Our enemies all over the World are inspired by what just happened in Afghanistan—the removal of the Military first, and our "gift" of $85 billion in Military equipment. We are no longer respected after the pathetic and incompetent withdrawal from Afghanistan. It will be a long time before we gain our reputation back. Just nine months ago, the United States was viewed as being strong, and now we are being viewed as weak and stupid.

The Taliban has totally retaken Afghanistan—a far more potent position than they had 20 years ago, after we spent trillions of dollars, with hundreds of thousands of lives lost (on both sides). This loss emboldens not only foreign terrorists, but also Antifa and BLM. It's sad that this is not what you hear from the Fake News Media who are only interested in talking about "terrorism" from the right and protecting an illegitimate president. Our reputation is gone, our Borders are broken, inflation is raging, and COVID continues, even with the vaccines (developed under "Trump"), to ravage our Nation. September 13, 2021

Donald J Trump @RealDonaldTrump

So interesting to watch former President Bush, who is responsible for getting us into the quicksand of the Middle East (and then not winning!), as he lectures us that terrorists on the "right" are a bigger problem than those from foreign countries that hate America, and that are pouring into our Country right now. If that is so, why was he willing to spend trillions of dollars and be responsible for the death of perhaps millions of people? He shouldn't be lecturing us about anything. The World Trade Center came down during his watch. Bush led a failed and uninspiring presidency. He shouldn't be lecturing anybody! September 13, 2021

Donald J Trump @RealDonaldTrump
Does anybody really believe the California Recall Election isn't rigged? Millions and millions of Mail-In Ballots will make this just another giant Election Scam, no different, but less blatant, than the 2020 Presidential Election Scam! September 13, 2021

Donald J Trump @RealDonaldTrump
These kids tricked Biden just like the Taliban did! [picture of Biden with a bunch of schoolchildren, with most of them wearing Trump hats and T-shirts!] September 13, 2021

Donald J Trump @RealDonaldTrump
"The Big Lie" is the Presidential Election of 2020. When the Fake News Media uses that term, always remember that this was the Election that is destroying our Country, both inside and out! September 13, 2021

September 14, 2021

Donald J Trump @RealDonaldTrump
The inept Afghan government, led by corrupt President Ghani, released 5,000 prisoners—not the Trump Administration. Secretary of State Blinken is doing everything in his power to make the most inept withdrawal in history look, at least, acceptable. It never will. Now it is understood, on top of everything else, that billions of dollars will be paid to Afghanistan to help them along the way. The so-called leaders of our Country have gone crazy! September 14, 2021

Donald J Trump @RealDonaldTrump
People don't realize that, despite the Rigged voting in California (I call it the "Swarming Ballots"), I got 1.5 Million more votes in 2020 than I did in 2016. The place is so Rigged, however, that a guy who can't even bring water into their State, which I got federal approval to do (that is the hard part), will probably win. Billions of gallons of water coming to California from the North is being sent out to sea, rather than being spread throughout the State. This is to protect the tiny delta smelt, which is doing far worse now without the water.

In any event, it all doesn't matter because the California Election is totally Rigged. Many people are already complaining that when they go to vote they are told, "I'm sorry, you already voted" (Just like 2020, among many other things). They then leave angry, but fortunately, even the Fake News Media has been reporting it. September 14, 2021

Donald J Trump @RealDonaldTrump
So now it's determined in a major Wall Street Journal article that Facebook is secretly protecting its so-called "Elite," making them exempt from rules. Facebook and Big Tech are so corrupt ("unlocked boxes," etc.), this should help my lawsuit against Big Tech, and those people who hate America. September 14, 2021

Donald J Trump @RealDonaldTrump
If we didn't have RINOs, the Republican Party would totally dominate politics. The good news is there are far less than there were four years ago—it is a dying breed—but nevertheless, and unfortunately, they still exist! September 14, 2021

September 15, 2021

Donald J Trump @RealDonaldTrump
If the story of "Dumbass" General Mark Milley, the same failed leader who engineered the worst withdrawal from a country, Afghanistan, in U.S. history, leaving behind many dead and wounded soldiers, many American citizens, and $85 Billion worth of the newest and most sophisticated Military equipment in the world, and our Country's reputation, is true, then I assume he would be tried for TREASON in that he would have been dealing with his Chinese counterpart behind the President's back and telling China that he would be giving them notification "of an attack." Can't do that!

The good news is that the story is Fake News concocted by a weak and ineffective General together with two authors who I refused to give an interview to because they write fiction, not fact. Actions should be taken immediately against Milley, and better generals in our Military, of which we have many, should get involved so that another Afghanistan disaster never happens again. Remember, I was the one who took out 100% of the ISIS Caliphate. Milley said it couldn't be done!

For the record, I never even thought of attacking China—and China knows that. The people that fabricated the story are sick and demented, and the people who print it are just as bad. In fact, I'm the only President in decades who didn't get the U.S. into a war—a well known fact that is seldom reported. September 15, 2021

September 16, 2021

Donald J Trump @RealDonaldTrump
Milley never told me about calls being made to China. From what I understand, he didn't tell too many other people either. He put our Country in a very dangerous position but President Xi knows better, and would've called me. The way Milley and the Biden Administration handled the Afghanistan withdrawal, perhaps the most embarrassing moment in our Country's history, would not exactly instill fear in China. Milley is a complete nutjob! The only reason Biden will not fire or court-martial Milley is because he doesn't want him spilling the dirty secrets on Biden's deadly disaster in Afghanistan. September 16, 2021

Donald J Trump @RealDonaldTrump
Congratulations to General Don Bolduc on his incredible presentation regarding Mark Milley, the Taliban and China's all-time favorite General! Watch the interview here:
https://video.foxnews.com/v/6272827874001
Fox News. Retired general calls for Milley's resignation, says military has lost confidence in Joint Chiefs chair,
Retired Gen. Don Bolduc reacts to allegations Gen. Mark Milley overstepped his power during the end of Trump's presidency. September 16, 2021

Extended Comment
Mark Milley

The preceding Statements are in regard to a new book reporting General Milley had contacted his counterpart in China after J6, telling him that he would warn China if Trump decided to launch a nuclear attack against China in the final days of his presidency. Milley promised that if Trump ordered such an attack, he would stop it, as had told his underling to contact him if such an order was ever given,

Milley has been at the center of a firestorm amid reports he made two calls to Gen. Li Zuocheng of the People's Liberation Army to assure him that the United States was not going to suddenly go to war with or attack China.

Descriptions of the calls made last October and in January were first aired in excerpts from the forthcoming book "Peril" by Washington Post journalists Bob Woodward and Robert Costa. The book says Milley told Li that he would warn Li in the event of an attack (AP. Milley).

However, as Trump indicates, he had no such plans. It was just Milley being hyperbolic in his Trump hatred. But Milley contacting China and telling his underlings to listen to him rather than the Commander-in-Chief was an act of treason. But with the inept Biden administration, he was never prosecuted for it nor even fired, and he remains at his post to this day.

The bias of the MSM can be seen in its reporting of this situation:

It seems that Milley, according to published accounts from those who have read the book, became convinced his tantrum-throwing, spittle-spewing, reality-denying commander-in-chief was in a state of mental collapse and as such, was an immediate threat to world peace. So the general went around him, twice reaching out via back channel to his Chinese counterpart, Gen. Li Zuocheng (Trib Live. Leonard).

But conservative news outlets have a different take:

As the embattled Gen. Mark Milley took a defiant tone regarding reports that he surreptitiously tried to circumvent the authority of his then-commander-in-chief, President Donald Trump, critics increasingly demanded his resignation while the White House offered him full support.

Milley's alleged actions include making secret calls to the top military officer in Beijing, and holding a clandestine gathering of military officers to demand that they only obey command orders that came through Milley, according to the authors of a forthcoming book....

"If he really thought that Trump was so unstable that he was going to start a nuclear war, there was a way to address that," the senior official told Just the News. "We have provisions for that as spelled out in the U.S. Constitution, namely that the Cabinet would remove him under the 25th Amendment. But instead of doing that, he ran his own independent operation" (Just the News. Milley).

Trump Fights Back with Statements

Donald J Trump @RealDonaldTrump

Interesting that everyone is quitting at Homeland Security. They know what a mess our Border is, and they will never be able to fix it. All they had to do is "go to the beach" and leave it alone—it was so good—the best in history! September 16, 2021

To comment, Trump's comment here echoes his comment elsewhere that all Biden had to do when he took office was nothing, and the country would have been just fine. The southern border, the vaccine distribution, the economy, the Afghan withdrawal, and more had all been taken care of by Trump and his administration. He just needed to follow Trump's plans. But, instead, Biden reversed all of Trump's plans, leading to disasters on all of those fronts.

This is why the subtitle to my *Biden Tweets* books is "Revering Trump, While Dividing and Destroying America." Trump sums up what Biden should have done by saying he have just "gone to the beach" and did nothing, while leaving all his (Trump's) plans in place.

Donald J Trump @RealDonaldTrump

Our hearts and minds are with the people being persecuted so unfairly relating to the January 6th protest concerning the Rigged Presidential Election. In addition to everything else, it has proven conclusively that we are a two-tiered system of justice. In the end, however, JUSTICE WILL PREVAIL! September 16, 2021

Extended Comment
Justice for J6 Rally

I address the unfair treatment of those arrested for protesting at the Capitol on January 6, 2021 in my *Tragic Ending* book. Their prosecution and treatment stand in sharp contrast to the BLM/ Antifa rioters from the summer of 2020, most all of whom were left off Scot-free.

But their mistreatment was the subject of a rally on Saturday, September 18, 2021. The MSM vilified it as being an attempt to "rewrite" the history of J6. But it was really about the protestors being treated unjustly.

The architect of a Washington protest planned for Saturday that aims to rewrite history about the violent January assault on the U.S. Capitol is hardly a household name.

Matt Braynard worked as an analyst for the Republican Party, crunched data for a small election firm and later started a consulting business that attracted few federal clients, records

167

show. He started a nonprofit after he was dismissed by Donald Trump's 2016 campaign following several months on the job but struggled to raise money. The group's tax-exempt status was revoked last year.

But Braynard's fortunes changed abruptly after Trump's 2020 election loss. He joined an aggrieved group of Trump allies seeking to overturn the election — and in the process reaped recognition, lucrative fees and a fundraising windfall that enabled him to rekindle his nonprofit.

Now, Braynard and his group, Look Ahead America, are using his newfound platform and resources to present an alternate history of the Jan. 6 attack that was meant to stop Congress from certifying Joe Biden's victory, rebranding those who were charged as "political prisoners" (AP. Organizer).

Despite his seeming support in this Statement, Trump later expressed misgivings about this rally in an interview with The Federalist.

During the interview, Trump acknowledged the widespread disgust that most Americans have for the professional political class in Washington, D.C.

"There's a discontent with everything having to do with politics," Trump said about the general political situation in the country. "People are so disgusted with the way people are being treated from the Jan. 6 situation. It's a combination of that compared to how Antifa and BLM were treated. When you compare the treatment, it is so unjust, it is so unfair. It's disgraceful."

Trump also characterized the planned Sept. 18 rally at the U.S. Capitol as a "setup" meant to denigrate Republican voters regardless of what transpires.

"On Saturday, that's a setup," Trump said, referring to the rally. "If people don't show up they'll say, 'Oh, it's a lack of spirit.' And if people do show up they'll be harassed" (Federalist. In Exclusive).

This time, the Capitol Police were ready for any potential violence, despite the organizer calling for all to act peacefully:

Newsmax reported Friday that Defense Secretary Lloyd Austin has approved a Capitol Police request to provide 100 D.C. National Guard troops for Saturday's event. In addition, responding to fears of potential violence, security fencing has been installed in front of the Capitol, and other measures have been taken.

Fox News reported that Braynard issued a statement via video that called those facing charges for their alleged actions during the deadly riot "political prisoners." He said they have been treated unfairly. He urged anyone planning to attend Saturday's event to behave peacefully (Newsmax. Capitol).

What Braynard is referring to situations like the following:

A lawyer representing several defendants arrested in connection with the Jan. 6 U.S. Capitol breach is sounding alarm bells over conditions he says cannot be called "anything other than cruel and unusual," as suspects who have no criminal history and who are charged in non-violent crimes are allegedly held in solitary confinement for up to 23 hours per day and denied bail....

Though some defendants have been charged with serious violations such as assault or conspiracy, many are awaiting trial on charges such as knowingly entering or remaining in restricted grounds without authority or obstruction of an official proceeding.

"Unfortunately, this process has been unequally meted out by the courts and many of those who continue to be detained were not violent, have no criminal history, and many have mental health vulnerabilities of significance," Watkins said. "The process appears to be optics driven" (Newsmax. Jan. 6 Detentions).

In the end, only a few hundred showed up for the rally, with many scared off that it could be a set up.

In the shadow of a fortified Capitol, a few hundred demonstrators turned up Saturday for a rally to support those charged in January's riot, but were vastly outnumbered by the media and a heavy police presence.

U.S. Capitol Police were taking no chances, with hundreds of officers brought into Washington in an effort to avoid a repeat of the pre-inauguration attack. The fence around the Capitol was put back up, the city police force was fully activated and Capitol Police requested assistance from the National Guard (AP. Heavy).

But still, the rally did put a focus on the differing treatment of the J6 protestors versus the BLM/ Antifa rioters, despite the latter's riots being much more extensive and dangerous than the J6 uprising.

Not only are January 6 defendants generally enduring longer periods behind bars for lesser charges than racial rioters, but some of their lawyers seem to believe judges will treat them more favorably if they publicly recant their political beliefs.

A new RealClearInvestigations database contrasts the January 6 prosecutions, in which "dozens" of defendants have been held in pretrial detention for months, with those of Floyd rioters ("several" long detentions) and long-forgotten rioters at President Trump's inauguration (none).

"The summer 2020 riots resulted in some 15 times more injured police officers, 30 times as many arrests, and estimated damages in dollar terms up to 1,300 times more costly than those of the Capitol riot," not to mention "more sophisticated and dangerous tactics," the database's introduction reads.

Yet across 2,000 police officers assaulted or injured and 16,000 arrests, only 44 federal assault charges were filed against racial rioters, a quarter of the total for January 6 defendants. The former had more weapons charges, though.

At least 90% of citations or charges were "dropped, dismissed or otherwise not filed" in most of the dozen major jurisdictions prosecuting racial rioters, while D.C. prosecutors dropped most felony rioting charges. They're on track to dismiss charges in most cases from riot-friendly Portland, Ore (Just the News. 'Justice).

September 17, 2021

Donald J Trump @RealDonaldTrump

RINO Congressman Anthony Gonzalez, who has poorly represented his district in the Great State of Ohio, has decided to quit after enduring a tremendous loss of popularity, of which he had little, since his ill-informed and otherwise very stupid impeachment vote against the sitting President of the United States, me. This is no loss for Ohio or our Country and, most importantly, we have a great candidate who was substantially leading Gonzalez in the polls, Max Miller, who I have given my Complete and Total Endorsement. Max is a tremendous person who will represent Ohio well. Good riddance to Anthony, he can now get himself a job at ratings-dead CNN or MSDNC! September 17, 2021

Trump Fights Back with Statements

Donald J Trump @RealDonaldTrump
1 down, 9 to go! September 17, 2021

To comment, Trump is referring to the ten Senators who voted to convict in the second impeachment trial. One has bailed on running for reelection. More are sure to follow.

Donald J Trump @RealDonaldTrump
Letter to Georgia Secretary of State Brad Raffensperger
Read the report here: "43,000 Absentee Ballot Votes Counted in DeKalb County, Georgia 2020 Election Violated Chain of Custody Rule" –
https://georgiastarnews.com/4300-absentee-ballot-votes-counted-in-dekalb-county-2020-election-violated-chain-of-custody-rule.html
September 17, 2021

September 19, 2021

Donald J Trump @RealDonaldTrump
After many years of allowing China to rip off the United States on trade and so much else, I was very tough on China, by far the toughest of any U.S. President in history. During my administration, China paid us hundreds of billions of dollars and finally respected the U.S. again. Before me, they never gave us "ten cents."

For Lightweight General Mark Milley to have called the Chinese to "bring down the temperature" of my negotiations with them, negotiations that were having a major positive impact on large-scale benefits to the United States, is outrageous. We were not going to make any Military moves—never even thought of it, but we were hitting them so hard in all other ways. While every other President caved to China, China was caving to me and the U.S. for the first time ever.

"Dumbo" Milley inserted himself right in the middle of my trade negotiation, and if he did what is reported, he would have had a profound negative effect on those negotiations. Milley is an idiot with no common sense or ability to negotiate—that's why he left $85 Billion of the World's best Military equipment in the hands of the Taliban for no reason whatsoever. That's also why 13 young Warriors are not with their families tonight.

Mark Milley hurt our Country very badly, and he should pay a big price, just like the crooked politicians and lawyers on the Hillary Clinton campaign for the years of Fake Russia, Russia, Russia stories that are now being revealed with the arrest yesterday of Attorney Michael Sussmann of the Democrat's Law Firm Perkins Coie, who was one of the heads of the operation.

I have had the same fake "[expletive]" going on for years with the Witch Hunt by New York District Attorney Cyrus Vance and Attorney General Letitia James, headed by Never Trumper Mark Pomerantz, who now shockingly works for the DA's office, but is a partner of the Hillary Clinton and DNC's Democrat Party Never Trumper Law Firm Paul, Weiss, Rifkind, Wharton & Garrison. This is unprecedented!

Over three million pages of documents have been examined by them (a record fishing expedition!), Never Trumper lawyers and law firms are used by the DA and AG to "Get Trump," in their prosecutorial misconduct Witch Hunt, anti-Trump political campaigns are viciously waged by them to get elected—and they have NOTHING!

Murder and all forms of crime are "through the roof" in New York, and their focus is on "Trump," despite numerous other political investigations that went nowhere. They are spending tens of millions of dollars with a vast army of Trump Haters. This has been going on for years and the people of our Country are not going to take it anymore! September 19, 2021

Donald J Trump @RealDonaldTrump

The largest number of illegal aliens in the history of our Country are pouring in by the millions. They are totally unchecked and unvetted, can do whatever they want, and go wherever they want. Our Country is rapidly becoming a cesspool of humanity. Murderers, drug dealers, and criminals of all shapes and sizes are a big part of this massive migration. Tens of thousands of people are coming from Haiti, and many now from countries in Africa, even more so now than South America. Nothing is done and the corrupt Mainstream Media is giving almost no attention to what will be perhaps the greatest Crisis in the history of our Country. This is not just a Border Crisis, this is a Crisis Crisis. God Bless America! September 19, 2021

Donald J Trump @RealDonaldTrump

It is incredible that our National Guard is standing at the empty Capitol, not at our Southern Border, where the number of illegals coming into our Country is at a level that has never been seen before! September 19, 2021

To comment, great observation! Not only are there 100,000s of illegal aliens crossing the border every month from Central America, but now we have the human disaster of 14,000 Haitians living under a

bridge in Texas. Even the AP is now recognizing the Biden-caused disaster. See: "Trib Live/ AP. Official: U.S. will fly 'massive' number of Haitians to Haiti" –
https://triblive.com/news/world/official-u-s-will-fly-massive-number-of-haitians-to-haiti/

September 21, 2021

Donald J Trump @RealDonaldTrump
The United States will soon be considered a Third World Nation. There has never been anything like what is happening at our Border. Millions of people have already poured in, but many more than that are coming! September 21, 2021

Donald J Trump @RealDonaldTrump
Anybody that changes the name of the once storied Cleveland Indians to the Cleveland Guardians should not be running for the United States Senate representing the Great People of Ohio. The Atlanta Braves didn't change their name, and the Florida State Seminoles didn't change their chant, but Cleveland has, and they were there first.
Despite this, a man named Matt Dolan, the son of the owner of the team, said he is against Cancel Culture. Do those two things really work together? In any event, I know of at least one person in the race who I won't be endorsing. The Republican Party has too many RINOs! September 21, 2021

September 23, 2021

Donald J Trump @RealDonaldTrump
Why is the Fake News Media continuing on their path of saying, "baseless and disproven lies," concerning the Presidential Election of 2020, no matter how much evidence they see? These phrases are coordinated propaganda by Lamestream. It is an automatic phrase they use about the 2020 Election Scam when in fact it was just the opposite. The proof is massive and staggering. The Presidential Election of 2020 was Rigged! When the information becomes public, people will see that it wasn't even close. September 23, 2021

Donald J Trump @RealDonaldTrump
RINO former President George "Dubya" Bush and his flunky Karl Rove are endorsing warmongering and very low polling, Liz Cheney. Bush is the one who got us into the quicksand of the Middle East and,

after spending trillions of dollars and killing nearly a million people, the Middle East was left in worse shape after 21 years than it was when he started his stupidity. It ended with Biden's most embarrassing in history withdrawal from Afghanistan, a total surrender, leaving $85 Billion dollars of equipment and many young Warriors lives behind.

Bush is the person who did not have the courage to give a pardon to his Vice President's Chief of Staff, Scooter Libby, even though Cheney begged for him to do so. He wouldn't, they didn't talk for years.

I didn't know Scooter, but gave him a full pardon—not at their request, but because he deserved it. He suffered greatly. Former Vice President Cheney called to effusively thank me. Now he is on the side of his daughter who is so bad for Wyoming and the United States that she is polling at record lows. September 23, 2021

Donald J Trump @RealDonaldTrump

I spent virtually no time with Senators Mike Lee of Utah, or Lindsey Graham of South Carolina, talking about the 2020 Presidential Election Scam or, as it is viewed by many, the "Crime of the Century." Lindsey and Mike should be ashamed of themselves for not putting up the fight necessary to win. Look at the facts that are coming out in Arizona, Georgia, Michigan, Pennsylvania, Wisconsin, and other States.

If this were Schumer and the Democrats, with the evidence we have of Election Fraud (especially newly revealed evidence), they would have never voted to approve Biden as President, and had they not, all of the mistakes that were made over the last month, which are destroying our Country, would not have happened.

Mike Lee, Lindsey Graham, and all of the other Republicans who were unwilling to fight for the Presidency of the United States, which would have included at least an additional four Republican Senators, two in Georgia, one in Michigan, one in Arizona, are letting the Democrats get away with the greatest Election Hoax in history—a total con job!

We are losing our Country! The Democrats are vicious and fight like [expletive], and the Republicans do nothing about it. RINOs fight harder against Republicans than they do against Democrats. They want to be so politically correct, even if that means losing our Country, which is happening now. The evidence on determinative and wide-ranging Election Fraud is staggering. Your Republican Presidential candidate won in a landslide, but has so little backing from Republican "leadership." They should be ashamed of themselves. Why don't they have hearings? Or even if just Republicans had open public sessions, we would all hear the irrefutable facts. Remember, the Fake News Media does not report the truth! September 23, 2021

September 24, 2021

Donald J Trump @RealDonaldTrump

Dear Governor Abbott,

Despite my big win in Texas, I hear Texans want an election audit! You know your fellow Texans have big questions about the November 2020 Election. Bills to audit elections in your great state's House and Senate were considered during Texas' Second Special Session. Instead, the legislature passed a watered-down amendment that doesn't even apply to the 2020 Presidential Election. This short amendment doesn't answer the questions Texans have about the last election. Texans demand a real audit to completely address their concerns.

We need HB 16, which was just filed in the Third Special Session. This legislation specifically addresses the 2020 Presidential Election, and enables audits for future elections. The bill creates a process for candidates and party chairs to initiate an audit, and uses the same language as SB 97, which already passed the Texas State Senate, but did not have enough time to make it through the House during the Second Special Session.

Texas needs you to act now. Your Third Special Session is the perfect, and maybe last, opportunity to pass this audit bill. Time is running out. Paper ballots in your state are only kept for 22 months after the election. Your citizens don't trust the election system, and they want your leadership on this issue, which is the number one thing they care about. It is their most important issue—one that will affect 2022 and 2024.

Governor Abbott, we need a "Forensic Audit of the 2020 Election" added to the call. We're quickly running out of time and it must be done this week. Texans know voting fraud occurred in some of their counties. Let's get to the bottom of the 2020 Presidential Election Scam! September 24, 2021

To comment, Trump won Texas, so this shows he is not only concerned about states he did not win but about election integrity in general.

Donald J Trump @RealDonaldTrump

The "Unselect Committee" of highly partisan politicians, a similar group that perpetrated the now proven lie of Russia, Russia, Russia, Ukraine, Ukraine, Ukraine, Impeachment Hoax #1, Impeachment Hoax #2, and many other Scams, has sent out Harassment Subpoenas on Jan. 6th so that the Government of the United States can continue wasting time while Russia, China, and virtually every other country that deals with our Nation can continue to "eat our lunch," and laugh at the stupidity of what is going on at our Southern Border, and the worst withdrawal from a war zone by any Nation in history—all of this while the Democrats persecute and prosecute Republicans which is, together with Rigging Elections, essentially all they know how to do.

We will fight the Subpoenas on Executive Privilege and other grounds, for the good of our Country, while we wait to find out whether or not Subpoenas will be sent out to Antifa and BLM for the death and destruction they have caused in tearing apart our Democrat-run cities throughout America.

Hopefully the Unselect Committee will be calling witnesses on the Rigged Presidential Election of 2020, which is the primary reason that hundreds of thousands of people went to Washington, D.C. in the first place. Let the people of the United States see the real facts, which cannot happen because the Fake News refuses to write about them.

The Witch Hunt will never end! In the meantime, the Democrats get away with the Russia Scam, and all of the other corruption they have perpetrated on our Country for so many years. MAKE AMERICA GREAT AGAIN! September 24, 2021

To comment, many conservatives, including this writer, have decried having a Commission to investigate J6, but the so more extensive and destructive BLM/ Antifa riots have gone uninvestigated and the rioters unpunished.

Donald J Trump @RealDonaldTrump

Interesting that the Unselect Committee of political hacks "dropped" their subpoena request the night before Arizona is expected to announce its findings from the Forensic Audit on voter fraud in the 2020 Presidential Election Scam. This is what they do, this is what they are good at—but everybody will be watching Arizona tomorrow to see what the highly respected auditors and Arizona State Senate found out regarding the so-called Election! September 24, 2021

Donald J Trump @RealDonaldTrump

Our Country can never make progress because all the Democrats do are these Scams and Hoaxes. It's the only thing they're good at! September 24, 2021

To comment, the political timing and nature of the J6 Commission will become more and more apparent as time goes on. I will address much more about all of these issues in my *J6 Commission* book.

September 25, 2021

Donald J Trump @RealDonaldTrump

Huge findings in Arizona! However, the Fake News Media is already trying to "call it" again for Biden before actually looking at the facts—just like they did in November! The audit has uncovered significant and undeniable evidence of FRAUD! Until we know how and why this happened, our Elections will never be secure. This is a major criminal event and should be investigated by the Attorney General immediately. The Senate's final report will be released today at 4:00PM ET. I have heard it is far different than that being reported by the Fake News Media. September 25, 2021

Donald J Trump @RealDonaldTrump

The Fake News is lying about the Arizona audit report! The leaked report conclusively shows there were enough fraudulent votes, mystery votes, and fake votes to change the outcome of the election 4 or 5 times over. The number includes 23,344 mail-in ballots, despite the person no longer living at that address. Phantom voters! The official canvass does not even match who voted, off by 11,592—more than the entire Presidential Election margin.

Voters who voted in multiple counties totaled 10,342, and 2,382 ballots came from people who no longer lived in Maricopa County. There were also 2,592 "more duplicate ballots than original ballots." Just those fraudulent ballots alone total 50,252, and is fraud many more times than the so-called margin of "victory," which was only 10,457.

In addition, election data appears to have been intentionally deleted, and ballot images were "corrupt or missing." This is not even the whole state of Arizona, but only Maricopa County. It would only get worse! September 25, 2021

Donald J Trump @RealDonaldTrump

There is fraud and cheating in Arizona and it must be criminally investigated! More is coming out in the hearing today.

Donald J Trump @RealDonaldTrump

CNN, New York Times, Washington Post, and other Lamestream Media are feeding large-scale misinformation to the public about the Arizona Audit. The Audit was a big win for democracy and a big win for us. Shows how corrupt the Election was. Arizona State Senate hearing going on now and the information about what took place is terrible—a bigger Scam even than anticipated! September 25, 2021

Donald J Trump @RealDonaldTrump

It is not even believable the dishonesty of the Fake News Media on the Arizona Audit results, which shows incomprehensible Fraud at an Election Changing level, many times more votes than is needed. The Fake News Media refuses to write the facts, thereby being complicit in the Crime of the Century. They are so dishonest, but Patriots know the truth! Arizona must immediately decertify their 2020 Presidential Election Results. September 25, 2021

Donald J Trump @RealDonaldTrump

Massive fraud was found in the Arizona Forensic Audit, sometimes referred to as "Fraudit." The numbers are Election Changing! September 25, 2021

Donald J Trump @RealDonaldTrump

I will be discussing the winning results of the Arizona Forensic Audit, which will show 44,000 possibly illegal ballots cast, tomorrow at the Great State of Georgia rally, which will be packed! September 25, 2021

Extended Comment
Arizona Election Audit

As mentioned previously, there is much dispute about the results of the Arizona election audit. Following are news reports indicating these differing perspectives.

AP. GOP review finds no proof Arizona election stolen from Trump

A draft report of an election review in Arizona's largest county by supporters of former President Donald Trump found that President Joe Biden did indeed win the 2020 race there, an embarrassing end to a bizarre quest to find evidence supporting Trump's false claim that he lost because of fraud.

The final report was set to be released Friday [9/24/21], the result of a monthslong partisan review funded partly by taxpayers. The draft circulated Thursday night, showing the results of the review's chaotic hand-count of all 2.1 million ballots in

Maricopa County, home to Phoenix. The tally in the draft document showed a net gain of 360 votes for Biden over the official results....

The draft claims a number of shortcomings in election procedures, suggested the final tally still could not be relied upon and recommended several changes to state law. But the review previously made a series of false allegations that have since been retracted about how the election was handled in Maricopa County.

"Unfortunately, the report is also littered with errors & faulty conclusions about how Maricopa County conducted the 2020 General Election," county officials said on Twitter.

Election officials say that's because the review team is biased, has no experience in the complex field of election audits and ignored the detailed vote-counting procedures in Arizona law....

The Arizona review did not uncover a single example of fraud, but the draft report makes misleading assumptions about the reliability of the election that Trump amplified in a series of statements — claiming it demonstrated "fraud" (AP. GOP).

CNN. Final report from partisan Arizona review confirms Biden defeated Trump in Maricopa County last November.

The final report produced by Cyber Ninjas, the company hired by Arizona Senate Republicans to conduct a months-long, partisan review of the 2.1 million ballots cast in Maricopa County in the 2020 election, shows that the results of reviewers' hand recount are nearly identical to the county's tally.

The state Senate released the report Friday during a presentation by Cyber Ninjas and its subcontractors of its findings.

"The ballots that were provided to us to count in the coliseum very accurately correlate with the official canvass numbers," Cyber Ninjas CEO Doug Logan said during the presentation. He noted that the hand recount found President Joe Biden gaining 99 votes in Maricopa County and former President Donald Trump losing 261 votes – which he called "very small discrepancies." ...

One critical example that illustrates how the sham audit has given birth to conspiracy theories that have taken hold on the right: In an earlier meeting, Logan, the Cyber Ninjas CEO, said that Maricopa County had received and counted more than 74,000 mail-in ballots "where there is no clear record of them being sent" to voters, and said the discrepancy merited a massive door-knocking campaign to check the veracity of the votes.

That claim was false. In fact, those 74,000 ballots were early votes cast in-person. Election experts explained that Logan had failed to understand the purpose of the early voting data Maricopa County had collected – a mistake an experienced auditor would have been unlikely to make. Still, Logan had provided fodder for Trump, who publicly repeated the claim about 74,000 ballots at his Phoenix rally just 10 days later, even though it had already been immediately and widely proven as false (CNN. Final).

NYT. Republican Review of Arizona Vote Fails to Show Stolen Election.

After months of delays and blistering criticism, a review of the 2020 election in Arizona's largest county, ordered up and financed by Republicans, has failed to show that former President Donald J. Trump was cheated of victory.

Instead, the report from the company Cyber Ninjas said it found just the opposite: It tallied 99 additional votes for President Biden and 261 fewer votes for Mr. Trump in Maricopa County, the fast-growing region that includes Phoenix.

"Truth is truth and numbers are numbers," Karen Fann, the Republican Senate president who commissioned the vote review, said as the findings were presented to the State Senate on Friday [9/24/21]…

Officials with the review claimed that duplicate ballots might have been counted, that signatures on ballot envelopes were suspect, that 23,344 mail-in ballots might have come from wrong addresses and that 10,342 voters might have voted in multiple counties. They said thousands of voters might have moved out of the county or the state, that mail ballots never sent to voters might have been counted and that 282 voters might have been dead.

At the presentation's end, Ms. Fann called for Arizona's attorney general, a Republican, to investigate the claims of irregularities. None of the claims held up, according to experts on election administration who monitored the proceedings (NYT. Republican).

Newsmax. Arizona Vote Auditors Raise Biden Total, Claim Numerous Anomalies.

Trump Fights Back with Statements

Auditors who reviewed voting results cast in Maricopa County, Arizona, in last November's election said Joe Biden's vote total was 99 more than officially certified — and Donald Trump's was 261 fewer.

But at the same time, they maintained they'd found multiple election anomalies, among them more than 17,000 duplicate ballots.

The findings of the audit, commissioned by Arizona Senate Republicans and conducted by Florida-based Cyber Ninjas, were both hailed and decried by Trump critics. At once, they said the review debunked the former president's claim of fraud, but also disputed other assertions of irregularities at the polls....

Biden beat Trump by fewer than 11,000 votes — by the certified count — in the nominally Republican state, and about 45,000 in Maricopa County — its most populous — out of more than 2 million cast.

Cyber Ninja representatives outlined their findings in a hearing before the Arizona Senate late Friday. The presentation was led by company CEO Doug Logan.

One slide during the presentation indicated there were 17,322 duplicate votes (Newsmax. Arizona Vote).

September 28, 2021

Donald J Trump @RealDonaldTrump

The Republicans in the Senate have the cards, including political cards, to stop the onslaught of Democrat Legislation that will further lead to the destruction of the United States. The 19 Senators who voted for the (non) Infrastructure Bill, of which only 11% is infrastructure as we know it, have created a big setback for Republicans. They can't make mistakes like that again. They must play every card in the deck! September 28, 2021

To comment, again, I detail what is in the infrastructure bill now law in my *Biden Tweets* books. By my calculations, less than half deals with traditional infrastructure. That is more than what Trump claims, but I am looking at major categories, like road and bridge repair, while maybe Trump has access to the specifics, with some of what is listed under road and bridge repair not really being about roads and bridges.

Donald J Trump @RealDonaldTrump

All 17,000 illegal immigrants who entered our Country from Haiti and other places unknown have now been released into our Country with no vetting, checking, or even minimal understanding of who they are. Some are very sick with extremely contagious diseases, even worse than the China Virus. They are not masked or mandated, but just let free to roam all over our Country and affect what was just a year ago, a great Nation. Now we are a Nation humiliated like never before, both with the historically embarrassing "withdrawal" from Afghanistan, and our Border where millions of people are pouring in. Our Country is being destroyed! September 28, 2021

Donald J Trump @RealDonaldTrump

Just eight months ago, the whole world knew that if you illegally violated America's borders, no matter where you came from, you'd be immediately caught, promptly detained, and swiftly removed—perfect precision clockwork. Our border was the envy of nations. Now, our border is the laughingstock of the globe. Anyone, from anywhere, can just illegally walk across our border, turn themselves in, and then be on to the city of their choice. No testing, no masking, no mandates. Free healthcare, deliveries, and medical services in our emergency rooms, all paid for by taxpayers. Drugs pour through like water. Our border agents are disrespected, denigrated, and demoralized.

Now, news reports indicate another 20,000 Haitians are staged in Columbia preparing to make the trek to our Southern Border. But that's just the beginning. Wave after wave are heading our way, INVITED here to break our laws by Biden, Mayorkas, and the Marxist Democrats. Indeed, at this very moment, House Democrats are preparing to pass a Reconciliation Bill that includes total amnesty for millions of illegal aliens, and removes all limits on green cards and chain migration. Democrats are playing for keeps—Republicans better fight hard, fight strong, and stay united for America, or we won't have a Country left. September 28, 2021

Extended Comment
Haitian Mass Migration

Trump is referring to a wave of migrants from Haiti coming from Central American, through Mexico, through our southern border during September. Thousand were gathered under a bridge at one point. It was a humanitarian crisis created by Biden's open border policy.

Trump Fights Back with Statements

The number reported on Newsmax was 60,000 Haitians came our way. That is the equivalent of a rural town being imported into our country, all at our expense, with no idea who they are or if they are infected with Covid. I detail this Biden created crisis in my *Biden Tweets* books.

September 29, 2021

Donald J Trump @RealDonaldTrump
The botched and embarrassingly incompetent withdrawal from Afghanistan had nothing to do with past Administrations or things that happened "from 20 years ago," (other than we should not have been in the Middle East in the first place!).

The horrible "withdrawal" was caused, in particular, because the Military was taken out before American citizens and $85 Billion worth of the highest-grade Military equipment anywhere in the world. This withdrawal was developed by a child's mind, and only the Biden Administration is responsible for it.

When I left office, the Taliban was held at bay, we had as long as we wanted, there was no reason to rush, no soldiers were killed or even shot at for over 18 months, and if they didn't meet certain conditions, we would have hit them very hard. But then Biden and Milley removed the Military in one of the dumbest Military moves in history, and it all began. So sad for our Nation! September 29, 2021

Donald J Trump @RealDonaldTrump
No wonder the Afghanistan withdrawal was such a disaster. "General" Milley spent all of his time talking to these Fake Book writers. That's not a Soldier or General, that's a Public Relations agent. America will continue losing with Milley and woke television Generals who are only looking to be stars! September 29, 2021

To comment, Milley is more concerned about getting before the camera and being woke than about leaving our people behind in Afghanistan. He is a disgrace.

Donald J Trump @RealDonaldTrump
Rather than the political January 6th Unselect Committee of Radical Left Democrats and Democrat wannabes (Warmonger Liz Cheney and Cryin' Adam Kinzinger), Congress should set up a "Commission On the Disastrous Withdrawal From Afghanistan," to figure out what went wrong, why so many of our Warriors were killed, and why so much money (85 BILLION DOLLARS), in the form of Weapons and Military

equipment, was left behind for the Taliban to use—and to sell to other countries. This is without question something that needs to be investigated further. Thirteen dead AMERICAN HEROES, billions of dollars of equipment, and hundreds of Americans still left behind in Afghanistan with the Taliban! September 29, 2021

To comment, don't forget droning ten Afghan civilians, including seven children. That gave the Taliban the talking point that Americas are the true terrorists and child-killers. And thanks to Biden, they would be correct. Despicable. I address this debacle in my article, "Worst Foreign Policy Debacle in USA History" –
https://www.zeolla.org/politics/articles/2021/worst.htm

Chapter Ten
Trump's Statements
October 2021

These Trump Statements are continued from Chapter Nine.

October 1, 2021

Donald J Trump @RealDonaldTrump
    If Democrats are able to piece together their huge tax hikes, called by another name, it will mean an additional 40 Republican seats in the House and at least a few additional Republican Senators in the U.S. Senate. October 1, 2021

    To comment, I hope that proves to be the case. But take nothing for granted. Repubs need to campaign hard in 2022 and keep reminding people about all of the disasters of the Biden administration and the radicalism of the House and Senate Dems. I list several of the more recent of them in my article, "Biden Administration Tragedies and Missteps" - https://www.zeolla.org/politics/articles/2021/tragedies-missteps.htm

Donald J Trump @RealDonaldTrump
    Snuck into the government funding bill, or CR [Continuing resolution], the Democrats are trying to pass, and just found, is unlimited money to random, unscreened, unvetted Afghan nationals. Republicans can't let this happen. This is a further insult after Biden's humiliating withdrawal from Afghanistan, that needlessly killed 13 Americans.
    This is not a "clean" government funding bill. It's a major immigration rewrite that allows Biden to bring anyone he wants from Afghanistan for the next year—no vetting, no screening, no security—and fly them to your community with free welfare and government-issued IDs. We've already seen some of the horrible assaults and sex crimes that have taken place. But these terrible assaults will just be the tip of the iceberg of what's coming if this isn't shut down.
    The CR even covers people who don't live in Afghanistan and haven't in many years, as long as they used to live there. So Biden and Blinken can load up planes of former Afghans from Pakistan or elsewhere without any limits, checks or even a lawful visa or refugee status.

The only "rule" is that Mayorkas—an incompetent radical—give them a green light. This bill must be opposed! October 1, 2021

To comment, sadly, this bill passed, and 13 RINOs in the Senate voted for it, all the usual suspects, plus Mitch McConnel and Linsdey Graham.

Mitch was great in getting Trump's judicial nominees confirmed. But otherwise, he's proving to be a big disappointment. As for Graham, after shining during the Kavanaugh hearings, he is also proving to be a big disappointment. I address his role and that debacle in book *Tearing the USA Apart*, hereafter referred to as my *Tearing Apart* book.

October 2, 2021

Donald J Trump @RealDonaldTrump

Just heard Patriots are moving the Texas Audit Bill forward. Texas State Senator Paul Bettencourt filed Senate Bill 47, legislation that authorizes Texans to initiate a strong and real Forensic Audit of the 2020 Presidential Election Scam—not a weak risk-limiting audit that is being slow-walked through the Secretary of State's office. Lt. Gov. Dan Patrick, a great guy, sent the bill to the State Affairs Committee the very same day, and it should quickly pass through the Senate. There is still time for the House to take up the issue in the Third Special session with House Bill 16.

I'd like to thank Dan and Paul for their bold leadership, and for listening to Texans who are demanding answers about Nov. 3. Everyone feels certain Governor Abbott will follow suit. This will have a big impact on the upcoming 2022 and 2024 elections in Texas. Texas will always be red, but we must stop the cheating.

Keep it up and get this bill over the finish line. Passing the audit bill will be a Big Win for Texas! Let's make sure the great people of Texas believe and trust their elections. October 2, 2021

Donald J Trump @RealDonaldTrump

The Progressives gain far more power with the legislation being currently talked about by failing than if it passes. It makes them a true powerhouse. Next up, AOC running against Chuck Schumer for his US Senate Seat! October 2, 2021

To comment, Trump is referring to Biden's Build Back Better plan. I address it depth in my *Biden Tweets* books. But here, that's an interesting take. But I still want it to fail, as it will be a giant step towards socialism and government control of all aspects of our lives, literally from womb to tomb, as depicted in a Biden-released cartoon about Linda and Leo that I discuss in those books.

October 3, 2021

Donald J Trump @RealDonaldTrump
The Democrat plan, if approved at any level, will push our Country towards socialism! October 3, 2021

To comment, exactly.

Donald J Trump @RealDonaldTrump
Because the Election was rigged, and America now has weak and corrupt leadership, we may very well end up in a war with China who no longer respects the USA. They witnessed firsthand our television generals' complete surrender to the Taliban with the loss of 13 great Warriors and the handing over of $85 billion of the best and most expensive Military equipment in the World—China and Russia are already reverse engineering the equipment so they can build it for themselves.
The only thing the Radical Left Democrats, who are destroying our Nation, are good at is rigging Elections and criminal activity, while always blaming the other side through corrupt prosecutors and prosecutions. Our Country is in big trouble—we better get going fast! October 7, 2021

October 7, 2021

Donald J Trump @RealDonaldTrump
Looks like Mitch McConnell is folding to the Democrats, again. He's got all of the cards with the debt ceiling, it's time to play the hand. Don't let them destroy our Country! October 7, 2021

To comment, Trump is referring to the deal to raise the debt limit, so that the USA does not default on October 18, 2021. But it only pushes the default date back to December 6. Mitch had promised to not hold such a vote and to force Dems to go it alone, just as they have throughout Biden's presidency. But Mitch folded. But he has vowed again that this is the only time he will allow such a vote. By December, he says the Dems will have to go it alone once again. Only time will tell if he holds to his guns then.

October 8, 2021

Donald J Trump @RealDonaldTrump

Fiona Hill was terrible at her job. The first time I remember hearing her name was during Impeachment Hoax # 1, where she worked hard to say anything bad, but there wasn't much. It was a total con job. She may have been in the Oval and conference rooms with me, but this was not anybody who I recognized. Then she acted like she was a know-it-all, but in reality, she had no influence whatsoever.

She was very close to one of the dumbest and most "crazed" people in Washington, John Bolton. Both of them didn't say much and what they did say wasn't listened to, especially after Bolton's statement that he wants the "Libya Model" on North Korea in the midst of my negotiation with Kim Jong Un. He made that statement on "Deface the Nation", or "Meet the Fake Press"—it doesn't matter, they're all the same. Fortunately, Kim Jong Un understood how stupid he was, and wouldn't allow him at meetings or dinners (I liked that).

Fiona Hill was a Deep State stiff with a nice accent. Books are being written by people like her who had virtually no access to me, and who I didn't even know. They write it as if they're experts on "Trump," but they know absolutely nothing about me. My function was to save our Country and Survive. Unfortunately, when you look at what is happening now with Afghanistan, the Border, inflation, etc., our Country is not being saved. It is in big trouble! October 8, 2021

To comment, Trump is correct that Hill and Bolton were dumb deep staters who were just looking for their 15 minutes of fame.

I discuss Fiona Hill's role in the impeachment in detail in volumes one and two of my *Impeach* trilogy." I discuss Bolton, his bias book, and the media frenzy over it, in detail in Volume Three.

Donald J Trump @RealDonaldTrump

Republican Senators, do not vote for this terrible deal being pushed by folding Mitch McConnell. Stand strong for our Country. The American people are with you! October 8, 2021

To comment, Trump is again referring to that debt cealing deal. Sadly, ten senators voted with Mitch to move the bill forward. It then passed with only Dem votes, went to the House, was passed there, and was then signed by Biden. But wait until December for the rematch.

Trump Fights Back with Statements

Donald J Trump @RealDonaldTrump

I have sent a letter to the U.S. National Archives and Records Administration in defense of the Office of the Presidency, the Constitution, vital principles of separation of powers, and on behalf of our great Nation. The Radical Left Democrats tried the RUSSIA Witch Hunt, they tried the fake impeachments, and now they are trying once again to use Congress to persecute their political opponents. Their requests are not based in law or reality—it's just a game to these politicians. They don't care about our Country or the American people.

The Democrats are drunk on power, but this dangerous assault on our Constitution and important legal precedent will not work. This Committee's fake investigation is not about January 6th any more than the Russia Hoax was about Russia. Instead, this is about using the power of the government to silence "Trump" and our Make America Great Again movement, the greatest such achievement of all time. We won two elections, did far better in the second than the first, and now perhaps have to do it a third time

It is also about trying to deflect blame from Biden's surrender in Afghanistan and the failures to address COVID, the border, crime, and the economy that is leaving Americans dead or broke. It's another grand distraction, because Biden and the Democrats don't want you to see how badly America is losing due to their incompetence.

My administration, and the great patriots who worked on behalf of the American people, will not be intimidated. We will not allow Biden or the Radical Democrats to get off without accepting blame for their incompetence and failures. I will always fight for America First, and the Constitution. Together, we will Make America Great Again, Again!

Read the letter here.

https://cdn.nucleusfiles.com/7a/7afce14c-07a3-4292-bdb2-8560e007ec4f/letter_to_archivist_of_the_united_states.pdf October 8, 2021

Donald J Trump @RealDonaldTrump

Biden has rejected our request to withhold White House information from the House Unselect Committee investigating the January 6th protest, but has not taken a stance on the insurrection that took place on November 3rd, often referred to as the Crime of the Century.

This will put the current White House in a terrible position when the inevitable request for information comes concerning the massive corruption by Hunter Biden and the already well-documented crimes committed by the Biden family, the least of which are Hunter's paintings selling for as much as $500,000 a piece. With our Country collapsing, with our Military disgraced, with our Borders nonexistent, when will the American people have had enough? October 8, 2021

Extended Comment
Hunter Biden's Artwork

I predicted such corruption would be forthcoming from the Biden crime family when I documented Biden's previous corruption in my *Corruption* book.

Here, that renewed corruption is in the form of paintings looking like they were drawn by a two-year-old being sold for five or six figures. Really, Hunter sells five such paintings for $75,000 each, yet the media tells us it is not to buy influence with Joe. Are we really that stupid? Just how did Joe Biden become a millionaire on a Senator's and VP's salary?

At least five reproductions of Hunter Biden's artwork have garnered $75,000 each as lawyers vet people who plan to attend his spring gallery show in New York City, The New York Post reported.

The Georges Berges Gallery sold the prints before the Oct. 1 opening of a "pop-up" exhibition in Los Angeles, a source told the Post on Thursday [107/21].

It was unclear who bought the reproductions or if any more were sold after the L.A. event began....

The younger Biden's recent schmoozing with attendees at his debut exhibition caught the attention of Richard Painter, who was President George W. Bush's chief ethics lawyer.

Painter said it was clear that a White House attempt to prevent influence-peddling by maintaining anonymity for the buyers won't work, as the L.A. opening "just illustrates how this veil-of-secrecy idea is not happening" (Newsmax. Hunter).

October 9, 2021

Donald J Trump @RealDonaldTrump
Heading to the Great State of Iowa, big crowd of Patriots. See you soon! Will be broadcast live on OAN, Newsmax, Right Side Broadcasting, and Real America's Voice, among others, at 7:00PM CDT. October 9, 2021

Donald J Trump @RealDonaldTrump

Just landed in Iowa. Beautiful weather. Massive crowd. See you soon! October 9, 2021

Extended Comment
Iowa Rally

This was a great rally. I watched it on Newsmax, the only station that aired it.

Former President Donald Trump on Saturday night gave unqualified praise to Iowa voters at a massive rally in that state, offering the electorate the strongest sign yet that he intends to run in the next presidential election.

"Boy, we did really good," Trump told a crowd at the Iowa state fairgrounds, commending attendees for the state's strong turnout in his favor in November.

Trump praised his "eight-point landslide victory" in the state, which he called "a big beautiful victory in November."

"You proved why Iowa should continue to vote first in the nation," he told the raucous crowd.

The former president returned to some familiar tenets of his campaign platforms, warning that Democrats in control of Washington espouse an open-border policy that threatens the safety of Americans, unlike when he was in office and imposed a travel ban for some counties that was upheld by the Supreme Court....

He also repeated the 2020 election he lost was "rigged" and that he "never conceded" the race.

Trump also retuned to lambasting "fake news," and said Washington Democrats' multi-trillion spending bill would give money to such media companies allowing reporters at the rally and others to buy a "new car" (Just the News. Trump rallies).

Donald J Trump @RealDonaldTrump

The Thursday House hearing of the Arizona Election Scam turned sharply against the Democrats when Congressman Andy Biggs and others started asking questions about all the damning findings of the audit and the people for Maricopa County were unable to give an answer. It was incredible.

They could not answer why they deleted and moved election data after they received a subpoena, or why they have never delivered chain of custody documents for millions of ballots. Congressman Andrew Clyde exposed the Democrats' "Big Lie" that Biden "won" the recount, because no matter how many times you count counterfeit money, "you may have 100 pieces of paper in your pocket, but you sure don't have $100 dollars in legal tender."

The hearing exposed how numerous laws were broken during the Arizona voting, how blank mail-in ballot envelopes were approved, and how there are tens of thousands of suspected fraudulent ballots.

The Fake News, however, refuses to cover those questions and answers because they prove, without question, that we won Arizona (and many other states). October 9, 2021

Donald J Trump @RealDonaldTrump

Texas Speaker of the House Dade Phelan is another Mitch McConnell. He is not fighting for the people of Texas. Speaker Phelan should immediately move the Forensic Audit bill, SB 47 by Senator Bettencourt that passed out of the State Senate this week, to the floor. The Speaker knows the bill will overwhelmingly pass the House with Republican support.

While standing in the way of a real election audit, Speaker Phelan just weakened the penalty for voting illegally in the state of Texas from a felony to a misdemeanor, siding with the Democrats and calling their amendment that makes a mockery of our election laws "thoughtful." After the 2020 Presidential Election Scam we need tougher penalties for cheating in our elections, not weaker ones.

Texans are tired of Phelan's weak RINO leadership in the State House. Texas is a very red state, even more than people know.

If this doesn't pass soon, we look forward to seeing him in the Texas primary. It will get done one way, or the other! October 9, 2021

October 11, 2021

Donald J Trump @RealDonaldTrump

The highly partisan Unselect Committee is just a sideshow to distract America from MASSIVE failures by Biden and the Democrats. What happened to the Capitol would have never happened if the people in charge did their job and looked at the intelligence. They abandoned the officers on the ground, just like Biden abandoned Americans in Afghanistan. Instead of holding bad leaders accountable, the Democrats are going after innocent staffers and attacking the Constitution.

Why is the just released bombshell January 6th whistleblower report being ignored by the mainstream media? Based on this high ranking

Capitol Police official's report, these partisan hearings must stop at once. This is yet another continuation of the Radical Left's Witch Hunt—led by Shifty Adam Schiff and his crew who misled America on RUSSIA, RUSSIA, RUSSIA, the "Perfect" Ukraine phone call, the Mueller report scam, and so much else. Now Shifty, who couldn't get a job with the administration, is at it again. Radical Left Democrats are rapidly destroying America! October 11, 2021

October 13, 2021

Donald J Trump @RealDonaldTrump

Our Border has gone from the safest and most secure in history, by far, to a broken, dirty, and disgusting wreck with thousands of unknown people from unknown countries, including from their now emptied prisons all over the world, unsustainably pouring in. No country has ever seen anything like what is happening on the Southern Border of the United States—and no country is stupid enough to allow such a thing to happen. Crime will go up at levels that the U.S. has never seen before (it is actually already there), and terrorism will be the next big wave to lead the way.

Despite this, and incredibly, the very expensive and high-tech Border Wall, which has been 100% successful in areas where it was completed, is being lifted from installation points and moved to storage dumps where it will begin the process of rotting and rusting away. Putting it in place would have been far less expensive, and the Wall would have been quickly completed—there was very little left to do. Billions of dollars are being paid to contractors to NOT build the Wall, specifically, $6 million per day.

The "leaders" of our Country have gone crazy! Everything is falling apart, our Military is in shambles, the shelves of our stores are empty, COVID continues to rage at levels higher than last year, we have no oil, we have no courage, we have nothing. Our Country is a laughingstock all over the world, and is certainly no longer great, but we will Make America Great Again! October 13, 2021

To comment, Trump is correct about it costing more to not finish the wall than to finish it. That is because much of the border wall had already been constructed. All that had to be done was to lift it into place in the already dug trenches, then painted. But the pieces were left lying on the ground, rusting away, because they had not yet been painted.

See the references under "Border Wall Construction Stoppage" in Appendix One for much more on this subject.

Donald J Trump @RealDonaldTrump

Big rally in Michigan yesterday, unbelievable spirit and knowledge of what went on with respect to voting and vote counting in the 2020 Presidential Election. Detroit, considered for many years to be one of the most corrupt places in the United States for elections (and many other things!), had large-scale irregularities so much so that two officials, at great risk to themselves and their families, refused to certify the results, and were sadly threatened. Wasn't it a fact that aside from other things, there were far more votes than voters? Even the RINOs on the Senate Committee found 289,866 absentee ballots that were sent to people who never requested them, "something that would be illegal." Why did they viciously kick out the Republican poll watchers? Seventy percent of Detroit's mail-in ballot counting boards didn't match, it was a total mess.

Why won't they give respected professionals and representatives at yesterday's rally the right to do a Forensic Audit of Wayne County (Detroit) and Macomb County? That includes the RINOs in the State Senate and House who for, whatever reason, do nothing but obstruct instead of seeking the truth. Hopefully, each one of these cowardly RINOs, whose names will be identified and forthcoming, will be primaried, with my Complete and Total Endorsement, in the upcoming election. Congratulations on the great rally yesterday! October 13, 2021

To comment, see under "Michigan Voter Irregularities" in Appendix One for much more on this subject.

Donald J Trump @RealDonaldTrump

COVID is raging out of control, our supply chains are crashing with little product in our stores, we were humiliated in Afghanistan, our Border is a complete disaster, gas prices and inflation are zooming upward—how's Biden doing? Do you miss me yet? October 13, 2021

October 14, 2021

Donald J Trump @RealDonaldTrump

Here we go again. After a very long wait, a judge in Georgia refuses to let us look at the ballots, which I have little doubt are terrible. This whole situation is a disgrace to our Country. Why can't the public see the ballots? Our Country is going to hell and we are not allowed transparency even in our Elections. The people of Georgia deserve to know the truth. So unfair to them and our Country. The fight continues, we will never give up. Our Elections are so corrupt and nobody wants to do anything about it! October 14, 2021

Donald J Trump @RealDonaldTrump

Why isn't the January 6th Unselect Committee of partisan hacks studying the massive Presidential Election Fraud, which took place on November 3rd and was the reason that hundreds of thousands of people went to Washington to protest on January 6th? Look at the numbers now being reported on the fraud, which we now call the "Really Big Lie."

You cannot study January 6th without studying the reason it happened, November 3rd. But the Democrats don't want to do that because they know what took place on Election Day in the Swing States, and beyond. If we had an honest media this Election would have been overturned many months ago, but our media is almost as corrupt as our political system! October 14, 2021

Donald J Trump @RealDonaldTrump

If we don't solve the Presidential Election Fraud of 2020 (which we have thoroughly and conclusively documented), Republicans will not be voting in '22 or '24. It is the single most important thing for Republicans to do. October 14, 2021

Donald J Trump @RealDonaldTrump

How come the Fake News Media doesn't talk about Afghanistan anymore? October 14, 2021

To comment, the late great Rush Limbaugh often described the media as a spotlight. It will shine its light on a particular situation for a short while, then it will move onto something else, forgetting the previous story.

In this case, the media had to report about the Afghan debacle, as it was just too tragic to ignore completely. But having believed they did their jobs and did some real journalism for a short while, they had to move on, less they disparage their favored faux President and party too much.

But we on the right will not let the American people forget how much Biden screwed up the withdrawal, leading to the deaths of 13 of our brave soldiers and that he left Americans behind, who are still in hiding in Afghanistan out of fear for their lives.

Sean Hannity in particular continues to open his radio show with a count of the number of days it has been since Biden left Americans behind in Afghanistan, even now, almost a year later (August 5, 2022).

October 15, 2021

Donald J Trump @RealDonaldTrump

Today, the highly respected Dr. Shiva Ayyadurai, MIT PhD, is having an event on the big findings from the Arizona Audit. He has invited the RINOs on the Maricopa County Board of Supervisors to participate. If they have nothing to hide, and if this was the "most secure election" in history, they would show up and answer the many questions raised by the audit, like how there were over 17,000 duplicate mail-in ballots and why they poured in after Election Day, how there were over 6,000 more ballots than there were envelopes, or why some were stamped "verified and approved," even though they had no signature, which is against the law.

Maricopa County has refused to answer these questions (and so much more!), and instead "shoots the messenger." Tune in to Dr. Shiva's open forum from 12-4PM EDT. We must fix our elections to save our Country!

These massive irregularities and corruption are now in the hands of the Attorney General Mark Brnovich of Arizona. Everybody knows what the right answer is, both in Arizona and other places! October 15, 2021

October 16, 2021

Donald J Trump @RealDonaldTrump

New information found from public records, documents, and votes in Arizona. It is damning and determinative! Will be discussing this today. October 16, 2021

Donald J Trump @RealDonaldTrump

Isn't it terrible that all of Andrew McCabe's benefits, pensions, salary, etc., were just fully reinstated by the Justice Department? This is yet another mockery to our Country. Among other things, McCabe's wife received hundreds of thousands of dollars in campaign contributions from Hillary Clinton and the Democrats while Crooked Hillary was under investigation, which was quickly dropped, of course. What a bad chapter this has been for the once storied FBI—I hate to see it happening, so many GREAT people work there.

Next thing you know the two lovers, Peter Strzok and Lisa Page, will be getting awards for what they did, and Hunter Biden will be given a clean bill of health on everything done by him, with everyone to receive as payment a beautiful Hunter Biden inspired painting selling at your local art gallery for $500,000.

While I have never painted before, Hunter has inspired me to immediately begin painting because I've always felt I have a talent at that, and could surely get at least $2 million dollars per canvas—and probably a lot more. I will begin immediately. Our Country is crooked as hell! October 16, 2021

Donald J Trump @RealDonaldTrump

A new analysis of mail-in ballots in Pima County, Arizona means the election was Rigged and Stolen from the Republican Party in 2020, and in particular, its Presidential Candidate.

This analysis, derived from publicly available election data, shows staggering anomalies and fictitious votes in Pima County's mail-in returns, making it clear they stuffed the ballot box (in some precincts with more ballots than were ever sent!).

Your favorite Republican candidate was steadily outperforming the Republican share of mail-in ballots by 3%, while Joe Biden was underperforming Democrats by 3%. But when mail-in ballots started pouring in way higher than normal (at over 87%), this trend flipped. In other words, when it was clear Trump was going to win, that's when they swung into action. As more mail-in ballots poured in and increased by 1%, Trump's performance decreased by 1%, while Biden's increased.

As more and more mail-in ballots were stuffed into the system, Biden's numbers shot way up. But they overplayed their hand, and got caught. Two precincts in Pima had over 100 percent turnout for mail-in ballots -- which is impossible -- and 40 precincts had over 97% returned. The national mail-in ballot return rate was 71%, but in Pima County the mail-in ballot return rate was 15% higher, and 19% higher than all the counties combined in the entire state of Arizona. One precinct with 99.5% mail-in turnout had 9,812 ballots counted. Another precinct with 100.6% turnout had 2,182 ballots returned, but only 2,170 mail-ins were ever sent. These two total 11,994 ballots, alone more than the margin needed to win.

Turnout rates of 99% and 100% is what you get in a Third World Country, and that's what we're becoming (look at crime, the Border, Afghanistan, food prices, energy prices, and the empty store shelves, etc.), unless this is fixed immediately!

The precincts above 92% mail-in return rate represented 264,000 votes. If just 2% are fraudulent, meaning Trump votes went to Biden, that would be enough to change the so-called margin in Arizona of 10,457 votes.

The Department of Justice has had this information since the November 2020 Election, and has done nothing about it. The Pima County GOP should start a canvass of Republican voters, in order to identify and remove the obvious fictitious voters from the system.

In addition, the Arizona Audit found tens of thousands of illegal votes, including 6,545 mail-in ballots with no envelopes, 2,580 bad signatures on mail-in ballot envelopes, and 1,919 mail-in ballot envelopes with no signature, which is also determinative and more than the margin.

Either a new Election should immediately take place or the past Election should be decertified and the Republican candidate declared the winner. October 16, 2021

October 18, 2021

Donald J Trump @RealDonaldTrump
"The Klu Klux Klan dressed protester case should have never been brought as the plaintiffs have no one to blame but themselves. Rather than protest peacefully, the plaintiffs intentionally sought to rile up a crowd by blocking the entrance to Trump Tower on 5th Avenue, in the middle of the day, wearing Klu Klux Klan robes and hoods. When security tried to deescalate the situation, they were unfortunately met with taunts and violence from the plaintiffs themselves.

Seeing this for what it is, prior to my deposition today, the Court dismissed almost all of the plaintiffs' claims—except for a baseless claim for injuries they never suffered, and the temporary loss of a worthless cardboard sign which was soon thereafter returned to them. After years of litigation, I was pleased to have had the opportunity to tell my side of this ridiculous story—Just one more example of baseless harassment of your favorite President." — Donald J. Trump October 18, 2021

To comment, this statement is in regard to the following story: Newsmax. Trump Ordered to Give Deposition in NYC Protesters' Lawsuit. https://www.newsmax.com/politics/trump-deposition-protester-lawsuit/2021/10/14/id/1040540/

Donald J Trump @RealDonaldTrump
Wacky Senator Bill Cassidy from Louisiana is a RINO Republican who begged for my endorsement in 2020 and used it all over the place to win re-election, much like Little Ben Sasse, and then voted to impeach your favorite President.

Trump Fights Back with Statements

I have done so much for the State of Louisiana, including making it possible to build major energy facilities that would never have happened without me filling up the strategic petroleum reserve at record low prices, and making sure they received huge amounts of hospital supplies and ventilators to aid the people of Louisiana in fighting the China Virus. Even the Democrat governor thanked me for all I did.

Now, Wacky Bill Cassidy can't walk down the street in Louisiana, a State I won by almost 20 points. He could not even be elected dog catcher today, the great people curse him.

Wacky Bill is a totally ineffective Senator, but Louisiana does have a great Senator in John Kennedy. October 18, 2021

To comment, do not miss Trump referring to "filling up the strategic petroleum reserve at record low prices." If Trump had not done this, Biden would not have later been able to release a million barrels a day from the SPR in an effort to lower gasoline prices. Prices did come down; but eventually, Biden will have to refill those reserves, and at a much higher price than Trump filled them. When Biden does so, gasoline prices will begin to skyrocket again.

October 19, 2021

Donald J Trump @RealDonaldTrump

General Keith Kellogg has written a sweeping and powerful account of the Trump Presidency. He spent four years with me in the White House and in the 2016 Campaign for the Presidency. His narrative is factual and indisputable. Unlike other Fakers and Slimeballs that write fictional books without knowing me or virtually anything about me, The General knew me and my administration well, and he was there for every major National Security decision.

Finally we have a real and inside account of our very successful four years. An incredible read published today. I strongly recommend this important book that will set a historic standard. Go get War By Other Means by General Keith Kellogg—it's really good! October 19, 2021

Donald J Trump @RealDonaldTrump

Wonderful to see Colin Powell, who made big mistakes on Iraq and famously, so-called weapons of mass destruction, be treated in death so beautifully by the Fake News Media. Hope that happens to me someday. He was a classic RINO, if even that, always being the first to attack other Republicans. He made plenty of mistakes, but anyway, may he rest in peace! October 19, 2021

Donald J Trump @RealDonaldTrump

The fake, highly partisan Unselect Committee continues to rock and roll. They were unable to make a deal with Kevin McCarthy to put real Republicans on the Committee, so they got stuck with low-polling warmonger Liz Cheney and Cryin' Adam Kinzinger who have no idea what our Party stands for. Cheney is polling in the low 20's in Wyoming, the State she doesn't represent. This is just a continuation of the Witch Hunt which started with the now fully debunked and discredited Russia, Russia, Russia Scam, quickly reverting to a perfect phone call with Ukraine, Ukraine, Ukraine, Impeachment Hoax #1, Impeachment Hoax #2, and now this. The Unselect Committee is composed of absolute political hacks who want to destroy the Republican Party and are decimating America itself. I am the only thing in their way. MAKE AMERICA GREAT AGAIN! October 19, 2021

October 20, 2021

Donald J Trump @RealDonaldTrump

Isn't it terrible that a Republican Congressman from Nebraska just got indicted for possibly telling some lies to investigators about campaign contributions, when half of the United States Congress lied about made up scams, and when Mark Zuckerberg, in my opinion a criminal, is allowed to spend $500 million and therefore able to change the course of a Presidential Election, and nothing happens to them?

Comey lied, Schiff lied, Crooked Hillary lied, McCabe lied, the two lovers, Peter and Lisa, lied. They all lied having to do with Russia, Russia, Russia, because they knew it was a SCAM, and they all lied having to do with Ukraine, Ukraine, Ukraine, because they knew it was a SCAM—and they made up fairy tales about me knowing how badly it would hurt the U.S.A.—and nothing happens to them. Is there no justice in our Country? October 20, 2121

To comment, I discuss that scam Ukraine impeachment in-depth in my *Impeach* trilogy. It truly was a despicable display of a lack of due process. I also touch on the other scams Trump mentions in those books and on my politics website: "Biblical and Constitutional Politics" https://www.zeolla.org/Politics/index.html

All of these false attacks on Trump should not be forgotten, as Dems, the media, and Big Tech will use the same tactics against whoever runs in 2024, be it Trump or someone else. For that matter, they will use the same tricks in the 2022 midterms. That is why I am chronicling as many of them as possible in my books and on my website.

October 21, 2021

Donald J Trump @RealDonaldTrump
> The insurrection took place on November 3, Election Day. January 6 was the Protest! October 21, 2121

To comment, I document the many irregularities that give credence to Trump's claim here in my *Corruption* book.

The way Dems, the media, and Big Tech banded together to hand the election to Biden should not be forgotten, as they will use the same tactics in 2022 and again in 2024. But my book will stand as a reminder of those tactics and what to look out for next time.

October 22, 2021

Donald J Trump @RealDonaldTrump
> Isn't it funny that Meghan McCain, who has always been a bully and basically a lowlife, is now complaining that it was she who was bullied by the Slobs and Radical Left maniacs of "The View."
> At the request of many of her representatives, I made it possible for her father to have the world's longest funeral, designed and orchestrated by him, even though I was never, to put it mildly, a fan. In his own very special way, he was a RINO's RINO. Despite his fighting against me, I won Arizona by a lot in 2016 and won Arizona by even more in 2020—unfortunately the vote counters in 2020 were far more important than the candidate (See the determinative Report issued Wednesday by the Arizona Auditors!).
> I have since found out that McCain, who was close to last in his class at Annapolis, sent the fake and totally discredited scam Dossier to the FBI, hoping to stop the "Trump Train."
> In any event, Meghan should fight the Communists instead of explaining how they beat her, hurt her, and made her "physically ill." She should fight back against the Losers of The View the way she fights against very good and well-meaning Republicans, and she would do herself a world of good! October 22, 2121

October 23, 2021

Donald J Trump @RealDonaldTrump
> General Keith Kellogg's book is a true and insightful record of our incredibly successful four years. It is a truly accurate account of my

Presidency and brings to full light what my Administration accomplished in the face of constant attacks from mainstream media and political opportunists. What we did was right for America and our great citizens, and the record proves it. Kellogg was with me for every critical decision I made on behalf of our great Nation. Kellogg's bestselling book, War By Other Means, published this week, is a must read. Get it now! October 23, 2121

October 24, 2021

Donald J Trump @RealDonaldTrump

Our Country is being poisoned with the millions of people that are illegally flowing through our Borders, in most cases not even questioned or stopped. Many are criminals from the emptied prisons of other countries, most of these are very dangerous people. Our Country is dying from within and nobody is doing anything to stop it.

The first thing that should be done, and it can be done quickly, is FINISH THE WALL. A deal must be made with Mexico, where Mexico serves as a 2,000 mile barrier, not a launching pad for the illegals that are coming in.

Also, 97 percent of the people that came in from Afghanistan rushed the planes and should not be here. Those people must be checked very carefully because many of them will turn out to be strongly related to high-level terrorism.

How stupid our Country has become, so sad to watch when just 10 months ago we had none of these problems, and none either with bad economy, inflation, fuel prices going through the roof, and so much else.

And never forget, because the Fake News will not talk about it any longer, those needlessly killed in Afghanistan and the thousands of people and the $85 Billion worth of Military equipment left behind in the complete and total surrender by the United States of America. We would have been out but we would have been out with dignity and strength. Our Country is now a laughingstock all over the world! October 24, 2021

October 25, 2021

Donald J Trump @RealDonaldTrump

The largest caravan in history is coming towards us, and we are totally unprepared and doing nothing about it. Complete the wall and get tough. Our Country is being systematically destroyed before our very eyes! October 25, 2021

To comment, I discuss such caravans in depth in my *Tearing Apart* book. But back then (2018), Trump was in charge. He brought the border under control, and his policies stopped the caravans. But now, with Biden playing President and no one really in charge, those caravans will keep coming and coming, as our border gets overrun with illegal aliens.

CBS Evening News reported 1.66 million illegal aliens had been arrested year to date as of 10/24/21. That is a record for one year, and there's still over two months to go. It also does not include illegals that were not caught by Border Patrol. That is a lot of unvetted aliens entering the country, with 10% of them testing positive for Covid. Yet, the Biden administration is letting them in nevertheless, even spreading them (and Covid) around the country.

It is truly a despicable situation that was totally preventable. All Biden had to do was to leave Trump's policies in place., They worked at bringing the crisis under control, as I detail in that book.

Donald J Trump @RealDonaldTrump

What good is it if FOX News speaks well of me when they continually allow horrible and untruthful anti-Trump commercials to be run—and plenty of them. In the good old days, that would never have happened and today it happens all of the time. Ratings-challenged CNN and MSNBC would never run a positive Trump ad—never. With so many forces against us, Big Tech, the Fake News Media, the Radical Left, the RINOs, and more, we are at such a disadvantage, but we will win anyway! October 25, 2021

October 26, 2021

Donald J Trump @RealDonaldTrump

President Jair Bolsonaro and I have become great friends over the past few years. He fights hard for, and loves, the people of Brazil—Just like I do for the people of the United States. Brazil is lucky to have a man such as Jair Bolsonaro working for them. He is a great President and will never let the people of his great country down! Oct 26, 2021

October 29, 2021

Donald J Trump @RealDonaldTrump

I hope everyone is watching the MASSIVE Caravan pouring through Mexico and headed to our Country. This must be stopped before they reach our Border, or before. Just nine months ago, we had the strongest Border in our Nation's history. This should have never happened! October 29, 2021

Donald J Trump @RealDonaldTrump

What country will be the primary beneficiary from a "Billionaires Tax," or Wealth Tax? Where will wealthy people and companies move to, leaving the United States high and dry? Most don't need to be in the U.S. anyway. I know all of those very smartly run countries, and they are all thrilled by what the Radical Left maniacs are doing in Congress. I just wonder, will I be allowed to run for president again if I move to another country? No, I guess I'll just stick it out, but most others won't! October 29, 2021

Donald J Trump @RealDonaldTrump

Vito Fossella is running as the very popular Republican nominee for Staten Island Borough President. Under the failed leadership of Mayor Bill de Blasio, Staten Island, a place I know and love so much, has become New York's forgotten Borough. The Radical Left is defunding our police, corrupting our schools, and endangering our children. It can come back strongly, but New York City is now a filthy and dangerous place. This is what happens under a corrupt one-party rule.

Vito is the only true Conservative Republican in the race who will stand up to the Radical Liberal Mob. I have been a proud supporter of Vito Fossella because he is Strong, Tough, and Loves the incredible people of Staten Island. Vito has my Complete and Total Endorsement. He will not disappoint you! October 29, 2021

Donald J Trump @RealDonaldTrump

Chanting, "We love Trump" in Arlington, Va. Thank you, Arlington, see you soon! October 29, 2021

Donald J Trump @RealDonaldTrump

$7.59 gasoline in various parts in California—a record, and going higher. All over the Country gasoline is spiking. If the Trump Administration were in there, it would right now be $2 a gallon or less. October 29, 2021

To comment, all Biden can do is beg OPEC and Russia to pump more oil. If he hadn't reversed Trump's policies and kept us energy-independent like Trump left us, we would not need to depend on those who hate us for the lifeblood of our economy.

October 30, 2021

Donald J Trump @RealDonaldTrump

The statement that I made a few weeks ago saying that Republicans will not vote if the Election Fraud of 2020 is not fixed, was in no way meant to imply that I would tell them not to vote, but rather that they may not have the incentive to vote if the election process is not fully remedied, and quickly. It was the Crime of the Century. We are working on solving that problem every day—it will be done! People do not want to spend their time and money to have a SCAM like that happen again. Regardless of anything or anyone, we must get out the Republican and SANE VOTE! October 30, 2021

To comment, I am glad you posted this clarification. Republicans need to vote in each and every election. But we also need to be sure they are fair elections.

October 31, 2021

Donald J Trump @RealDonaldTrump
2 down, 8 to go! October 31, 2021

Extended Comment
Adam Kinzinger

Trump is referring to Adam Kinzinger announcing he will not run for reelection. That is because he knows he will lose in the Republican primary, as redistricting has him facing off against a Trump supporter.

Adam was one of the ten Repub representatives who voted to impeach Trump in the second impeachment proceedings. The other who already said he is not running for reelection is Anthony Gonzalez of Ohio. Adam is also on the J6 Commission.

Six-term Republican U.S. Rep. Adam Kinzinger, an ardent opponent of former President Donald Trump and his continued leadership of the GOP, announced Friday [10/29/21] he would not seek reelection.

Kinzinger's announcement came just hours after state legislators passed a new congressional map drawn by Illinois Democrats that put him into a new district with Trump-supporting U.S. Rep. Darin LaHood...

Kinzinger, one of 10 Republicans to vote to impeach Trump over the Jan. 6 insurrection at the Capitol and one of two GOP members on the House select committee investigating the insurrection, indicated he would be focusing on his One Country political action committee, which is aimed at supporting opponents of the former president....

Though he voted with the Trump administration's policies 92% of the time, he became a sharp critic of the former president as Trump geared up for reelection and openly called out his Republican colleagues for backing him, including party leadership. (Yahoo! News/ Chicago Tribune).

Republican Rep. Adam Kinzinger of Illinois, a critic of Donald Trump's who is on the panel investigating the deadly Jan. 6 Capitol attack by the former president's supporters, announced Friday that he will not seek reelection next year.

The military veteran, who has represented his northern Illinois congressional district since 2013, was one of 10 House Republicans who voted to impeach Trump on a charge of inciting the insurrection at the Capitol. Kinzinger joins GOP Rep. Anthony Gonzalez of Ohio as one of the 10 who have decided to bow out of Congress.

The Illinois Republican announced his decision in a video, saying the "time is now" to move on. "My disappointment in the leaders that don't lead is huge," he said (Yahoo! News. GOP).

But cry as he might, Adam is wrong that backing Trump is bad for the GOP, as will be seen in the next chapter. Back to Trump.

Donald J Trump @RealDonaldTrump

There is far too much corruption and irregularities in Arizona to put in this letter, so we are attaching a copy of the just released and totally determinative report pertaining to the Election Audit.

Not included in the Audit was Pima County, which had multiple precincts with OVER 100 percent turnout for mail-in ballots—which is not possible (or legal!). These alone total 11,994 ballots, more than the election margin. Precincts with anomalous high turnout laughably went from 6% of Republicans voting for Biden to 40% of Republicans "voting" for Biden in mail-in ballots. No one in the Fake News Media pretends to believe this, so they just ignore the facts. It is all just part of the 2020 Presidential Election Scam.

Trump Fights Back with Statements

We are not talking about one state, Pennsylvania, we are talking about numerous states, far more than is necessary to win, which we did, but which the Fake News media and the Wall Street Journal refused to talk about and are doing everything within their power to cover up. They don't want the facts because if they had them, we win!

The Wall Street Journal does not properly refute the numbers in Pennsylvania and doesn't even address the fact that there are still at least 120,000 excess voters not accounted for by the Pennsylvania Department of State, meaning more votes than voters!

The thing the Wall Street Journal is right about is the statement that "their attempts to censor Mr. Trump have done nothing to diminish his popularity," and "our advice would be to examine [the Democrats'] own standards after they fell so easily for false Russian collusion claims." October 31, 2021

To comment, I address the situation in PA and those "excess voters" in my *Corruption* book and follow up on it in my *Tragic Ending* book.

Donald J Trump @RealDonaldTrump
The Wall Street Journal just did a white-washed statement, so incorrectly, almost as incorrect as their views on tariffs against China, a country that has been ripping off the United States for years (not even including the disaster of the China Virus), trying to justify the fraud of an election in Pennsylvania, but also saying "even if" we are right, "Mr. Trump would be two states short of victory."

Wrong! We were only talking about Pennsylvania, we weren't talking about other states, which are also wrapped up in large scale fraud or election improprieties. As an example take a look at what happened yesterday in Racine, Wisconsin, where a brave Patriot Sheriff and his staff found fraud and criminal activity with regard to what took place with ballot harvesting and other things in nursing homes, which the Wisconsin Election Commission ordered to be done throughout the state. This is just the tip of the iceberg.

There are many other improprieties in Wisconsin, including numerous laws broken, according to a new report from the Legislative Audit Bureau, who identified at least 44,272 illegal "indefinitely confined" votes who did not show Voter ID. Almost 7% of a sample of mail-in ballots were missing information required by law, and therefore should not have counted, which would amount to 32,431 illegal ballots.

Just one example of fraud in Georgia (and there is so much more!) is enough to swing the election, as 43,907 ballots from Facebook funded drop boxes violated Chain of Custody requirements, and were thus illegally counted? In Michigan, even the RINOs in the state senate confirmed roughly 45,000 ballots were delivered to the TCF Center in Detroit with no Chain of Custody at 3:30 and 4:30 a.m on Nov. 4, and an estimated 289,866 absentee ballots were illegally sent to people who never requested them, far more votes than needed to win the state.

Also in Arizona, the Maricopa County Board of Supervisors were caught spreading "outright lies" about the Audit, and caught illegally deleting election data and records in defiance of a subpoena. They cannot explain away the findings of the Arizona Audit, which include:

- 23,344 "Mail-In Ballots Voted from Prior Address"
- 9,041 "More Ballots Returned by Voter Than Received"
- 284,412 ballot images "were corrupt or missing"
- 17,322 duplicate ballot envelopes (which surged after Election Day)
- 5,295 "Voters That Potentially Voted in Multiple Counties"
- 2,382 "In-Person Voters Who Had Moved out of Maricopa County"
- 2,081 "Voters Moved Out-of-State During 29-Day Period Preceding Election"
- "Official Results Does Not Match Who Voted" (off by at least 3,432 ballots) October 31, 2021

Donald J Trump @RealDonaldTrump

Is everybody watching the soon to be fact that the Biden Administration is going to give illegal aliens $450,000 each? October 31, 2021

Extended Comment
Separation Settlement

In this Statement, Trump is talking about Biden settling with the ACLU and "families" separated at the border, agreeing to pay $450,000 for each separated family member. That is $50,000 more than Gold Star families receive after the death of their loved ones.

If Trump was still in office, he would have fought this ridiculous settlement. But Biden just caved and agreed to pay people for breaking our laws, while law-abiding US citizens are suffering.

The Biden administration is in talks to offer immigrant families that were separated during the Trump administration around $450,000 a person in compensation, according to people familiar with the matter, as several agencies work to resolve lawsuits filed on behalf of parents and children who say the government subjected them to lasting psychological trauma....

The total potential payout could be $1 billion or more....

Many of the lawsuits describe lasting mental-health problems for the children from the trauma of the months without their parents in harsh conditions, including anxiety, a fear of strangers and nightmares. The lawsuits seek a range of payouts, with the average demand being roughly $3.4 million per family, some of the people said (WSJ. U.S. in).

According to a piece in this afternoon's Wall Street Journal, the Biden administration has decided to pay reparations to illegal aliens. In other words, foreigners who came here without invitation, who came in willful violation of legal statutes passed by our Congress per our Constitution, those people are about to get a groveling apology and huge amounts of cash. Why? Because our government dared to enforce its own laws, which now apparently is immoral.

So the Biden White House is going to pay criminals for committing crimes (Tucker Carlson, quoted in Breitbart. FNC's].

President Biden on Sunday [10/31/21] was asked about the administration's plan to pay illegal immigrants who had been separated from their families under the Trump administration $450,000 per person. Instead of responding, Biden just scratched his head.

"Mr. President, is it true we're going to give $450,000 to border crossers who are separated?" Fox News's Peter Doocy asked the president as he rode down an escalator at the G20 summit.

Instead of responding, Biden gave a blank stare and scratched his head (Townhall. How).

But what could Biden say? This plan is so ridiculous, it sounds like something you would read in the Babylon Bee. But it is real.

I discuss these "family" separations in my *Tearing Apart* book. In it, I explain why I am putting "family" in quotes here.

Against Lies of Biden, Attacks from Dems, and Bias of Media

Chapter Eleven
Trump's Statements
November 2021

These Trump Statements are continued from Chapter Ten.

November 1, 2021

Donald J Trump @RealDonaldTrump
It's wonderful to see the moderate Democrats take such total advantage of the ultra Liberal Progressives in the House. They promised the Progressives everything and are giving them nothing. No wonder AOC +3 are so angry! November 1, 2021

Donald J Trump @RealDonaldTrump
Looking forward to being at the World Series in Atlanta tonight. Thank you to the Commissioner of Baseball Rob Manfred, and Randy Levine of the great New York Yankees, for the invite. Melania and I are looking forward to a wonderful evening watching two great teams! November 1, 2021

To comment, it was nice to see you and your lovely wife doing the Tomahawk Chop. That really set the MSM off, which is always fun to watch. It was also nice to see the Braves stick it to the MLB by winning the World Series, after the MLB pulled the All-Star game out of Atlanta. Add in the Youngkin victory in Virginia (more on that in a moment) and the race being too close to call in New Jersey on election night, and it's been a good time for the MAGA movement.

November 2, 2021

Donald J Trump @RealDonaldTrump
It is very interesting that Afghanistan, and our horrible and incompetent withdrawal, losing soldiers and leaving $Billions of military equipment, was when people really began to realize how horrible this Socialism/Communism direction for America has become.
We have never been thought of so poorly as we are right now, including the fact that the leaders of foreign countries, all of whom are at the top of their game, are laughing at Biden as he makes the rounds in

Europe. So low and so bad for America. There has never been a time like it! November 2, 2021

To comment, after the Afghanistan debacle, there is no way anyone can take Biden seriously as a leader anymore. I discuss that debacle in depth in my article: "Worst Foreign Policy Debacle in USA History' – https://www.zeolla.org/Politics/articles/2021/worst.htm

I then chronicle many of his other recent screw-ups in my article "Biden Administration Tragedies and Missteps' – https://www.zeolla.org/Politics/articles/2021/tragedies-missteps.htm

Donald J Trump @RealDonaldTrump

Even Biden couldn't stand hearing so much about the Global Warming Hoax, the 7th biggest Hoax in America, followed closely behind by the 2020 Presidential Election Scam, Russia, Russia, Russia, Ukraine, Ukraine, Ukraine, Impeachment Hoax #1, Impeachment Hoax #2 and, of course, the "No Collusion' finding of the Mueller Report.

Biden went to Europe saying Global Warming is his highest priority, and then promptly fell asleep, for all the world to see, at the Conference itself. Nobody that has true enthusiasm and belief in a subject will ever fall asleep! November 2, 2021

Extended Comment
My Books and Biden Sleeping

I chronicle many of hoaxes Trump mentions in my various political writings. I address the election scam, Impeachment Hoax #1, and Impeachment Hoax #2 in my books. I also address Biden's failing presidency, including his falling asleep at the conference in my books: https://www.zeolla.org/Politics/subject/books.html

I address Russia, Russia, Russia and the "No Collusion' finding of the Mueller Report on my politics website: https://www.zeolla.org/Politics/index.html

It is true Biden fell asleep during the conference:

Presidents — they're just like us: Social media erupted on Monday [11/1/21] when a viral video appeared to show President Biden dozing off during opening speeches at the 2021 United Nations Climate Change Conference.

The 78-year-old Biden – who warned military service members this summer that top Pentagon officials consider climate change to be the "greatest threat' to America's national security in the coming years – sat with his arms crossed, appearing to drift in and out of sleep, in video shared by Washington Post reporter Zach Purser Brown.

"Biden appears to fall asleep during COP26 opening speeches,' Purser Brown wrote to caption a video that showed Biden closing his eyes for extended periods of time before an aide approached him with some type of message. Biden was also seen wiping his eyes and the video quickly went viral, with many mocking the president for appearing to take a quick nap.

Former President Trump has long referred to his political rival as "Sleepy Joe' and Monday's video presumably won't help make that nickname go away anytime soon. However, many conservatives joked that Biden nodding off during the climate conference was the most relatable thing he's done as president (Fox News. Biden appears). Back to Trump.

November 3, 2021

Donald J Trump @RealDonaldTrump

Early indications are that MAGA voters are turning out big for Glenn Youngkin, let's see what happens. All eyes are on Fairfax, why the delay? November 3, 2021

Donald J Trump @RealDonaldTrump

I would like to thank my BASE for coming out in force and voting for Glenn Youngkin. Without you, he would not have been close to winning. The MAGA movement is bigger and stronger than ever before. Glenn will be a great governor. Thank you to the people of the Commonwealth of Virginia and most particularly, to our incredible MAGA voters! November 3, 2021

Extended Comment:
Virginia Gubernatorial Race

The preceding two Statements are in regard to the gubernatorial race in Virginia. In a surprise victory, Republican Glenn Youngkin beat Democratic and former Governor of Virginia Terry McAuliffe.

This was an important race nationally, as it was considered a "bellwether' for the 2022 midterm elections. It was also important, in that McAuliffe thought tying Youngkin to Trump would hurt Youngkin. But it did not. In fact, it probably helped him. The most important issues to Virginians are also important to most Americans.

Throughout the campaign, McAuliffe sought to cast Youngkin as overly supportive of former President Trump. Youngkin, on the other hand, emphasized tax cuts, education, and tried to tap into the feeling that the country was on the wrong track under Biden. Youngkin's approach was more successful, leading to an upset victory in a state that has trended Democratic in recent years.

Overall, voters said the economy was the top issue facing the state, followed distantly by the pandemic and education (Fox News. How).

Republican Glenn Youngkin's victory in Virginia's gubernatorial election Tuesday [11/2/22] night dealt another blow to President Biden and Democrats, as the political newcomer flipped a typically blue state red in a signal of what could be to come in the 2022 midterms.

Youngkin's victory is the first statewide for the Republican Party in Virginia in 12 years – in what some saw as a referendum on Biden's presidency and his legislative agenda pending in Congress.

"The Youngkin win in Virginia sends a signal to Democrats: Americans want to get back to work and want their kids to succeed and don't want policies that are aimed to pit people against each other,' a senior House GOP aide told Fox News. "If I were a moderate Democrat, I'd take tonight as a clear sign that a vote for trillions of dollars of socialist spending while inflation is already hurting Americans' pocketbooks is a vote in the wrong direction' (Fox News. Youngkin victory).

The following poll on my local newspaper's website is instructive:

Do you think Republican Glenn Youngkin's victory in Virginia's gubernatorial election demonstrates the most effective post-Trump strategy for Republicans to win statewide and national elections?

Yes, I think so: 55%
Maybe, I'm not sure: 22%
No, I don't think so: 14%
Other / No opinion: 9% (Trib Live).

Therefore, Fox News is correct. This was as signal to Dems they are on the wrong track while Repubs are on the right track. Back to Trump.

214

Trump Fights Back with Statements

Donald J Trump @RealDonaldTrump
   Big congratulations to my friend Steve Bovo on his election as Mayor of Hialeah, Florida. He ran a great race. Steve has been a loyal supporter and is a great Patriot. He is tough on crime, will always protect our Second Amendment Rights, supports our America First agenda, knows the value of a strong economy, and understands the evils of socialism. Good luck to Steve, and I look forward to seeing you soon! November 3, 2021

November 6, 2021

Donald J Trump @RealDonaldTrump
   So interesting to watch the so-called Democrat "Progressives' being lied to and played by the Democrat Moderates. It used to be the other way around. Let's see if the Progressives fold, and how long it will take them to do so? November 6, 2021

   To comment, it is fun watching the in-fighting in the Dem Party. Here's hoping they continue to shoot each other in the foot through the 2022 midterms. That will ensure a red wave.

November 9, 2021

Donald J Trump @RealDonaldTrump
   CNN just aired a Fake documentary on the Presidential Election Fraud of 2020. The only thing they didn't discuss were the tremendous number of findings indicating what a complete Sham the Election was. Would've been nice to have discussed the facts that have been pouring in from each of many States concerning the Crime of the Century. Are we supposed to have a Fraudulent Election that is allowed to stand while our Country is being simultaneously destroyed? November 9, 2021

   To comment, it was to counter fake news about the 2020 election from the likes of CNN that I knew would be forthcoming that I wrote my *Corruption* book. It will forever stand as a documentation of the many irregularities in that election.

Donald J Trump @RealDonaldTrump
   The Unselect Committee of politically ambitious hacks continues to subpoena people wanting to know about those protesting, on January 6th, the insurrection which took place during the Presidential Election

of November 3rd. There is so much proof, but the Fake News Media refuses to print it or show it in any way, shape, or form. Just read the findings of the Arizona report, or look at what's happening in Wisconsin, Pennsylvania, Georgia, and numerous other States. That's right, the Committee is studying the PROTEST when it should be studying the Fraudulent Election that led to the protest. As the LameStream Media knows, the facts are there for all to see! November 9, 2021

J6 Commission Subpoenas

Trump is referring to the following:

The Democrat-controlled House committee investigating the Jan. 6 Capitol riot on Tuesday [11/9/21] issued another round of subpoenas, this time for top Trump administration officials including former White House press secretary Kayleigh McEnany and adviser Stephen Miller, according to news reports.

Others subpoenaed were issued to Nicholas Luna, a personal assistant to Trump; Molly Michael a special assistant to Trump; Ben Williamson, a deputy assistant to Trump and senior adviser to former Chief of Staff Mark Meadows; Christopher Liddell, a former White House deputy chief of staff; John McEntee, a former White House personnel director; Keith Kellogg, who served as former Vice President Pence's national security adviser; Cassidy Hutchinson, a special assistant to Trump for legislative affairs; and Kenneth Klukowski, a former senior counsel to assistant Attorney General Jeffrey Clark, according to NBC News....

The subpoenas were issued one day after the select committee issued subpoenas to six former Trump administration and campaign officials including Bill Stepien, Trump's 2020 reelection campaign manager; Jason Miller, a senior campaign adviser; John Eastman, a conservative lawyer who was reported to have advised Trump and others in the administration; and former Trump national security adviser Michael Flynn, NBC also reports (Just the News. Jan. 6).

It is clear Dems are on a fishing expedition, looking for someone, anyone, to say something negative about Trump to be able to tie him to J6, after having failed in their second fake impeachment to do so. They need to do so, as they know they cannot beat Trump if he runs again in

2024. That was the impetus for the first fake impeachment, as summarized by the title of my trilogy on it: *Dems Cannot Beat Trump, So They Impeach Trump*. Back to Trump.

Donald J Trump @RealDonaldTrump

Why is it that Old Crow Mitch McConnell voted for a terrible Democrat Socialist Infrastructure Plan, and induced others in his Party to do likewise, when he was incapable of getting a great Infrastructure Plan wanting to be put forward by me and the Republican Party? He continuously said he couldn't get it passed, just like I had to go around him to get the very popular Southern Border Wall built (which caused great delay—but could now be completed in one month by Biden).

All of the Infrastructure money, $2 Trillion, would have gone into real Infrastructure (roads, bridges, tunnels, airports, etc). Also, why did Mitch give the Democrats a two-month hiatus, just long enough for them to figure it all out, when they were completely ready to fold? November 9, 2021

November 11, 2021

Donald J Trump @RealDonaldTrump

With an approval rating at 19% in Wyoming, people are wise to Liz Cheney. She is a threat to Free and Fair elections, which are the cornerstone of our Country, because she caved so easily on the Crime of the Century. She is happy to join the Democrats in the Unselect Committee (the next RUSSIA, RUSSIA, RUSSIA Hoax), and spread more of their lies. Cheney is far more unpopular than her father, who just lost his position as the least popular Vice President in American history to Kamala Harris. Democrats would never put up with a Liz Cheney in their ranks. If we had a Free and Fair media, instead of a corrupt media, those election results would never have been allowed to happen. The proof of irregularities and fraud is massive! November 11, 2021

November 13, 2021

Donald J Trump @RealDonaldTrump

The lawsuit brought by a woman who made up false accusations against President Trump for publicity or money has just been dropped in its totality. The Fake News Media totally and completely distorted the facts—they are corrupt. President Trump has been totally vindicated. No money of any kind, or legal fees, were paid by President Trump, who stated, "It is so sad when things like this can happen, but so incredibly important to fight for the truth and justice. Only victory can restore one's reputation!' November 13, 2021

November 14, 2021

Donald J Trump @RealDonaldTrump
Looks like Lyin' Brian Williams is leaving ratings-challenged MSNBC to search for new employment. Never had the credibility to do what he is doing after he was caught lying about his involvement in a fake military airplane skirmish. He later confessed, it never happened. He's tired of his current show and they're obviously tired of him— won't be missed! November 14, 2021

Donald J Trump @RealDonaldTrump
Mitch McConnell has stated that he will not go to the signing of the "Non-Infrastructure' Bill (only 11% for real Infrastructure) or, as it is sometimes called, the Elect Democrats in 2022/24 Act. It gives Biden and the Democrats a victory just as they were falling off the cliff.
Based on the fact that the Old Crow convinced many Republican Senators to vote for the Bill, greatly jeopardizing their chance of winning re-election, and that he led the way, he should go to the signing and put up with the scorn from Great Republican Patriots that are already lambasting him. Our Country is being destroyed while Mitch McConnell gives lifelines to those who are destroying it! November 14, 2021

To comment, again, I detail that the actual infrastructure expenditures in the plan only constituted less than half of the total spending in Volume Two of my *Biden Tweets* books.

Donald J Trump @RealDonaldTrump
Any interest from good and SMART America First Republican Patriots to run primary campaigns against Representatives Tom Rice, John Katko, Don Bacon, Don Young, Fred Upton (challenge accepted), Andrew Garbarino, Peter Meijer (challenge accepted), David McKinley (challenge accepted), Nancy Mace, Jaime Herrera Beutler (challenge accepted) and Chris Smith? You will have my backing! Gonzalez, Kinzinger, and Reed already QUIT, they are out of politics, hopefully for good.
Warmonger Liz Cheney (challenge accepted) is on the SKIDS with a 19% approval rating. Saving America starts by saving the GOP from RINOs, sellouts, and known losers! In the Senate, the "Disaster from

Alaska,' Lisa Murkowski (challenge accepted), must go. There is "almost' nobody worse! November 14, 2021

Donald J Trump @RealDonaldTrump
Why aren't they investigating the people and states who cheated on the election causing the protest of January 6th? Why aren't they investigating the people who ruthlessly and violently burned down and took over Democrat-run cities, beating and murdering people along the way? Instead they are viciously investigating those who protested the November 3rd Presidential Election, the Crime of the Century.
No investigations on Election Fraud, but if anybody was near the Capitol waving an American flag, they've had nothing but trouble. American Patriots are not going to allow this subversion of justice to continue, including the use of prosecutors, local, state, and federal, to torment and destroy innocent people. All this, while our Country is going to hell! November 14, 2021

Donald J Trump @RealDonaldTrump
This Country has perhaps never done to anyone what they have done to Steve Bannon and they are looking to do it to others, also. If they would be so tough with China, Russia, and the world, who no longer respects us, maybe our Country would not be failing at a level at which we have never seen before. We never talk about making our Country great, and it is now heading in an unthinkable direction with the Afghanistan withdrawal, open Borders, Inflation, Woke everything, and so much more. The USA is a radicalized mess! November 14, 2021

To comment, I will address the treatment of Steve Bannon and others tied to J6 in my forthcoming *J6 Commission* book.

November 16, 2021

Donald J Trump @RealDonaldTrump
From Election Day, November 3rd, the day I realized that the 2020 Presidential Election was rigged, I would never have agreed to go to Joe Biden's Inauguration. This decision was mine, and mine alone. The old broken-down Crow, Mitch McConnell, had nothing to do with it. According to third-rate reporter Jonathan Karl of ABC Fake News, McConnell unsuccessfully tried getting a letter signed by others for me not to go. This was nothing I ever heard of and actually, if he ever did get it signed, I probably would have held my nose and gone. The Election was rigged, the facts are clear, and Mitch McConnell did nothing.

He was probably too busy working on deals with China for his wife and family! November 16, 2021

To comment, I knew it too. That is why I was first out of the blocks with a book about it with my *Corruption* book.

November 17, 2021

Donald J Trump @RealDonaldTrump

Heard that Alyssa Farah was terrible on The View—they could have asked the people who know her and saved a lot of time. She was a "back-bencher' in the White House, and is now a nobody again. We put her out there to face the public as little as possible.

It's amazing how these people leave with respect and adoration for me and others in the White House, but as soon as CNN or other cameras get shoved in their face, or the losers from the The View ask a question, or money gets thrown at them, or someone writes a fake book, inglorious lightweights like Farah change so quickly. I watched this clown on television saying exactly what they wanted her to say and I watched the lies. Was she paid by low-ratings CNN?

By the way, as soon as the Crime of the Century happened on November 3rd, I knew the Election was Rigged and Stolen, and never changed my view on that one bit. I did not go soft on the "Real' Big Lie, the Election Scam, and never will. Backbencher said I told her I lost the Election—never did. I virtually never even spoke to Farah (it's like she didn't even exist in the White House). Anybody who ever says that I thought the Election was legit, even for a moment, is wrong. All you have to do is look at the thousands of pages of documents and evidence—which continues to mount.

When we told Alyssa to "hit the road,' she wrote a very nice letter stating that working for "Trump' was "the honor of a lifetime' and she was "deeply proud of the incredible things we were able to accomplish to make our country stronger, safer, and more secure.' Show the rest of the letter Alyssa, and explain why you wrote it! November 17, 2021

Donald J Trump @RealDonaldTrump

A very sad sight watching yesterday as the Taliban had a major Military parade displaying much of the $85 Billion of Military equipment the United States surrendered to them. The handling of the Afghanistan withdrawal was the greatest embarrassment in the history of our Country! November 17, 2021

Trump Fights Back with Statements

To comment, Biden and the media have forgotten about Afghanistan, but it good to see you haven't. It is such a tragedy you weren't in office to oversee the withdrawal. If you had been, it would not have been such a debacle, and all of that military gear would not have been left behind. But as it is, just wait until terrorists begin using it against us. Then we'll see how honest the media is, if they report it or not.

November 18, 2021

Donald J Trump @RealDonaldTrump

When the Broken Old Crow, Mitch McConnell, agreed to a two-month extension, he allowed the Democrats to get their act together and pass the $1.2 Trillion "Non-Infrastructure' Green New Deal Bill, which is a disaster for America in that only 11% of the money will be spent on REAL Infrastructure, with most being spent on Green New Deal nonsense, with big tax increases. Its actual cost is over $2 Trillion, but the bigger disaster is yet to come in the next, much larger version of the Green New Deal, which some people say will be $5 Trillion.

This was all allowed by Mitch McConnell's incompetence and now I understand that a couple Republican Senators may get on board so that they can have yet another and even bigger victory, for the Democrats, while at the same time ensuring massive Inflation and the destruction of our Country as we know it. This is what happens when you allow a guy who lost an Election to take over the Office of the President. He obviously had no mandate, but they're changing our Country and everything it stands for.

Mitch McConnell couldn't stop the first Bill so 19 Senators, including himself, joined in. That's what he does—if you can't beat them, join them. If he wasn't so stupid and didn't give the two-month extension, he could have stopped it all. Now he and his RINO friends will allow a much bigger and far worse Bill to pass, ruining our Country while giving the Democrats a great political lift, all at the same time. People, with the help of the Fake News Media, have already forgotten about the horrendous Afghanistan withdrawal, an economy and jobs that are in shambles, and so many other things.

The good news is, they can't forget about Inflation because it's hitting them right in the face. This is the Broken Old Crow's fault. He could have won it all using the Debt Ceiling—they were ready to fold. Now the Democrats have a big victory and the wind at their back. McConnell is a fool and he [expletive] well better stop their "Dream of Communism Bill' and keep his Senators in line, or he should resign now, something he should have done a long time ago.

Use the Debt Ceiling like it should have been used, you Old Broken Crow, to do so would hurt our Country far less than this horrible Bill. Any Republican in the House or Senate who votes for this Bill will never ever get a Trump Endorsement. Thank you, and good luck! November 18, 2021

To comment, Biden claims the cost of his Build Back Better plan is "just" $3.5 trillion. However, that assume most of the provisions will sunset after a certain period of time. But everyone knows that once a government program begins, it almost never ends. A more honest assessment of the cost without those sunsets is $5 trillion, just as Trump indicates. I document all of this in my *Biden Tweets* books.

November 19, 2021

Donald J Trump @RealDonaldTrump

Congratulations to Tim Ramthun, State Representative of Wisconsin, for putting forward a powerful and very popular, because it's true, resolution to decertify the 2020 Presidential Election in Wisconsin based on the recently found absolute proof of large scale voter fraud that took place.

Rep. Ramthun's resolution details tremendous amounts of election fraud, including 44,272 voters who did not show proper voter identification (which alone is more than twice the margin necessary to win), thousands of emails that show election manipulation by Mark Zuckerberg's funding, irregularities in the state's voter registrations like 400 registered voters at a single address, the Wisconsin Election Commission committing felony crimes by knowingly ordering illegal voting at nursing homes, and so much more.

Only one state senator needs to cosponsor the resolution for it to be put to a vote in each chamber. Which American Patriot from the State Senate will step forward?

Great job, Rep. Ramthun! Even the Democrats and RINOs cannot object to all the evidence that has been exposed! November 19, 2021

Donald J Trump @RealDonaldTrump

Congressman Paul Gosar has been a loyal supporter of our America First agenda, and even more importantly, the USA. Paul is a Congressman who is highly respected in Arizona, strong on Crime, Borders, our Military, and our Veterans. He continually fights for Lower Taxes, Less Regulations, and our great, but under siege, Second Amendment. Paul Gosar has my Complete and Total Endorsement! November 19, 2021

November 20, 2021

Donald J Trump @RealDonaldTrump
Looks like the Democrats are getting far more than they ever dreamed possible, largely because of Mitch McConnell's idiotic move of giving in on the Debt Ceiling and giving them two months to get their act together. They are destroying our Country! We have been put in a much worse negotiating position, but we have the "Trump Card,' and it's called the Debt Ceiling. If they don't drop this horrendous, Communistic style Bill that will be ruinous to all we stand for as a Country, we should not approve a Debt Ceiling increase.

The Old Broken Crow has to be willing to play this hand, not like last time when he folded up like a cheap umbrella. Play it and mean it, because the Debt Ceiling is far less destructive than the Bill that they will otherwise successfully pass, especially when added to the "Unfrastructure' Bill that was just so stupidly approved. Republicans should not have allowed the separation, McConnell should not have given a two month reprieve, but it is what it is. Win with the Debt Ceiling, or resign! November 20, 2021

Donald J Trump @RealDonaldTrump
Great job by Kevin McCarthy last night, setting a record by going over 8 hours of speaking on the House Floor in order to properly oppose Communism. We must never forget what the Democrats have done, at the highest level of evil. If Mitch McConnell had fought, you would have a different Republican President right now. November 20, 2021

Donald J Trump @RealDonaldTrump
Congratulations to Kyle Rittenhouse for being found INNOCENT of all charges. It's called being found NOT GUILTY—And by the way, if that's not self defense, nothing is! November 20, 2021

To comment, absolutely true. It was a clear-cut case of self-defense. In fact, it should never have been brought to trial.

November 21, 2021

Donald J Trump @RealDonaldTrump
The Communist Democrats are engaging in yet another Witch Hunt, this time going after my Administration's unprecedented and incredible

coronavirus response, despite the fact that, sadly, more Americans have died this year from Covid than in all of 2020.

It is a Witch Hunt that's been going on for years. Why don't they investigate Crooked Hillary, when so much has now been proven about her and her campaign's lies and dealings with Russia to smear me and spy on my campaign? I'm telling Peter Navarro to protect executive privilege and not let these unhinged Democrats discredit our great accomplishments. The Witch Hunts must end! November 21, 2021

To comment, I can well remember how the media, Dems, and Biden himself tried to vilify Trump for his Covid response. But those attacks, like all of the rest on him, were unjustified. We see that clearly now, as the death toll under Biden climbs higher than it was under Trump. But don't expect an apology from any of them, though Trump deserves one.

Donald J Trump @RealDonaldTrump

The whole world is watching the tragedy which just took place in Waukesha, Wisconsin, it is devastating, horrible, and very very sick! My heart goes out to the people of this great, beautiful, and hardworking community. We must find the answers to this terrible crime, and stop these violent and depraved acts from happening again. I am with you Waukesha, and always will be! November 21, 2021

Extended Comment
Waukesha Christmas Parade Massacre

This Statement is in regard to the black man who drove a car through a Christmas parade composed of mostly white parade goers, killing six. The media ignored the racial issue. But if the skin shades had been reversed, you can be sure that is all they would have talked about. But as it was, the MSM quickly move on from this story, as it did not fit their narrative of white supremacy and guns being our nation's biggest threats.

However, the real issue here was bail reform. The thug should not have been on the streets, let alone allowed to drive a car, but he was out on bail.

The suspect in a Christmas parade crash in suburban Milwaukee that killed five people was free on $1,000 bail posted just two days before the deadly event, a fact that is leading to a review of what happened and renewed calls for giving judges more power to set higher bails.

One pending case against Darrell Brooks Jr. included an allegation that he deliberately hit a woman with his car in early November after a fight. Prosecutors in Milwaukee County on Monday called their bail recommendation "inappropriately low" given the facts of that case and the Sunday crash, and said they would review it (AP. Waukesha).

The people of Waukesha, Wisconsin, paid a "horrific price" for the "stupidity" of Milwaukee County District Attorney John Chisholm and his push for lowering bonds and allowing violent criminal suspects like Darrell Brooks Jr., the man accused of driving his car into a Christmas parade Sunday [11/21/21] and killing several people, out on bail, Rep. Glenn Grothman said on Newsmax Wednesday [11/24/21]....

Darrell Brooks Jr., 39, of Milwaukee, is accused of driving an SUV into a Christmas parade in Waukesha, a suburban Milwaukee community, on Sunday, killing at least six people and injuring 48 others. He has two open criminal cases in Milwaukee County, including being released on a $1,000 bond on Friday, just days before the killings.

He's now being held under a $5 million bond (Newsmax. Rep. Grothman).

The massacre happened just two days after Kyle Rittenhouse was found not guilty of reckless homicide and intentional homicide after he fatally shot two people and injured another in Kenosha, which is just 52 miles south of Waukesha....

Brooks is a violent 39-year-old career criminal, registered sex offender and amateur rapper from north Milwaukee with a rap sheet going back to 1999, who allegedly punched the mother of his child in the face early last month and then drove over her, leaving tire marks on her leg. Despite the severity of that crime, he was released five days before the Waukesha rampage on a cash bail of just $1,000 set by liberal Milwaukee County prosecutors....

Millard [who witnessed the attack] said Brooks' skin color and the politics of the case don't matter to her and shouldn't matter to anyone. She only wishes she could forget the nightmare she and so many others at the parade experienced.

"He drove down the middle (of the parade) and aimed to get as many people as he could," said Millard, who has been speaking out whenever she can, even on live TV shoots that terrify her.

"They should put him in a room and let us have a go at him. I think he deserves the death penalty. He will burn in hell."

But Waukesha residents also admit they just don't know why Brooks did what he allegedly did, and are wary of appearing racist (NYP. 'Not fitting). Back to Trump.

November 23, 2021

Donald J Trump @RealDonaldTrump

Fake News refusing to cover the Presidential Election Fraud is the Russia Hoax in REVERSE: No coverage of a real scandal, versus endless coverage of a Democrat Fake News scandal! November 23, 2021

Donald J Trump @RealDonaldTrump

For decades our Country's very important Strategic Oil Reserves were low or virtually empty in that no President wanted to pay the price of filling them up. I filled them up three years ago, right to the top, when oil prices were very low. Those reserves are meant to be used for serious emergencies, like war, and nothing else.

Now I understand that Joe Biden will be announcing an "attack' on the newly brimming Strategic Oil Reserves so that he could get the close to record-setting high oil prices artificially lowered. We were energy independent one year ago, now we are at the mercy of OPEC, gasoline is selling for $7 in parts of California, going up all over the Country, and they are taking oil from our Strategic Reserves. Is this any way to run a Country? November 23, 2021

To comment, no it is not. Remember when we had a real President? It wasn't too long ago, but it seems like a lifetime.

That said, Trump hit the nail on the head with this Statement, but this was when Biden only released a few million barrels. But later, he would begin releasing a million barrels a day for six months. That will bring down oil prices, but at the cost of draining our SPR. Then once he begins to refill those reserves, prices will skyrocket again.

Meanwhile, if we have a real emergency, like a hurricane wiping out oil rigs, then we will have no reserves to fall back on.

Donald J Trump @RealDonaldTrump

The Democrats are feasting on January 6th, with no Republicans on the Unselect Committee (Cheney and Kinzinger are not Republicans!) but they are refusing to even discuss the root cause of that protest, which was the insurrection that took place during the November 3rd Presidential Election. We had a Rigged and Stolen Election in our Country, the proof is voluminous and everywhere, but the Democrats refuse to even mention or discuss it. It's called Cancel Culture, and until that is done, this Country will never heal! November 23, 2021

Donald J Trump @RealDonaldTrump

Whatever happened to the Rigged and Stolen Arizona Presidential Election that is being investigated, or maybe the words should properly be "looked at,' by Attorney General Mark Brnovich? When will the legislature vote to decertify? People are very upset in Arizona that it is all taking so long, especially when the findings of the State Senate's Forensic Audit were so conclusive, not even including the recent revelation of 35,000 fictitious votes in Pima County, and precincts with over 100 percent turnout (how do you like that one?).

The people of Arizona are anxiously awaiting the decision of the Attorney General. They know what really went on during that Election! November 23, 2021

Donald J Trump @RealDonaldTrump

Saving America starts with saving the GOP from RINOs, sellouts, and known losers. My great Trump-endorsed candidate in Ohio, Max Miller, is doing both. After I endorsed Max, his RINO opponent, Anthony Gonzalez, was forced into early retirement. A big win for the GOP! Now, with Ohio's new Congressional lines, Max will be running in the 13th District where he will help lead the path back to a strong GOP majority. Max will be a powerful voice for America First and will fight to rein in the Communist Democrats' radical agenda. Max has my Complete and Total Endorsement! November 23, 2021

Donald J Trump @RealDonaldTrump

Media advisory. I will be interviewed tonight by Sean Hannity at 9pm EST. November 23, 2021

November 24, 2021

Donald J Trump @RealDonaldTrump

The Unselect Committee issued a subpoena to Bernie Kerik, an American Patriot and great former Police Commissioner of New York City, for its Jan. 6th Witch Hunt, but didn't realize what they were demanding is a massive trove of evidence of Voter Fraud. According to Bernie's lawyer, these documents show significant indicators of fraud in the 2020 Presidential Election Scam, but have remained hidden from the public. It is exactly what the Unselect Committee should be interested in—if this was a real investigation.

Bernie wants to comply with the subpoena with a public hearing, and asked me to waive attorney-client privilege so Bernie can testify and provide documents, which I grant him. The Unselect Committee will not like what they asked for! November 24, 2021

To comment, I am sure Schiff, et al. will try to muffle any talk about election fraud and will not allow it to be broadcasted. But it would be interesting to watch if they did.

November 25, 2021

Donald J Trump @RealDonaldTrump

A very interesting time in our Country, but do not worry, we will be great again—and we will all do it together. America will never fail, and we will never allow it to go in the wrong direction. Too many generations of greatness are counting on us. Enjoy your Thanksgiving knowing that a wonderful future lies ahead! November 25, 2021

To comment, great message! But the reason we can be so confident is because the LORD God Almighty is watching over this great nation. It is to Him that all thanksgiving should be directed, as from Him all blessing flow.

I detail the LORD's sovereignty in my book, *The LORD Has It Under Control: What the Bible Teaches About the Sovereignty of God* - https://www.zeolla.org/christian/books/preview/teaches/8-control.htm

I include George Washington's Thanksgiving Proclamation in this book, as it is a great testament to God's providence in the founding of this great country.

November 26, 2021

Donald J Trump @RealDonaldTrump

Does anybody really believe that longtime Con Man Bob Woodward, and his lightweight lapdog assistant Robert Costa, are implying in their book of fiction that I was planning to go to war with China, but that one of the dumber generals in the military called the Chinese to tell them that he will inform them if this action proceeds further. Milley may have called, but if so, he should be tried for treason.

Trump Fights Back with Statements

I never had even a thought of going to war with China, other than the war I was winning, which was on TRADE. To make up stories like this and to sell it to the public is disgraceful. I watched that craggy smug face of Woodward as he [expletive] the public and said to myself, "I wonder if history will really believe this stuff?' How do you get your reputation back? I was the only President in decades to not get us into a war—I got us out of wars!

Our Country has been taken over by Scammers and Hoaxsters, and we have to take it back. Just like the Russia, Russia, Russia Scam has now been totally debunked and discredited as a FAKE Democrat/Crooked Hillary Plot, the "go to war with China' story is even more ridiculous. It's incredible that someone is even allowed to write this stuff. We no longer talk about greatness for our Country, everything is about political investigations, hoaxes, and scams. We will Make America Great Again! November 26, 2021

Donald J Trump @RealDonaldTrump
Great news for Arizona, Senator Paul Boyer, a RINO obstructionist, is done. Congratulations to Karen Fann and all of the other Republican Patriots who have worked so hard to reveal the Presidential Election Fraud of November 3rd! November 26, 2021

Donald J Trump @RealDonaldTrump
I view the story being concocted by the Unselect Committee about the so-called insurrection of January 6th (actually, November 3rd!) the same way as the Democrats' Russia, Russia, Russia Hoax, now fully debunked and discredited! November 26, 2021

To comment, there was no insurrection. The FBI made that clear. There was no organized attempt to overthrow the US government, which is what an insurrection is supposed to be. It was a riot, in some places. But most of those who entered the Capitol Building were peaceful and acting more like tourists than terrorists. But you will never hear that from the fake news media.

November 29, 2021

Donald J Trump @RealDonaldTrump
The Fake News Media cannot stand the fact that so many people in our Country know the truth, that the 2020 Election was rigged and stolen, yet almost every article written contains the words the "Big Lie' or "unsubstantiated facts,' etc., always trying to demean the real results.

Against Lies of Biden, Attacks from Dems, and Bias of Media

I am willing to challenge the heads of the various papers or even far left politicians, who have perpetuated the Real Big Lie, which is voter irregularities and fraud on a massive and determinative scale. This includes members of the highly partisan Unselect Committee of Democrats who refuse to delve into what caused the January 6th protest—it was the Fake Election results!

While I am willing to do it, they will never agree because they cannot argue that facts in states including Wisconsin, Pennsylvania, Michigan, Georgia, Arizona, Nevada, New Hampshire, and others such as New Mexico, where the Democrat Secretary of State changed the voting laws without legislative approval just prior to the Election, making it virtually impossible for the Republican presidential candidate to win. If anyone would like a public debate on the facts, not the fiction, please let me know. It will be a ratings bonanza for television! November 29, 2021

To comment, I would love to watch such a debate!

November 30, 2021

Donald J Trump @RealDonaldTrump

Arizona State Senator Wendy Rogers is doing everything in her power to find out the truth of the 2020 Election, and to hold people accountable for Election Fraud in Arizona. Wendy is a MAGA warrior who loves our Country and listens to her constituents. She has a truly great fighting spirit, is strong on Law and Order, securing our Border, and gun rights. Wendy Rogers has my Complete and Total Endorsement for reelection to the Arizona State Senate because she FIGHTS! November 30, 2021

Chapter Twelve
Trump's Statements
December 2021

These Trump Statements are continued from Chapter Eleven.

December 1, 2021

Donald J Trump @RealDonaldTrump
It's really interesting, everybody wants me on television, I get the highest ratings by far, they need ratings to survive, and yet I put out a challenge to debate me about the massive election fraud, which took place in the 2020 Presidential Election, and there are no takers—think of it, zero takers for the so-called "ratings machine."
The reason is, they know they can't win. All I have to do is lay out the facts—they are irrefutable. I've supposedly won all my political debates, but this would be the easiest of them all! Swing state by swing state, they get decimated. This is the Hoax and the Scam and the Crime of the Century. Just remember, no takers! December 1, 2021

To comment, you could use my *Corruption* book to document those claims, if you ever get taken up on that offer, which I doubt.

Donald J Trump @RealDonaldTrump
If Democrats don't immediately stop smash-and-grab robberies, which are taking place in their cities, the National Guard must be called out. There has never been such a thing that has happened in our Country. Large numbers of stores are leaving San Francisco and other cities. Some chains are closing most of their stores, it is all not even believable. December 1, 2021

To comment, in the Bibliography in Appendix One is a series of news articles about these smash and grab robberies in Chicago, Los Angeles, and Minnesota, all very blue areas.

Donald J Trump @RealDonaldTrump
Congresswoman Ilhan Omar should apologize for marrying her brother, committing large-scale immigration and election fraud, wishing death to Israel, and for essentially abandoning her former country,

which doesn't even have a government—Exactly what she'd like to see for the United States! December 1, 2021

Donald J Trump @RealDonaldTrump
Interesting to watch the Unselect Committee go after the gentleman at the Department of Justice who thought the Election was RIGGED, but not go after the people who did the RIGGING. Just look at the numbers that the Fake News does everything possible NOT to report. They are overwhelming! The Unselect Committee itself is Rigged, stacked with Never Trumpers, Republican enemies, and two disgraced RINOs, Cheney and Kinzinger, who couldn't get elected "dog catcher" in their districts. Kinzinger has already quit! December 1, 2021

To comment, the makeup of the J6 Commission truly is disgraceful. As soon as Jim Jordan and Jim Banks were refused as being members, I knew this was just a witch hunt. I knew then the conclusion would be, "It was all Trump's faulty." Just wait for it. It is coming. But it will be a meaningless, forgone conclusion. I predicted such would be the case in my *Tragic Ending* book and will detail it in my *J6 Commission* book.

Donald J Trump @RealDonaldTrump
Great news for television viewers, they have just suspended Chris Cuomo indefinitely! The big question is, was it because of his horrendous ratings, which in all fairness have permeated CNN and MSDNC, or was it because his brother is no longer Governor? Probably both. In any event, Fredo is gone! December 1, 2021

December 2, 2021

Donald J Trump @RealDonaldTrump
The story of me having COVID prior to, or during, the first debate is Fake News. In fact, a test revealed that I did not have COVID prior to the debate. December 2, 2021

Donald J Trump @RealDonaldTrump
Stacey "The Hoax" Abrams has just announced that she's running for Governor of Georgia. I beat her single-handedly, without much of a candidate, in 2018. I'll beat her again, but it will be hard to do with Brian Kemp, because the MAGA base will just not vote for him after what he did with respect to Election Integrity and two horribly run elections, for President and then two Senate seats. But some good Republican will

run, and some good Republican will get my endorsement, and some good Republican will WIN! December 2, 2021

December 3, 2021

Donald J Trump @RealDonaldTrump
America fell 340,000 jobs short of the very modest expectations set by economists. That's because Joe Biden is a one trick pony, "Get the vaccine." But no one trusts this administration. I developed the vaccine when everyone said it wasn't possible, now without "Trump," that's their only solution. This administration is destroying America before our very eyes because there is no leadership.

Besides my vaccine, this is the administration of no jobs and massive layoffs, high gas and energy prices, high crime, empty shelves, open borders, and a horrendous surrender and evacuation from Afghanistan. A lot of effort and money went into RIGGING the 2020 Presidential Election, only to destroy the Country. Was it worth it? December 3, 2021

To comment, Trump is referring to the November jobs report. Over half a million jobs were expected, but only 210,000 were created. But you would think those making such predictions would have learned by now that the Biden economy will always underperform expectations.

As for the vaccines, if Biden would call them the "Trump vaccines" (which is what they are), maybe there will be less vaccine hesitancy among Trump supporters. But Biden cannot bring himself to give credit to Trump for anything. As for that hesitancy, I will address it in my forthcoming *Coronavirus* book.

December 4, 2021

Donald J Trump @RealDonaldTrump
I thought Joe Biden was "put in office" to eradicate the Coronavirus, despite the fact that he previously had failed so badly with the H1N1 pandemic. Well, I guess that didn't work out too well because it was just announced that we've had more cases than ever before. The only difference is, the Fake News doesn't like reporting the real facts. They are the enemy of the people and more dishonest than they have ever been before. December 4, 2021

To comment, in my forthcoming *Coronavirus* book I will have a chapter on "Trump vs. Biden on Covid." It will ask the question, "Who has done a better job on the Coronavirus in the USA? Former President Donald J. Trump or current President Joseph R. Biden?" My answer will be, "I will take Trump. At least he did not make grandiose promises about shutting down virus like Biden did, who should have known better. And it is Biden, not Trump, who contributed to vaccine hesitancy, extending this pandemic."

Donald J Trump @RealDonaldTrump
Do you believe that Shifty Adam Schiff is on the Committee concerning the 2020 protest when he was the one that scammed America and the World on the Russia, Russia, Russia Hoax? He's a sleezeball that has no credibility and is so bad for our Nation! December 4, 2021

December 6, 2021

Donald J Trump @RealDonaldTrump
Anybody that doesn't think there wasn't massive Election Fraud in the 2020 Presidential Election is either very stupid, or very corrupt! December 6, 2021

Donald J Trump @RealDonaldTrump
The Fake News continues to push the false narrative that I had Covid prior to the first debate. My Chief of Staff Mark Meadows confirmed I did not have Covid before or during the debate, saying, "And yet, the way that the media wants to spin it is certainly to be as negative about Donald Trump as they possibly can while giving Joe Biden a pass." Biden goes around coughing on people all over the place, and yet the Corrupt News doesn't even cover it. They continue to shield Biden, who has been a disaster not just on Covid, where we have more deaths this year than last, but on the Border, the Economy, Inflation, Afghanistan, Gas prices, and everything else. Probably because he's not supposed to be in office in the first place! December 6, 2021

Extended Comment
When Did Trump Test Positive?

The full story is as follows:
[Chief of Staff Mark] Meadows says the positive test had been done with an old model kit. He told Trump the test would be repeated with "the Binax system, and that we were hoping the first test was a false positive".

Trump Fights Back with Statements

After "a brief but tense wait", Meadows called back with news of the negative test. He could "almost hear the collective 'Thank God' that echoed through the cabin", he writes (Guardian. Trump tested).

The possibility of false positives and false negatives is why I have never been a fan of widespread testing. There are just too many uncertainties. But here, with the more reliable test being negative, Trump had every reason to go on with the debate. Back to Trump.

Donald J Trump @RealDonaldTrump
Biden said that he was going to "beat the virus," but instead, the virus has beaten him—and badly. Far more people died this year than last, despite tremendous help from vaccines and therapeutics developed under "Trump." He said anybody with his results should leave office. Well Joe, what are you waiting for! December 6, 2021

To comment, this claim is true. There were 400,000 American Covid deaths under Trump. By January 1, 2022, there were 825,000 Covid deaths. That means there have been 425,000 Covid deaths under Biden. By the end of his first year, there will be 458,000 Covid deaths under Biden, or 58,000 more than under Trump's year of dealing with Covid. I will document all of these points in my forthcoming *Coronavirus* book.

Donald J Trump @RealDonaldTrump
Wow, it looks like highly respected Senator David Perdue will be running against RINO Brian Kemp for Governor of Georgia. David was a great Senator, and he truly loves his State and his Country. This will be very interesting, and I can't imagine that Brian Kemp, who has hurt election integrity in Georgia so badly, can do well at the ballot box (unless the election is rigged, of course). He cost us two Senate seats and a Presidential victory in the Great State of Georgia. December 6, 2021

December 7, 2021

Donald J Trump @RealDonaldTrump
I'm watching Republican Senators talk about fighting the horrendous Build Back Better Bill that the Democrats will push forward, made much easier for them by the 19 Republican Senators who voted for the Democrats Unfrastructure Plan, which is only 11% Infrastructure, and

also by McConnell incredibly giving the Democrats a two-month extension, which allowed them to get their act together.

Now the Republicans start fighting a much harder war, and I told them this would happen. It's pathetic!

Those 19 Republicans, including the Broken Old Crow, should not be forgotten for what they have done and the absolutely horrible ramifications this Bill will have on the future of our Nation. Just like McConnell blew two Senate seats in Georgia, and wouldn't fight the Rigged Presidential Election, he gave this one away also. December 7, 2021

Donald J Trump @RealDonaldTrump

Vladimir Putin looks at our pathetic surrender in Afghanistan, leaving behind dead Soldiers, American citizens, and $85 billion worth of Military equipment. He then looks at Biden. He is not worried! December 7, 2021

To comment, this Statement is in regard to Putin amassing his troops on the Russian border with Ukraine.

December 8, 2021

Donald J Trump @RealDonaldTrump

Mitch McConnell just folded on the Debt Ceiling, a total victory for the Democrats—didn't use it to kill the $5 Trillion Dollar (real number!) Build Back Worse Bill that will essentially change the fabric of our Country forever. The Old Crow's two-month extension, and the break up of the Bill into two parts, gave the Democrats everything they needed.

The Dems would have folded completely if Mitch properly played his hand, and if not, the Debt Ceiling scenario would be far less destructive than the Bill that will get passed. He has all the cards to win, but not the "guts" to play them. Instead, he gives our Country away, just like he did with the two Senate seats in Georgia, and the Presidency itself. The Old Crow is a disaster! December 8, 2021

December 11, 2021

Donald J Trump @RealDonaldTrump

Mitch McConnell, the Broken Old Crow, has just conceded, for absolutely nothing and for no reason, the powerful Debt Ceiling negotiating block, which was the Republicans' first-class ticket for victory over the Democrats. He was afraid to play that card even though, without question, they would have completely FOLDED on the Build Back Worse Bill, which will destroy the fabric of our Country and virtually anything else that the Republicans wanted. It should have been used on the Unfrastructure Deal also.

Proudly, House Republicans voted 100% like true patriots (Kinzinger, in my mind, is not a Republican!). The Old Crow also allowed a breaking up of the filibuster, which allows the Democrats now to establish precedent for changing the number of Justices on the Supreme Court and, perhaps most importantly of all, a so-called Voting Rights Bill, which will make it almost impossible for Republicans to get elected in the future.

He lost two seats in Georgia, didn't fight for the presidency, and now gave away our most powerful negotiating tool—the Debt Ceiling. Other than fundraising, where he buys senatorial support, the Broken Old Crow is a loser, and very bad for the Republican Party! December 11, 2021

To comment, I discuss each of these issues in my *Biden Tweets* books, the debt ceiling fight and looming government shutdown, the Infrastructure bill (now law), Biden's BBB plan and how it not only will bankrupt American but would fundamentally change it, the Dem voting rights bills, the filibuster fight, and related issues.

December 13, 2021

Donald J Trump @RealDonaldTrump
See you in Sunrise, FL, in a little while and tomorrow, Orlando. Big crowds! December 13, 2021

Donald J Trump @RealDonaldTrump
We had a great time in Sunrise, FL yesterday. Very exciting, informative, and fun. We will be back in the area for a major rally in the not too distant future. See you then! December 13, 2021

Donald J Trump @RealDonaldTrump
It's amazing how inaccurately the Fake News Media covers my statements. They will take something I say and literally write the exact opposite. They truly are a disgrace and disaster for our Country. Make America Great Again! December 13, 2021

Against Lies of Biden, Attacks from Dems, and Bias of Media

To comment, the MSM's propensity to take Trump's words out for context is one of the reasons for this book. I am presenting Trump's entire Statements, unedited, except to sometimes add paragraphing and to redact foul language.

Donald J Trump @RealDonaldTrump

Mitch McConnell is giving the Democrats victory on everything. What is wrong with this Broken Old Crow? He's hurting the Republican Senators and the Republican Party. When will they vote him out of Leadership? He didn't have the guts to play the Debt Ceiling card, which would have given the Republicans a complete victory on virtually everything. The Dems were ready to fold! Watch, they will use the Debt Ceiling against us at their first opportunity, and they won't fold. It will not be pretty. GET RID OF MITCH! December 13, 2021

To comment, Repubs play nice. Dems paly dirty. Repubs think that means they are taking the high ground, when I fact, it just means they are conceding to the agenda of the Dems.

Donald J Trump @RealDonaldTrump

Not even believable how bad the morning television ratings are for Psycho Joe Scarborough and his lovely wife, Mika. MSDNC is doing badly, but "Morning Joe" is in particular peril! How much longer can a show like that survive—are the advertisers not watching? The only good news is that CNN, believe it or not, is doing even worse! December 13, 2021

December 14, 2021

Donald J Trump @RealDonaldTrump

Isn't it ironic that Liz Cheney is supporting the same people, Radical Left Democrats, that did everything possible to destroy her father when he was Vice President, and after? When they are finished using "Liz," they will destroy her also. This is all happening as her poll numbers have reached an all-time low in the Great State of Wyoming! December 14, 2021

To comment, for those who don't know, Liz is the daughter of Dick Cheney, VP under George W. Bush. The MSM vilified Cheney as a warmonger, especially attacking him in regard to his support for the Iraqi war. But now Liz seems to have forgotten all of that and is doing all she can to chummy up to the MSM.

December 15, 2021

Donald J Trump @RealDonaldTrump

Letitia James wants to politically weaponize her position as Attorney General instead of exemplifying impartiality and protecting the interests of all New Yorkers. While she pretends that she suspended her short-lived campaign for New York Governor to go after me, she conveniently fails to mention that she couldn't garner any support and her poll numbers were abysmal—she had no chance of even coming close to winning. Despite weeks of campaigning, she was losing to Governor Hochul by what would have been a massive landslide.

She didn't drop out of the race for a higher purpose, or to "finish existing business" (I wonder what that would be?). She dropped out because her campaign was a complete failure, possibly because the citizens of New York saw how unfairly and viciously she and other highly partisan New York Democrat prosecutors were treating President Donald J. Trump. It's called Prosecutorial Misconduct.

Rather than continue to waste her time and taxpayer resources on a long continuing Witch Hunt against the Republican Party and me, she should focus her attention on helping to resurrect the once Great State of New York where crime and poverty continue to wreak havoc, with murder, rape, drug sales, and just about every other form of crime at record levels, and now with a just-announced highest unemployment rate in the Nation. New York is dying before our very eyes, and all the Democrat Prosecutors are focused on is how we can get and punish Donald Trump, who many would say has done, over the years, a spectacular job for New York! December 15, 2021

To comment, the rise in crime in blue cities like NYC is truly disturbing. Therefore, Trump is correct that focusing on trying to pin something on him is wrongheaded.

Donald J Trump @RealDonaldTrump

Mitch McConnell has given away the Unfrastructure Bill and will soon be giving away the Build Back Worse Bill, which will change the very fabric of our society. This was all made possible by the two-month extension he gave the Democrats, the separation of the two Bills, and, most importantly, his lack of courage in playing the Debt Ceiling Card. He has grabbed defeat from the jaws of victory! How this guy can stay as Leader is beyond comprehension—this is coming not only from me, but from virtually everyone in the Republican Party. He is a disaster and should be replaced as "Leader" ASAP! December 15, 2021

To comment, fortunately, the BBB bill will be defeated, thanks to Senator Joe Minchin (D. WV). But later, Manchin will cave for a smaller version of the bill. I address the defeat of the BBB at the end of Volume Two of my *Biden Tweets* books. I will address the reduced version of it in my follow-up set, if I do such a follow-up.

Donald J Trump @RealDonaldTrump
Congresswoman Lauren Boebert @LaurenBoebert has done a fantastic job in her first term representing Colorado's Third District. She is a fearless leader, a defender of the America First Agenda, and a fighter against the Loser RINOs and Radical Democrats. She will continue to be tough on Crime, strong on Borders, and always protect our under-siege Second Amendment. Lauren has my Complete and Total Endorsement for her reelection! December 15, 2021

December 17, 2021

Donald J Trump @RealDonaldTrump
I'm hearing great things about Matt DePerno from delegates and party leaders in Michigan. He has been all over the Great State of Michigan gathering delegate and Republican Party endorsements and commitments. For far too long the Democrats have taken control of Michigan and pushed radicalism. Enough is enough!

Matt is the true America First Agenda candidate and will make a great Attorney General. He is a patriot and the fierce fighter Michigan needs to overturn the failed policies of Dana Nessel and Gretchen Whitmer. I urge all Michigan delegates and party leaders to support Matt DePerno in the April Republican Endorsement Convention. December 17, 2021

December 19, 2021

Donald J Trump @RealDonaldTrump
The Democrats are now on a new kick with their so-called Voting Rights Bill, which is a disaster for our Country and certainly the Republican Party. The problem is, good old Mitch gave away our primary negotiating weapon—the debt limit, and he got nothing for it.

Trump Fights Back with Statements

This is Democrat controlled legislation that will make it virtually impossible for Republicans to win elections. It is a scam, as is everything else being put forth by the Democrats. McConnell is the best thing that ever happened to them! December 19, 2021

To comment, the two voting bills going through Congress are based on the lie that voting laws being passed in red states are designed to "suppress voters." But in fact. they are election integrity laws. They will make our elections fair and free. But Dems don't want the former, as they know they cannot win fair elections.

Donald J Trump @RealDonaldTrump

All the Democrats want to do is put people in jail. They are vicious, violent, and Radical Left thugs. They are destroying people's lives, which is the only thing they are good at. They couldn't get out of Afghanistan without disgracing our Country. The economy and inflation are a disaster. They're letting thugs and murderers into our Country— their DA's, AG's, and Dem Law Enforcement are out of control.

This is what happens in communist countries and dictatorships, and they don't think they'll be held accountable for rigging the 2020 Presidential Election. The Jan. 6 Unselect Committee is a coverup for what took place on November 3rd, and the people of our Country won't stand for it. December 19, 2021

To comment, "destroying people's lives" is what Democrats are all about. They used the Trump/ Russian collusion hoax and the first impeachment hoax to ruin the lives of many people. All of those people they called to testify on the latter had to pay lawyer fees of $10,000s. I discuss this point in my trilogy of books on that hoax.

I hadn't thought of it before, but now that you mention it, they are doing the same with the J6 Commission. Every person they call before the committee needs to hire an expensive lawyer. Not all of those people are rich like you. But no matter to the Dems if someone goes broke because of their investigation. They ruined Michael Flynn's life that way, so why not others?

Donald J Trump @RealDonaldTrump

Word is that CNN and its new owners want Jeff Zucker out, not only because of the turmoil of Fredo Cuomo, the Don Lemon ("the dumbest man on television") escapades, and so much else, but primarily because his ratings have gone to an all-time low, and the so-called "network" is rudderless.

In any event, that's great news for America. Maybe CNN can be brought back to what it was in the good old days of the legendary Ted Turner. Jeff will always bomb, just as he did at NBC years before! December 19, 2021

To comment, even though you have been out of office for almost a year, CNN cannot stop talking about you. Every time I put it on, its either Covid or you. That's it. That's all they can talk about, as they know it is only you that brought them any ratings. Without you in office, their ratings are tanking.

That is because of the way they focused on the Trump-Russia collusion hoax for four years, and still have not admitted they were wrong in pushing that hoax. I discuss it throughout my politics website, but especially in my two-part article, "I Told You It Was a Hoax" – https://www.zeolla.org/Politics/articles/2019/hoax/part_one.htm

December 22, 2021

Donald J Trump @RealDonaldTrump

Why isn't the Unselect Committee of highly partisan political hacks investigating the CAUSE of the January 6th protest, which was the rigged Presidential Election of 2020? Does anybody notice that they want to stay as far away from that topic as possible, the numbers don't work for them, or even come close. The only thing they can do is not talk about it.

Look at what is going on now in Pennsylvania, Arizona, Georgia, Wisconsin, and, to a lesser extent, Michigan where the numbers are horrendously corrupt in Detroit, but the weak Republican RINOs in the Michigan House and Senate don't want to touch the subject.

In many ways a RINO is worse than a Radical Left Democrat, because you don't know where they are coming from and you have no idea how bad they really are for our Country. The good news is there are fewer and fewer RINOs left as we elect strong Patriots who love America.

I will be having a news conference on January 6th at Mar-a-Lago to discuss all of these points, and more. Until then, remember, the insurrection took place on November 3rd, it was the completely unarmed protest of the rigged election that took place on January 6th. December 22, 2021

To comment, I address all of these points in in my *Corruption* and *Trump's Tweets* books

Donald J Trump @RealDonaldTrump
Joe Biden was supposedly "elected" because he was going to quickly get rid of COVID-19, sometimes referred to as the China Virus. How's that working out? December 22, 2021

To comment, again, I will address "Trump vs. Biden on Covid" in my forthcoming *Coronavirus* book.

December 24, 2021

Donald J Trump @RealDonaldTrump
Wacko Bette Midler said horrible things about the great people of West Virginia and Joe Manchin, but when I say much less offensive things about her, everybody goes wild. Don't worry, I'll tell the real facts about her in my book. I love you, West Virginia! December 24, 2021

To comment, I'm not sure what book Trump is referring to. As far as I know, he has not written a book.

Donald J Trump @RealDonaldTrump
The people being persecuted by the January 6th Unselect Committee should simply tell the truth, that they are angry about the RIGGED Presidential Election of 2020. People are entitled to Freedom of Speech, and perhaps there has been no time in our Country's history where Freedom of Speech has been so totally violated. They don't want to talk about election results because they know they can't win. December 24, 2021

Donald J Trump @RealDonaldTrump
Has it been at all noticed that I offered to debate anybody, on television or otherwise, about the RIGGED Presidential Election of 2020. This was a publicly stated challenge—I have been called a "ratings machine," and therefore would be good for television economics—which have not been doing so well lately. With all the bravado out there, I have not had one credible person willing to stand up and debate me in order to defend the CROOKED election.
All involved, like those on the Unselect Committee of January 6th, know that it is a losing proposition for them. The election numbers are not defensible. Arizona, Michigan, Pennsylvania, Wisconsin, Georgia, Nevada, and probably New Hampshire, Minnesota, New Mexico, and

others were all won, and in some cases big, by a certain Republican Presidential Candidate, me.

So, after one month, a very public offer to debate, I have no takers—not even the sleazebags you see on the January 6th Commission who speak with such fake reverence about the day. This is Cancel Culture. They think they got away with the Crime of the Century, and they don't want it to be talked about or discussed. Look at what has happened to our Country, and what a shame it is! December 24, 2021

To comment, that would be an interesting debate, and it is a shame there are no takers. But if you are planning on running again in 2024, at some point, you need to put 2020 behind you and start focusing on how you will turn the country around from the disaster Biden is creating.

December 25, 2021

Donald J Trump @RealDonaldTrump

Merry Christmas to all. We will Make America Great Again! December 25, 2021

Extended Comment
The Real Reason for the Season

MAGA is important, but Christmas Day is about the birth of our Lord and Savior, Jesus Christ, as I detail in the newsletter I sent out on this day. The Christmas portion reads as follows:

The Real Reason for the Season
By Gary F. Zeolla

Merry Christmas Everyone!

In the midst of all of the hustle and bustle of this day, don't forget to take a few minutes to meditate on The Real Reason for the Season:

[18]Now the generation [or, birth] of Jesus Christ was in this manner: For His mother Mary, having been promised in marriage to Joseph, before they came together [fig., had sexual relations], was found having in [the] womb [fig., to have become pregnant] by [the] Holy Spirit. [19]But Joseph her husband being righteous and not wanting to publicly disgrace her, intended to privately send her away [or, to secretly divorce her].

Trump Fights Back with Statements

[20]But while he was thinking about these [things], look!, an angel [or, a messenger] of [the] Lord appeared to him in a dream, saying, "Joseph, son of David, you should not be afraid to take Mary [as] your wife, for the [Baby] in her was conceived by [the] Holy Spirit. [21]And she will give birth to a Son, and you will call His name Jesus ["Yahweh saves"], for He will save His people from their sins" (Matthew 1:18-21).

[4]But when the fullness [or, completion] of the time came, God sent forth His Son, having been born of a woman, having been born under [the] Law, [5]so that He should redeem [or, set free] the [people] under [the] Law, so that we shall receive the adoption [or, the formal and legal declaration that we are His children] (Galatians 4:4-5).

[5]Indeed, be letting the frame of mind [or, attitude] be in you* which [was] also in Christ Jesus, [6]who existing in the nature of God, did not consider being equal to God something to be held onto, [7]but He emptied Himself, having taken the nature of a bondservant, having come to be in the likeness of people, [8]and having been found in appearance as a person, He humbled Himself, having become obedient to the point of death—even of death of a cross.
[9]And so God highly exalted Him [or, put Him in the most important position] and gave to Him a Name, the [Name] above every name, [10]so that at the Name of Jesus every knee shall bow, of heavenly [ones] and of earthly [ones] and of [ones] under the earth, [11]and every tongue [fig., person] shall confess that Jesus Christ [is] Lord to [the] glory of God [the] Father! [cp. Isaiah 45:23; Rom 10:9] (Philippians 2:3-11).

[15]Trustworthy [is] the word and worthy of all acceptation, that Christ Jesus came into the world to save sinful [people], of whom I am first [fig., the foremost of all]. [16]But because of this, I was shown mercy, so that in me first [fig., as the foremost of all] Jesus Christ should demonstrate all His patience, as a pattern for the ones about to be believing on [or, trusting in] Him to life eternal. [17]Now to the King of the ages [fig., the King eternal], incorruptible, invisible, [the] only wise God, [be] honor and glory into the ages of the ages! [fig., forever and ever!] So be it! (1Timothy 1:15-17; ALT3). Back to Trump.

December 29, 2021

Donald J Trump @RealDonaldTrump
The Unselect Committee of Radical Left Democrats, and two failed Republicans, has just dropped a large portion of their request for my

records and documents—a very big story even though the New York Times refused to put it on the front page. The reason that they dropped the records request is that they don't want this horror show to happen to Biden and Hunter in three years. This also changes the entire complexion of their request, not that there are any documents that would be incriminating or a problem for me—but the Witch Hunt continues! December 29, 2021

To comment, in my *Impeach* trilogy, I warned that with the way Dems lowered the bar for impeachment, it would become a normal political tool, whenever Congress and the President are of different parties.

Donald J Trump @RealDonaldTrump
More cases of COVID-19, sometimes referred to as the China Virus, are recorded in the U.S. today than ever before—not even close, and the Fake News Media refuses to print the real numbers. Do you remember when the Democrats campaign was based on the fact that they would quickly and easily get rid of the China Virus?
Their whole campaign was a lie from Religion, to the Border, to the Military, to the Economy, to Inflation, to the loss of Energy Independence and, of course, most embarrassing of all, to the inept, grossly incompetent withdrawal from Afghanistan. All of those things, together with the Rigged 2020 Presidential Election, are the REAL BIG LIE! December 29, 2021

To comment, the left-wing media is reporting "the real numbers." They are doing all they can to scare the American people into compliance with the new Covid restrictions.
On the other hand, the right-wing media is downplaying the surging Covid cases, hospitalizations, and deaths, wrongly proclaiming the Omicron variant is just a cold, while disparaging the Trump vaccines.
Both approaches are misguided and are leading to unnecessary suffering and death. I will detail such in my *Coronavirus* book.

December 30, 2021

Donald J Trump @RealDonaldTrump
The United States just set a record high for coronavirus infections. Remember when Biden said that he would quickly and easily solve this problem? How's he doing? He now says that it is up to the states, not the Federal Government, exactly the opposite of what he said during the campaign! December 30, 2021

Chapter Thirteen
Trump's Statements
January 2022

These Trump Statements are continued from Chapter Twelve.

January 4, 2022

Donald J Trump @RealDonaldTrump
Anyone want to run for Congress against Don Bacon in Nebraska? January 3, 2022

Donald J Trump @RealDonaldTrump
Twitter is a disgrace to democracy. They shouldn't be allowed to do business in this Country. Marjorie Taylor Greene has a huge constituency of honest, patriotic, hard-working people. They don't deserve what's happened to them on places like low-life Twitter and Facebook. Everybody should drop off of Twitter and Facebook. They're boring, have only a Radical Left point of view, and are hated by everyone. They are a disgrace to our Nation. Keep fighting, Marjorie! January 4, 2022

To comment, for two different takes on this move by Twitter, see the following two articles, the first conservative, the second liberal:

Newsmax. Matt Gaetz to Newsmax: Greene Kicked Off Twitter for 'Challenging the Regime'. https://www.newsmax.com/newsmax-tv/newsmaxtv-mattgaetz-bigtech-censorship/2022/01/03/id/1050875/

NYT. Twitter Permanently Suspends Marjorie Taylor Greene's Account. https://www.nytimes.com/2022/01/02/technology/marjorie-taylor-greene-twitter.html

January 5, 2022

Donald J Trump @RealDonaldTrump
In light of the total bias and dishonesty of the January 6th Unselect Committee of Democrats, two failed Republicans, and the Fake News Media, I am canceling the January 6th Press Conference at Mar-a-Lago

on Thursday, and instead will discuss many of those important topics at my rally on Saturday, January 15th, in Arizona—It will be a big crowd!

What has become more and more obvious to ALL is that the LameStream Media will not report the facts that Nancy Pelosi and the Capitol Sergeant-at-Arms denied requests for the D.C. National Guard or Military to be present at the Capitol. Their emails and correspondence with the Department of Defense exist, but the media won't ask for this evidence, or report the truth!

This is the Democrats' Great Cover-Up Committee and the Media is complicit. Why did Adam "Shifty" Schiff forge and change the statement of Congressman Jim Jordan without any consequence? Why will Crazy Nancy Pelosi not provide her communications with the House Sergeant-at-Arms and the House Chief Administrative Officer, or promise to retain these vital messages, which many feel she has already destroyed—perhaps illegally? Also, why is the primary reason for the people coming to Washington D.C., which is the fraud of the 2020 Presidential Election, not the primary topic of the Unselect Committee's investigation? This was, indeed, the Crime of the Century.

I look forward to seeing our Great American patriots in Arizona next weekend for a big rally to Save America! January 5, 2022

Donald J Trump @RealDonaldTrump

What is happening in Chicago with all the school closures is devastating. Democrats are congregating in mass tomorrow to fan the flames of a divide that THEY created, while our kids sit at home watching their futures vanish. It must stop. Educate our children in person or give every dollar spent on education directly to the students so they can get out of these failing government schools! January 5, 2022

Donald J Trump @RealDonaldTrump

The Biden Administration's response to COVID is getting worse every day. Joe Biden said, "there is no federal solution" to the pandemic, but he then federalized the distribution of antibodies, and red states are getting the short end of the stick. In my administration, we respected the role of Governors to take care of their own states, and they could request antibodies and therapeutics depending on what they needed. That's the way our Country is supposed to be run.

Now, there's talk by the Biden Administration again about closing schools and even vaccine mandates for school children. This is an outrage, and MAGA nation should rise up and oppose this egregious federal government overreach. The Democrats are so incredibly mandate happy—there is discussion about a vaccine mandate for school kids this year in Detroit and other Democrat-run places.

248

Trump Fights Back with Statements

Our administration did what they said could not be done—vaccines in record time. But we never issued mandates, and I never would! People should be able to choose how they want to govern their own health. The federal government must be reined in and give the people back the freedom to decide whether they want to be vaccinated or not.

Joe Biden said he would never issue mandates, but he did it anyway like so many other things. January 5, 2022

To comment, the response of the Biden administration to Covid has been atrocious. As a result, more people have died from Covid under Biden than under Trump, as detailed previously.

January 6, 2022

Donald J Trump @RealDonaldTrump

To watch Biden speaking is very hurtful to many people. They're the ones who tried to stop the peaceful transfer with a rigged election. Just look at the numbers. Does anybody really think that Biden beat Obama with the Black population in select Swing State cities, but nowhere else? That he would lose 18 out of 19 bellwether counties, and 27 out of 27 "toss up" House races, but somehow miraculously receive the most votes in American history with no coattails? That he would lose Florida, Ohio, and Iowa and win, even though it has never been done before?

They spread a "web of lies" about me and Russia for 4 years to try to overturn the 2016 election, and now they lie about how they interfered in the 2020 Election, too. Big Tech was used illegally.

Where did all those votes show up from in Georgia, where it was just revealed they sold ballots for $10 a piece, or in Pennsylvania, and Arizona, and Wisconsin. He acts like he's aggrieved, but we're the ones who were aggrieved and America is suffering because of it with poisonous Borders, record Inflation, a humiliating surrender in Afghanistan, $5 a gallon gas and higher, empty stock shelves, and rampant crime.

America is a laughingstock stock of the world, and it's all because of the real insurrection, which took place on November 3rd, but this is an election year and MAGA Republicans should get elected and work with me to fix this horror that Joe Biden and the Democrats have brought us.

Never forget the crime of the 2020 Presidential Election. Never give up! January 6, 2022

To comment, in his speech on this day, the one-year anniversary of J6, Biden put the blame for the events of J6 on Trump. If you want to know if this claim is true, read Trump's own words. I record them in my *Trump's Tweets* book.

It was the big deal the MSM, Biden, and Dems made of this anniversary that led me to finish my *Tragic Ending* book. I wasn't going to bother, as I figured J6 was old news. But it is clear those three will never let go of it, as it is all Dems and Biden have to run on, given Biden's failing presidency, which I detail in my *Biden Tweets* books.

January 7, 2022

Donald J Trump @RealDonaldTrump

What we witnessed yesterday was the last gasps of a corrupt and discredited left-wing political and media establishment that has, for decades, driven our country into the ground—shipping away our jobs, surrendering our strength, sacrificing our sovereignty, attacking our history and values, and trying to turn America into a country that our people can barely recognize.

These radical leftists in Washington care NOTHING for American Democracy. All they care about is control over you, and wealth and riches for themselves.

But they are failing. No one believes them anymore. And the day is quicky coming when they will be overwhelmingly voted out of power.

Joe Biden's voice is now the voice of desperation and despair.

His handlers gave him that speech to read yesterday because they know the unprecedented failures of his presidency and the left-wing extremism of the Pelosi-Schumer Congress have destroyed the Democrat Party.

Part of their panic is motivated by the realization that, just like the Russia Collusion Hoax, they cannot sustain the preposterous fabrications about January 6 much longer. The truth is coming out.

But for them, the worst part of it all is the knowledge that the American People are seeing right through their phony media event—which despicably compared a Pelosi-led security failure at the Capitol to the darkest days in American history and the deaths of 3,000 Americans.

The people see right through that sham. They see a cynical politician who ran for office promising unity who is now doing the most divisive thing possible—slandering his political opponents as domestic terrorists, just like insecure dictators do in communist countries.

The American People also see that January 6 has become the Democrats' excuse and pretext for the most chilling assault on the civil liberties of American citizens in generations. It is being used to justify outrageous attacks on free speech, widespread censorship, de-platforming, calls for increased domestic surveillance, appalling abuse of political prisoners, labeling opponents of COVID lockdowns and mandates as national security threats, and even ordering the FBI to target parents who object to the radical indoctrination of their children in school.

And this week, January 6 is also the Democrats' excuse for trying to pass a radical Federal takeover of state election law. They are trying to BAN voter ID and other basic measures that can ensure the sacred integrity of the vote. The reason the Democrats are doing all of this is not because they believe they will win a fair and honest election. It's because they know they will overwhelmingly LOSE one.

Remember, I am not the one trying to undermine American Democracy—I am the one trying to SAVE American Democracy. January 7, 2022

To comment, in his speech yesterday, Biden called claims of fraud in the 2020 election "The Big Lie." But is it? I present evidence for irregularities in that election in my *Corruption* book. Read the evidence and decide for yourself.

I discuss Trump's authorization of the National Guard and the refusal of Pelosi and Mayor Bowser to accept that authorization in my *Tragic Ending* book and will elaborate on it in my *J6 Commission* book.

I address the Dem voting bills in my *Biden Tweets* books.

I don't mean to keep referring to my other books in this one, but if I repeated all of that information here, it would extend this book by many pages, probably to being a two-volume set.

Donald J Trump @RealDonaldTrump

Today, I am more confident than ever in the strength and common sense of the American People. They are counting the days until we will no longer have to be constantly lectured, lied to, and dictated to by corrupt politicians and their media partners. When we will no longer have to put up with this broken establishment's hoaxes and its manufactured media narratives—And as Biden and his radical handlers know, that day is coming fast. Because in the months and years ahead, the American People are going to speak up, take action, and VOTE in massive numbers, and we are going to TAKE BACK OUR COUNTRY.

From the very beginning, all that Americans have wanted is great jobs, safe neighborhoods, strong borders, good schools, a proud nation, and a government that LISTENS to the American People. That is what our movement has always been about—and that is what we are focused on to this day.

Joe Biden and the Radical Democrats have failed on every front. But do not lose hope. America WILL be Great Again. January 7, 2022

To comment, Amen on all points!

January 8, 2022

Donald J Trump @RealDonaldTrump

Congratulations to Darren Beattie and @RevolverNews who have exposed so much of the Fake News' false narrative about January 6th. Because of Darren's work, and others, Americans aren't buying into the Unselect Committee's attempts to smear 75 million (plus!) Americans. The newly minted term "Fedsurrection," was even trending! January 8, 2022

To comment, my *Trump's Tweets*, *Tragic Ending*, and forthcoming *J6 Commission* books also expose that false narrative.

January 10, 2022

Donald J Trump @RealDonaldTrump

"Senator" Mike Rounds of the Great State of South Dakota just went woke on the Fraudulent Presidential Election of 2020. He made a statement this weekend on ABC Fake News, that despite massive evidence to the contrary, including much of it pouring in from Wisconsin, Georgia, Arizona, Michigan, Pennsylvania, and other states, he found the election to be ok—just fine.

Is he crazy or just stupid? The numbers are conclusive, and the fraudulent and irregular votes are massive. The only reason he did this is because he got my endorsement and easily won his state in 2020, so now he thinks he has time, and those are the only ones, the weak, who will break away. Even though his election will not be coming up for 5 years, I will never endorse this jerk again.

It's RINOs like this that are allowing the Democrats to destroy our Nation! Our Borders, our Military, our Economy, Inflation, the horrible handling of the China Virus and Afghanistan, and rampant crime throughout our Democrat-run cities are ripping our Country apart. We are a laughingstock throughout the world when we were respected and even feared just 1 year ago. There were no thoughts of Russia with

252

Ukraine, China with Taiwan, Iran with nuclear weapons, or North Korea with nasty statements.

The Radical Left Democrats and RINOS, like "Senator" Mike Rounds, do not make it easy for our Country to succeed. He is a weak and ineffective leader, and I hereby firmly pledge that he will never receive my Endorsement again! January 10, 2022

To comment, your paragraph about the failures of the Biden administration is where you and all Republicans need to focus. Continuing to harp about 2020 will not enable us to retake the House and Senate this year. But emphasizing Biden's failures and tying all Dem candidates to them will do the trick. That is the reason for my *Biden Tweets* books.

Donald J Trump @RealDonaldTrump

Matt DePerno, running for Attorney General in the Great State of Michigan, is doing a great job. He has energized the Republican base against the RINOs and Crooked Democrats, especially as it pertains to Election Integrity. I have fully endorsed Matt because of his past accomplishments as a warrior lawyer. He is exactly what Michigan needs! January 10, 2022

January 11, 2022

Donald J Trump @RealDonaldTrump

Stacey Abrams helped Biden steal the 2020 Election in Georgia but now she won't even share a stage with Joe. Stacey knows that Biden actually lost BIG in Georgia, and in the 2020 Presidential Election as a whole, and he's been so terrible she now wants nothing to do with him. Even the woke, radical left realizes that Joe Biden's Administration is an embarrassment! January 11, 2022

To comment, your last sentence is probably the main reason Stacy did not attend. She knows the Biden administration is already a sinking ship, and she does not want to go down with it as she prepares to run for governor again in Georgia.

January 13, 2022

Donald J Trump @RealDonaldTrump

The Supreme Court has spoken, confirming what we all knew: Biden's disastrous mandates are unconstitutional. Biden promised to shut down the virus, not the economy but he has failed miserably on both—and mandates would have further destroyed the economy. We are proud of the Supreme Court for not backing down. No mandates! January 13, 2022

Extended Comment
SCOTUS Mandates Rulings

SCOTUS struck down Biden's mandate that all businesses with over 100 employees must make sure their employees are vaccinated. But it left in place the mandate for healthcare workers to be vaccinated. That is because most all hospitals receive Medicare reimbursements, and with government money always comes government control.

The Supreme Court has stopped the Biden administration from enforcing a requirement that employees at large businesses be vaccinated against covid-19 or undergo weekly testing and wear a mask on the job.

At the same time, the court is allowing the administration to proceed with a vaccine mandate for most health care workers in the U.S.

The vaccine mandate that the court will allow to be enforced nationwide scraped by on a 5-4 vote, with Chief Justice John Roberts and Justice Brett Kavanaugh joining the liberals to form a majority. The mandate covers virtually all health care workers in the country, applying to providers that receive federal Medicare or Medicaid funding. It potentially affects 76,000 health care facilities as well as home health care providers. The rule has medical and religious exemptions (AP. Supreme).

January 14, 2022

Donald J Trump @RealDonaldTrump

Look forward to seeing everyone in Arizona tomorrow! Many topics will be discussed including the Rigged Presidential Election of 2020, the fake Big Lie, the corrupt LameStream Media, the Afghanistan disaster, Inflation, the sudden lack of respect for our Nation and its leaders, and much more. Big crowds, will also be covered on TV. See you Saturday evening! January 14, 2022

To comment, this rally was aired on Newsmax. But that is the only station I know of that did so. Newsmax also discussed the rally on its website:

Making his return to campaign-style rallies Saturday [1/15/22], former President Donald Trump told his large crowd to "get out and vote, and make sure it's not a rigged vote, please."

Making his return to campaign-style rallies Saturday, former President Donald Trump told his large crowd to "get out and vote, and make sure it's not a rigged vote, please."

"This crowd is a massive symbol of what took place, because the people are hungry for the truth: They want their country back," Trump told his Save America rally in Florence, Arizona, which lasted almost two hours. "I want their country back, between the open borders and the bad elections, and we were always thought of as a beautiful country that had fair elections, and now we're laughing stock all over the world for many reasons."

At the end of his speech, he teased a return to the campaign trail in the 2024 presidential election (Newsmax. Trump: 'In).

January 19, 2022

Donald J Trump @RealDonaldTrump
How come Biden picks a reporter off a list, in all cases softball questions, and then reads the answer? I would never have been allowed to get away with that, nor would I have to!

`To comment, Trump is referring to Biden's press conference on January 19, 2022, the day before the end of Biden's first year in office. I cover that press conference in detail in the final chapter of my book *Biden Tweets: Volume Two*.

Here, I will say, to be fair, Biden did go off-script in the second hour and call on one reporter each from Fox News and Newsmax, but he didn't answer their questions.

January 20, 2022

Donald J Trump @RealDonaldTrump
President Biden admitted yesterday, in his own very different way, that the 2020 election may very well have been a fraud, which I know it was. I'm sure his representatives, who work so hard to make it look legit, are not happy.

To comment, Trump is probably referring to the following:

President Joe Biden is facing heat after he said during a rare press conference Wednesday that the 2022 midterm elections could be "illegitimate."

The president then went on a tangent speculating what would have happened after the 2020 election if then-Vice President Mike Pence submitted to pressure by Trump and his allies to try and block electoral votes on the day of the Capitol riot.

When the reporter, RealClearPoltics's Philip Wegmann, formerly of the Washington Examiner, told Biden he meant solely the 2022 election, the president did not back down from his assertion that there could be problems with the midterm elections....

"Oh, yeah, I think it could easily be illegitimate," Biden said, stumbling through his response....

"The prospect of being an illegitimate is in direct proportion to us being able to get these reforms passed, but I don't think ... you're going to see the Democratic Party give up on coming back," Biden said (Washington Examiner. Biden says).

January 21, 2022

Donald J Trump @RealDonaldTrump

My phone call to the Secretary of State of Georgia was perfect, perhaps even more so than my call with the Ukrainian President, if that's possible. I knew there were large numbers of people on the line, including numerous lawyers for both sides. Although I assumed the call may have been inappropriately, and perhaps illegally, recorded, I was not informed of that. I didn't say anything wrong in the call, made while I was President on behalf of the United States of America, to look into the massive voter fraud which took place in Georgia.

Just last week, it was further determined that they are looking into ballot harvesting in Fulton County, after supposedly watching tapes of it actually taking place. This alone could be tens of thousands of votes. What this Civil Special Grand Jury should be looking into is not my perfect phone call, but the large scale voter fraud that took place in Georgia. Then they would be doing a great job for the people. No more political witch hunts! January 21, 2022

To comment, I record the transcript for the Georgia call, along with my running commentary, in my *Trump's Tweets* book.

Trump Fights Back with Statements

I record the transcript for the Ukrainian call in my Volume One of my *Impeach* trilogy.

Read what Trump said and decide for yourself if he said anything wrong, illegal, or impeachable in those two phone calls.

Donald J Trump @RealDonaldTrump
Meat Loaf was a great guy—got to know him very well doing Celebrity Apprentice. He was smart, talented, open, and warm.

His success was enormous—we all loved him. Meat Loaf will be greatly missed! January 21, 2022

To comment, this Statement is in regard to the death of Classic Rocker Meat Loaf. He is best known for his song, "Paradise by the Dashboard Light." Though "Bat Out of [Expletive]" is great too, despite the foul language.

January 22, 2022

Donald J Trump @RealDonaldTrump
So let me get this straight, I am being investigated in Georgia for asking an Attorney General with many lawyers and others knowingly on the phone to look for corruption, which definitely took place in the Georgia Presidential election—but the people who committed the crime are in no way, shape, or form under investigation and are instead being protected? The people looking for the crime are being hounded and the people who committed the crime are being protected. This is not the American way. January 22, 2022

Donald J Trump @RealDonaldTrump
As you gather together today for the March for Life, I am with you in spirit! January 22, 2022

To comment, Trump was the first President to actually attend the March for Life. And his three great Supreme Court appointments later finally ended the nationwide holocaust, though it remains in blue states.

January 24, 2022

Donald J Trump @RealDonaldTrump
Some RINO Republicans in Wisconsin are working hand in hand with others to have drop boxes again placed in Wisconsin. These fools

are playing right into the Democrats' hand. Drop boxes are only good for Democrats and cheating, not good for Republicans. January 24, 2022

To comment, the Wisconsin Supreme Court will later rule those drop boxes are illegal, as I will report in my *J6 Commission* book.

January 25, 2022

Donald J Trump @RealDonaldTrump
What's happening with Russia and Ukraine would never have happened under the Trump Administration. Not even a possibility! January 25, 2022

Donald J Trump @RealDonaldTrump
Really big crowd expected in Texas this weekend. The rallies are bigger than ever before—so much to talk about! January 25, 2022

Donald J Trump @RealDonaldTrump
Jessie Watters Primetime launches tonight at 7PM on Fox News. The show will be a great success! January 25, 2022

To comment, Jessie is okay. I preferred the rotating hosts. It made it more interesting to tune in just to see who was hosting that week.

January 26, 2022

Donald J Trump @RealDonaldTrump
Ted Budd, who I endorsed many months ago for the U.S. Senate, is now leading the pack in North Carolina. He is the true America First fighter who stands strong for the Second Amendment, fights for our great Military and Law Enforcement, and has tremendous courage fighting against the Woke Mob who wants to destroy America. I am proud of him, and he is going to win big. Ted Budd is the ONLY U.S. Senate candidate in North Carolina who has my Complete and Total Endorsement! January 26, 2022

Donald J Trump @RealDonaldTrump
I am told the very strong and impressive Morgan Ortagus is exploring a run for Congress in Tennessee's 5th Congressional District. I couldn't be happier because she's an absolute warrior for America First and MAGA! Morgan was fantastic in her role working with Secretary Mike Pompeo at the U.S. State Department and understands the threats

posed by China, Russia, Iran and others, and will be tough, not just roll over like the Democrats and RINOs. She serves in the U.S. Navy Reserves and will fight for our Military. She won't bow to the Woke Mob or the Leftist LameStream Media. Morgan Ortagus will have my Complete and Total Endorsement if she decides to run! January 26, 2022

Donald J Trump @RealDonaldTrump
Looking forward to seeing everyone in Conroe, Texas. Will be big! January 26, 2022

January 28, 2022

Donald J Trump @RealDonaldTrump
BIG news out of Pennsylvania!
The practice of no-excuse mail-in ballots, put in place by Democrats right before the stolen 2020 Election, has been ruled UNCONSTITUTIONAL by the Pennsylvania Commonwealth Court.
Here is the key question: If widespread mail-in balloting is unconstitutional in Pennsylvania now, how could mail-in balloting have been constitutional in the RIGGED 2020 Presidential Election then?
We all know the answer—it wasn't!
All American Patriots are thanking the Commonwealth Court of Pennsylvania for having the courage to do the right thing! January 28, 2022

Extended Comment
PA Mail-in Balloting Rulings

I discuss this unconstitutional changing of our election laws in my *Corruption* book. Here, I want to update this issue.
Previously, PA only allowed absentee ballots for those with one of several possible "excuses" as to why they could not make it to their polling place in person, such as disability or truly being absent from their precinct on Election Day. But that was changed in 2019 to allow "no excuse" mail-in ballots. That led to a massive increase in the number of people voting via mail-in ballots.

Mail-in voting has been heavily used since the beginning of the pandemic in the spring of 2020. In that year's general election, 2.6 million mail-in ballots were cast in Pennsylvania. As of August, there were more than 1.3 million voters on Pennsylvania's permanent mail-in ballot list....

In the past, absentee voting was allowed only for people who were unable to go to the polls because of illness or disability, or were away because of work, religious holiday or election day duties (Trib Live. Pa.).

A challenge was made to that change in our absentee ballot/ mail-in ballot law after the 2020 election, and that challenge was successful. But it took over a year to occur.

> Pennsylvania's Commonwealth Court on Friday [1/28/22] ruled that the state's system of mail-in voting, passed in 2019, is unconstitutional and the only way to implement it is by constitutional amendment.
> The court's opinion said the decision "explains how a system of no-excuse mail-in voting may be constitutionally implemented in the commonwealth and expresses no view on whether such a system should, or should not, be implemented as a matter of public policy."
> The 3-2 Republican majority opinion was immediately appealed to the state Supreme Court, said Attorney General Josh Shapiro (Trib Live. Pa.)

This was a correct ruling. However, the Supreme Court of Pennsylvania (SCOPA) has a 5-2 Dem majority and will most certainly overturn this ruling.

> The Commonwealth Court of Pennsylvania on Friday found the state's mail-in voting law unconstitutional.
> The lawsuit was filed by Doug McLinko, vice chairman of the Bradford County Board of Commissioners in Pennsylvania. His argument was that he was unable to perform his duties as commissioner and certify the 2020 election because Pennsylvania's 2019 election reform law is unconstitutional....
> In October 2019, Act 77 was signed into law by Democratic Gov. Tom Wolf with support from both parties. The law, described by PennLive "as the most significant change to Pennsylvania's election laws in more than 80 years," greatly expands mail-in voting by allowing a citizen to vote by mail without an excuse....
> The act "should have been put on the ballot, and the constitution should have been changed to allow it, like bulk case laws," the Bradford County Commissioner said (Just the News. Court).

What McLinko says is exactly what I said in my prior book. Since Act 77 amounted to a change to the PA Constitution, it required a constitutional amendment to be enacted. That requires for it to be passed by two successive state legislatures, to be announced in two newspapers in every one of our 67 counties, and to be placed on a state-wide ballot.

However, none of that was done. Act 77 was just passed with a vote of the legislature and signed into law by Gov. Wolf, and that was that. That was nowhere near sufficient for such a major change in our elections. Hence why the Commonwealth Court's ruling was correct.

However, as a later update, sadly but just as I predicted, our Dem-majority SCOPA voted to overturn that ruling.

> The state Supreme Court has upheld Pennsylvania's mail ballot law, preserving for the time being a popular voting method that passed the legislature with bipartisan support but was later challenged by Republican elected officials.
>
> In a 5-2 decision released Tuesday [8/3/22], the justices rejected the GOP argument that the legislature did not have the power under the state constitution to allow Pennsylvanians to vote by mail without an excuse.
>
> The 2019 law, known as Act 77 and employed for the first time during the contentious 2020 presidential election, ushered in the most sweeping expansion of voting access in Pennsylvania in decades.
>
> More challenges to the law are on the horizon. Republican elected officials who brought the suit said Tuesday that they plan to appeal to the U.S. Supreme Court. (Trib Live. Pa. Pa. Supreme).

Predictably, that 5-2 vote was along party lines. Courts should not be political, but apparently, SCOPA is political.

I seriously doubt SCOTUS will even take the case, as it has been reluctant to get involved in state election issues, so most likely, this ruling will stand and PA will remain open to the potential fraud that no-excuse mail-in balloting facilitates.

January 29, 2022

Donald J Trump @RealDonaldTrump
Big crowd already gathering in Texas for tonight, see you there! January 29, 2022

January 31, 2022

Donald J Trump @RealDonaldTrump

If the Vice President (Mike Pence) had "absolutely no right" to change the Presidential Election results in the Senate, despite fraud and many other irregularities, how come the Democrats and RINO Republicans, like Wacky Susan Collins, are desperately trying to pass legislation that will not allow the Vice President to change the results of the election? Actually, what they are saying, is that Mike Pence did have the right to change the outcome, and they now want to take that right away. Unfortunately, he didn't exercise that power, he could have overturned the Election! January 31, 2022

Extended Comment
Pence and the 2020 Election

This statement is in regard to the following:

There is a movement in Congress to reform the Electoral Count Act, which was enacted in 1887 and deals with the counting of electoral votes after a presidential election. It allows lawmakers to object to certifying electoral votes while Congress oversees the count of the states' votes.

Rep. Zoe Lofgren, D-Calif., told NPR that "this is a statute that's over 100 years old. It has ancient language that may not be as clear as we'd want, and we are now observing the potential of threats to the orderly running of elections and apolitical running of elections in the future" (Newsmax. Trump: Effort).

Former President Donald Trump issued a statement Sunday firing back against Sen. Susan Collins (R-Maine) and blaming former Vice President Mike Pence for not overturning the 2020 election....

`Collins spoke with ABC's George Stephanopoulos on Sunday about her efforts to lead a bipartisan group of 16 senators to reform the Electoral College Act.

"We saw, on January sixth of 2021, how ambiguities… were exploited. We need to prevent that from happening again," she told Stephanopoulos. "I'm hopeful that we can come up with a bipartisan bill that will make very clear that the vice president's role is simply ministerial, that he has no ability to halt the count."

Trump Fights Back with Statements

The House Jan. 6 panel is also reportedly discussing how to limit the vice president's role in certifying election results (Just the News. Donald).

Whether Trump's reasoning here is correct or not is hard to say. But Collins is correct that the language needs to be clarified, so as to avoid confusion in the future.

Moreover, Pence, in his first public disagreement with his former boss, emphatically declared he did not have such authority. He declared:

> President Trump is wrong. I had no right to overturn the election...
>
> January 6, 2021 was a dark day in the history of the United States Capitol....
>
> The American people must know that we will always keep our oath to the Constitution, even when it would be politically expedient to do otherwise.... "Elections are conducted at the state level, not by Congress" ... "the only role of Congress with respect to the Electoral College is to open and count votes submitted and certified by the states. No more, no less....
>
> Frankly there is no idea more un-American than the notion that any one person could choose the American president. Under the Constitution, I had no right to change the outcome of our election. And Kamala Harris will have no right to overturn the election when we beat them in 2024...
>
> The truth is, there's more at stake than our party or political fortunes. Men and women, if we lose faith in the Constitution, we won't just lose elections — we'll lose our country (adapted from Trib Live/ AP. Pence).

Pence is correct in the last paragraph—if we lose faith in our Constitution, we lose our country. However, he is a bit confused as to what Trump was asking him to do. It was not for Pence "to overturn the election" or for "one person" to "choose the American president."

What Trump wanted was for Pence to declare the Electoral votes of several states to be invalid due to irregularities in each of those state's voting. He wanted each of those states to be given the opportunity to review their vote counts to be sure they were indeed accurate, then resend them back to Congress after that review.

The only dispute was if in fact Pence had the authority to require such a review. The AP is probably correct in its comments in this regard:

Vice presidents play only a ceremonial role in the the [sic] counting of Electoral College votes, and any attempt to interfere in the count would have represented a profound break from precedent and democratic norms (Trib Live/ AP. Pence).

The AP comments here echo mine in my *Corruption* book. No matter how much Trump might argue otherwise, Pence's only role was that of a MC at an awards show, that being to read the results of the previous vote, and that is it. Thus, Pence is correct that Trump was wrong, even if he was a bit confused as to what Trump was asking of him.

Back to Trump.

Donald J Trump @RealDonaldTrump

AT&T is closing the very popular One America News Network (OAN) because too many people are watching. They couldn't put up with that any longer. Conservatives/Republicans should boycott Direct TV, and while you're at it, "Concast's" Xfinity as well. These are Radical Left Lunatics who are destroying our Nation! January 31, 2022

To comment, my Xfinity/ Comcast system does not carry OAN, so I have never watched it. But it does carry Newsmax and Fox News, which are my two main sources of TV News. I also watch my local ABC affiliate (WTAE) and *CBS Evening News* every day. That gives me a variety of perspectives.

Chapter Fourteen
Trump's Statements
February 2022

These Trump Statements are continued from Chapter Thirteen.

February 1, 2022

Donald J Trump @RealDonaldTrump
Highly respected Dinesh D'Souza, working together with Catherine Engelbrecht of True the Vote, just released a trailer to their new movie, "2,000 Mules," that shows the world exactly how the 2020 Presidential Election was Rigged and Stolen. The movie exposes the lies of the Democrats, RINOs, and Fake News who say it was the "most secure election in history." It was, perhaps, the least secure in history. The ballot box was stuffed, and stuffed like never before—and it's all on video. Ballots were trafficked and sold in a massive operation in each Swing State.

The evidence is so damning, what will the cowards who sat and did nothing about the stolen election say now? The way our votes were taken away is a disgrace to our Nation. It must be fixed. February 1, 2022

Donald J Trump @RealDonaldTrump
So pathetic to watch the Unselect Committee of political hacks, liars, and traitors work so feverishly to alter the Electoral College Act so that a Vice President cannot ensure the honest results of the election, when just one year ago they said that "the Vice President has absolutely no right to ensure the true outcome or results of an election." In other words, they lied, and the Vice President did have this right or, more pointedly, could have sent the votes back to various legislators for reassessment after so much fraud and irregularities were found.

If it were sent back to the legislators, or if Nancy Pelosi, who is in charge of Capitol security, had taken my recommendation and substantially increased security, there would have been no "January 6" as we know it! Therefore, the Unselect Committee should be investigating why Nancy Pelosi did such a poor job of overseeing security and why Mike Pence did not send back the votes for recertification or approval, in that it has now been shown that he clearly had the right to do so! February 1, 2022

Donald J Trump @RealDonaldTrump

The Fake News Media has done everything in their power not to report the record setting $122 million that has been raised for Save America and publicly announced last night, they hate that I broke all records. The Failing New York Times refuses to acknowledge that the power of the Trump endorsement is far stronger today than ever before—it is virtually unblemished! Our Country can never be strong again unless we have an honest, open, and fair media and sadly, our media is largely fake and corrupt. The people of our Country demand the truth! February 1, 2022

To comment, Trump is referring to the following:

Former President Trump's political operation raised over $51 million in the second half of 2021, according to new federal filings.

The fundraising haul brings Trump's total campaign war chest entering 2022 to $122 million — roughly double the Republican National Committee's cash on hand, according to The New York Times.

The millions give Trump, who has continued to solicit online political contributions since leaving office about 13 months ago, a solid head start on other possible 2024 presidential contenders should he seek reelection (Just the News. Trump raised).

February 3, 2022

Donald J Trump @RealDonaldTrump

Jeff Zucker, a world-class sleazebag who has headed ratings and real-news-challenged CNN for far too long, has been terminated for numerous reasons, but predominantly because CNN has lost its way with viewers and everybody else. Now is a chance to put Fake News in the backseat because there may not be anything more important than straightening out the horrendous LameStream Media in our Country, and in the case of CNN, throughout the World. Jeff Zucker is gone—congratulations to all! February 3, 2022

Donald J Trump @RealDonaldTrump

I wouldn't! [photoshopped picture of Biden in an airline pilots uniform. The captions askes, "If this were the pilot, would you get on the airplane?] February 3, 2022

Trump Fights Back with Statements

Donald J Trump @RealDonaldTrump

Why isn't the corrupt Unselect Committee of political hacks and highly partisan sleazebags in Washington investigating the massive voter fraud and irregularities that took place in the 2020 Presidential Election, rather than spending all of its time investigating those who were protesting its result? It was the Crime of the Century! Large-scale proof of fraud and serious irregularities exist all over the place. Also, why is Crazy Nancy Pelosi and her files, which reportedly have been largely destroyed and deleted, not under investigation for not properly securing the Capitol with Soldiers or the National Guard that were strongly recommended to her by me and others?

I knew the crowd would be extraordinarily large because they were protesting the RIGGED ELECTION. Capitol security was her job, not the President's, and the American people now know that. If she did with security what she should have, there would have been no "January 6" as we know it. The Fake Unselect Committee wants nothing to do with that subject because they know it was the fault of Nancy Pelosi and, to a lesser extent, the Mayor of D.C. So, if I recommend Soldiers and if she refused to use them, why am I, and those around me, responsible for anything? We're not, plain and simple! February 3, 2022

Donald J Trump @RealDonaldTrump

Why isn't the Unselect Committee investigating the massive ballot harvesting operation that has just been irrefutably reported, on tape, in Georgia and other Swing States? Game changer, among many other game changers! February 3, 2022

To comment, ballot harvesting, the collecting of multitudes of ballots, is the subject of the aforementioned *2000 Mules* documentary.

Donald J Trump @RealDonaldTrump

Jeff Zucker is not out at CNN for "concealing a relationship" as the Fake New York Times writes on its front page headline. Zucker is happy and proud (and lucky!) that he can have a relationship. He is out because of horrible ratings down 90%, an all-time low! February 3, 2022

February 4, 2022

Donald J Trump @RealDonaldTrump

Bernie Moreno of Ohio is leaving the race for Senate, but I would like to thank him for his time and effort, and that of his wonderful family. I was very impressed with Bernie who was tough on illegal immigration which, after the Biden disaster at the Border, has become a big issue for all candidates. He has done much for Ohio and loves his State and our great MAGA Movement. His decision will help ensure the MAGA Ticket wins BIG, as it is all over the Country. Thank you, Bernie, for your support and keep fighting! February 4, 2022

Donald J Trump @RealDonaldTrump

The stench of Jeff Zucker is finally leaving CNN. The air over there, the Radical Left will be happy to hear, is being made more "environmentally friendly." The carbon footprint is looking better. But the stench remains, and also at low-rated MSDNC, where weak leaders like Brian Roberts, of "Concast," who are under the thumb of the Left, don't allow the truth to be told. Stockholders should not treat these companies well. We need a free and open press in our Country, and we need it now! February 4, 2022

February 5, 2022

Donald J Trump @RealDonaldTrump

If Nancy Pelosi does her job on security, there is no "January 6." So the corrupt Unselect Committee should stop its work immediately! The Committee is nothing but a cover up for Pelosi's failure to act and Biden's failed Administration. The more time the Fake News Media spends talking about this, the less time they have to talk about Inflation, the horrendously implemented Afghanistan withdrawal, rising gas prices, loss of energy independence, Woke military leaders, etc. That's what the Radical Left Dems want! February 5, 2022

To comment, all correct observations. I cover each of these failures in my *Biden Tweets* books.

Donald J Trump @RealDonaldTrump

Just saw Mike Pence's statement on the fact that he had no right to do anything with respect to the Electoral Vote Count, other than being an automatic conveyor belt for the Old Crow Mitch McConnell to get Biden elected President as quickly as possible. Well, the Vice President's position is not an automatic conveyor if obvious signs of voter fraud or irregularities exist. That's why the Democrats and RINOs are working feverishly together to change the very law that Mike Pence and his unwitting advisors used on January 6 to say he had no choice. The reason they want it changed is because they now say they don't want the Vice President to have the right to ensure an honest vote.

In other words, I was right and everyone knows it. If there is fraud or large scale irregularities, it would have been appropriate to send those votes back to the legislatures to figure it out. The Dems and RINOs want to take that right away. A great opportunity lost, but not forever, in the meantime our Country is going to [expletive]! February 5, 2022

February 6, 2022

Donald J Trump @RealDonaldTrump
Mike Pence said he had no authority other than to send the votes forward to the Old Crow, Mitch McConnell. If so, why are the Dems and RINOs fighting so hard to make it impossible for a VP to do so in the future? February 6, 2022

To comment, these statements were Trump's response to Pence's comments that I quoted in the previous chapter. Even though these two seemed to have made up shortly after J6, as I reported in my *Tragic Ending* book, it is clear there is still animosity between them. Things could get really heated if they both decide to run in 2024.

Donald J Trump @RealDonaldTrump
Republicans are getting absolutely creamed with the phony redistricting going on all over the Country. Even the Fake New York Times is having a hard time believing how ridiculous things have gotten. We were expecting to do well in New York and now, we'll lose 4 seats and the Old Broken-Down Crow, Mitch McConnell, sits back and does nothing to help the Party. The only thing the Democrats are good at is cheating on elections, and the proof is out for everybody to see but hold on, you haven't seen anything yet! February 6, 2022

Donald J Trump @RealDonaldTrump
The ballot harvesting scam will go down as the biggest political scandal in history. It is totally determinative, and the Democrats are doing everything they can to stop the news from coming out. Republicans must be strong and unified in order to save our Country! February 6, 2022

Donald J Trump @RealDonaldTrump
Congratulations to the Republican National Committee (RNC) and its Chairwoman, Ronna McDaniel, on their great ruling in censuring Liz Cheney and Cryin' Adam Kinzinger, two horrible RINOs who put themselves ahead of our Country. They have almost no approval ratings,

and the Republican Party would be far better off without them! February 6, 2022

Donald J Trump @RealDonaldTrump
On Monday [2/7/22] the incredible people of Iowa exercise their sacred right to peaceably assemble and participate in the great Iowa Caucus! One of the most time-honored and American of traditions. Neighbors will join together to cast their votes and determine their future. However, the corrupt and elitist Democrat Establishment wants to steal Iowa's First-in-the-Nation status. They want to limit your freedoms, silence your voices, strangle your livelihoods, and restrict your God-given right to nominate your political leaders.
Coastal Democrats allow illegal aliens to vote in California and New York, but are attempting to stifle the free speech of great American Patriots. With me, Iowa will ALWAYS keep its first-in-the-Nation status. The great people of Middle America will have a powerful vote and voice. Iowans, make sure you go out on Monday and participate in your precinct caucus!
Thank you to Governor Reynolds, Senator Grassley, and Chairman Kaufmann for fighting hard against the Radical Democrats! February 6, 2022

February 7, 2022

Donald J Trump @RealDonaldTrump
My Ambassador to Israel, David Friedman, has written a memoir in which he explains how our foreign policy of "peace through strength" brought about unprecedented support for Israel and once-in-a-lifetime peace agreements between Israel and five Muslim nations (with more to come)—the Abraham Accords. His book is aptly named, Sledgehammer: How Breaking with the Past Brought Peace to the Middle East. Go to http://Sledgehammerbook.com to order your copy and learn more about how American foreign policy is supposed to work—making us stronger, safer, and more prosperous at home and abroad. Congrats to David on a great new book! http://sledgehammerbook.com/ February 7, 2022

Donald J Trump @RealDonaldTrump
There would have been no January 6, as we know it, if Nancy Pelosi heeded my recommendation to bring 10,000 Soldiers, or the National Guard, into the Capitol. End the Unselect Committee January 6th Witch Hunt right now. Pelosi and the Dems are responsible! February 7, 2022

270

Trump Fights Back with Statements

To comment, I postulate in my *Tragic Ending* book that J6 was a setup. Nancy and Mayor Bowers did not want the National Guard to prevent any possible disturbance, as they wanted something to happen, just so they could pin it on Trump and Republicans in general.

That is why both of them need to be interviewed by the "Unselect Committee" (or J6 Commission as I call it). But don't hold your breath, as that Commission is not searching for the truth. Its forgone conclusion will be that Trump was responsible. That was predetermined when Jim Banks and Jim Jordan were not allowed on the Commission.

Donald J Trump @RealDonaldTrump

If AT&T/DirecTV cancels OAN, I hope that everyone will boycott and cancel DirecTV. It is a very popular channel, far more popular than most would understand, and they are being treated horribly by the Radical Left lunatics running the networks. Instead of being allowed to grow, their voice is being shuttered. Don't let it happen, cancel DirecTV. If you feel infringed by what this Communist movement is doing, cancel DirecTV! February 7, 2022

Donald J Trump @RealDonaldTrump

Joe Rogan is an interesting and popular guy, but he's got to stop apologizing to the Fake News and Radical Left maniacs and lunatics. How many ways can you say you're sorry? Joe, just go about what you do so well and don't let them make you look weak and frightened. That's not you and it never will be! February 7, 2022

Extended Comment
Joe Rogan and Spotify

Trump is referring to the following:

Popular U.S. podcaster Joe Rogan has apologized amid a backlash against COVID-19 misinformation in his program, while his platform, Spotify Technology SA , said it would add a "content advisory" to any episode with discussion of COVID.

Rogan, a prominent vaccine skeptic, has stirred controversy with his views on the pandemic and on vaccines and government mandates to control the spread of the virus.

Singer-songwriters Neil Young and Joni Mitchell announced last week that they were removing their music from Spotify in protest at coronavirus misinformation broadcast on the platform..

"If I p***ed you off, I'm sorry," Rogan said. "I will do my best to try to balance out these more controversial viewpoints with other people's perspectives so we can maybe find a better point of view" (Newsmax. Joe Rogan).

Rogan's interviews with Malone and another scientist skeptical of COVID vaccines, Peter McCullough, prompted a campaign by some scientists to deplatform him from Spotify, which said his podcast was its most popular globally last year.

Veteran musicians Neil Young and Joni Mitchell notably demanded the removal of their catalogs from Spotify for platforming Rogan. The streaming giant split the baby Sunday [1/30/22], imposing new COVID content warnings that resemble Facebook's without overtly penalizing its cash-cow host.

The "advisory" will point listeners to its COVID hub with "data-driven facts [and] up-to-date information as shared by scientists, physicians, academics and public health authorities around the world, as well as links to trusted sources," CEO Daniel Ek wrote (Just the News. Big Tech).

Rogan responded to the fallout on Sunday, saying in a video on Instagram that he was only seeking to have conversations on his podcast with people who have "differing opinions."

"I'm not trying to promote misinformation, I'm not trying to be controversial," Rogan said. "I've never tried to do anything with this podcast other than to just talk to people."

He also said that he schedules the guests on his podcast himself, and that he would try to book doctors with different opinions right after he talks to "the controversial ones." Rogan noted that he earlier sat down on the show with Dr. Sanjay Gupta, the chief medical correspondent for CNN, Dr. Michael Osterholm, who is a member of President Joe Biden's COVID-19 advisory board, and Dr. Peter Hotez from Baylor College of Medicine.

Rogan additionally welcomed the idea of adding advisories before podcasts related to COVID-19 (WTAE/ AP. Joe Rogan).

In 2020, Spotify purchased the exclusive rights to Rogan's podcast in a deal reportedly worth over $100 million.

Rogan, whom critics have accuses [sic] of promoting COVID misinformation on his podcasts, said Sunday that he consistently seeks out individuals to come on his show who have "differing opinions" but that he's "very happy" with Spotify's decision.

"I'm not trying to promote misinformation," he said in an Instagram video post. "I'm not trying to be controversial. I've never tried to do anything with this podcast other than to just talk to people" (Just the News. Spotify).

I have never listened to Rogan. But I will say, in general, it is never wise to say you're sorry to the woke mob. It will never do any good, as it will never be enough. The mob knows nothing about grace and forgiveness. But wait until one of them needs grace and forgiveness, and then they will learn that such is needed for all of us, as we all mess up sooner or later.

Moreover, lost in all of the ruckus is that Rogan did give the other side a say.

He has also interviewed medical figures aligned with the COVID establishment, Sanjay Gupta and Michael Osterholm, because his goal is having "interesting conversations with people that have differing opinions," he said. What interests Rogan is "how people come to these conclusions and what the facts are" (Just the News. Big Tech).

I think it is good for people to hear both sides then decide. That is the whole point of my Covid writings, to counteract the false misinformation pushed by both the right and the left. But Rogan appears to have presented both sides, if you listen to him long enough. But the left picks and choses only those guests they deem to have presented misinformation, while ignoring the guests they probably would agree with.

Finally, this is a complicated case, made more complicated by the complexities of the music industry.

Though Peter Frampton and David Crosby voiced support for Young, their albums remain available for Spotify's millions of subscribers.

The reasons why more artists haven't abandoned Spotify include a stew of political hesitancies, music ownership complications and business incentives. The issues speak to the trickiness of the debate over covid-19 misinformation, free speech, music rights and the role of Spotify in the modern music industry....

Even when artists want to leave Spotify — and some do — it isn't as simple as pressing the skip button. The top musicians typically don't have direct relationships with streaming services; their music appears on the app through licensing deals with their labels and publishers.

The big labels — Universal Music, Sony Music and Warner Music — all have licensing deals with Spotify, as do the indies through music rights agency Merlin. Artists such as Mitchell have to go through their labels to get their tunes off the platform.

Many artists don't even own their catalogs, creating additional difficulties (Trib Live/ Los Angeles Times. Why).

February 8, 2022

Donald J Trump @RealDonaldTrump

The Biden Administration now says "conspiracy theories" about elections are the greatest threat to the homeland. Does the Department of Homeland Security include in its list of conspiracy theories the on tape irrefutable evidence of massive "Ballot Harvesting" in the Swing States? Do they include more votes than voters, and the fact that in Georgia thousands of duplicate votes were scanned and voter fraud was committed with 100-0 falsified vote counts for Joe Biden?

Do they include in Wisconsin more than twice the election margin voted without ever showing Voter ID, which is illegal, or the widespread fraud uncovered in nursing homes? Or how 23,344 mail-in ballots were counted, despite the person no longer living at that address in Arizona, and that there was over 100% turnout for mail-in ballots in precincts in Pima County. What about the many violations of the Constitution, and the millions poured into Swing States by the Facebook CEO to hijack our elections?

The Biden Administration will do anything to keep the eye away from the massive irregularities and voter fraud that took place in the 2020 Presidential Election, even so ridiculously as going after its own citizens as "terrorists" using DHS, which should instead be focusing on the Border, where millions of people, from places unknown, are pouring into our Country. They are so desperate to hide the truth, they'll make it criminal to speak it! February 8, 2022

To comment, I don't know if Trump's numbers are accurate. But I discuss his claims about Georgia in my *Trump's Tweets* book. I explain Trump is getting his numbers from his lawyers, so he is not making them up. But Georgia election officials dispute his numbers, saying they are greatly exaggerated. My book gives both sides.

However, there is no doubt here were irregularities in the 2020 election. There are five major issues I address in my books on this subject that could have affected the outcome. They are:

1. Change of election laws by entities other than state legislatures.
2. Election observers not being given meaningful access to observe the vote counts
3. The allowing of "curing" of mail-in ballots in a partisan manner
4. Lowered standards for signature verification for mail-in ballots versus in-person ballots
5. The coverup of the Hunter Biden laptop story by the mainstream media and Big Tech

I document each of these irregularities in my *Corruption* and *Tragic Ending* books.

Donald J Trump @RealDonaldTrump
Kristi Noem has done a great job as Governor of South Dakota. She is strong on Borders, the Second Amendment, preserving land and Energy Dominance, Medical Freedom, and kept South Dakota open during COVID. She fully supports our great Law Enforcement, Military, our wonderful Vets—and is a fighter for the incredible people of South Dakota. Kristi has my Complete and Total Endorsement! February 8, 2022

Donald J Trump @RealDonaldTrump
Congressman Jim Jordan's book is doing very well. Go get a copy of *Do What You Said You Would Do: Fighting for Freedom in the Swamp*. It is fantastic! February 8, 2022

February 9, 2022

Donald J Trump @RealDonaldTrump
Mitch McConnell does not speak for the Republican Party, and does not represent the views of the vast majority of its voters. He did nothing to fight for his constituents and stop the most fraudulent election in American history. And he does nothing to stop the lawless Biden Administration, the invasion of our Borders, rising Inflation, Unconstitutional mandates, the persecution of political opponents, fact finding on the incompentent Afghanistan withdrawal, the giving away our energy independence, etc., which is all because of the fraudulent election. Instead, he bails out the Radical Left and the RINOs.

If Mitch would have fought for the election, like the Democrats would have if in the same position, we would not be discussing any of the above today, and our Country would be STRONG and PROUD instead of weak and embarrassed. February 9, 2022

Donald J Trump @RealDonaldTrump
For the Old Crow Mitch McConnell to say that the RNC should not censure walking Democrat sound bites, Liz Cheney and Cryin' Adam Kinzinger, is so against what Republicans are about. It's not as bad as the two-month extension he gave the Democrats when they were ready to fold, but the censure of Cheney and Kinzinger is a good and very appropriate thing to do as it pertains to our great Republican Party! February 9, 2022

February 10, 2022

Donald J Trump @RealDonaldTrump
Following collaborative and respectful discussions, the National Archives and Records Administration (NARA) openly and willingly arranged with President Trump for the transport of boxes that contained letters, records, newspapers, magazines, and various articles. Some of this information will someday be displayed in the Donald J. Trump Presidential Library for the public to view my Administration's incredible accomplishments for the American People.

The media's characterization of my relationship with NARA is Fake News. It was exactly the opposite! It was a great honor to work with NARA to help formally preserve the Trump Legacy.

The papers were given easily and without conflict and on a very friendly basis, which is different from the accounts being drawn up by the Fake News Media. In fact, it was viewed as routine and "no big deal." In actuality, I have been told I was under no obligation to give this material based on various legal rulings that have been made over the years. Crooked Hillary Clinton, as an example, deleted and acid washed 32,000 emails and never gave that to the government. Then, they took large amounts of furniture out of the White House. And Bill Clinton kept numerous audio recordings that the archives wanted, but were unsuccessful at getting after going to court. We won't even mention what is going on with the White House in the current, or various past administrations.

Also, another fake story, that I flushed papers and documents down a White House toilet, is categorically untrue and simply made up by a reporter in order to get publicity for a mostly fictitious book. The Democrats are just using this and the Unselect Committee of political hacks as a camoflauge for how horribly our Country is doing under the Biden Administration.

In the United States there has unfortunately become two legal standards, one for Republicans and one for Democrats. It should not be that way! February 10, 2022

Extended Comment
Handling of Documents

Trump is referring to the following:

President Joe Biden is ordering the release of Trump White House visitor logs to the House committee investigating the riot of Jan. 6, 2021, once more rejecting former President Donald Trump's claims of executive privilege.

The committee has sought a trove of data from the National Archives, including presidential records that Trump had fought to keep private. The records being released to Congress are visitor logs showing appointment information for individuals who allowed to enter the White House on the the [sic] day of the insurrection (AP. Biden orders).

The Biden administration is rejecting former President Trump's argument that his White House visitor logs are protected by executive privilege and has ordered the National Archives to give them to the Democrat-led House committee investigating the Jan. 6 Capitol riot.

In a letter to the National Archives, White House counsel Dana Remus said President Biden has rejected Trump's executive privilege claims and that "in light of the urgency" of the committee's work, the agency should provide the material within 15 days, according to The Washington Post.

Biden last year did not to back Trump's attempt to use executive privilege to protect White House documents and records sought by the committee. The former president failed in his attempt in federal court to have their release blocked, the newspaper also reports (Just the News. Biden orders).

The Washington Post reported Wednesday [2/9/22] that the National Archives and Records Administration has asked the Justice Department to investigate whether former President

Donald Trump violated federal law in the handling of documents.

The Associated Press was unable to independently confirm the report.

The referral followed several Post stories chronicling how then-President Trump dealt with documents, including tearing them up. In one report, since confirmed by the National Archives, the agency arranged the transport of 15 boxes of documents from the Mar-a-Lago property in Florida after Trump's representatives discovered them and notified the archives.

The Post says the referral is asking the Justice Department to investigate whether Trump violated the Presidential Records Act, which requires that all presidential records of an administration be turned over to the archives when a president leaves office.

The Archives did not return multiple messages seeking comment. The Justice Department declined comment (AP. Report: Archives).

To comment, do not miss the use of the word "insurrection" at the end of the first block quote. I explain in my *Tragic Ending* book that J6 was not an insurrection, despite the Deems and the MSM always using that word to deceive that day.

Also do not miss that even the AP was not able to collaborate WaPo's claims about Trump mishandling documents, in which Trump denies any improprieties.

February 11, 2022

Donald J Trump @RealDonaldTrump

Even more Voter Fraud was just discovered in Wisconsin. It shows the Election was Rigged and Stolen. A hearing this week revealed at least 50,000 illegal phantom votes were cast in the 2020 Presidential Election, which is more than twice the "victory" margin.

Incredible problems were also uncovered within Wisconsin's voter rolls, including an apartment building with 102 percent turnout rate (not possible), 113 ballots cast from an address where no one lives, 3,713 "voters" registered to U.S. Post Offices, and 625,000 dead people on Wisconsin's voter rolls. In addition, 46,000 votes were cast on Nov. 3rd based on voter information that was never verified by the state.

Trump Fights Back with Statements

This is on top of massive ballot harvesting, rigged "indefinitely confined" votes, the Wisconsin Election Commission instructing election officials to break the law, Zuckerberg drop boxes, etc.

So who in Wisconsin is leading the charge to decertify this fraudulent Election? It's time for RINOs to step forward and save our Country! February 11, 2022

Donald J Trump @RealDonaldTrump

The Unselect Committee and Nancy Pelosi are completely out of control, harassing innocent people, seizing private phone and bank records, and using the Capitol Police to spy on members of Congress. The RINOs, who were recently given support by Mitch McConnell, are trying to give legitimacy to a totally illegitimate and Marxist exercise.

All the real questions about January 6 are being ignored, like why they are hiding 14,000 hours of video footage, and why Nancy Pelosi left the Capitol completely unsecured and denied up to 20,000 National Guard troops as requested by me.

They should be looking at the massive evidence of Voter Fraud, which continues to come out daily, and is why everyone was there in the first place. The Unselect Committee is a cover up of the real insurrection, which took place on Nov. 3rd! February 11, 2022

To comment, the important new point here is the "14,000 hours of video footage." We have only seen selective clips with violent behavior. But the bulk of those 14,000 hours is probably of people peacefully entering, milling around, and leaving the Capitol Building, without engaging in any kind of violence or vandalism.

Such video would be boring to watch, but very instructive. It would show the vast majority of those who entered the Capitol Building were not part of the uprising and should not be charged in any way.

That latter point would be buttressed by video showing Capitol police officers moving barriers and waving in protesters, standing by idly as protestors peacefully walk by them, or moving away and letting rioters do their thing.

I know such video exists as I saw it on J6 and in video clips since then, as I report in my *Tragic Ending* book and will reiterate in my *J6 Commission* book. But the MSM and J6 commission are not very fond of airing such videos. They only want to show the violent stuff.

Donald J Trump @RealDonaldTrump

Yet another fake book, by a reporter who knows nothing about me, Maggot Haberman of the New York Times, is making up stories about my relationship with foreign leaders. She claims I speak with Kim Jong

Un of North Korea, but not other world leaders. Wrong! February 11, 2022

February 12, 2022

Donald J Trump @RealDonaldTrump

The latest pleading from Special Counsel Robert Durham provides indisputable evidence that my campaign and presidency were spied on by operatives paid by the Hillary Clinton Campaign in an effort to develop a completely fabricated connection to Russia. This is a scandal far greater in scope and magnitude than Watergate and those who were involved in and knew about this spying operation should be subject to criminal prosecution. In a stronger period of time in our country, this crime would have been punishable by death. In addition, reparations should be paid to those in our country who have been damaged by this. February 12, 2022

February 13, 2022

Donald J Trump @RealDonaldTrump

What Hillary Clinton and the Radical Left Democrats did with respect to spying on a President of the United States, even while in office, is a far bigger crime than Watergate. It will be interesting to see how it was covered by the media and what Mitch McConnell and the RINOs will be doing about it. This is an insult to the Republican Party, but a far greater insult to our Nation. Covered very powerfully this morning by Fox and Friends and, of course, Maria Bartiromo. February 13, 2022

February 14, 2022

Donald J Trump @RealDonaldTrump

Could somebody please inform the low-rated political shows that plague our Sunday morning programming that my Endorsement of candidates is much stronger today than it was even prior to the 2020 Election Scam. I am almost unblemished in the victory count, and it is considered by the real pollsters to be the strongest endorsement in U.S. political history. There are plenty of existing politicians who wouldn't be in power now were it not for my Endorsement (like the Old Crow!).

The Fake News does everything within their power to diminish and belittle but the people know, and the politicians seeking the Endorsement really know! February 14, 2022

Donald J Trump @RealDonaldTrump
THEY SPIED ON THE PRESIDENT OF THE UNITED STATES!
February 14, 2022

February 15, 2022

Donald J Trump @RealDonaldTrump
Can you imagine that, what should be the biggest story of our time, bigger than Watergate, is getting absolutely no mention, ZERO, in the New York Times, Washington Post, ABC Fake News, NBC Fake News, CBS Fake News, ratings-dead CNN, and MSDNC. This in itself is a scandal, the fact that a story so big, so powerful, and so important for the future of our Nation is getting zero coverage from LameStream, is being talked about all over the world.

Just like they wouldn't talk about the many Biden corruption scandals prior to the Election, (or for that matter now!), they won't talk about this, which is potentially even bigger. It shows how totally corrupt and shameless the media is.

Can you imagine if the roles were reversed and the Republicans, in particular President Donald Trump, got caught illegally spying into the Office of the President? All [expletive] would break loose and the electric chair would immediately come out of retirement. The good news is, everybody is talking about not only this atrocity against our Nation, but that the press refuses to even mention the major crime that took place. February 15, 2022

Donald J Trump @RealDonaldTrump
I was proven right about the spying, and I will be proven right about 2020! February 15, 2022

Donald J Trump @RealDonaldTrump
Is the Unselect Committee still talking about January 6 when a bigger scandal than Watergate has just been unearthed? February 15, 2022

Extended Comment
Durham Report

The preceding Statements are about the Durham report, parts of which were just released at this time. I have been mentioning about his investigation since the first volume of my *Impeach* trilogy, written in the fall of 2019. He is looking into the origins of the Trump/ Russia collusion hoax. But it took until now for the first parts of the report to be released. Since I have been waiting so long for this report to emerge, I will cover it in some detail here, as it is a very important story and investigation that is finally coming to fruition.

Trump/ Russia Collusion Hoax:

The main issue for this portion of the Durham investigation is the indictment of former Clinton campaign lawyer Michael Sussmann for lying to the FBI. He claims he did not have ties to the Clinton campaign when he had interactions with a Kremlin based tech firm. But Durham claims he has evidence that he did. That is important, as it shows the Clinton campaign was behind the Trump/ Russia collusion hoax.

This hoax is the real scandal, not J6. Following are news reports about what should be the greatest political scandal ever, if the MSM was not intent on covering it up.

A filing from Justice Department special counsel John Durham says Hillary Clinton's presidential campaign paid a technology company to "infiltrate" Trump Tower servers, and later the White House, Fox News reports.

Durham in a motion filed Feb. 11 said the purpose of the infiltration was to establish a "narrative" of collusion between then-Republican presidential candidate Donald Trump and Russia (Newsmax. Durham).

The filing relates to Mr. Durham's September indictment of Michael Sussmann, a lawyer who represented the Clinton campaign while he worked for the Perkins Coie law firm. Mr. Sussmann is accused of lying to the FBI at a September 2016 meeting when he presented documents claiming to show secret internet communications between the Trump Organization and Russia-based Alfa Bank. The indictment says Mr. Sussmann falsely told the FBI he was presenting this information solely as a good citizen—failing to disclose his ties to the Clinton campaign. (He has pleaded not guilty.)....

The filing says the new allegations Mr. Sussmann provided—claiming suspicious ties between a Russian mobile phone operator and the White House—were also bogus, and that Mr. Sussmann again made the false claim that he wasn't working on behalf of a client...

Mr. Durham's legal filing is related to certain conflicts of interest in Mr. Sussmann's legal team, and it remains unclear where else his probe is going. But the unfolding information underscores that the Russia collusion story was one of the dirtiest tricks in U.S. political history. Mr. Durham should tell the whole sordid story (WSJ. Trump Really).

A filing from Justice Department special counsel John Durham says Hillary Clinton's presidential campaign paid a technology company to infiltrate Trump Tower servers, and later the White House, Fox News reports.

Durham in a motion filed Feb. 11 said the purpose of the surreptitious intrusion was to establish a "narrative" of collusion between then-Republican presidential candidate Donald Trump and Russia.

Durham, appointed by then-Attorney General William Barr to lead a review into the Russia investigation, made the claim in his investigation that brought charges against an FBI attorney and former Clinton campaign lawyer Michael Sussman, who is currently charged with making a false statement to a federal agent (Newsmax. Durham Report).

John Durham, the special counsel appointed under former President Trump to investigate the FBI's probing of Russian interference in the 2016 election, alleged in court that a tech executive "exploited" access to White House data in order to find damning information about Trump.

In a court filing submitted Friday, Durham's office said that the executive, who is referred to in legal filings only as "Tech Executive-1" but has been identified in news reports as Rodney Joffe, used his company's access to nonpublic government domain name system (DNS) data through a pending cybersecurity contract as he was analyzing supposed links between the Trump Organization and a Russian bank.

"Tech Executive-1's employer, Internet Company-1, had come to access and maintain dedicated servers for the EOP as part of a sensitive arrangement whereby it provided DNS resolution services to the EOP," Durham's office wrote, using an acronym for the White House's Executive Office of the President....

Sussmann is accused of falsely telling the FBI's top attorney in a 2016 meeting that he was not representing any client when he presented data that researchers believed could have established a connection between Trump's business and the Moscow-based Alfa Bank.

Sussmann has pleaded not guilty and denied any wrongdoing. His attorney did not immediately respond when asked for comment (Hill. Durham alleges).

Clinton campaign paid to 'infiltrate' Trump Tower, White House servers to link Trump to Russia, Durham finds…

Former chief investigator of the Trump-Russia probe for the House Intelligence Committee under then-Rep. Devin Nunes, R-Calif., Kash Patel, said the filing "definitively shows that the Hillary Clinton campaign directly funded and ordered its lawyers at Perkins Coie to orchestrate a criminal enterprise to fabricate a connection between President Trump and Russia."

"Per Durham, this arrangement was put in motion in July of 2016, meaning the Hillary Clinton campaign and her lawyers masterminded the most intricate and coordinated conspiracy against Trump when he was both a candidate and later President of the United States while simultaneously perpetuating the bogus Steele Dossier hoax," Patel told Fox News, adding that the lawyers worked to "infiltrate" Trump Tower and White House servers.

The anti-Trump dossier, authored by ex-British intelligence officer Christopher Steele, commissioned by opposition research firm Fusion GPS, was funded by the Democratic National Committee and Hillary Clinton's campaign through Elia's law firm, Perkins Coie.

Patel added that Sussmann relayed the "false narrative" to U.S. government agencies "in the hopes of having them launch investigations of President Trump" (Fox News. Clinton campaign).

Trump Really Was Spied On:

This evidence shows beyond any doubt the Trump campaign was indeed "spied upon" just as Trump claimed, but just as the MSM denied.

The disclosures raise troubling questions far beyond the Sussmann indictment. How long did this snooping last and who had access to what was found? Who approved the access to White House data, and who at the FBI and White House knew about it? Were Mrs. Clinton and senior campaign aides personally aware of this data-trolling operation?

Mr. Durham's revelations take the 2016 collusion scam well beyond the Steele dossier, which was based on the unvetted claims of a Russian emigre working in Washington. Those claims and the Sussmann assertions were channeled to the highest levels of the government via contacts at the FBI, CIA and State Department. They became fodder for secret and unjustified warrants against a former Trump campaign official, and later for Robert Mueller's two-year mole hunt that turned up no evidence of collusion.

Along the way the Clinton campaign fed these bogus claims to a willing and gullible media. And now we know its operatives used private tech researchers to monitor White House communications. If you made this up, you'd be laughed out of a Netflix story pitch (WSJ. Trump Really).

WSJ Opinion: Durham's New Revelations About Spying on Trump

Strassel: "The filings show that the Clinton campaign was involved not just in feeding the bogus Steele dossier and the Sussmann allegations to the FBI, but also internet snooping" ...

In a new legal filing, the special counsel says a tech company that had access to Trump's internet communications shared that data with operatives working for the Clinton campaign in 2016 (WSJ. Who).

Lesley Stahl, a correspondent for CBS' "60 Minutes," is receiving backlash over an unearthed interview with Donald Trump in which she dismissed claims that the former president was spied on during his 2016 campaign.

The backlash comes after new allegations by special counsel John Durham in the inquiry into the origins of the Russia investigation gjzg support the former president's suspicions.

In the October 2020 interview, Trump declared that "the biggest scandal was when they spied on my campaign."

"There is no real evidence of that," Stahl responded.

"Of course there is. It's all over the place," Trump said as Stahl quickly shot back with a defiant "No."

The back and forth continued until Stahl reiterated once more that she disapproved of Trump's comments and "didn't know" if what he said was true (Newsmax. Lesley).

About 20 minutes after his initial statement, Trump released another one-line statement: "I was proven right about the spying, and I will be proven right about 2020!" (Newsmax. Trump: 'Zero').

(From Twitter) Eric Trump @EricTrump
Lesley Stahl should apologize to Donald Trump. Feb 13, 2022.

Americans Want Hillary Investigated:

Despite the MSM's attempt to downplay this scandal, a majority of Americans, including Republicans, Democrats, and Independents, want this scandal and Hillary herself investigated.

Former President Donald Trump tore into the mainstream media Monday [2/14/22] for refusing to report on Hillary Clinton's campaign being accused of paying a technology company to infiltrate Trump Tower servers and later, the White House (Newsmax. Trump: 'Zero').

An increasing number of Democrats believe Hillary Clinton should be investigated by special counsel John Durham in connection with her alleged involvement in manufacturing ties between 2016 presidential rival Donald Trump and the Russia, according to a recent survey.

The survey, by TechnoMetrica Institute of Policy and Politics, found 75% of respondents who follow the story think Clinton and her campaign advisers should be investigated for her role in so-called Russiagate, according to several news reports.

Among them, 66% are Democrats – a 20-point rise from last October when the same question was asked.

About the same percentage of independent voters agreed that Clinton should be probed, and 91% of Republicans said the same (Just the News. Fast growing).

A full 66% of Democrats want to see Hillary Clinton investigated for any role she might have had in trying to manufacture former President Donald Trump's ties to Russia in an attempt to smear him, according to a new poll by TechnoMetrica Institute of Policy and Politics (Newsmax. TIPP).

Sussman Trial and Verdict:

To give a later update in order to finish this story here, on May 31, 2022, Sussman was found not guilty. But that has been attributed to the case being tried in Washington DC, where 93% of citizens are Democrat. That does not bode well for future Durham indictments, which will also be tried in DC.

Despite former FBI lawyer Jim Baker testifying he was "100% confident" Sussmann was lying about not acting on behalf of candidate Hillary Clinton's campaign, Sussmann's lawyers ultimately won the case on the premise FBI agents [acted] independently and were widely aware Sussmann had ties to Clinton (Newsmax. Durham 'Disappointed').

Sussmann's lawyers won with the argument that the FBI agents were aware Sussmann was tied to Clinton (Newsmax. Rep. Mace).

The acquittal of attorney Michael Sussmann by a Washington D.C. jury effectively means that no Democrat can ever be convicted of any crime involving corruption as long as the crime has political implications and the trial is before a D.C. jury. We now have one-party justice in America.

Despite overwhelming evidence that he lied to the FBI, Sussmann was found not guilty by a jury filled with Democrats (Newsmax. Sussmann Acquittal).

Durham might have taken the high road from Tuesday's verdict, but that wasn't the case with former federal prosecutor Brett Tolman.

While speaking to Newsmax, Tolman said Americans shouldn't be surprised that a Washington D.C.-based judge and jury followed their political affiliations, instead of established law.

(Various reports say that three jurors were Hillary Clinton donors in the past.)

"It's not surprising to me that the D.C. court impaneled the jury that it did," Tolman told Newsmax's "John Bachman Now" program. "You look at the facts of the case, and it's overwhelming, so you have to actually have a jury that's willing to ignore the evidence and ignore the law."

Tolman also criticized the Sussmann trial judge for failing to extract the bias in the jury pool.

"When you select a jury, you want to be able to point out potential bias and existing bias and typically a judge would say to someone like you know, the Hillary campaign can't be contributors," Tolman also told Newsmax.

"The woman whose daughter was on the same athletic team as Sussmann's daughter, you would say, 'You know what, the connection is too close; I'm going to eliminate that juror.'

"But in this case that didn't happen. And so John Durham was left to use just a few challenges that he had to try to make a fair and consistent jury, and it proved to be impossible to do so in Washington, D.C" (Newsmax. Trump Slams).

Rep. Nancy Mace, speaking to Newsmax after a Washington, D.C., court's verdict that former Hillary Clinton-connected attorney Michael Sussmann was found not guilty of lying to the FBI, said she does not feel that special counsel John Durham or his prosecutors got their fair day in court, and that "no one is ever held accountable" for breaking laws.

"No one is ever held accountable in this country for breaking the law, particularly in the highest echelons of campaigns and the federal government," the South Carolina Republican said on Newsmax's "John Bachman Now." "It's inexcusable, really, and the frustration of the American people I'm sure will be palpable with this verdict. We just want someone, anyone, to be held accountable for the laws that they're breaking." …

"I hope that it doesn't end here today, and I hope that in the next case or in the future, they will allow every single piece of evidence entered into the record," Mace said. "The American people deserve to have the right to know what did and did not happen" (Newsmax. Rep. Mace).

Trump posted sarcastically about this verdict on his new social media site Truth Social:

Donald J Trump @RealDonaldTrump
Our Legal System is CORRUPT, our Judges (and Justices!) are highly partisan, compromised or just plain scared, our Borders are OPEN, our Elections are Rigged, Inflation is RAMPANT, gas prices and food costs are "through the roof," our Military "Leadership" is Woke, our Country is going to HELL, and Michael Sussmann is not guilty. How's everything else doing? Enjoy your day!!! June 1, 2022

There are many more references in Appendix One about the Sussman trial and its relation to the Trump/ Russia collusion hoax than I have quoted here. But here, back to Trump and his Statements from February 2022.

Donald J Trump @RealDonaldTrump
MAGA will never accept RINO Governor Doug Ducey of Arizona running for the U.S. Senate—So save your time, money, and energy, Mitch! February 15, 2022

Donald J Trump @RealDonaldTrump
Get Ready! Your favorite President will see you soon! February 15, 2022

To comment, this post is in regard to Trump's new social media site Truth Social being about to go online. At this point, I was not sure if Trump would continue to issue Statements and if Gab would continue to repost them.

Donald J Trump @RealDonaldTrump
Funny thing about Susan Collins, who is absolutely atrocious, and has been for a long time, I won Maine 2, by a lot, and those hard working people attended a rally of many thousands. Just one word about her and the fact that she didn't help the fisherman, as their rights were taken from them from the federal government, and the lumberjacks, she would have had no chance to win. But I remained silent and positive and allowed her to have her victory. She would have lost in a landslide. Gee, aren't I nice? February 15, 2022

February 16, 2022

Donald J Trump @RealDonaldTrump
Much of the now-uncovered espionage campaign of the Democrats breaking into the White House and my New York City apartment, took place after the 2016 Election as yet another way to undermine the upcoming 2020 Election. This spying into the Oval Office continued for a long period of time and further served to undermine and discredit the 2020 Election, along with massive ballot harvesting, phantom voters, and so many other things that made the Election a sham. The voting numbers were big and determinative! February 16, 2022

Donald J Trump @RealDonaldTrump
Why isn't the media asking who gave Crooked Hillary Clinton's "plumbers" their orders? With Watergate it was the coverup that turned out to be the far bigger crime. With Hillarygate it is the Mainstream Media Coverup that is almost as big of a crime as the act of treasonous

espionage itself. It is showing the world why our media is truly the enemy of the people! February 16, 2022

February 17, 2022

Donald J Trump @RealDonaldTrump

The Wyoming State Senate is considering SF0097, introduced by Patriot Senator Bo Biteman, to protect the integrity of Wyoming primary elections. This critically important bill ensures that the voters in each party will separately choose their nominees for the General Election, which is how it should be! It makes total sense that only Democrats vote in the Democrat primary and only Republicans vote in the Republican primary. This bill has my Complete and Total Endorsement and Support. Every Member of the Wyoming Senate should vote for SF0097. Thank you! February 17, 2022

To comment, I totally agree, and this is the way it is here in PA. Dems should not choose Repub candidates, nor vice versa. It is called a "closed primary." The only argument for an "open primary" is Independent are left out in the primary. But again, Independents should not be choosing either Dem or Repub candidates. Let each party chose its own candidates.

Donald J Trump @RealDonaldTrump

So, Crooked Hillary Clinton, one of the most corrupt politicians ever to run for President, can break into the White House, my apartment, buildings I own, and my campaign—in other words, she can spy on a Presidential candidate and ultimately, the President of the United States—and the now totally discredited Fake News Media does everything they can not to talk about it.

On the other hand, failed Gubernatorial candidate, Letitia James, can run for the office of AG on saying absolutely horrendous and false things about Donald Trump, a man she doesn't know and has never met, go on to get elected, and then selectively prosecute him and his family.

After viewing millions of pages of documents over many years, they come up with a "Fringe Benefits" case on a car, an apartment, and on grandchildren's education. She is doing everything within their corrupt discretion to interfere with my business relationships, and with the political process. With the rest of the case, even Cy Vance, who just left the DA's office without prosecuting anything additional, because there isn't anything additional to prosecute—THERE IS NO CASE!

Trump Fights Back with Statements

The targeting of a President of the United States, who got more votes while in office than any President in History, by far, and is a person that the Radical Left Democrats don't want to run again, represents an unconstitutional attack on our Country—and the people will not allow this travesty of justice to happen. It is a continuation of the greatest Witch Hunt in history—and remember, I can't get a fair hearing in New York because of the hatred of me by Judges and the judiciary. It is not possible! February 17, 2022

To comment, the situation in regard to Letitia James is as follows:
"[New York state Attorney General] Letitia James got elected by violently attacking 'Donald J. Trump,' even though she knew nothing about me," Trump wrote. "Likewise, District Attorney Alvin Bragg 'bragged' that he has sued President Trump over 100 times, more than anybody else. He is now working hand-in-hand with people from the law firm which is one of Hillary Clinton's biggest donors."

Trump concluded by saying that law enforcement should focus on "murderers, drug dealers and rapists instead" of continuing the "sham investigation" against him, which he said is the "continuation of a Witch Hunt" (Just the News. Donald).

February 18, 2022

Donald J Trump @RealDonaldTrump
Congressman Jim Hagedorn was a strong and effective legislator for the great people of Southern Minnesota. I campaigned with Jim in 2018, and enjoyed working with him in Congress. May he rest in Peace, and his family find comfort during this difficult time. He will be greatly missed! February 18, 2022

Donald J Trump @RealDonaldTrump
When is Lesley Stahl of 60 Minutes going to apologize for saying that my campaign was not spied upon? On top of that, they spied on the White House! February 18, 2022

Donald J Trump @RealDonaldTrump
Congratulations to Kevin McCarthy and Elise Stefanik on their strong and powerful endorsement of Harriet Hageman of Wyoming. Loser Liz Cheney is a RINO and warmonger who doesn't deserve to serve in the House of Representatives. Harriet will be an outstanding Representative for the Great State of Wyoming! February 18, 2022

Donald J Trump @RealDonaldTrump

Remember when Paul Krugman, the highly overrated op-ed columnist for the New York Times, told everybody to get out of the stock market fast and completely after I was elected President in 2016. Anybody that took this losers advice would have approximately one-third of the money they have right now—or even less assuming bad investments. The New York Times probably told him what to say because nobody could be so dumb, and nobody has attacked their credibility like me. They are truly Fake News. They got a Pulitzer Prize for Russia, Russia, Russia, and it turned out to be a total scam.

The Pulitzer Committee, which has no credibility left anyway, should demand all of the Russia, Russia, Russia prizes back because the facts were the exact opposite. Likewise, Krugman, should apologize to all of those people that followed his advice and lost a fortune doing so. Maybe they should all get together and sue him for what they have lost. Apologize, Paul! February 18, 2022

February 21, 2022

Donald J Trump @RealDonaldTrump

My long-term accounting firm didn't leave me for any other reason than they were harassed, abused, and frightened by DA's and AG's that for years have been threatening them with indictment and ruination.

They were "broken" by these Radical Left racist prosecutors, and couldn't take it anymore. Even the letter they sent stated, "Mazars performed its work in accordance with professional standards. A subsequent review of those work papers confirms this." Further, their disclaimer clause in the financial statements has for years stated much the same.

My company is incredible with some of the greatest assets in the world and very low debt. Also, we're loaded with cash. The Fake News Media hates talking about it! February 21, 2022

February 23, 2022

Donald J Trump @RealDonaldTrump

If properly handled, there was absolutely no reason that the situation currently happening in Ukraine should have happened at all. I know Vladimir Putin very well, and he would have never done during the Trump Administration what he is doing now, no way!

Trump Fights Back with Statements

Russia has become very very rich during the Biden Administration, with oil prices doubling and soon to be tripling and quadrupling. The weak sanctions are insignificant relative to taking over a country and a massive piece of strategically located land.

Now it has begun, oil prices are going higher and higher, and Putin is not only getting what he always wanted, but getting, because of the oil and gas surge, richer and richer. The U.S. was energy independent under the Trump Administration, an independence that we had never obtained before, and oil prices would have remained low. Now, what a mess our Country is in! February 23, 2022

To comment, most likely, Putin would not have invaded Ukraine if Trump was still President. How do I know that? Because Putin didn't invade Ukraine while Trump was President. But he invaded Crimea while Obama was President, and then the rest of Ukraine while Biden was President. He even made military moves while Bush 43 was President. But during Trump, no new military moves. Those are the facts.

February 24, 2022

Donald J Trump @RealDonaldTrump
Our Country has totally lost its self-confidence! February 24, 2022

Donald J Trump @RealDonaldTrump
Putin is playing Biden like a drum. It is not a pretty thing to watch! February 24, 2022

February 25, 2022

Donald J Trump @RealDonaldTrump
If I were in Office, this deadly Ukraine situation would never have happened! February 25, 2022

To comment, I've written two articles so far about this tragedy. In them, I make this very same point:

"Why is Russia Poised to Invade Ukraine?" Putin's sense of entitlement to annex Ukraine is emboldened by a weak US President and a weakened USA.
https://www.zeolla.org/Politics/articles/2022/putin_ukraine.htm

"Full-Scale Invasion." Despite USA and worldwide sanctions and threats of more severe sanctions, Russia invaded Ukraine at 5:00 am local time on February 24, 2022.

February 26, 2022

Donald J Trump @RealDonaldTrump

What is happening in the City of Atlanta is nothing short of disgraceful. It's national news and a regional embarrassment. The good people of Buckhead don't want to be a part of defunding the police and the high crime that's plaguing their communities.

However, RINOs like Governor Brian Kemp, the man responsible, along with his puppet master Mitch McConnell, for the loss of two Senate Seats and 2020 Presidential Vote, Lt. Governor Jeff Duncan, Speaker David Ralston, and State Senators Butch Miller, Jeff Mullis, and John Albers always talk a big game but they don't deliver.

What good is having Republican leaders if they are unwilling to fight for what they campaigned on? Every RINO must go! Let the voters decide on the very popular City of Buckhead proposal! Feb 26, 2022

February 28, 2022

Donald J Trump @RealDonaldTrump

Just heard about an incredible effort underway that will strengthen the Republican Party. The "Precinct Strategy" is enlisting America First Patriots to their local County Republican Party committees, positions which are too often left vacant. If members of our Great movement start getting involved (that means YOU becoming a precinct committeeman for your voting precinct), we can take back our great Country from the ground up.

The Precinct Strategy, as explained by Dan Schultz at http://www.PrecinctStrategy.com, is a great way to restore our Republic by transforming our Party from currently at less than half-strength at the precinct level into a full-strength Get Out The Vote powerhouse—as it should be. http://www.precinctstrategy.com/ February 28, 2022

Donald J Trump @RealDonaldTrump

I hope everyone is able to remember that it was me, as President of the United States, that got delinquent NATO members to start paying their dues, which amounted to hundreds of billions of dollars. There would be no NATO if I didn't act strongly and swiftly. Also, it was me that got Ukraine the very effective anti-tank busters (Javelins) when the previous Administration was sending blankets. Let History so note! February 28, 2022

Chapter Fifteen
Trump's Statements
March 2022

These Trump Statements are continued from Chapter Fourteen.

March 1, 2022

Donald J Trump @RealDonaldTrump
If my energy policy had remained in place, where we were energy independent, and would have soon been bigger in production than Saudi Arabia and Russia combined, the world would have had no problems whatsoever. This war should never have started in the first place. If the Election wasn't Rigged, America would right now continue to have record-low gas prices, as it was under my Administration, and we would be supplying the world with oil and gas. Also, Russia would not have attacked Ukraine. Instead, we have a horribly tragic and unnecessary war, record-high energy prices, Inflation, no Border, crime, and chaos. Make America STRONG Again! March 1, 2022

March 2, 2022

Donald J Trump @RealDonaldTrump
The State of Wisconsin just announced massive Election Fraud in the 2020 Presidential Election.
See the findings from the Office of the Special Counsel Second Interim Investigative Report On the Apparatus & Procedures of the Wisconsin Elections System here.
Read carefully because, despite the findings, the Fake News will never allow you to see what is happening. The Media is corrupt, and so was our Presidential Election!
http://email.m.saveamerica45.com/c/eJxVUV2PnSAU_DXcN
March 2, 2022

To comment, Trump might be referring to the following:
The special counsel investigating suspected irregularities in Wisconsin's 2020 election has found that 91 nursing homes in the counties of Milwaukee, Racine, Dane, Kenosha, and Brown had voter turnout rates ranging from 95% to a 100% in 2020 —

as compared to overall nationwide participation rates of 67% in 2020 and 60% in 2016.

The nursing home data only reflects voting at the facilities that the special counsel "has been able to vet to this juncture," according to the report compiled by retired state Supreme Court Justice Michael Gableman for the state Assembly. "There are more facilities in these counties, and after auditing the votes from other facilities, the above percentages may change." ...

The sheriff found that facility staff, under the guise of "helping" residents to vote, coaxed votes from some whom family members believed incapable of voting (Just the News. Wisconsin).

Donald J Trump @RealDonaldTrump

The RINOs, Warmongers, and Fake News continue to blatantly lie and misrepresent my remarks on Putin because they know this terrible war being waged against Ukraine would have never happened under my watch. They did absolutely nothing as Putin declared much of Ukraine an "independent territory."

There should be no war waging now in Ukraine, and it is terrible for humanity that Biden, NATO, and the West have failed so terribly in allowing it to start. Instead of showing strength and toughness, they declared the Global Warming Hoax as the #1 threat to global security, killed American Energy Independence, and then made Europe, the U.S., and the rest of the World dependent on Russian oil. They laid down the welcome mat and gave Russia the opening, now Putin may be getting everything he wanted, with Ukraine and the rest of the World suffering the consequences. It's terrible, but this is what you get with Biden, the Democrats, and RINO warmongers! March 2, 2022

To comment, Trump is most likely correct there would not be war in Ukraine now if he were President. I discuss this point and present the background to the war in my two articles on the Russian/ Ukrainian war:

"Why is Russia Poised to Invade Ukraine?" - Putin's sense of entitlement to annex Ukraine is emboldened by a weak US President and a weakened USA.
https://www.zeolla.org/Politics/articles/2022/putin_ukraine.htm

"Full-Scale Invasion" – Despite USA and worldwide sanctions and threats of more severe sanctions, Russia invaded Ukraine at 5:00 am local time on February 24, 2022.
https://www.zeolla.org/Politics/articles/2022/invasion.htm

Donald J Trump @RealDonaldTrump
Big night in Texas! All 33 candidates that were Trump endorsed have either won their primary election or are substantially leading in the case of a runoff. Governor Abbott and Lieutenant Governor Dan Patrick have won in a landslide. Thank you, and congratulations to all! March 2, 2022

Donald J Trump @RealDonaldTrump
All 33 Trump-Endorsed candidates won last night in Texas, or are substantially leading. Big night! How will the Fake News make it look bad? March 2, 2022

To comment, these statements are correct but a bit misleading.

Mr. Trump's record was mixed. The former president endorsed 33 Texas Republicans ahead of their primaries, but virtually all of them were widely expected to win before receiving the Trump seal of approval. As of early Wednesday [3/2/22] morning, all of Mr. Trump's picks for Congress were on pace to win their nominations.

But other races raised doubts that Mr. Trump's approval alone could secure a victory. Attorney General Ken Paxton, who was endorsed by Mr. Trump, and Dawn Buckingham, Mr. Trump's choice for land commissioner, were both headed to runoffs in May, after failing to get more than 50 percent of the vote (NYT. Takeaways).

March 4, 2022

Donald J Trump @RealDonaldTrump
The actual conspiracy to defraud the United States was the Democrats rigging the Election, and the Fake News Media and the Unselect Committee covering it up. Few things could be more fraudulent, or met with more irregularities, than the Presidential Election of 2020. They refuse to cover the facts, such as just this week the special counsel in Wisconsin called for the decertification of the 2020 Election because of massive illegality, including election bribery, and the preying on the elderly for votes, which resulted in fraud of "95-100 percent turnout," an impossibility, in at least 91 nursing homes.

This is true with many other states, especially swing states. In Arizona, 204,430 mail-in ballots had mismatched signatures that were never sent to review, and 740,000 mail-in ballots had broken chain of custody, all far more necessary than the votes needed, 10,457, for "President Trump to win." In Georgia, over 240 ballot harvesters have been identified in an illegal operation spanning multiple swing states, all caught on video.

The evidence is monumental but the Unselect Committee of politically partisan hacks, and someone who had a steaming hot affair with a Chinese spy, hides the facts. Judges and even justices of the United States Supreme Court, are afraid to even look, as was the Attorney General of the United States, who was so petrified of being held in contempt or being impeached by the Democrats, which they were constantly threatening him with, that he was virtually a broken man who allowed for the systemic violation of election laws and other things to take place.

The reason for January 6th was that millions of people in our Country know the Election was Rigged and Stolen, and Nancy Pelosi refused to put the requested 10,000+ troops in the Capitol three days earlier, as strongly recommended by me. She didn't like "the look."

The Unselect Committee's sole goal is to try to prevent President Trump, who is leading by large margins in every poll, from running again for president, if I so choose. By so doing they are destroying democracy as we know it. Their lies and Marxist tactics against political opponents will not stop the truth, or the biggest political movement, Make America Great Again/America First, in the history of our Country. And now we have a war waging in Ukraine that would have never happened, record-setting inflation, an embarrassingly poorly executed withdrawal from Afghanistan, and an economy that is teetering, at best. All because of a corrupt Election result. March 4, 2022

To comment, Trump is correct that the goal of the "Unselect Committee" is to keep him from running again, as Dems know they cannot beat him. That was the reason for the first impeachment. I detail such in my *Impeach* trilogy.

Also, Trump was not responsible for J6, as I demonstrate in my *Trump's Tweets* and *Tragic Ending* books. I will add to that with my forthcoming *J6 Commission* book.

Donald J Trump @RealDonaldTrump

Governor Doug Ducey of Arizona saw the big Primary numbers in Texas, where "Trump Endorsements" went 33 wins and 0 loses, and he said, knowing I would never endorse him, "No thanks, I am not going to run for Senate!" Smart move, Doug—there's no room for RINOs. I guess that means we can call this week 34 and 0! March 4, 2022

March 5, 2022

Donald J Trump @RealDonaldTrump

Former Attorney General Bill Barr wouldn't know voter fraud if it was staring him in the face—and it was. The fact is, he was weak, ineffective, and totally scared of being impeached, which the Democrats were constantly threatening to do. They "broke" him. He should have acted much faster on the Mueller Report, instead of allowing the fake Russia, Russia, Russia, Hoax to linger for so long, but it was the Election Fraud and Irregularities that he refused to act on because he wanted to save his own hide—and he did.

He never got impeached, contempt charges never went forward, and the Democrats were very happy with him—but I wasn't. The Unselect Committee of Political Hacks continues to spin its wheels in trying to fabricate a narrative that doesn't exist. The only thing they refuse to look into is the massive Election Fraud that took place in the 2020 Presidential Election. March 5, 2022

March 8, 2022

Donald J Trump @RealDonaldTrump

Bill Barr said, and just reiterated, that the Trump campaign was "spied on", but did nothing about it. He then said, "mail-in ballots are prone to fraud," and then did nothing to catch the fraudsters. He was so afraid of being impeached, that he went to the other side—and they left him alone. Barr was a "Bushie" who never had the energy or competence to do the job that he was put in place to do. March 8, 2022

To comment, we have known "mail-in ballots are prone to fraud" ever since the "2005 Carter/ Baker Election Fraud Report." I discuss that report in detail in my *Corruption* book.

That report detailed the steps that needed to be taken to secure our elections. But sadly, Congress never followed those steps. That led to the 2020 election debacle. In fact, I quote Rush Limbaugh in my book as saying that report was the blueprint Dems followed in the 2020 election as to how to commit fraud and steal the election.

BREAKING NEWS: HIGHEST GAS PRICES IN HISTORY! DO YOU MISS ME YET? March 8, 2022

To comment, from energy independent and a net exporter of oil under Trump to energy dependent on tyrants and a net importer of oil under Biden, all in less than a year. Such is life under Joe Biden.

March 9, 2022

Donald J Trump @RealDonaldTrump

The Fake News Media refuses to report that I was the one who very early and strongly gave the anti-tank busters (Javelins) to Ukraine, while Obama/Biden was giving blankets, to great and open complaints. Then Biden came in, and canceled the remaining military equipment that was packed, loaded, and ready to be shipped. Now the Fake News Media is trying to say that Trump gave Ukraine nothing and it was Biden who is their great friend and gave them weaponry. The dishonesty is so unbelievable. All I can do is report it! March 9, 2022

To comment, Trump is absolutely correct here. Javelins were made available to Ukraine by Trump not Obama. Moreover, the purchase of those Javelins was not part of the "pause" in military aid to Ukraine, as Dems made it out to be during the impeachment proceedings. I detail all of this my *Impeach* trilogy.

Those books are even more important now, as they provide the background to what is happening in Ukraine now but did not happen under Trump. That is how we know if Trump were still President, none of this would be happening. Ukrainians would not be suffering under Putin's invasion, we would not be experiencing pain at the pump, and millions of Africans would not staving due to the stoppage of grain shipments form Ukraine.

Donald J Trump @RealDonaldTrump

Just confirmed that most of Europe won't go along with the United States in boycotting Russian oil and gas. As usual the United States will be left out there alone, being taken advantage of by Europe, as we defend them, while we read in the Fake News how everyone has come together under Biden to fight Russia. March 9, 2022

Donald J Trump @RealDonaldTrump

Congratulations and thank you to Robin Vos, Speaker of the Wisconsin State Assembly, and State Assemblywoman Janel Brandtjen, Chair of the Committee on Campaigns and Elections, for standing by highly respected Justice Michael Gableman on the incredible findings just announced on Election Fraud in the great State of Wisconsin. I feel confident that Robin will exercise his moral duty to follow up on Justice Gableman's findings.

In addition to announcing that they will stay in session and take action to get rid of ERIC and the WEC, which have done some very bad things and made review very difficult (as also noted by the Legislative Audit Bureau), based on the Gableman report, I would imagine that there can only be a Decertification of Electors. This is one of the biggest stories of our generation, even though the Fake News Media will try to play it down as much as they can.

Also, this past October the Racine County Sheriff, Christopher Schmaling, referred felony criminal charges against five of the six members of the Wisconsin Election Commission ("WEC") for their scheme to violate Wisconsin law and allow illegal vote harvesting in nursing homes. The Sheriff stated that the governing "election statute was in fact not just broken but shattered" in all 72 counties across Wisconsin.

Read the full story here.

Wisconsin election law violations, Racine County sheriff alleges https://www.fox6now.com/news/wisconsin-election-law-violations-racine-county-sheriff-reveals-findings

Numerous other states are likewise finding large scale Election Fraud and irregularities. Interesting time! March 9, 2022

March 10, 2022

Donald J Trump @RealDonaldTrump
Nigel Farage. Donald Trump was right about everything. [picture of Nigel with a link to a YouTube video – you.tu.be/9PVFqpOHPBg. But the link doesn't work. Maybe YouTube took it down] March 10, 2022

March 11, 2022

Donald J Trump @RealDonaldTrump
Big rally in South Carolina this weekend. Will be honoring Katie Arrington, who is running against the absolutely horrendous Nancy Mace, and Russell Fry, who is likewise running against "doesn't have a clue" Tom Rice. Big crowds at the Florence Regional Airport, starts at 7:00PM ET. See you there! March 11, 2022

Donald J Trump @RealDonaldTrump
Whatever happened to free speech in our Country? Incredibly, but not surprisingly, the Big Tech lunatics have taken down my interview

with the very popular NELK Boys so that nobody can watch it or in any way listen to it. In the 24 hours that it was up it set every record for them, by many times.

Interestingly on the show I told them this would happen because Big Tech and the Fake News Media fear the truth, they fear criticism about Biden, and above all, they don't want to talk about the Rigged 2020 Presidential Election, all topics discussed. In Russia, the people are not allowed to know that they're fighting a war with Ukraine, that's where our media is going, and that's where our Country is going because it quickly follows—just study history.

Are we going to allow this to happen? Our Country is going to [expletive]! Look at your gas prices, Inflation, the Afghanistan debacle, our Border, the war with Ukraine, which should have never happened, and so much more. We need freedom of speech again, we don't have it and it's getting worse every day! March 11, 2022

March 12, 2022

Donald J Trump @RealDonaldTrump
Big crowds for Rally in Florence, South Carolina. Will be there soon! March 12, 2022

March 13, 2022

Donald J Trump @RealDonaldTrump
A winner from Save America PAC WAS chosen for dinner and that winner, and family, will soon be coming to Palm Beach, Florida. Reporting by the Washington Post was inaccurate and, Fake News. These arrangements were handled directly by President Trump's representatives. March 13, 2022

Donald J Trump @RealDonaldTrump
The story is Fake News about my plane being "mothballed" in Stewart Airfield in Newburgh, New York because "I didn't think I would need it until 2025." My plane, a Boeing 757, is going through a major scheduled maintenance program, which will be completed in approximately 90 days. It will then be put back into service. I was not allowed to use it during the Presidency, and didn't. March 13, 2022

Donald J Trump @RealDonaldTrump
Such Fake News and stories about me on Google. Anything positive does not get reported. Even the NELK Boys record-setting interview

with me was taken down because I told the TRUTH, which the Radical Left cannot handle. The Media and Big Tech is doing everything possible to destroy our Country. They are truly the ENEMY OF THE PEOPLE! March 13, 2022

Donald J Trump @RealDonaldTrump
We demand Freedom of the Press! March 13, 2022

March 15, 2022

Donald J Trump @RealDonaldTrump
Time Warner, the owner of Fake News CNN, has just announced that they will be terminating a very popular and wonderful news network (OAN). Between heavily indebted Time Warner, and Radical Left Comcast, which runs Xfinity, there is a virtual monopoly on news, thereby making what you hear from the LameStream Media largely FAKE, hence the name FAKE NEWS!
I believe the people of this Country should protest the decision to eliminate OAN, a very important voice. Likewise, Comcast is terrible and expensive. Let them know that you're sick and tired of FAKE NEWS! In this modern age of technology, they are no longer necessary. Demand that OAN be allowed to stay on the air. It is far bigger and more popular than anyone knows, and importantly, it represents the voice of a very large group of people! March 15, 2022

March 16, 2022

Donald J Trump @RealDonaldTrump
Breaking News: Russia just sanctioned Joe Biden. While that is a terrible thing, in so many ways, perhaps it will now be explained why the Biden family received 3.5 million dollars from the very wealthy former Mayor of Moscow's wife. During our Presidential Debate, "moderator" Chris Wallace, then of Fox, would not let me ask that question. He said it was inappropriate. Perhaps that's why Biden has been so "slow on the draw" with Russia. This is a really bad conflict of interest that will, perhaps now, be fully and finally revealed! March 16, 2022

Donald J Trump @RealDonaldTrump
Now with what's going on with Russia and Ukraine, among many other things, the great and wonderful people of Hungary need the continued strong leadership of Prime Minister Viktor Orban more than ever.

He is TOUGH, SMART, AND LOVES HIS COUNTRY. In the upcoming Election next month, he already has my Complete and Total Endorsement! March 16, 2022

Donald J Trump @RealDonaldTrump
Congratulations to Paul Mango on his new book, Warp Speed: Inside the Operation that Beat Covid, the Critics, and the Odds, which tells the story of how my Administration, in record time, delivered vaccines and therapeutics to the American people to fight the China Virus. What we achieved was incredible, but it is sad to see what Biden has done with it (no mandates!). Great job, Paul! March 16, 2022

Donald J Trump @RealDonaldTrump
People forget so quickly, with the help of the Fake News, that it was me that got the 20 out of 28 delinquent NATO countries to start paying the money that they owed in order to rebuild a floundering NATO.
Nobody knew things would happen so rapidly, but NATO was poor and now it is rich, and all of the Fake News commentators that said Trump was tearing down NATO should be ashamed of themselves for telling lies. Not only was the United States being taken advantage of by the EU on trade, but it was forced to pay the costs of the many delinquent NATO countries. Bush and Obama did nothing but make speeches and talk—I acted, and acted strongly. I said to them, "if you don't pay up, no protection." They all paid up, and paid up quickly. It's a story that's never reported, but that's only because we have a corrupt press in our Country! March 16, 2022

March 17, 2022

Donald J Trump @RealDonaldTrump
Fox News is putting on the terrible Nancy Mace of South Carolina at every opportunity they get. Fox Board Member (too bad!) Paul Ryan is pushing her so hard it's ridiculous. She's nasty, disloyal, and bad for the Republican Party. Her opponent, Katie Arrington, is wonderful and will do a much better job for both South Carolina and the Republican Party. Katie Arrington has my Complete and Total Endorsement! March 17, 2022

Donald J Trump @RealDonaldTrump
Speaker Robin Vos, of the Great State of Wisconsin, just said there was "widespread fraud" in the 2020 Presidential Election, but that the State Legislature cannot do anything about it. Wrong! If you rob the

diamonds from a jewelry store, if you get caught, you have to give the diamonds back, votes should be no different. There is already a very powerful resolution in the Wisconsin State Assembly that calls for the decertification of the 2020 Election and reclaiming of Wisconsin's 10 electoral votes. There is so much fraud, as Vos knows, that this should be done quickly and easily.

The highly respected Special Counsel, Michael Gableman, has exposed so much already, including election bribery with Mark Zuckerberg's $8.8 million, horrific fraud stealing votes from the elderly in nursing homes, and rampant ballot harvesting and phantom votes. Far more votes than is needed for the Republican candidate, me, to win.

Our Country would not be in the mess it's in if Republicans had the courage to act. We would be energy independent, no inflation, the Ukraine desecration would not be happening, our economy would be strong, there would have been no surrender in Afghanistan, and so much else. Speaker Vos should do the right thing and correct the Crime of the Century—immediately! It is my opinion that other states will be doing this, Wisconsin should lead the way! March 17, 2022

March 18, 2022

Donald J Trump @RealDonaldTrump
The New York Times just admitted that it participated in an effort to rig the election for Joe Biden. Read the article by the New York Post here.

Now that Joe Biden's president, the Times finally admits: Hunter's laptop is real. https://nypost.com/2022/03/17/the-times-finally-admit March 18, 2022

To comment, the NYT's article is, "Hunter Biden Paid Tax Bill, but Broad Federal Investigation Continues" –
https://www.nytimes.com/2022/03/16/us/politics/hunter-biden-tax-bill-investigation.html
The NYT should have read my *Corruption* book. It was published in May of 2021 and explained why this story could not be a "Russian disinformation campaign." But now that Biden's presidency is failing, as my *Biden Tweets* books detail, the NYT probably figures they can admit the corruption of the Bidens, in hopes Joe doesn't run again.

Donald J Trump @RealDonaldTrump
When is the Attorney General of Arizona going to rule on all of the Election Fraud and large-scale Election Irregularities that wait before

him? People want to know whether or not Attorney General Brnovich is up to doing the right thing, or is it just politics as usual.

As an example, the strongly Trump-Endorsed Kari Lake, who is running for Governor, has made the Fraudulent 2020 Election a primary part of her campaign. She is leading by massive numbers over her weak RINO competitors. This is both the issue of the day and the Crime of the Century! And now, on top of everything else, it was just announced by the New York Times that they, in collusion with other Fake News Media, covered up the Hunter Biden crime story prior to the Election (a 15 point difference!). Wow, what a Country. March 18, 2022

To comment, I detail in my *Corruption* book that if more people knew about the Hunter scandal, enough of them say they would not have voted for Biden to have turned the election to Trump.

March 20, 2022

Donald J Trump @RealDonaldTrump
Looking forward to seeing the big crowd tonight at the FLA Live Arena for the American Freedom Tour at 5:00pm ET! So much to talk about! March 20, 2022

March 22, 2022

Donald J Trump @RealDonaldTrump
Arizona Senate President Karen Fann is asking the exact right question about the corrupt Maricopa County Board of Supervisors, "What are they hiding now?"

Based on the already released information regarding the Rigged and Stolen 2020 Presidential Election, including mail-in ballots without signatures and forgeries, as well as the disgusting refusal to turn over documents, now is finally the time for the Arizona Attorney General to issue warrants and take his investigation to the next level. The supervisors just won't release the information—it must really be bad!

The American people deserve answers, and there is no time to waste! March 22, 2022

Donald J Trump @RealDonaldTrump
Mo Brooks of Alabama made a horrible mistake recently when he went "woke" and stated, referring to the 2020 Presidential Election Scam, "Put that behind you, put that behind you," despite the fact that

the Election was rife with fraud and irregularities. If we forget, the Radical Left Democrats will continue to Cheat and Steal Elections. Just look at what is happening in Wisconsin, Arizona, Pennsylvania, Georgia, and elsewhere, but tremendous progress has been made that will help us in 2022 and 2024. The 2020 Election was rigged, and we can't let them get away with it.

When I endorsed Mo Brooks, he took a 44-point lead and was unstoppable. He then hired a new campaign staff who "brilliantly" convinced him to "stop talking about the 2020 Election." He listened to them. Then, according to the polls, Mo's 44-point lead totally evaporated all based on his "2020" statement made at our massive rally in Cullman, Alabama.

When I heard his statement, I said, "Mo, you just blew the Election, and there's nothing you can do about it." Very sad but, since he decided to go in another direction, so have I, and I am hereby withdrawing my Endorsement of Mo Brooks for the Senate. I don't think the great people of Alabama will disagree with me. Election Fraud must be captured and stopped, or we won't have a Country anymore. I will be making a new Endorsement in the near future! March 23, 2022

March 24, 2022

Donald J Trump @RealDonaldTrump

Mo Brooks was a leader on the 2020 Election Fraud and then, all of sudden, during the big rally in Alabama, he went "woke" and decided to drop everything he stood for—when he did, the people of Alabama dropped him, and now I have done so also. The people get it, but unfortunately, Mo doesn't.

As far as Mitch McConnell, I am not a fan and there's been no harsher critic than me. He has been absolutely terrible, and very bad for the GOP. The sooner he leaves "Leadership," the better off the Republican Party will be. March 24, 2022

Extended Comment
Mo Brooks

These Statements about Mo Brooks are in regard to the following:

Republican Rep. Mo Brooks of Alabama said on Wednesday [3/23/22] that former President Donald Trump pressed him to illegally remove President Joe Biden from office and hold a new presidential election, moves that are both unconstitutional.

"President Trump asked me to rescind the 2020 elections, immediately remove Joe Biden from the White House, immediately put President Trump back in the White House, and hold a new special election for the presidency," Brooks said in a statement responding to Trump's withdrawal of his endorsement of Brooks' US Senate campaign (Insider. Mo Brooks).

Trump backed Brooks, one of his close congressional allies in his failed effort to overturn his 2020 election loss, early on in the race to replace retiring GOP Sen. Richard Shelby.

But despite Brooks' former loyalty, Trump has increasingly soured on the Alabama congressman over his poor fundraising and poll numbers, openly airing some of his frustrations in a recent interview with the Washington Examiner (Insider. Trump rescinds).

Trump referenced Brooks' comments at an Alabama rally last summer when the lawmaker told attendees to move past the 2020 election. According to a local news report, Brooks was booed by the crowd.

"There are some people who are despondent about the voter fraud and election theft in 2020," Brooks said then, according to AL.com. "Folks, put that behind you, put that behind you" (Insider. Trump calls).

"When I endorsed Mo Brooks, he took a 44-point lead and was unstoppable. He then hired a new campaign staff who 'brilliantly' convinced him to 'stop talking about the 2020 Election.' He listened to them. Then, according to the polls, Mo's 44-point lead totally evaporated," wrote Trump.

"Very sad but, since he decided to go in another direction, so have I, and I am hereby withdrawing my Endorsement of Mo Brooks for the Senate," he continued (Just the News. Trump un-endorses). Back to Trump.

Donald J Trump @RealDonaldTrump
Have the great people of Missouri been considering the big, loud, and proud personality of Congressman Billy Long for the Senate? Do they appreciate what they have in him, a warrior and the first major political leader to say, "You better get on the Trump Train, it's leaving the station." That was before I even announced I was running for President. This is not an Endorsement, but I'm just askin'? March 24, 2022

March 26, 2022

Donald J Trump @RealDonaldTrump
Highly respected Nigel Farage when asked on Fox and Friends this morning about Trump, he stated, "Trump was 100% right." Thank you, Nigel! March 26, 2022

Donald J Trump @RealDonaldTrump
Getting ready to leave now. Hearing there are tremendous crowds in Commerce, Georgia, for our Save America Rally. Make America Great Again! March 26, 2022

March 27, 2022

Donald J Trump @RealDonaldTrump
Massive crowd last night in Georgia even despite the cold weather, the enthusiasm was unbelievable. David Perdue, running against horrendous Governor Brian Kemp, who let the Election be Rigged and Stolen, is seeing a very big surge. Will be interesting, but why would anybody want to vote for somebody who unnecessarily allowed a really bad and unfair consent decree, but wouldn't allow a special session as requested by the State Senate. Kemp is a disaster for Georgia. March 27, 2022

Donald J Trump @RealDonaldTrump
We had a massive crowd last night in Georgia, but as usual, the Fake News Media absolutely refuses to show it. People are estimating 25,000 to 35,000 people, but our record so far is Texas with 87,000 people with 50,000 being turned away. This is really fun! March 27, 2022

March 28, 2022

Donald J Trump @RealDonaldTrump
Glad to see Clarence Thomas is healthy and doing well. March 28, 2022

March 30, 2022

Donald J Trump @RealDonaldTrump
So the Radical Left Democrats in Congress and the Unselect Committee continue to seek the destruction of lives of very good people, but have no interest in going after the criminals and thugs who cheated like

mad dogs on the 2020 Presidential Election. All the evidence is in and conclusive, but they, and the Fake News Media, refuse to look at or report it. They call it the Big Lie, but the Big Lie is the exact opposite— they are the liars, they are the cheaters, and they are the ones who are destroying our Country at the Voting Booths, the Borders, the Gas Stations, with our Military, our Vets, Foreign Relations, and everywhere else! March 30, 2022

Donald J Trump @RealDonaldTrump
Many people are asking, so I'll give it to you now, it is 100% true. While playing with the legendary golfer, Ernie Els, winner of four Majors and approximately 72 other tournaments throughout the world, Gene Sauers, winner of the Senior U.S. Open, Ken Duke, and Mike Goodes, both excellent tour players, I made a hole-in-one. It took place at Trump International Golf Club in West Palm Beach, Florida, on the 7th hole, which was playing 181-yards into a slight wind. I hit a 5-iron, which sailed magnificently into a rather strong wind, with approximately 5 feet of cut, whereupon it bounced twice and then went clank, into the hole.
These great tour players noticed it before I did because their eyes are slightly better, but on that one hole only, their swings weren't. Anyway, there's a lot of chatter about it, quite exciting, and people everywhere seem to be asking for the facts. Playing with that group of wonderful, talented players was a lot of fun.
The match was Ernie and me (with no strokes) against Gene, Mike, and Ken. I won't tell you who won because I am a very modest individual, and you will then say I was bragging- and I don't like people who brag! [0:39 video of Trump being congratulated for the shot] March 30, 2022

Donald J Trump @RealDonaldTrump
Shifty Adam Schiff and the same "scum" who fought us on Russia, Russia, Russia, Ukraine, Ukraine, Ukraine, Impeachment Hoax #1, Impeachment Hoax #2, and more, coupled with Crazy Liz Cheney and Cryin' Adam Kinzinger, have gone on, as the Unselect Committee, to try and destroy the lives of many wonderful people. It can't be allowed to happen! March 30, 2022

Donald J Trump @RealDonaldTrump
While they say that January 6 was an "attempted coup," which it was not, they should add that the Election on November 3 was the actual coup. All you have to do is look at the massive evidence in Swing States,

available upon request (with much more to come). Our Country is paying a big price for that Rigged Election! March 30, 2022

March 31, 2022

Donald J Trump @RealDonaldTrump

I hear that VERY low-rated "Morning Joe" and his psycho wife, Mika, think that I should not be asking Russia what the $3.5 million that Hunter and Joe got from the Mayor of Moscow's wife was for. In time, Russia may be willing to give that information. The Fake News is also saying I called Putin a "genius," when actually, and to be precise, I called his build-up on the Ukraine Border before the war started genius because I assumed he would be easily able to negotiate a great deal for Russia. The U.S. and NATO would agree to give Russia what they wanted.

Unfortunately, and tragically, Putin went too far, acting on the WEAK Foreign Policy of the Biden Administration. The Fake News said I called him a genius during the war. No, I was describing the great negotiating posture he had prior to the unfortunate decision to enter Ukraine and fight. There was nothing "genius" about that! March 31, 2022

Donald J Trump @RealDonaldTrump

Breaking News: Wow! Just out that the 2016 Clinton Campaign and the DNC paid the FEC today for violating the law by failing to disclose that their payments for "legal advice and services" to law firm Perkins Coie was, in fact, a guise to hire numerous companies, all of whom are now named Defendants in my lawsuit, to try and take down and illegally destroy your favorite President, me. This was done to create, as I have stated many times, and is now confirmed, a Hoax funded by the DNC and the Clinton Campaign. This corruption is only beginning to be revealed, is un-American, and must never be allowed to happen again. Where do I go to get my reputation back? March 31, 2022

Chapter Sixteen
Trump's Statements
April 2022

These Trump Statements are continued from Chapter Fifteen.

April 1, 2022

Donald J Trump @RealDonaldTrump
So after 50 years of being virtually empty, I built up our oil reserves during my administration, and low energy prices, to 100% full. It's called the Strategic National Reserves, and it hasn't been full for many decades. In fact, it's been mostly empty. It's supposed to only be used for large-scale emergency or conflict. Now I see where Biden has just announced he's going to take what we so carefully and magically built, and what will be a futile attempt to reduce oil and gasoline prices. They will soon bring it down to empty again. It just never ends! April 1, 2022

April 3, 2022

Donald J Trump @RealDonaldTrump
Great night in Michigan—with 7,000 inside and 21,000 outside trying to get in! [two pictures of the packed rally] April 3, 2022

April 4, 2022

Donald J Trump @RealDonaldTrump
Wonderful patriot Sarah Palin of Alaska just announced that she is running for Congress, and that means there will be a true America First fighter on the ballot to replace the late and legendary Congressman Don Young. Sarah shocked many when she endorsed me very early in 2016, and we won big. Now, it's my turn!
Sarah has been a champion for Alaska values, Alaska energy, Alaska jobs, and the great people of Alaska. She was one of the most popular Governors because she stood up to corruption in both State Government and the Fake News Media. Sarah lifted the McCain presidential campaign out of the dumps despite the fact that she had to endure

some very evil, stupid, and jealous people within the campaign itself. They were out to destroy her, but she didn't let that happen.

Sarah Palin is tough and smart and will never back down, and I am proud to give her my Complete and Total Endorsement, and encourage all Republicans to unite behind this wonderful person and her campaign to put America First! April 4, 2022

April 6, 2022

Donald J Trump @RealDonaldTrump

UPTON QUITS! 4 down and 6 to go. Others losing badly, who's next? April 6, 2022

Extended Comment
Fred Upton/ Yes Impeachment Votes

Trump is referring to Rep. Fred Upton (R. MI). He is one of the ten Repub representatives who voted "Yes" on impeachment in the second House impeachment, as discussed in my *Tragic Ending* book. Trump has made it his goal to get all ten out of office.

Michigan GOP Rep. Fred Upton announced Tuesday he will retire from the House instead of seeking another term in the 2022 election cycle.

Upton was one of 10 House Republicans who voted to impeach then-President Donald Trump following the Jan. 6 Capitol riot.

He joins three other Reps. in that group who have announced they will not be seeking reelection this cycle. Reps. Anthony Gonzalez (R-Ohio), John Katko (R-N.Y.), and Adam Kinzinger (R-Ill.) are also stepping back from public office.

Upton, who has been in Congress since 1986, says his retirement decision is unrelated to his impeachment vote.

"This was our decision, independent of what I did with Trump," he said. (Just the News. GOP).

A few weeks after voting to impeach Donald Trump, the 10 House Republicans who supported charging the now-ex-president with inciting the Capitol riot gathered with a conservative luminary who told them not to worry.

314

Trump Fights Back with Statements

"Former presidents just sort of fade away," Arthur Brooks, the former president of the American Enterprise Institute, told the anti-Trump Republicans over breakfast.

"Not this guy," Rep. Fred Upton (R-Mich.) interjected, politely predicting the exact path Trump would follow. "It's going to be scorched earth, election was stolen."

On Tuesday [4/5/22], after more than 35 years in Congress, Upton declared that he had reached the end of this ideological fight for the soul of the Republican Party (WaPo. Fred).

It's been more than a year [as of 3/1/22] since the House of Representatives impeached then-President Trump for his role in the Jan. 6 attack. Ten House Republicans voted to impeach him, a remarkably high number (five House Democrats voted to impeach Bill Clinton in 1998.). After a trial, the Senate acquitted Trump.

But Trump critics in the Republican Party tend not to stay in office for very long.

Four have retired; six are running or are likely to run for reelection, all of them facing primary challengers because of their impeachment vote — including some endorsed by Trump (WaPo. What).

To comment, Upton can claim his decision to not run again is unrelated to Trump, but the pattern is hard to miss, with three others of the ten making the same decision.

New York Republican Rep. John Katko's surprise retirement announcement Friday [1/14/22] is simply the latest proof that there's no room in the Republican Party for people who are insufficiently loyal to former President Donald Trump.

Katko is one of 10 House Republicans who voted to impeach Trump for his actions (and inaction) during the January 6 riot at the US Capitol. He is now one of three -- Reps. Anthony Gonzalez of Ohio and Adam Kinzinger of Illinois are the others -- who have announced they will leave Congress at the end of this term (CNN. Another). Back to Trump.

Of the other six, they have either already lost their reelection bids or are way behind in the polls, such as Liz Cheney. Last I heard, she was down by 23 percentage points. Back to Trump.

Against Lies of Biden, Attacks from Dems, and Bias of Media

Donald J Trump @RealDonaldTrump

I want to congratulate Congressman Bob Gibbs of Ohio on a wonderful and accomplished career. His retirement, after serving in Congress for more than a decade, should be celebrated by all. He was a strong ally to me and MAGA, voting to support my America First agenda and fighting strongly against the Radical Left. Thank you for your service, Bob—a job well done! April 7, 2022

April 7, 2022

Donald J Trump @RealDonaldTrump

New approval rating—96% in the Republican Party, much of it a STRONG approval! April 7, 2022

April 8, 2022

Donald J Trump @RealDonaldTrump

This is just a continuation of the greatest Witch Hunt of all time, by a failed Attorney General, who continues to use her office for political gain following a disastrous and embarrassing attempt to run for Governor, in which she only received a 3% approval rating, and was forced to drop out of the race by her own party, in disgrace. This Democrat prosecutorial misconduct began the second I came down the escalator in Trump Tower, and has continued in an attempt to silence a President who is leading in every single poll. Never before has this happened to another President, and it is an absolute violation of my civil rights.

As President I had two jobs—to run our Country well, and to survive. I've been investigated by the Democrats more than Billy the Kid, Jesse James, and Al Capone, combined. This has been going on for years, and in all cases, I have been innocent. After having survived so many investigations, numerous people have said to me, "You must be the cleanest person alive. Nobody else could have survived this." But how do I get my reputation back as this unfair persecution endlessly continues?

Letitia James is no longer working as Attorney General, she is an operative for the Democrat Party in a political prosecution. New York has been through [expletive], and she is an embarrassment to our legal system. James uses her office for political gain, while New York crime is up over 50 percent, a bigger increase than any other place in the Nation. Much of it is violent crime—murder, rape, and drug trafficking (which is at the highest level ever).

316

Trump Fights Back with Statements

When will the Witch Hunt against a popular former President, who had our Country Energy Independent, with no Inflation, a strong Southern Border, and no Wars (such as that which is now raging uncontrollably in Ukraine), who rebuilt our Military (including Space Force), cut Taxes, Regulations, and so much more, ever end. When will horrible and unfair political harassment and persecution in our Country finally be over. Instead, MAKE AMERICA GREAT AGAIN! April 8, 2022

Donald J Trump @RealDonaldTrump
What the Fake News Media doesn't tell you, and they are doing everything within their power to force prosecutors throughout the Country to do a terrible injustice to our Nation and its people, is that a low-life attorney named Mark Pomerantz, who is a "Never Trumper" and a Hillary Clinton sycophant (together with his wife), left a Never Trumper, Crooked Hillary law firm, Paul, Weiss, Rifkind, Wharton & Garrison, with two young associates who were also Never Trumpers, in order to go into the District Attorney's office to unjustly prosecute a man named Donald J. Trump, who also just happens to be the 45th President of the United States, and is leading in every poll to be the 47th.

The Fake News also didn't reveal the fact that this is virtually unprecedented for private lawyers to take an unpaid leave of absence from an opposing party law firm in order to prosecute anyone, let alone a former President. They also didn't tell you that a principal leader of the firm is Robert Schumer, the brother of Chuck Schumer, that the firm is a Never Trumper firm and works for the Democrat Party, that for lawyers to go into the New York City's District Attorney's office to prosecute an opponent is unprecedented in NYC history because the District Attorney's office has hundreds of lawyers already working there, and that a number of Assistant District Attorneys refused to work on the case because they felt I was being treated extremely unfairly, and that indeed, there was no case.

Can you imagine a Never Trumper Democrat-only law firm sending a Never Trumper law partner with two associates to the District Attorney's office to prosecute their political opponent, Donald J. Trump, and the firm represents the Democrat Party, and is headed by Robert Schumer, Chuck Schumer's brother, and many other Never Trumpers? What kind of Country are we living in? April 8, 2022

Extended Comment
Manhattan Criminal and Civil Probes

Trump is referring to the following:

Against Lies of Biden, Attacks from Dems, and Bias of Media

Former President Trump, members of his family, and the real estate business that bears his name remain under criminal investigation in Manhattan despite the recent resignations of the two experienced prosecutors leading the case, Manhattan District Attorney Alvin Bragg insisted Thursday [4/7/22] in his first public statement about the case since the resignations in February....

The Trump Organization and Trump's long-serving chief financial officer, Allen Weisselberg, have each pleaded not guilty to charges they've faced in connection with the probe, which has been looking into whether proper taxes were paid on perks given to certain Trump Organization executives.

The case also examines how Trump valued his real estate holdings when he sought loans and tax breaks. The New York Attorney General's office is conducting a parallel civil investigation (ABC News. Manhattan).

Former President Donald Trump should be held in contempt for failing to respond to a subpoena as instructed, the New York Attorney General's office said Thursday in a new court filing.

New York Attorney General Letitia James also asked the judge to impose a daily $10,000 fine until Trump complies.

The subpoena, issued as part of James' civil investigation into the way Trump values his real estate portfolio, sought personal documents from Trump, including tax records and statements of financial condition. The original deadline of March 3 was pushed to March 31 after Trump asked for an extension (ABC News. NY Attorney).

As a later update for the last point:

Former President Donald Trump must pay a $110,000 fine to the New York state attorney and meet other conditions to purge a contempt of court order for his failure to comply with a subpoena in a civil probe into his business practices, a New York judge said on Wednesday [5/11/22].

Judge Arthur Engoron held Trump in contempt, imposing a fine of $10,000 a day, after the former president failed to comply with New York Attorney General Letitia James' subpoena.

If Trump pays the fine and meets other requirements, the judge said he would lift the contempt order (Newsmax. NY Judge).

Former President Trump has paid the $110,000 in fines he accrued for being found in contempt of court for being slow to respond to a civil subpoena in New York, the state attorney general's office that issued the subpoena said Friday [5/20/22].

Trump paid the fine Thursday [but still must submit additional paperwork to have the contempt order lifted, according Attorney General Letitia James' office (Just the News. Trump pays).

This case is still ongoing as of this writing (8/2/22).

April 10, 2022

Donald J Trump @RealDonaldTrump
Getting ready for our big rally tonight in North Carolina. Heavy support for Ted Budd for Senate, big crowd! April 10, 2022

Donald J Trump @RealDonaldTrump
This is all about winning elections in order to stop the Radical Left maniacs from destroying our Country. The Great Commonwealth of Pennsylvania has a tremendous opportunity to Save America by electing the brilliant and well-known Dr. Mehmet Oz for the United States Senate. I have known Dr. Oz for many years, as have many others, even if only through his very successful television show. He has lived with us through the screen and has always been popular, respected, and smart. He even said that I was in extraordinary health, which made me like him even more (although he also said I should lose a couple of pounds!).

He is a graduate of Harvard University and earned a joint MD and MBA from the University of Pennsylvania School of Medicine and Wharton School of Finance. He has authored more than 350 original publications, written 8 New York Times bestsellers, and received patents for developing medical devices that have improved countless lives and performed thousands of life-saving heart operations.

Dr. Oz is Pro-Life, very strong on Crime, the Border, Election Fraud, our Great Military, and our Vets, Tax Cuts, and will always fight for and support our under-siege Second Amendment. He will ensure America will become Energy Independent again. Dr. Oz also passionately believes in high-quality education and protecting parent involvement throughout the process. Perhaps most importantly, I believe that Mehmet Oz will be the one most able to win the General Election against a Radical Left Democrat looking to do unthinkable harm to our Country.

Women, in particular, are drawn to Dr. Oz for his advice and counsel. I have seen this many times over the years. They know him, believe in him, and trust him. Likewise, he will do very well in Philadelphia and

Pittsburgh, where other candidates will just not be accepted. He knows his job is to serve every single Pennsylvanian. Dr. Oz is smart, tough, and will never let you down, therefore, he has my Complete and Total Endorsement. Good luck, Dr. Oz. our Country needs you! April 10, 2022

April 12, 2022

Donald J Trump @RealDonaldTrump

Is the Unselect Committee of January 6th going to see the movie that was just released by Citizens United, called "Rigged," or the movie coming out shortly concerning True the Vote and produced by Dinesh D'souza called "2,000 Mules"? When you watch the movies, or look at any of the other mountains of evidence on the Rigged Election, you would realize that their standard and boring sound bite, "The Big Lie," is actually the Big Lie in reverse! April 12, 2022

April 13, 2022

Donald J Trump @RealDonaldTrump

One person in Pennsylvania who I will not be endorsing is Bill McSwain for Governor. He was the U.S. Attorney who did absolutely nothing on the massive Election Fraud that took place in Philadelphia and throughout the commonwealth. He said Barr told him not to do anything (because Barr was afraid of being impeached by the Democrats), but he should have done his job anyway. Without free and fair Elections, we don't have a Country. Do not vote for Bill McSwain, a coward, who let our Country down. He knew what was happening and let it go. It was there for the taking and he failed so badly. Many of the U.S. Attorneys were probably told not to do anything by Barr. Hence, our Country is going to hell [expletive]. April 13, 2022

April 15, 2022

Donald J Trump @RealDonaldTrump

PRESIDENT DONALD J. TRUMP ENDORSES J.D. VANCE FOR THE UNITED STATES SENATE IN OHIO. April 17, 2022

Donald J Trump @RealDonaldTrump

MAGA patriots from across the nation are set to deliver an election landside for Republicans that will serve as a devastating rebuke of the failures of Joe Biden and the Radical Left Democrats. In the Great State

320

of Ohio, the candidate most qualified and ready to win in November is J.D. Vance. We cannot play games. It is all about winning!

Like some others, J.D. Vance may have said some not so great things about me in the past, but he gets it now, and I have seen that in spades. He is our best chance for victory in what could be a very tough race. The Democrats will be spending many millions of dollars, but the good news is that they have a defective candidate who ran for President and garnered exactly zero percent in the polls. The bottom line is, we must have a Republican victory in Ohio.

This is not an easy endorsement for me to make because I like and respect some of the other candidates in the race—they've said great things about "Trump" and, like me, they love Ohio and love our Country. I've studied this race closely and I think J.D. is the most likely to take out the weak, but dangerous, Democrat opponent—dangerous because they will have so much money to spend. However, J.D. will destroy him in the debates and will fight for the MAGA Movement in the Senate. He's strong on the Border, tough on Crime, understands how to use Taxes and Tariffs to hold China accountable, will fight to break up Big Tech, and has been a warrior on the Rigged and Stolen Presidential Election.

J.D. is a Marine who served in the Iraq War, a graduate of The Ohio State University, and earned a Law Degree from Yale—a great student. With J.D. Vance, Ohio gets both brains and brawn. Ohio has been good to me, I won it twice, really BIG, and I have likewise been GREAT for Ohio. Let's keep it going!

It is time for the entire MAGA movement, the greatest in the history of our Country, to unite behind J.D.'s campaign because, unlike so many other pretenders and wannabes, he will put America First. In other words, J.D. Vance has my Complete and Total Endorsement. He will not let you down. MAKE AMERICA GREAT AGAIN! April 15, 2022

April 17, 2022
Easter Sunday

Donald J Trump @RealDonaldTrump

Happy Easter to all including the Radical Left Maniacs who are doing everything possible to destroy our Country. May they not succeed, but let them, nevertheless, be happy, healthy, wealthy, and well! April 17, 2022

Donald J Trump @RealDonaldTrump

Happy Easter to failed gubernatorial candidate and racist Attorney General Letitia James. May she remain healthy despite the fact that she will continue to drive business out of New York while at the same time keeping crime, death, and destruction in New York! April 17, 2022

Extended Comment
Easter Not for Political Fights Again

I must once again rebuke Trump for using Easter as an occasion to attack his political opponents. It is a day for proclaiming and celebrating the resurrection of Jesus Christ, not political fights.

[1]Now after [the] Sabbaths, at the dawning into [the] first [day between the] Sabbaths [fig., the first day of the week; i.e., early Sunday morning], Mary the Magdalene and the other Mary went [or, came] to see the grave. [2]And look! A great earthquake occurred, for an angel of [the] Lord having come down out of heaven, having come to [the tomb], rolled away the stone from the entrance and was sitting on it. [3]Now his appearance was like lightning and his clothing white as snow. [4]But the ones keeping guard shook because of the fear of him, and they became as dead [men].
[5]Then answering, the angel said to the women, "You*, stop being afraid! For I know that you* seek Jesus, the One having been crucified. [6]He is not here! For He was raised, just as He said! Come, see the place where the Lord was lying. [7]And go quickly, say to His disciples, 'He was raised from the dead!' And listen! He is going before you* to Galilee; there you* will see Him. Listen! I told you*." [8]And having gone out quickly from the tomb, with fear and great joy, they ran to report to His disciples (Matthew 28:1-8). Back to Trump

April 19, 2022

Donald J Trump @RealDonaldTrump

With the horrible Subway Shootings and Violent Crime in New York being at an all-time high, where people are afraid to walk the streets, the racist and highly partisan Attorney General of New York State, failed Gubernatorial candidate Letitia James, should focus her efforts on saving the State of New York and ending its reputation as a Crime Capital of the World, instead of spending millions of dollars and utilizing a large portion of her office in going after Donald J. Trump and the Trump Organization (for many years!), who have probably done more for New York than virtually any other person or group, including employing many wonderful people and paying millions and millions of dollars in taxes. This never-ending Witch Hunt must stop.

We don't need racist political hacks going after good, hardworking people for highly partisan political gain. The people of our Country see right through it all, and won't take this Radical Left "sickness" anymore. Make New York Great Again! April 19, 2022

Donald J Trump @RealDonaldTrump

Attorney General Brnovich of Arizona was given massive information on the fraud and so-called "irregularities" that took place in the 2020 Presidential Election. Many people said that he would do nothing about it because that just seems to be the way he is. I felt differently because the numbers and sheer amount of crime committed is so compelling, irrefutable, and determinative—the election result would have been entirely different.

Well, he did a report, and he recites some of the many horrible things that happened in that very dark period of American history but, rather than go after the people that committed these election crimes, it looks like he is just going to "kick the can down the road" and stay in that middle path of non-controversy. He wants to be politically correct. Because of the amount of time that it took him to do the report, which was endless, his poll numbers have been rapidly sinking. Now, people are upset with the fact that while he states the problem, he seems to be doing nothing about it—he doesn't give the answers.

What a shame for the Great State of Arizona, and for our Country itself! Because of this election, the USA is "going to [expletive]" with Inflation, Russia attacking Ukraine, the loss of Energy Independence, 5-dollar gasoline, a wide-open Border and, of course, the incompetence with which our pull-out from Afghanistan was handled. With an honest election, none of these things would have been a problem, they were all self-inflicted wounds. The good news is Arizona has some very good people running for election to the U.S. Senate. I will be making an Endorsement in the not too distant future! April 19, 2022

Donald J Trump @RealDonaldTrump

It doesn't make sense that Russia and Ukraine aren't sitting down and working out some kind of an agreement. If they don't do it soon, there will be nothing left but death, destruction, and carnage. This is a war that never should have happened, but it did. The solution can never be as good as it would have been before the shooting started, but there is a solution, and it should be figured out now—not later—when everyone will be DEAD! April 19, 2022

April 22, 2022

Donald J Trump @RealDonaldTrump

Piers Morgan, like the rest of the Fake News Media, attempted to unlawfully and deceptively edit his long and tedious interview with me. He wanted to make it look like I walked out on the interview when my time limit of 20 minutes went over by an hour. The good news is that the interview was taped by us as a means of keeping him honest. The interview was actually very strong on the 2020 Election Fraud, with me calling him "a fool" if he truly believed those results. The evidence is massive and irrefutable (check out Truth the Vote and the Dinesh D'Souza documentary, which will all be coming out soon). For those who want to make Piers look bad, compare his video promo and how it was doctored to the real thing. Hopefully they will now be doing some big changes to their final product. It just shows, however, what I have to deal with in the Fake News Media. He went out of his way to deceptively edit an interview and got caught. That is a big story, isn't it?

Listen to the audio here:
https://m.soundcloud.com/breitbart/ending-audio-of-donald-trump-interview-with-piers-morgan
April 21, 2022

Donald J Trump @RealDonaldTrump

Congratulations to CNN+ on their decision to immediately FOLD for a lack of ratings, or viewers in any way, shape, or form. It was like an empty desert out there despite spending hundreds of millions of dollars and the hiring of low-rated Chris Wallace, a man who tried so hard to be his father, Mike, but lacked the talent and whatever else is necessary to be a star. In any event, it's just one more piece of CNN and Fake News that we don't have to bother with anymore! April 22, 2022

To comment, this Statement is in regard to CNN's failed streaming service. It lasted all of three weeks due to subscribers being well below expectations. Chris Wallace left FNC for CNN on the promise of a show on CNN+. Now he is out of a job. After his dreadful performance as moderator in a presidential debate, which I discuss in my *Corruption* book, I cannot feel sorry for him.

Donald J Trump @RealDonaldTrump

The Governor of Georgia, Brian Kemp, and Secretary of State, Brad Raffensperger, perhaps in collusion with the Radical Left Democrats, have allowed a horrible thing to happen to a very popular Republican,

Trump Fights Back with Statements

Congresswoman Marjorie Taylor Greene. She is now going through [expletive] in their attempt to unseat her, just more of an election mess in Georgia, including the fact that they will still allow easily corruptible Ballot Boxes for all to cheat with, and have not been able to get a little thing called "Signature Verification" approved.

Unlike other Republicans, this Governor does everything possible to hurt the voting process in Georgia, including his approval of a disastrous Consent Decree, and not calling a Special Session that was requested by Georgia's Republicans Senators. He absolutely refused. Both of those failures were a disaster for the Republican Party, and for our Country.

Even the "True the Vote" people, great patriots, who will soon announce massive Ballot Harvesting in Georgia and other States, said Kemp was the worst of all Governors to deal with—he didn't want to do anything to help with finding this massive Ballot Harvesting fraud. Brian Kemp should be voted out of office—vote for David Perdue. REMEMBER, Brian Kemp will never be able to win the General Election against Stacey "The Hoax" Abrams because a large number of Republicans just will not vote for him. April 22, 2022

Donald J Trump @RealDonaldTrump

If I did what Piers Morgan did in his fake interview with me, rigging and redoing my words, and then making it sound like I walked out of an interview, the failed gubernatorial candidate and Radical Left Racist, Attorney General of New York State, Letitia James, would start an immediate investigation and demand the re-institution of the death penalty, or whatever may be worse than that. Piers got caught red-handed, and the interview that I rather enjoyed doing is now in shambles.

I especially enjoyed talking about the 2020 Presidential Election Fraud and his big mistake on the way he walked off his show when the "weatherman" made him look like a fool. I never walked out of my interviews with him, he's easy, but he tried to make it look like I did. Unlike others, I don't believe Piers is a complete slimeball, but he lost a lot of credibility. Interestingly, many of the Fake News Media outlets are covering his mistake. They view it as potentially fraudulent, and so do I. Piers is off to a bad start, but thanks to me, he may get a final burst of big ratings before it all comes crashing down! April 22, 2022

Donald J Trump @RealDonaldTrump

Looking forward to speaking at the Heritage Foundation Annual Leadership Conference in Amelia Island, Florida this evening. See you there! April 22, 2022

April 23, 2022

Donald J Trump @RealDonaldTrump
Heading to Ohio for a big rally tonight, great crowd. See you there! April 23, 2022

April 24, 2022

Donald J Trump @RealDonaldTrump
Why did Twitter quickly take down this video that I made on January 6th, and why isn't the Unselect Committee of political hacks talking about it? April 24, 2022

To comment, I discuss this video and all of Trump's tweets on that day in depth in my *Trump's Tweet* book.

April 25, 2022

Donald J Trump @RealDonaldTrump
The Special Counsel appointed by the Wisconsin Assembly to investigate the crimes of the 2020 Election did an outstanding job. He discovered many pieces of evidence that indicate foul play. Anyone calling themselves a Republican in Wisconsin should support the continued investigation in Wisconsin without interference. After all of the evidence the report brought to light, how could anyone want to stop it? I understand some RINOs have primary challengers in Wisconsin. I'm sure their primary opponents would get a huge bump in the polls if these RINOs interfere. April 25, 2022

April 26, 2022

Donald J Trump @RealDonaldTrump
Truth Social is number ONE in the Apple App Store! [screen shot of the top five apps in the iPhone app store, with Truth Social listed as number one.] April 26, 2022

To comment, Truth Social is Trump's new social media site. It went online in March. But, as far as I can tell, at this time, it was still only available for iPhone. But it would soon be available for Android and as well as a regular website. I usually access it from the latter. See Appendix Three for further details.

April 28, 2022

Donald J Trump @RealDonaldTrump
No, he's mentally ill, a very sick man. I don't know what Kellyanne did to him, but it must have been really bad. She has totally destroyed this guy—his mind is completely shot! [picture of George Conway looking fat and sad] April 28, 2022

To comment, Kellyanne is Kellyanne Conway, Trump's former campaign manager and advisor. George is her husband or maybe now ex-husband, I'm not sure. But I do know they had many disagreements over Trump.

April 29, 2022

Donald J Trump @RealDonaldTrump
I'M BACK! #COVFEFE [picture of Trump standing in the green yard in front of Mara logo] April 29, 2022

To comment, this was Trump's first post on his own social media site Truth Social. But it was cross-posted on Gab. The "Covfefe" is a reference to a typo he made in a Tweet a while back that the media went nuts over. This is Trump trolling them.

Donald J Trump @RealDonaldTrump
Remember when Bernie Sanders used to draw crowds of 3,000, 4,000 or even 5,000 people, and the press would go absolutely wild talking about how big Bernie's crowds were showing them from all different angles and making it sound like the greatest show on earth—but when I draw 30,000, 40,000, 50,000 or in one case 87,000 people, reporters do not report it and cameras are not allowed to show how big the crowds are. It is a constant complaint I make during speeches. Turn the cameras, I say, turn the cameras to show the crowd, but they refuse to do it, not even the networks that are even a little bit on our side. The good news is, the people of our Country get it, and they get it like never before! April 29, 2022

Donald J Trump @RealDonaldTrump
I immediately call for the release of all text messages sent to and from Barack Obama's Chief of Staff during their attempt to overturn the 2016 Presidential Election. They spied on my campaign, they spied on my transition team, and they even spied on the White House while I was

in the Oval Office. They did everything they could to disrupt the peaceful transfer of power, and stop the "Will of the People" with their Russia, Russia, Russia Hoax, Mueller Scam, and more. I wonder what the texts would reveal? Unlike my Chief of Staff, which show patriotic Americans concerned about illegal and massive Election Fraud in 2020, I say bad things would be revealed. April 29, 2022

April 30, 2022

Donald J Trump @RealDonaldTrump
The Democrats are the party of Disinformation. The Russia, Russia, Russia Scam, Impeachment Hoax #1, Impeachment Hoax #2, the Fake Dossier, and so much more, everything is a LIE – But their biggest LIE by far is the result of the 2020 election. They know it, and so does everyone else. April 30, 2022

To comment, I discuss Impeachment Hoax #1 in depth in my three-volume set on that fiasco. I discuss the irregularities in the 2020 election in my *Corruption* book

Donald J Trump @RealDonaldTrump
Just revealed that the Biden administration, on top of all of the other horrible things happening to our Country, will be putting a longtime political operative in charge of censoring Free Speech. They don't go after Facebook, Instagram, China's TikTok, or any of the others that are so unhinged, corrupt, or Radical Left. Our Fake News Media refuses to cover the facts as our Country spirals into [Expletive]! [picture of the new czar of the Ministry of Truth] April 30, 2022

Final Extended Comment

These last Statements end Trump communicating solely by issuing email Statements. He will now begin to post "Truths" regularly on Truth Social. I will not follow up this book with one containing those Truths as they are far different, mostly just consisting of links to news articles.

That said, it would be appreciated if the reader would write a review of this book on Amazon and/ or wherever you purchased it. Such reviews are a benefit to others who might be thinking of purchasing this book, and it is a help to me to know what readers like and do not like about this book. It would also be helpful if you would mention this book on whatever social media sites you participate in. Many thanks in advance for doing so.

Appendixes

Appendix One
Bibliography

Sources are cited in the text by being placed in parentheses using the first word or two of the main title of the source. For websites, the name of the website is given, followed by the first part of the webpage title. This Bibliography then gives the full biographical information.

For All Sections

Bible Versions:

All Scripture references in this book are taken from the *Analytical-Literal Translation of the Bible* (ALT). Copyright © 1999-2022 by Gary F. Zeolla (www.Zeolla.org).

TV News Channels:

CBS Evening News.
CNN.
Fox Business Network (FBN).
Fox News Channel (FNC).
Headline News.
KDKA TV Channel 2 (CBS affiliate for Pittsburgh, PA)
MSNBC.
Newsmax.
WPXI TV Channel 11 (NBC affiliate for Pittsburgh, PA)
WTAE TV Channel 4 (ABC/ CNN news affiliate for Pittsburgh, PA).

Radio News Reports:

America's First News (on 1320 AM, Pittsburgh, PA).
Answer, The 1250 AM (Pittsburgh, PA radio station)/
KDKA Radio, 1020 AM (CBS News affiliate radio station for Pittsburgh, PA and the world's first radio station).
NBC News Radio (on iHeartRadio).
News Talk 1320 AM (Pittsburgh, PA radio station).

Commentators (available on the iHeart app):

Bill O'Reilly.
Breakpoint.
Dan Bongino.
Dana Loesch (The Dana Show).

Megan Kelly.

Martin Gallagher (10:00 am to noon, 1250 The Answer, Pittsburgh).

Sean Hannity (3:00-6:00 pm, News Talk 1320 AM, Pittsburgh).

Town Hall Review (5:00-6:00 am weekdays, 5:00-6:00 am Saturdays, 101.5 WORD FM, Pittsburgh).

News Websites:

Trib Live is the website for three Pittsburgh area newspapers, including my hometown newspaper. I read their website most every day. That is why you see many references from Trib Live among the "For Chapters" sources. Note also, Trib Live is left-leaning in its perspective across all three of its newspapers and on its website.

The Trib often reprints articles from other news sources, most especially the AP. Those reprints are indicted by "Trib Live/ AP" (or whatever the original news source is) or "via Trib Live" at the end.

In addition, I subscribe to the websites for the *New York Times* (NYT), the *Wall Street Journal* (WSJ), and *Newsmax*. The NYT is very liberal, the WSJ is middle to right-leaning, while *Newsmax* is very conservative. That is why you see many references from these three sites.

Reuters is another go-to source, as it more moderate, giving me another perspective. That is why you see many references from it.

In addition, I check many other conservative, moderate, and left-leaning news websites regularly, as seen in the following references. All of these references give me a full-orbed view of the political landscape.

Book:

Unless otherwise indicated, all quotes from the US Constitution are from: Roosevelt, Franklin. 15 Documents and Speeches That Built America (Kindle edition).

English Reference:

Abbreviations.com

Dictionary.com.

Merriam-Webster. https://www.merriam-webster.com/

Oxford Dictionary (as found on Microsoft *Word 365*).

YourDictionary.com.

For Chapters

The following references are tied to specific chapters of this book.

Chapter Two
February 2021

RIP Rush Limbaugh:

Newsmax. Rush Limbaugh, Talk Radio Legend, Dies at 70 of Lung Cancer. https://www.newsmax.com/newsfront/rush-limbaugh-obituary-cancer/2021/02/17/id/1010398/

Media Bias Seen in Coverage of Rush's Death:

CNN. Rush Limbaugh, conservative media icon, dead at 70 following battle with cancer.
https://www.cnn.com/2021/02/17/media/rush-limbaugh-obituary/index.html

KDKA. Radio host Rush Limbaugh dies at 70.
https://www.radio.com/kdkaradio/news/national/polarizing-controversial-radio-host-rush-limbaugh-has-died

Newsmax. 'Fox & Friends' Rips NYT for Slams at Rush Limbaugh in His Obit. https://www.newsmax.com/politics/rush-limbaugh-newyorktimes-foxandfriends/2021/02/18/id/1010607/

NYT. Rush Limbaugh Dies at 70; Turned Talk Radio Into a Right-Wing Attack Machine. https://www.nytimes.com/2021/02/17/business/media/rush-limbaugh-dead.html

NYT. Rush Limbaugh's Legacy of Venom: As Trump Rose, 'It All Sounded Familiar.'
https://www.nytimes.com/2021/02/17/us/politics/limbaugh-death.html

Postmillennial. New York Times erases successful black man who produced Rush Limbaugh's shows.
https://thepostmillennial.com/new-york-times-erases-successful-black-man-who-produced-rush-limbaughs-shows/

Trib Live. Before making it big, Rush Limbaugh got his start in Pittsburgh as 'Jeff Christie.' https://triblive.com/local/rush-limbaugh-once-worked-in-pittsburgh-radio/

Trib Live/ AP. Even without listening, U.S. lives in Rush Limbaugh's media world. https://triblive.com/news/world/even-without-listening-u-s-lives-in-rush-limbaughs-media-world/

Trib Live/ AP. In Rush Limbaugh's home state, a flap over lowering flags. https://triblive.com/news/world/in-rush-limbaughs-home-state-a-flap-over-lowering-flags/

Dems and Celebrities on Rush:

Breitbart. Michael Moore Bashes Rush Limbaugh and His 'Brainwashed' Audience.

Against Lies of Biden, Attacks from Dems, and Bias of Media
https://www.breitbart.com/entertainment/2021/02/19/michael-moore-attacks-rush-limbaugh-i-cant-think-of-anybody-who-elevated-hate-racism-misogyny-more/

Chattanooga Conservative. Mayoral Candidate Kelly Mocks Death of Limbaugh; Supports Radical Agendas, Personal Gains At The Expense Of Chattanooga.
https://tennesseeconservativenews.com/mayoral-candidate-kelly-mocks-death-of-limbaugh-supports-radical-agendas-personal-gains-at-the-expense-of-chattanooga/

Just the News. Celebrity left rejoices in Limbaugh's death from cancer. https://justthenews.com/accountability/media/th-left-dance-grave-limbaugh-change-foto

Additional Tributes to Rush:

Breitbart. Ann Coulter: Rush Limbaugh Was 'Hilarious,' Taught Us to 'Forge Your Own Path.' https://www.breitbart.com/radio/2021/02/19/ann-coulter-rush-limbaugh-forge-own-path/

CNJ. Rush Limbaugh Remembered: 12 Standout Tributes to the Conservative Talk Radio Pioneer. https://christiannewsjournal.com/rush-limbaugh-remembered-12-standout-tributes-to-the-conservative-talk-radio-pioneer/

Creators. Limbaugh's Success Came in Spite of Big Media. https://www.creators.com/read/debra-saunders/02/21/limbaughs-success-came-in-spite-of-big-media

Fox News. Israel's Netanyahu sends condolences to Rush Limbaugh's family. https://www.foxnews.com/world/israel-netanyahu-rush-limbaugh

Fox News. Mike Pence: Rush Limbaugh's legacy – Here's how conservative Americans can repay the debt we owe to him. https://www.foxnews.com/opinion/mike-pence-rush-limbaugh-legacy-conservatives-repay-debt

Fox News. Rush Limbaugh to be honored at CPAC, inducted into Conservative Hall of Fame. https://www.foxnews.com/media/rush-limbaugh-to-be-honored-at-cpac

Just the News. Limbaugh became synonymous with talk radio during his career, transforming the medium in the process. https://justthenews.com/accountability/media/limbaugh-became-synonymous-talk-radio-during-his-career-transforming-medium

Just the News. Trump calls Limbaugh 'legend,' in first TV interview since Senate trial. https://justthenews.com/government/white-house/trump-calls-limbaugh-legend-first-tv-interview-leaving-white-house

Newsmax. 'Bo Snerdley': Rush Was a 'Phenomenon,' Great Human Being. https://www.newsmax.com/us/bosnerdley-rushlimbaugh-radio/2021/02/20/id/1010832/

Newsmax. David Limbaugh on Rush's Passing: 'My Brother Was the Real Deal.' https://www.newsmax.com/us/rush-limbaugh-death-david-limbaugh/2021/02/18/id/1010584/

Newsmax. DeSantis: Rush Limbaugh Was 'Obviously a Legend.' https://www.newsmax.com/us/desantis-limbaugh-florida-covid/2021/02/18/id/1010582/

Newsmax. Hannity: Rush Limbaugh Experienced 'Cancel Culture' Often. https://www.newsmax.com/us/hannity-rush-limbaugh-death-cancel-culture/2021/02/18/id/1010544/

Newsmax. Newt Gingrich Credits Rush Limbaugh With Helping GOP Take Control of House in '94. https://www.newsmax.com/politics/gingrich-limbaugh-houseofrepresentatives/2021/02/17/id/1010455/

Newsmax. Rush Limbaugh's Widow Speaks Out About His Final Days. https://www.newsmax.com/thewire/kathryn-limbaugh-cancer-death-marriage/2021/02/23/id/1011216/

Townhall. Rush Limbaugh - A Life Lived Not by Lies. https://townhall.com/columnists/kevingrieve/2021/02/21/rush-limbaugh--a-life-lived-not-by-lies-n2585012

Miscellaneous:

AP. Haley: Trump was 'badly wrong' in stoking crowd before riot (via Trib Live). https://triblive.com/news/world/haley-trump-was-badly-wrong-in-stoking-crowd-before-riot/

Breitbart. Trump Announces First Endorsement: Bob Paduchik for GOP Chair of Ohio. https://www.breitbart.com/politics/2021/02/24/trump-announces-first-endorsement-bob-paduchik-for-gop-chair-of-ohio/

Chapter Three
March 2021

Trump's CPAC Speech:
Liberal News Outlets:

CNN. 6 takeaways from the Trump-dominated CPAC. https://www.cnn.com/2021/02/28/politics/cpac-2021-takeaways-sunday/index.html

CNN. Fact check: Trump delivers lie-filled CPAC speech.

https://www.cnn.com/2021/02/28/politics/donald-trump-cpac-speech-fact-check/index.html

CNN. The specter of Trump's comeback raises a practical question. https://www.cnn.com/2021/02/28/world/meanwhile-in-america-february-26-intl/index.html

CNN. Trump and his CPAC fans lead GOP down a losing path. https://www.cnn.com/2021/02/28/opinions/trump-cpac-gop-jennings/index.html

CNN. Trump teases 2024 presidential run in lie-filled CPAC speech. https://www.cnn.com/2021/02/28/politics/trump-cpac-speech-2021/index.html

CNN. Trump unleashes new threat to American democracy. https://www.cnn.com/2021/03/01/politics/cpac-2021-trump-speech-american-democracy/index.html

NYT. A Quiet Life Out of the Spotlight? Not for This Former President. https://www.nytimes.com/2021/02/27/us/politics/donald-trump-cpac.html

NYT. CPAC and the New Republicanism. https://www.nytimes.com/2021/02/27/us/politics/cpac-trump-republicans.html

NYT. CPAC Takeaways: Trump Dominates, and DeSantis and Noem Stand Out. https://www.nytimes.com/2021/02/28/us/politics/cpac-trump-kristi-noem.html

NYT. Trump Loyalists Spurn 'Failed Republican Establishment of Yesteryear.' https://www.nytimes.com/2021/02/26/us/politics/trump-cpac-conservatices-cruz.html

NYT. Trump's Republican Hit List at CPAC Is a Warning Shot to His Party. https://www.nytimes.com/2021/02/28/us/politics/trump-cpac-republicans.html

NYT. Trump Revives Familiar Falsehoods in CPAC Speech. https://www.nytimes.com/2021/02/28/us/politics/trump-cpac-fact-check.html

NYT. Trump Targets Republicans Who Supported His Impeachment. Video. https://www.nytimes.com/video/us/politics/100000007629038/trump-cpac-speech.html

Reuters. Trump hints at 2024 bid, repeats election lies. https://www.reuters.com/article/us-usa-politics-conservatives-trump/trump-hints-at-2024-bid-repeats-election-lies-idUSKCN2AS0QC

Reuters. Trump proposes new voting limits, rails against "monster" voting rights bill.

Trump Fights Back with Statements

https://www.reuters.com/article/us-usa-politics-conservatives-trump-voti/trump-proposes-new-voting-limits-rails-against-monster-voting-rights-bill-idUSKCN2AT0XH

Reuters. Trump targets disloyal Republicans, repeats election lies and hints at 2024 run
https://www.reuters.com/article/us-usa-politics-conservatives/trump-targets-disloyal-republicans-repeats-election-lies-and-hints-at-2024-run-idUSKCN2AS0J5

Trib Live/ AP. Trump calls for GOP unity, repeats lies about election loss. https://triblive.com/news/politics-election/trump-calls-for-gop-unity-says-he-wont-start-another-party/

Trib Live/ AP. Trumps were vaccinated in January before leaving White House, adviser says.
https://triblive.com/news/trumps-were-vaccinated-in-january-before-leaving-white-house-adviser-says/

Conservative News Outlets:

Daily Wire. Trump Debunks Claims He Is Creating New Party: 'We're Not Starting New Parties,' 'We Have The' GOP.
https://www.dailywire.com/news/trump-debunks-claims-he-is-creating-new-party-were-not-starting-new-parties-we-have-the-gop

Fox News. CPAC: 5 biggest moments from weekend as Trump returns to stage, conservatives rail against Biden.
https://www.foxnews.com/politics/5-biggest-moments-all-week-at-cpac

Fox News. Trump slams 'establishment' Republicans McConnell, Cheney and others in CPAC speech as some deny GOP civil war.
https://www.foxnews.com/politics/trump-slams-establishment-republicans-mcconnell-cheney-and-others-in-cpac-speech-as-some-deny-gop-civil-war

Fox News. Trump uses CPAC speech to tear into Biden on border crisis, says he won't create new party.
https://www.foxnews.com/politics/trump-speech-cpac-2024-straw-poll

Just the News. He's back! Trump vows to work for election of 'strong, tough and smart Republican leaders.'
https://justthenews.com/politics-policy/all-things-trump/breaking-president-trump-speaks-cpac-marking-first-major

Newsmax. Trump: Biden 'Sold Out America's Children' to Teachers' Unions. https://www.newsmax.com/politics/trump-cpac-biden-schools/2021/02/28/id/1011852/

Newsmax. Trump: House Dems' Equality Act Hurting Women.
https://www.newsmax.com/politics/house-democrats-equalityact-women/2021/02/28/id/1011865/

Newsmax. Trump Reminds CPAC 'Endless Wars' Ended Under Him. https://www.newsmax.com/politics/trump-cpac-biden-wars/2021/02/28/id/1011855/

Newsmax. Trump Rips Biden for Being Clueless on Vaccines. https://www.newsmax.com/politics/covid-19-pandemic-operation-warpspeed/2021/02/28/id/1011853/

Newsmax. Trump Slams China, Biden Reentering WHO. https://www.newsmax.com/politics/trump-china-who-speech/2021/02/28/id/1011857/

Newsmax. Trump: 'Time to Break Up Big Tech Monopolies. https://www.newsmax.com/politics/bigtech-section230-monopolies-sanctions/2021/02/28/id/1011858/

Newsmax. Trump to CPAC: Rush Limbaugh Is 'Watching Closely.' https://www.newsmax.com/politics/conservative-radio-host-memorial/2021/02/28/id/1011854/

Newsmax. Trump: We All Knew Biden Would be Bad. https://www.newsmax.com/newsfront/trump-biden-speech-cpac/2021/02/28/id/1011850/

Newsmax. Trump: 'We're Not Starting a New Party.' https://www.newsmax.com/politics/gop-republican-thirdparty-con-servatives/2021/02/28/id/1011849/

Post-Millennial. WATCH: Trump to CPAC: 'We will be united and strong like never before.' https://thepostmillennial.com/watch-trump-to-cpac-we-will-be-united-and-strong-like-never-before

WSJ. Trump Teases 2024 Run as He Hits Biden's Early Moves. https://www.wsj.com/articles/at-cpac-trump-to-assert-dominance-of-gop-take-aim-at-biden-on-immigration-foreign-policy-11614513600

WSJ. Video: 'It Is Far From Being Over,' Trump Hints Comeback at CPAC. https://www.wsj.com/video/it-is-far-from-being-over-trump-hints-comeback-at-cpac/A9AB1283-1603-403F-B3F4-9186357B92DA.html

Trump on Greg Kelly:

Fox News. Trump reveals story behind Rush Limbaugh's Presidential Medal of Freedom honor. https://www.foxnews.com/media/trump-rush-limbaugh-medal-of-free-dom-lung-cancer

Just the News. YouTube removes new interview with President Trump, citing 'presidential election integrity policy.' https://justthenews.com/politics-policy/all-things-trump/youtube-re-moves-interview-president-trump-citing-presidential

Newsmax. Donald Trump to Newsmax TV: Biden Lying or 'Mentally Gone' on Vaccine Gaffe.

Trump Fights Back with Statements

https://www.newsmax.com/newsmax-tv/mentally-gone-inauguration-operation-warp-speed/2021/02/17/id/1010452/

Newsmax. Donald Trump to Newsmax TV: Rush Was Unique, Great Friend. https://www.newsmax.com/newsmax-tv/remembrance-conservative-radio-host-memory/2021/02/17/id/1010456/

Newsmax. Trump on Election: 'Really Bad, Dishonest Things Happened.' https://www.newsmax.com/us/election-fraud-voter-fraud/2021/02/17/id/1010460/

Newsmax. Trump Stops Short of Committing to 2024 Presidential Run. https://www.newsmax.com/newsmax-tv/2024-presidential-campaign-polling/2021/02/17/id/1010463/

OAN. Trump tells OAN: 'the [MAGA] movement is very strong and it's getting stronger.' https://thepostmillennial.com/trump-oan-conservative-movement-strong-getting-stronger

Record Voter Turnout in Georgia:

Axios. Republicans parade Georgia's record early turnout. https://www.axios.com/2022/05/24/republicans-parade-georgias-record-early-turnout

Newsmax. Early Primary Voting Surges in Georgia After 'Election Integrity' Law. https://www.newsmax.com/newsfront/early-primary-voting-georgia-election-integrity/2022/05/25/id/1071400/

Republicans argue that the results go against Democrats' early claims that the 2021 election law signed by Republican Gov. Brian Kemp would amount to voter suppression.

Georgia Secretary of State. Georgia Election Law Results in Record Early-Voting Turnout. https://sos.ga.gov/news/georgia-election-law-results-record-early-voting-turnout

Durham Investigation:

DJ Media. Authorities Admit Currently Investigating Members of Hillary Clinton's 2016 Campaign: Durham. https://djhjmedia.com/steven/authorities-admit-currently-investigating-members-of-hillary-clintons-2016-campaign-durham/

Fox News. Clinton campaign paid to 'infiltrate' Trump Tower, White House servers to link Trump to Russia: Durham. https://www.foxnews.com/politics/clinton-campaign-paid-infiltrate-trump-tower-white-house-servers

Human Events. Federal Authorities Arrest Russian Analyst Who Contributed to Steele Dossier.https://humanevents.com/2021/11/04/federal-authorities-arrest-russian-analyst-who-contributed-to-steele-dossier/

Just the News. Durham bombshell: Prosecutor unveils smoking gun FBI text message, 'joint venture' to smear Trump. https://justthenews.com/accountability/russia-and-ukraine-scandals/durham-bombshell-fbi-text-message-shows-clinton-lawyer

Just the News. Durham evidence creates timeline of relentless Democrat effort to sell Russia collusion hoax. https://justthenews.com/accountability/russia-and-ukraine-scandals/durham-evidence-creates-timeline-relentless-democrat

Just the News. Durham indicts Democrat lawyer for making false statement when he fed Russia dirt to FBI. https://justthenews.com/accountability/russia-and-ukraine-scandals/durham-indicts-democrat-lawyer-who-fed-fbi-russia-dirt

Just the News. Durham unmasks alliance between media, Democrat dirt diggers that triggered false Russia story https://justthenews.com/accountability/russia-and-ukraine-scandals/durham-unmasks-alliance-between-media-democrat-dirt

Just the News. New Durham indictment exposes second leg of Hillary Clinton's Russia collusion dirty trick. https://justthenews.com/accountability/russia-and-ukraine-scandals/new-durham-indictment-exposes-second-leg-hillary

Just the News. Trump demands prosecutions, reparations after explosive revelations in Durham court filing. https://justthenews.com/accountability/russia-and-ukraine-scandals/trump-demands-prosecutions-reparations-after-explosive

Newsmax. Durham 'Disappointed'; Thanks Jury, Team for 'Seeking Truth, Justice'. https://www.newsmax.com/newsfront/john-durham-michael-sussmann-special-counsel-verdict/2022/05/31/id/1072286/

Newsmax. Durham Report: Clinton Campaign Paid to 'Infiltrate' Trump Tower, White House Servers. https://www.newsmax.com/politics/durham-report-spying-steele-dossier-trump/2022/02/12/id/1056594/

Newsmax. Nunes to Newsmax: Durham Probe Will Bring 'More' Indictments Against Clinton Campaign. https://www.newsmax.com/newsmax-tv/johndurham-hillaryclinton-campaign-2016/2022/02/14/id/1056802/

Newsmax. Former DNI Ratcliffe Expects More Indictments From Durham Probe. https://www.newsmax.com/newsfront/intelligence-director-ratcliffe-russia-clinton/2022/02/14/id/1056768/

Newsmax. Judge Rejects Michael Sussmann's Motion to Strike Info From Durham Filing. https://www.newsmax.com/newsfront/michael-sussmann-john-durham-motion-indictment/2022/03/11/id/1060741/

Trump Fights Back with Statements

Newsmax. Lesley Stahl Slammed for Unearthed Trump Interview After Durham Report. https://www.newsmax.com/newsfront/durham-report-trump-mainstream-media/2022/02/14/id/1056800/

Newsmax. Probe: Hillary Lawyer Used Purported Russian Cellphone Data to Implicate Trump. https://www.newsmax.com/politics/durham-clinton-attorney-russian-cell-phones/2022/02/15/id/1056870/

Newsmax. Rep. Mace to Newsmax: Durham Didn't Get Fair Shot on Sussmann. https://www.newsmax.com/newsmax-tv/nancy-mace-durham-sussman-hillary-clinton/2022/05/31/id/1072302/

Newsmax. Sussmann Acquittal Gives Dems Immunity From Corruption Charges. https://www.newsmax.com/morris/acquittal-doj-venues/2022/06/01/id/1072382/

Newsmax. Trump: Clinton Campaign's Actions 'Would Have Been Punishable by Death' in Past. https://www.newsmax.com/newsfront/donaldtrump-hillaryclinton-russia-durham/2022/02/13/id/1056618/

Newsmax. Trump Slams 'Corrupt' Legal System After Sussmann's 'Not Guilty' Verdict. https://www.newsmax.com/newsfront/donald-trump-michael-sussmann-trial-durham/2022/05/31/id/1072322/

Newsmax. Trump: 'Zero' Media Coverage of Hillary Clinton Spying Scandal. https://www.newsmax.com/newsfront/trump-clinton-spying-news-outlets/2022/02/14/id/1056738/

Newsmax. White House Won't Answer Questions on Durham Report. https://www.newsmax.com/politics/durham-report/2022/02/14/id/1056812/

NYT. Authorities Arrest Analyst Who Contributed to Steele Dossier. https://www.nytimes.com/2021/11/04/us/politics/igor-danchenko-arrested-steele-dossier.html

Technofog. Special Counsel John Durham continues his focus on the Hillary Clinton Campaign. https://technofog.substack.com/p/special-counsel-john-durham-continues?s=w

Durham raises FEC ruling against Clinton and DNC in attorney-client privilege battle. https://www.washingtonexaminer.com/news/justice/durham-raises-fec-ruling-against-clinton-and-dnc-in-attorney-client-privilege-battle

Washington Examiner. Durham issues trial subpoenas to Clinton campaign and DNC. https://www.washingtonexaminer.com/news/justice/durham-issues-trial-subpoenas-to-clinton-campaign-and-dnc

Washington Examiner. Durham trial: FBI agents who opened Alfa-Bank inquiry testify about 'typos' in launch document.

https://www.washingtonexaminer.com/news/justice/durham-trial-fbi-agents-who-opened-alfa-bank-inquiry-testify-about-typos-in-launch-document

Washington Examiner. Ratcliffe says 1,000 intel documents given to Durham support more charges.
https://www.washingtonexaminer.com/news/john-ratcliffe-intelligence-documents-john-durham-charges

Washington Examiner. Russiagate investigator believes Durham cracked 'insurance policy' mystery.
https://www.washingtonexaminer.com/news/justice/russiagate-investigator-believes-durham-cracked-insurance-policy-mystery

Miscellaneous:

Fox News. House Democratic margin shrinks to 2 votes with swearing-in of Republican Julia Letlow.
https://www.foxnews.com/politics/house-democratic-majority-two-vote-margin-julia-letlow

Just the News. Missouri GOP Sen. Roy Blunt won't seek 2022 reelection. https://justthenews.com/government/congress/missouri-gop-sen-roy-blunt-wont-seek-2020-reelection

Chapter Four
April 2021

Arizona Audit:

AP. Arizona Supreme Court allows release of Senate audit records. https://triblive.com/news/politics-election/arizona-supreme-court-allows-release-of-senate-audit-records/

AP. Arizona election audit enters new phase as ballot count ends(via Trib Live). https://triblive.com/news/politics-election/arizona-election-audit-enters-new-phase-as-ballot-count-ends/

AP. Firm recounting Arizona ballots wants methods kept secret (via Trib Live). https://triblive.com/news/politics-election/firm-recounting-arizona-ballots-wants-methods-kept-secret/

AP. Inside Arizona's election audit, GOP fraud fantasies live on (via Trib Live). https://triblive.com/news/politics-election/inside-arizonas-election-audit-gop-fraud-fantasies-live-on/

AP. Judge has doubts on voter privacy in Arizona recount (via Trib Live). https://triblive.com/news/politics-election/judge-has-doubts-on-voter-privacy-in-arizona-recount/

Trump Fights Back with Statements

AP. Maricopa County refuses Arizona Senate's subpoena in election audit. https://triblive.com/news/world/maricopa-county-refuses-arizona-senates-subpoena-in-election-audit/

Epoch Times. 499 Arizonans Claim Stores as Legal Residences: 110 Voted in 2020, Study Finds. https://www.theepochtimes.com/499-arizonans-claim-stores-as-legal-residences-110-voted-in-2020-study-finds_4250646.html

Epoch Times. Arizona Senate Told of Multiple Inconsistencies Found in Election Audit. https://www.theepochtimes.com/arizona-senate-president-releases-audit-results_4015286.html

Just the News. Arizona Senate on the verge of beginning major audit of Maricopa County ballots. https://justthenews.com/politics-policy/elections/arizona-senate-verge-beginning-major-audit-maricopa-county-ballots

Just the News. New judge named in Arizona 2020 election audit suit, hearings resume Tuesday. https://justthenews.com/government/courts-law/new-judge-named-arizona-2020-election-audit-suit-hearings-resume-tuesday

Just the News. Trump praises 'brave and patriotic' Arizona Republicans for spearheading election audit. https://justthenews.com/government/state-houses/trump-praises-brave-and-patriotic-arizona-republicans-spearheading-election

Just the News. Trump praises judge's decision in Arizona to allow election audit to continue. https://justthenews.com/politics-policy/elections/former-president-trump-issues-statement-judges-decision-arizona-allow

Just the News. Trump says result of Arizona election audit 'won't be good for the Dems'. https://justthenews.com/politics-policy/elections/trump-arizona-election-audit-wont-be-good-dems

KTAR. Arizona Dems file suit to stop Senate audit of Maricopa County election. https://ktar.com/story/4343249/arizona-dems-file-suit-to-stop-senate-audit-of-maricopa-county-election/

Newsmax. Arizona Election Audit Pits McCain Widow vs. State GOP Head Kelli Ward. https://www.newsmax.com/politics/mccain-arizona-maricopa-electionaudit/2021/05/03/id/1019966/

Newsmax. Arizona Election Auditors Battling Courts, Media, Democrats. https://www.newsmax.com/newsfront/arizona-election-audit-media/2021/05/07/id/1020562/

Newsmax. Judge Won't Block Arizona Senate's 2020 Election Recount. https://www.newsmax.com/politics/election-2020-arizona/2021/04/28/id/1019407/

Newsmax. Rep. Andy Biggs: 'We Don't Know' 2020 Election Winner in Arizona. https://www.newsmax.com/politics/arizona-election-audit-house-biggs/2021/10/08/id/1039664/

Washington Examiner. Judge orders Arizona Senate to produce Maricopa audit records.
https://www.washingtonexaminer.com/news/judge-orders-arizona-senate-produce-maricopa-audit-records

Susan Wright:
Newsmax. Republican Susan Wright Makes US House Runoff in Texas. https://www.newsmax.com/newsfront/susanwright-congress-texas-special-election/2021/05/02/id/1019787/

Newsmax. Smear Calls, Anti-Trumpers Couldn't Stop Rep. Wright's Widow in TX-6. https://www.newsmax.com/johngizzi/wrighttx-6trumpsmearkinzingercheney/2021/05/02/id/1019801/

Reuters. Texas Republican first in U.S. Congress to die from COVID-19.https://www.reuters.com/article/us-health-coronavirus-usa-wright/texas-republican-first-in-u-s-congress-to-die-from-covid-19-idUSKBN2A81WE

Chapter Five
May 2021

GOP Conference Chair:
NYP. Chip Roy to challenge Elise Stefanik for ousted Cheney's House GOP post. https://nypost.com/2021/05/13/chip-roy-to-challenge-elise-stefanik-for-ousted-cheneys-house-gop-post/

NYP. Liz Cheney removed from position as House GOP conference chair over anti-Trump stance.
https://nypost.com/2021/05/12/house-republicans-remove-rep-liz-cheney-from-leadership-post/

NYP. Rep. Elise Stefanik wins GOP conference chair vote to replace Liz Cheney. https://nypost.com/2021/05/14/elise-stefanik-wins-gop-conference-chair-vote-to-replace-cheney/

Criminal Probes of Trump's Business Dealings:
AP. New grand jury seated as Trump criminal probe continues (via Trib Live). https://triblive.com/news/world/new-grand-jury-seated-as-trump-criminal-probe-continues/

AP. Trump, Ivanka, Don Jr. subpoenaed in New York AG's investigation (via Trib Live). https://triblive.com/news/world/trump-ivanka-don-jr-subpoenaed-by-n-y-attorney-general/

Insider. The Trump Org claimed an apartment was worth $25 million while also offering it to Ivanka Trump for $8 million, New York AG alleges in fraud case (via Yahoo! News). https://news.yahoo.com/trump-org-claimed-apartment-worth-125140363.html

Insider. Trump Organization produced just 3 documents from Donald Trump in response to New York AG probe, court filings show (via Yahoo! News). https://news.yahoo.com/trump-organization-produced-just-3-194747881.html

Just the News. New York Attorney General Letitia James subpoenas Ivanka Trump, Don Jr., in ongoing tax probe. https://justthenews.com/politics-policy/all-things-trump/new-york-attorney-general-letitia-james-subpoenas-ivanka-trump-don

Newsmax. Judge Warns Trump Org to Follow Subpoenas. https://www.newsmax.com/us/judge-trump-organization-new-york-subpoenas/2021/09/24/id/1037837/

Reuters. As impeachment begins, New York accelerates probes of Trump's property dealings. https://www.reuters.com/article/us-usa-trump-investigations-insight/as-impeachment-begins-new-york-accelerates-probes-of-trumps-property-dealings-idUSKBN2A91CS

Miscellaneous:

Fox Business. Michael Avenatti faces sentencing in Nike extortion scheme. https://www.foxbusiness.com/lifestyle/michael-avenatti-faces-sentencing-in-nike-extortion-scheme

Chapter Six
June 2021

Fauci Emails and the Origins of Covid:

Blaze. A lab accident causing the COVID-19 pandemic was 'certainly possible,' top US biosafety expert admitted in emails early last year. https://www.theblaze.com/news/lab-accident-covid-19-pandemic-certainly-possible-top-us-biosafety-expert-admitted

Breitbart. Fauci Emails: Mark Zuckerberg Says 'People Trust and Want to Hear from Our Experts'. https://www.breitbart.com/tech/2021/06/02/fauci-emails-mark-zuckerberg-says-people-trust-and-want-to-hear-from-our-experts/

Breitbart. Malliotakis: We Need to See Unredacted Fauci Emails on Wuhan Lab. https://www.breitbart.com/politics/2021/06/05/malliotakis-we-need-to-see-unredacted-fauci-emails-on-wuhan-lab/

Breitbart. Sen. Roger Marshall: Anthony Fauci's 'Damning' Emails Proves He Should Resign.

Against Lies of Biden, Attacks from Dems, and Bias of Media
https://www.breitbart.com/politics/2021/06/05/exclusive-sen-roger-marshall-anthony-faucis-damning-emails-proves-he-should-resign/

Dan Bongino. Tucker Slams Fauci – Says Emails Reveal He Lied Under Oath. https://bongino.com/tucker-slams-fauci-says-emails-reveal-he-lied-under-oath

Just the News. Emails show Fauci made urgent inquiry about gain-of-function research as pandemic began. https://justthenews.com/politics-policy/coronavirus/keep-your-cell-phone-emails-show-fauci-discussing-gain-function

NYP. Republican lawmakers blast Fauci after thousands of emails released. https://nypost.com/2021/06/02/gop-lawmakers-blast-fauci-after-covid-origin-emails-released/

Postmillennial. Tucker Carlson SLAMS Fauci for lying under oath after emails revealed. https://thepostmillennial.com/watch-tucker-carlson-slams-fauci-for-lying-under-oath-after-emails-revealed/

Postmillennial. White House press sec praises Fauci as an 'undeniable asset' after bombshell email revelations https://thepostmillennial.com/breaking-white-house-press-sec-praises-fauci-as-an-undeniable-asset-rejects-re-litigating-bombshell-emails

Washington Examiner. Emails: Fauci 'massively flipped and flopped and flipped'. https://www.washingtonexaminer.com/washington-secrets/emails-fauci-massively-flipped-and-flopped-and-flipped

Washington Examiner. No reporters ask White House about Fauci emails during press briefing, sparking outrage. https://www.washingtonexaminer.com/news/no-reporters-ask-fauci-emails-press-briefing-outrage

Trump and Facebook:
American Military News. Trump speaks out after Facebook upholds his account ban. https://americanmilitarynews.com/2021/05/trump-speaks-out-after-facebook-upholds-his-account-ban/

American Military News. Trump to sue Facebook's Mark Zuckerberg, Twitter's Jack Dorsey, Google's Sundar Pichai. https://americanmilitarynews.com/2021/07/trump-to-sue-facebooks-mark-zuckerberg-twitters-jack-dorsey-report/

AP. Facebook board upholds former President Trump's suspension (via Trib Live). https://triblive.com/news/world/facebook-boards-trump-decision-could-have-wider-impacts/

AP. Facebook suspends Trump accounts for 2 years (via Trib Live). https://triblive.com/news/world/facebook-suspends-trump-accounts-for-2-years/

Trump Fights Back with Statements

AP. Trump files suit against Facebook, Twitter and YouTube (via Trib Live). https://triblive.com/news/world/trump-announces-suits-against-facebook-twitter-and-google/

Bloomberg News. Facebook rules are 'shambles,' oversight board co-chairman says (via Trib Live). https://triblive.com/news/wire-stories/facebook-rules-are-shambles-oversight-board-co-chairman-says/

Breitbart. Facebook Has 'No Plans' to Lift Ban on Donald Trump. https://www.breitbart.com/tech/2021/01/12/facebook-has-no-plans-to-lift-ban-on-donald-trump/

Hannity. REPORT: Donald Trump Planning Major Lawsuit Against Facebook, Twitter, Google Over Censorship. https://hannity.com/media-room/report-donald-trump-planning-major-lawsuit-against-facebook-twitter-google-over-censorship/

Just the News. Zuckerberg says Facebook may block Trump 'indefinitely'. https://justthenews.com/politics-policy/all-things-trump/zuckerberg-says-facebook-may-block-trump-indefinitely

National Pulse. Facebook's Trump-Banning Oversight Board Is Virtually All Far-Left, Soros-Funded Activists. https://thenationalpulse.com/2021/05/05/facebook-oversight-board-is-overwhelmingly-anti-trump/

Newsmax. Facebook Suspends Trump's Account for 2 Years. https://www.newsmax.com/politics/facebook-trump-suspend/2021/06/04/id/1023939/

Postmillennial. 'Rules are in SHAMBLES': Facebook Oversight Board member speaks out against Trump ban https://thepostmillennial.com/rules-are-in-shambles-facebook-oversight-board-member-speaks-out-against-trump-ban

Trish Regan. Trump Responds to Facebook's Two-Year Ban Calling it An "Insult to 75 Million People". https://trishintel.com/trump-responds-to-facebooks-two-year-ban-calling-it-an-insult-to-75-million-people/

Trish Regan. Trump To Sue Facebook and Twitter CEOs Mark Zuckerberg, Jack Dorsey – Report. https://trishintel.com/breaking-trump-to-sue-facebook-and-twitter-ceos-mark-zuckerberg-jack-dorsey-report/

Trump and Lafayette Park:

AP. Judge tosses most claims over clearing protesters in Lafayette Square (via Trib Live). https://triblive.com/news/world/judge-tosses-most-claims-over-clearing-protesters-in-lafayette-square/

Just the News. 'Proven right': Trump savors post-presidency vindication streak. https://justthenews.com/politics-policy/all-things-trump/hcq-russian-bounties-lafayette-park-wuhan-lab-trump-rides-wave

Trump, Harris, and the Border:

AP. GOP embraces Trump during visit to Texas, border wall. https://triblive.com/news/world/gop-embraces-trump-during-visit-to-texas-border-wall/

AP. On border tour, VP Kamala Harris cites 'progress' in 'tough' situation (via Trib Live). https://triblive.com/news/politics-election/vp-kamala-harris-heads-to-border-after-facing-criticism-for-absence/

Daily Caller. Kamala Harris' Team Reportedly Panicked After Biden Gave Her Immigration Assignment. https://dailycaller.com/2021/06/01/harris-team-panicked-biden-immi-gration-border-mexico-illegal/

Fox News. Kamala Harris has gone 93 days without visit to border since being tapped for crisis role. https://www.foxnews.com/politics/kamala-harris-no-press-conference-border-crisis

Just the News. Former President Trump says he likely will visit the border in the coming weeks. https://justthenews.com/politics-policy/all-things-trump/former-presi-dent-trump-says-he-will-probably-visit-border-sometime

Just the News. Kamala Harris met with protests as she makes her first trip to the border as admin border czar. https://justthenews.com/government/white-house/kamala-harris-met-protests-she-makes-her-first-trip-border-admin-border-czar

Just the News. Harris says U.S. feeling 'disastrous effects' of Trump immigration policy. https://justthenews.com/government/white-house/harris-travels-bor-der-friday-after-facing-criticism-absence

Just the News. Trump may visit border soon, 'very concerned' by migrant surge, adviser says. https://justthenews.com/politics-policy/all-things-trump/trump-may-visit-border-soon-very-concerned-migrant-surge-adviser

Newsmax. Mark Morgan to Newsmax: Harris Won't Accomplish Anything at Border. https://www.newsmax.com/newsmax-tv/morgan-harris-el-paso-border/2021/06/25/id/1026400/

Newsmax. Rep. Gohmert to Newsmax: VP Harris Blames Trump for Border Crisis. https://www.newsmax.com/newsmax-tv/loui-egohmert-texas-border-kamalaharris/2021/06/25/id/1026494/

PJ Media. Harris Doesn't Even Consider Security In Her Laugha-ble Efforts to Deal With the Border Chaos.

Trump Fights Back with Statements
https://pjmedia.com/news-and-politics/rick-moran/2021/05/23/harris-doesnt-even-consider-security-in-her-laughable-efforts-to-deal-with-the-border-chaos-n1449028

Townhall. Texas Rancher: Biden and Harris Need to Visit the Border to See the 'Chaotic' Crisis for Themselves. https://townhall.com/tipsheet/juliorosas/2021/05/19/texas-cattle-rancher-biden-and-harris-need-to-visit-the-border-to-see-the-crisis-n2589539

Trib Live. Republican National Committee lambastes VP Harris for visiting Pittsburgh instead of border. https://triblive.com/local/regional/republican-national-committee-lambasts-vp-harris-for-visiting-pittsburgh-instead-of-border/

Chapter Seven
July 2021

Wisconsin Supreme Court and Drop Boxes:

AP. Wisconsin Supreme Court disallows absentee ballot drop boxes (via Trib Live). https://triblive.com/news/politics-election/wisconsin-supreme-court-disallows-absentee-ballot-drop-boxes/

CBS News. Wisconsin Supreme Court has disallowed absentee ballot drop boxes. https://www.cbsnews.com/news/wisconsin-supreme-court-disallows-absentee-ballot-drop-boxes-ruled-friday/

Federalist. Wisconsin Supreme Court Drops Hammer On 2020 Election Shenanigans: 'Ballot Drop Boxes Are Illegal' Under Wisconsin Law. https://thefederalist.com/2022/07/08/wisconsin-supreme-court-drops-hammer-on-2020-election-shenanigans-ballot-drop-boxes-are-illegal-under-wisconsin-law/

Gateway Pundit. Wisconsin Supreme Court Rules Public Absentee Drop Boxes ILLEGAL! https://www.thegatewaypundit.com/2022/07/breaking-big-wisconsin-supreme-court-rules-absentee-drop-boxes-illegal/

Chapter Eight
August 2021

2020/21 Olympics:

Newsmax. NBC's Olympics Coverage Continues to Suffer Poor Ratings. https://www.newsmax.com/us/nbc-tv-ratings-olympics-tokyo/2021/08/06/id/1031381/

NYT. NBC Tries to Salvage a Difficult Olympics.

Against Lies of Biden, Attacks from Dems, and Bias of Media
https://www.nytimes.com/2021/08/05/business/media/nbc-olympics-tv-ratings.html

Miscellaneous:

Newsmax. Trump's Man Carey Tops GOP Establishment in Ohio-15. https://www.newsmax.com/john-gizzi/mike-carey-ohio-special-election-primary/2021/08/03/id/1031044/

Chapter Nine
September 2021

Mark Milley:

AP. Milley: Calls to China were 'perfectly' within scope of job (via Trib Live. https://triblive.com/news/politics-election/milley-calls-to-china-were-perfectly-within-scope-of-job/

Dispatch. What the Milley Affair Says About the State of Our Politics. https://thedispatch.com/p/what-the-milley-affair-says-about

Just the News. Milley defiant amid increasing pressure to resign over China calls revelations. https://justthenews.com/government/security/milley-defiant-amid-increasing-calls-him-resign-wake-revelations-over-china

Trib Live. Leonard Pitts Jr.: Managing a mentally unbalanced president https://triblive.com/opinion/leonard-pitts-jr-managing-a-mentally-unbalanced-president/

Justice for J6 Rally:

AP. Heavy police presence as protesters trickle in for DC rally (via Trib Live). https://triblive.com/news/world/heavy-police-presence-as-protesters-trickle-in-for-dc-rally/

AP. Organizer of Capitol rally this weekend looks to rewrite Jan. 6 history (via Trib Live). https://triblive.com/news/world/organizer-of-capitol-rally-this-weekend-looks-to-rewrite-jan-6-history/

Federalist. In Exclusive Interview, Trump Calls Sept. 18 Rally A 'Setup,' Says GOP Senate Should Fire 'Disaster' McConnell. https://thefederalist.com/2021/09/16/in-exclusive-interview-trump-calls-sept-18-rally-a-setup-says-gop-senate-should-fire-disaster-mcconnell/

Just the News. 'Justice for J6' rally puts spotlight on evidence of political motives behind Jan. 6 prosecutions. https://justthenews.com/politics-policy/all-things-trump/justice-j6-rally-puts-spotlight-evidence-political-motivations

Trump Fights Back with Statements

Newsmax. Capitol Police Chief Defends Rights of J6 Rally Attendees. https://www.newsmax.com/newsfront/justice-for-j6-j6-capitolpolice/2021/09/17/id/1036943/

Newsmax. Defense Sec, Austin OKs 100 National Guard Troops If Needed at 'Justice for J6' Rally. https://www.newsmax.com/newsfront/defense-secretary-austin-national-guard-jan-6-capitol/2021/09/17/id/1036907/

Newsmax. Jan. 6 Detentions Called 'Cruel and Unusual' Punishment. https://www.newsmax.com/platinum/capitol-jail-solitary-confinement/2021/09/17/id/1036821/

Newsmax. Trump: 'Justice for J6' Rally a 'Setup'. https://www.newsmax.com/us/justice-for-j6-rally-setup-catch-22/2021/09/17/id/1036835/

Arizona Election Audit:

AP. GOP review finds no proof Arizona election stolen from Trump (via Trib Live). https://triblive.com/news/politics-election/draft-of-arizona-gops-vote-review-finds-wider-biden-win/

CNN. Final report from partisan Arizona review confirms Biden defeated Trump in Maricopa County last November. https://www.cnn.com/2021/09/24/politics/arizona-election-review-results/index.html

Just the News. Arizona's Maricopa County supervisors, state GOP Senate reach deal over routers in election audit https://justthenews.com/politics-policy/elections/arizonas-maricopa-county-supervisors-state-gop-senate-reach-deal-over

Just the News. Wisconsin audit to determine what was supposed to happen on Election Day, chief investigator says. https://justthenews.com/nation/states/gableman-audits-purpose-determine-what-was-supposed-happen-election-day

Newsmax. Arizona Republicans to Release Findings of 2020 Election Audit. https://www.newsmax.com/newsfront/arizona-gop-election-audit-results/2021/09/24/id/1037742/

Newsmax. Arizona Vote Auditors Raise Biden Total, Claim Numerous Anomalies. https://www.newsmax.com/politics/arizona-maricopa-audit-election/2021/09/24/id/1037862/

Newsmax. House Dems Ask Cyber Ninjas CEO to Testify on Arizona Audit. https://www.newsmax.com/politics/cyberninjas-arizona-election-review/2021/09/24/id/1037846/

Newsmax. Trump Calls Reports on Arizona Audit 'Fake News'. https://www.newsmax.com/politics/trump-arizona-audit-fraud/2021/09/24/id/1037804/

NYT. Republican Review of Arizona Vote Fails to Show Stolen Election. http://nytimes.com/2021/09/24/us/arizona-election-review-trump-biden.html?smid=fb-nytimes&smtyp=cur

Washington Examiner Maricopa County election audit findings presented to Arizona Senate. https://www.washingtonexaminer.com/news/watch-live-maricopa-county-election-audit-findings-presented-arizona-senate

Chapter Ten
October 2021

Border Wall Construction Stoppage:

Just the News. Biden halts work on border wall, thousands of migrants are sent home to Honduras from Guatemala. https://justthenews.com/world/biden-halts-work-border-wall-thousands-migrants-are-sent-home-honduras-guatemala

Newsmax. Incoming DHS Head Mayorkas Says Border Wall Decisions TBD. https://www.newsmax.com/us/alejandro-mayorkas-dhs-border-wall-senate/2021/01/19/id/1006284/

Newsmax. Chad Wolf to Newsmax TV: Border Wall Construction Needs to Continue. https://www.newsmax.com/newsmax-tv/chad-wolf-border-wall-construction-border-patrol/2021/02/01/id/1008120/

Reuters. Biden asks U.S. Supreme Court to cancel asylum, border wall arguments. https://www.reuters.com/article/us-usa-court-immigration/biden-asks-u-s-supreme-court-to-cancel-asylum-border-wall-arguments-idUSKBN2A13LU

Townhall. They 'Don't Give a Sh*t About Us': The Early Effects of Joe Biden Halting Border Wall Construction. https://townhall.com/tipsheet/juliorosas/2021/01/29/early-effects-of-joe-biden-halting-border-wall-construction-n2583899

Washington Examiner Promised a wall, left with a hole: Border rancher fears Biden order will funnel migrants through his land. https://www.washingtonexaminer.com/news/promised-wall-given-gap-border-rancher-fears-funnel-migrants-land

Michigan Voter Irregularities:

Federalist. Why Does Michigan Still Have 25,000 Dead People On Its Voter Rolls? https://thefederalist.com/2021/11/08/why-does-michigan-still-have-25000-dead-people-on-its-voter-rolls/

Just the News. Lawsuit filed against Michigan for over 25,000 suspected dead registered voters still on rolls.

Trump Fights Back with Statements

https://justthenews.com/government/courts-law/lawsuit-filed-against-michigan-over-25000-dead-registered-voters-rolls

Just the News. Over 7,000 affidavits delivered to Michigan lawmakers claim election fraud.

https://justthenews.com/nation/states/over-7000-affidavits-delivered-michigan-lawmakers-claim-election-fraud

Adam Kinzinger:

Yahoo! News/ Chicago Tribune. Republican U.S. Rep. Adam Kinzinger says he won't seek reelection after Democratic map puts him up against Rep. Darin LaHood, a supporter of Donald Trump.

https://news.yahoo.com/republican-u-rep-adam-kinzinger-154100325.html

Yahoo! News. GOP Trump critic Rep. Adam Kinzinger won't seek reelection.

https://news.yahoo.com/gop-trump-critic-rep-adam-143521001.html

Yahoo! News. Rep. Adam Kinzinger won't seek reelection.

https://news.yahoo.com/rep-adam-kinzinger-wont-seek-164351926.html

Separation Settlement:

Breitbart. FNC's Carlson: Biden Administration Illegal Immigrant Reparations Proposal the 'High-Water Mark of Political Lunacy.'

https://www.breitbart.com/clips/2021/10/29/fncs-carlson-biden-administration-illegal-immigrant-reparations-proposal-the-high-water-mark-of-political-lunacy/

Breitbart. Report: Biden Considers Paying Border Crossers $450K Each in Reparations.

https://www.breitbart.com/politics/2021/10/28/report-biden-considers-paying-border-crossers-450k-each-in-reparations/

Townhall. How Biden Responded When Asked About Plan to Give $450K to Illegal Immigrants.

https://townhall.com/tipsheet/leahbarkoukis/2021/11/01/biden-scratches-head-when-asked-about-450k-to-illegals-n2598345

WSJ. U.S. in Talks to Pay Hundreds of Millions to Families Separated at Border. https://www.wsj.com/articles/biden-administration-in-talks-to-pay-hundreds-of-millions-to-immigrant-families-separated-at-border-11635447591

Miscellaneous:

Just the News. Trump rallies Iowa voters, blasts Biden on border and economy in signal toward 2024 run.

https://justthenews.com/politics-policy/elections/trump-hold-weekend-rally-key-balloting-state-iowa

Just the News. Wisconsin lawmaker seeks to rescind state's electoral votes, Trump agrees.
https://justthenews.com/nation/states/rep-ramthun-calls-reclaim-wisconsins-electoral-votes-president-trump-agrees

Newsmax. Hunter Biden Sells 5 Art Reproductions for $75K Each. https://www.newsmax.com/politics/hunter-biden-art-president-pop-up/2021/10/08/id/1039745/

Chapter Eleven
November 2021

Miscellaneous 1:

Fox News. Braves win World Series thanks to power, pitching in Game 6. https://www.foxnews.com/sports/braves-astros-world-series-result-game-6

Fox News. Biden appears to fall asleep during climate speech despite claiming it's 'greatest threat' to US security.
https://www.foxnews.com/media/biden-appears-nod-off-during-climate-speech

Fox News. Election Day: New Jersey's governor's race too close to call: LIVE UPDATES. https://www.foxnews.com/live-news/election-day-voters-polls-contests-biden

Fox News. Democratic New Jersey Gov. Phil Murphy ekes out win over GOP challenger Ciattarelli. https://www.foxnews.com/politics/new-jersey-phil-murphy-win-jack-ciattarelli

Just the News. Five controversial policies tucked inside $1.2 trillion infra-structure bill passed by Congress.
https://justthenews.com/government/congress/five-policies-12t-infrastructure-bill-congress-passed-public-should-know-about

Just the News. Democrat-led House panel subpoenas six more Trump associates including Flynn, Eastman: Reports.
https://justthenews.com/government/congress/democrat-led-house-panel-subpoenas-six-more-trump-associated-including-flynn

Just the News. Jan. 6 select committee issues new round of subpoenas, this time for Miller, McEnany, eight others.
https://justthenews.com/government/white-house/jan-6-select-committee-issue-round-subpoenas-miller-mcenany-eight-others

Trump Fights Back with Statements
Kyle Rittenhouse Verdict:

AP. Acquitted and in demand, Kyle Rittenhouse ponders what's next (via Trib Live). https://triblive.com/news/world/acquitted-and-in-demand-kyle-rittenhouse-ponders-whats-next/

Newsmax. Rasmussen: Only 36 Percent Consider Media Coverage of Rittenhouse Trial Fair. https://www.newsmax.com/newsfront/poll-kylerittenhouse-kenosha-trial/2021/11/23/id/1045926/

Newsmax. Trump Meets With Rittenhouse, Slams Prosecutors' 'Misconduct.' https://www.newsmax.com/us/trump-rittenhouse-prose-cutors-trial/2021/11/24/id/1045978/

Waukesha Christmas Parade Massacre:

AP. Child is 6th death in Waukesha parade crash; suspect charged (via Trib Live). https://triblive.com/news/world/child-is-6th-death-in-waukesha-parade-crash-suspect-charged/

AP. Waukesha parade crash suspect's bail raises questions (via Trib Live). https://triblive.com/news/world/waukesha-parade-crash-suspects-bail-raises-questions/

Newsmax. Rep. Grothman to Newsmax: Waukesha Paid 'Horrific Price' for DA's 'Stupidity.' https://www.newsmax.com/newsmax-tv/grothman-waukesha-pa-rade/2021/11/24/id/1046038/

Newsmax. Trump: My Heart Goes Out to Waukesha. https://www.newsmax.com/headline/trump-parade-waukesha-wiscon-sin/2021/11/22/id/1045656/

NYP. 'Not fitting their narrative': Waukesha feels abandoned af-ter tragic parade attack. https://nypost.com/2021/12/13/why-waukesha-parade-attack-doesnt-fit-media-narrative/

Postmillennial. Career Criminal Darrell Brooks Charged With Five Counts of Intentional Homicide for Waukesha Christmas Parade Massacre Read more. https://thepostmillennial.com/breaking-darrell-brooks-charged-with-5-counts-of-intentional-homicide-for-waukesha-massacre?utm_campaign=64487

Virginia Gubernatorial Race:

Fox News. Glenn Youngkin wins Virginia governor's race, Fox News projects. https://video.foxnews.com/v/6280055728001#sp=show-clips

Fox News. How Virginia voters decided between Youngkin, McAuliffe: Fox News Voter Analysis. https://www.foxnews.com/politics/virginia-voters-youngkin-mcauliffe-fox-news-voter-analysis

Fox News. Youngkin victory deals another blow to Biden, as agenda stalls in Congress. https://www.foxnews.com/politics/youngkin-victory-another-blow-biden-agenda-congress#

Fox News. Youngkin defeats McAuliffe in race for Virginia governor. https://www.foxnews.com/politics/polls-close-in-virginia-with-eyes-of-the-nation-on-the-states-governors-election

Miscellaneous 2:

Breitbart. New York Times Admits More Coronavirus Deaths Under Joe Biden 'Despite Vaccines.' https://www.breitbart.com/politics/2021/11/24/new-york-times-admits-more-coronavirus-deaths-under-joe-biden-despite-vaccines/

Forbes. U.S. Covid-19 Deaths For 2021 Surpass Toll From 2020. https://www.forbes.com/sites/marisadellatto/2021/10/06/us-covid-19-deaths-for-2021-surpass-toll-from-2020/?sh=765e52886cc2

Newsmax. Trump: My Heart Goes Out to Waukesha. https://www.newsmax.com/headline/trump-parade-waukesha-wisconsin/2021/11/22/id/1045656/

Newsmax. Trump Waives Privilege for Kerik to Testify Before Jan. 6 Panel. https://www.newsmax.com/newsfront/trump-bernard-kerik-jan-6-committee/2021/11/24/id/1046036/

Postmillennial, The. House Approves Biden's MASSIVE Spending Bill 220-213. https://thepostmillennial.com/house-passes-bbb-mccarthy-marathon-speech

Trib Live/ AP. Democrats' sweeping social, climate bill passes divided House. https://triblive.com/news/world/democrats-sweeping-social-climate-bill-passes-divided-house/

Trib Live/ AP. Jury finds Kyle Rittenhouse not guilty in Kenosha shootings. https://triblive.com/news/world/jury-finds-kyle-rittenhouse-not-guilty-on-all-counts/

Chapter Twelve
December 2021

Smash and Grab Robberies:

Fox Business. Chicago burglars target a string of retail stores in upscale neighborhood on Black Friday. https://www.foxbusiness.com/retail/chicago-hit-string-retail-burglaries-black-friday

Fox Business. Chicago-area police searching for thieves accused of stealing $100,000 in Louis Vuitton merchandise.

https://www.foxnews.com/us/chicago-area-police-searching-for-band-of-thieves-accused-of-stealing-100000-in-louis-vuitton-merchandise

Fox Business. Shoplifters raid Chicago boutique in broad daylight, steal tens of thousands in luxury purses. https://www.foxnews.com/us/thieves-steal-purses-chicago-bottega-veneta

Fox News. California Apple store hit in latest smash-and-grab in broad daylight. https://www.foxnews.com/us/california-apple-smash-grab

Fox News. Los Angeles-area looters target Home Depot, Bottega Veneta stores on Black Friday: reports. https://www.foxnews.com/us/los-angeles-looters-home-depot-bottega-veneta-black-friday-smash-grab-flash-mob-robberies

Fox News. Two Best Buy stores in Minnesota looted, all get away, report says. https://www.foxnews.com/us/best-buy-minnesota-looters-suspects-burnsville

When Did Trump Test Positive?

Business Insider. Trump responds to report that he tested positive for COVID before debate, says 'Biden goes around coughing on people all over the place.' https://www.businessinsider.nl/trump-responds-to-report-that-he-tested-positive-for-covid-before-debate-says-biden-goes-around-coughing-on-people-all-over-the-place/

Business Insider. Trump tested positive for COVID-19 three days before his first debate against Biden, book says. https://www.businessinsider.com/trump-tested-positive-for-covid-19-3-days-before-biden-debate-book-2021-12?op=1

Guardian. Trump tested positive for Covid few days before Biden debate, chief of staff says in new book. https://www.theguardian.com/us-news/2021/dec/01/trump-tested-positive-covid-before-biden-debate-chief-staff-mark-meadows-book

NBC News. Trump tested positive for Covid three days before debating Biden, subsequently tested negative. https://www.nbcnews.com/politics/donald-trump/trump-denies-positive-covid-test-days-first-presidential-debate-n1285158

November Jobs Report:

Bongino. A Swing and a HUGE Miss – November Jobs Report Yet Another Bidenomics Disaster. https://bongino.com/a-swing-and-a-huge-miss-november-jobs-report-yet-another-bidenomics-disaster

Fox Business. Biden touts declining unemployment rate, despite huge job miss in November. https://www.foxbusiness.com/economy/biden-unemployment-rate-november-jobs-report

Fox Business. November jobs report expected to show another month of strong hiring momentum. https://www.foxbusiness.com/economy/november-jobs-report-2021-coronavirus-pandemic

Trib Live/ AP. U.S. jobless claims rise by 28,000, but still low at 222,000. https://triblive.com/news/wire-stories/u-s-jobless-claims-rise-by-28000-but-still-low-at-222000/

WSJ. Low Initial Jobless Claims Reflect Tight Labor Market. https://www.wsj.com/articles/weekly-jobless-claims-12-02-2021-11638389395

Chris Cuomo:

Fox News. New Chris Cuomo sexual misconduct allegation emerged days before CNN firing: report. https://www.foxnews.com/media/chris-cuomo-sexual-misconduct-allegation-cnn-firing

Postmillennial. BREAKING: CNN fires Chris Cuomo. https://thepostmillennial.com/breaking-cnn-fires-chris-cuomo

Trib Live/ AP. CNN fires Chris Cuomo for helping with brother's scandal. https://triblive.com/news/world/cnn-fires-chris-cuomo-after-helping-with-brothers-scandal/

Miscellaneous:

Trib Live/ AP. Virginia GOP completes sweep of elections with House win. https://triblive.com/news/politics-election/virginia-gop-completes-sweep-of-elections-with-house-win/

Chapter Thirteen
January 2022

Newsmax. Matt Gaetz to Newsmax: Greene Kicked Off Twitter for 'Challenging the Regime'. https://www.newsmax.com/newsmax-tv/newsmaxtv-mattgaetz-bigtech-censorship/2022/01/03/id/1050875/

Newsmax. Trump: 'In 2024, We Are Going to Take Back the White House.' https://www.newsmax.com/newsfront/save-america-rally-arizona-battleground/2022/01/15/id/1052581/

Newsmax. Trump Decries Cancellation of OAN. https://www.newsmax.com/newsfront/oan-att-t-trump-woke/2022/01/16/id/1052628/

NYT. Twitter Permanently Suspends Marjorie Taylor Greene's Account. https://www.nytimes.com/2022/01/02/technology/marjorie-taylor-greene-twitter.html

AP. Supreme Court blocks vaccine-or-test rule for U.S. businesses (via Trib Live). https://triblive.com/news/world/supreme-court-blocks-vaccine-or-test-rule-for-us-businesses-but-allows-vaccine-mandate-for-most-health-care-workers/

Washington Examiner. Biden says 2022 midterm elections 'could easily be illegitimate'. https://www.washingtonexaminer.com/news/white-house/biden-stirs-up-illegitimate-election-fracas

Chapter Thirteen
January 2022

PA Mail-in Balloting Rulings:

Just the News. Court finds Pennsylvania mail-in voting law unconstitutional. https://justthenews.com/politics-policy/elections/pennsylvania-mail-voting-law-found-unconstitutional

Trib Live. Pa. Commonwealth Court strikes down mail-in voting; State AG's office already filed notice of appeal. https://triblive.com/news/pennsylvania/pa-commonwealth-court-strikes-down-mail-in-voting-shapiro-said-state-will-appeal/

Trib Live. Pa. Pa. Supreme Court upholds no-excuse mail voting ahead of midterms. https://triblive.com/news/pennsylvania/pa-supreme-court-upholds-no-excuse-mail-voting-ahead-of-midterms/

Pence and the 2020 Election:

Just the News. Donald Trump fires back against Susan Collins, Mike Pence about overturning 2020 election https://justthenews.com/politics-policy/all-things-trump/donald-trump-fires-back-against-susan-collins-mike-pence-about

Newsmax. Trump: Effort to Change Election Rules Prove VP Could Change Results. https://www.newsmax.com/newsfront/donald-trump-mike-pence-electoral-count/2022/01/30/id/1054689/

Trib Live/ AP. Pence: Trump is 'wrong' to say election could be overturned. https://triblive.com/news/politics-election/pence-trump-is-wrong-to-say-election-could-be-overturned/

Chapter Fourteen
February 2022

Joe Rogan and Spotify:
 Just the News. Big Tech purges anti-lockdown scientists as Rogan defends his interview choices.
https://justthenews.com/accountability/cancel-culture/big-tech-bans-anti-lockdown-scientists-rogan-defends-his-interview
 Just the News. Spotify yields, puts advisories on COVID podcasts, Rogan responds to uproar sparked by his episodes.
https://justthenews.com/accountability/media/spotify-and-joe-rogan-respond-controversy-surrounding-covid-19-episodes
 Newsmax. Joe Rogan Apologizes, Spotify to Add Advisory to COVID Podcasts. https://www.newsmax.com/newsfront/joe-rogan-spotify-covid-podcast/2022/01/31/id/1054710/
 Trib Live/ Los Angeles Times. Why more musicians haven't joined Neil Young's Spotify boycott over Joe Rogan.
https://triblive.com/business/why-more-musicians-havent-joined-neil-youngs-spotify-boycott-over-joe-rogan/
 WTAE/ AP. Joe Rogan responds to Spotify protest, COVID-19 advisories. https://www.wtae.com/article/joe-rogan-responds-to-spotify-protest-covid-19-advisories/38943329

Handling of Documents:
 AP. Biden orders release of Trump White House logs to Congress (via Trib Live). https://triblive.com/news/world/biden-orders-release-of-trump-white-house-logs-to-congress/
 AP. Report: Archives asks Justice Department to probe Trump record handling (via Trib Live).
https://triblive.com/news/world/report-archives-asks-justice-depart-ment-to-probe-trump-record-handling/
 Just the News. Biden orders Trump White House logs turned over to Jan 6 panel, rejects executive privilege argument.
https://justthenews.com/government/white-house/biden-orders-trumps-white-house-logs-turned-over-jan-6-panel-rejects-exec

Durham Report:
Trump/ Russia Collusion Hoax:
 Fox News. Clinton campaign paid to 'infiltrate' Trump Tower, White House servers to link Trump to Russia: Durham.
https://www.foxnews.com/politics/clinton-campaign-paid-infiltrate-trump-tower-white-house-servers

Hill. Durham alleges cyber analysts 'exploited' access to Trump White House server.
https://thehill.com/regulation/court-battles/594126-durham-alleges-cyber-analysts-exploited-access-to-trump-white-house/

Just the News. Clinton campaign hired techs to 'mine' data about Trump servers to fuel collusion suspicions: Durham.
https://justthenews.com/politics-policy/all-things-trump/durham-says-clinton-campaign-hired-techs-infiltrate-trump-servers

Just the News. GOP Senate Chairman Johnson, Grassley request more Crossfire Hurricane FBI briefing notes.
https://justthenews.com/government/security/sens-ron-johnson-and-chuck-grassley-request-additional-crossfire-hurricane-fbi

Just the News. Hillary Clinton lashes out at Donald Trump, Fox News over Durham probe: 'Spinning up a fake scandal'.
https://justthenews.com/politics-policy/all-things-trump/hillary-clinton-attacks-donald-trump-fox-news-over-durham-probe

Just the News. Latest Durham revelations put Biden's national security adviser in uneasy light.
https://justthenews.com/accountability/russia-and-ukraine-scandals/latest-durham-revelations-put-bidens-national-security

Just the News. Sussmann: Durham filing alleging mining of Trump server fuels 'conspiracy' with 'false allegations'.
https://justthenews.com/government/courts-law/sussman-says-durham-filing-alleged-trump-server-tampering-are-politicized

Just the News. Trump demands prosecutions, reparations after explosive revelations in Durham court filing.
https://justthenews.com/accountability/russia-and-ukraine-scandals/trump-demands-prosecutions-reparations-after-explosive

Newsmax. Durham Report: Clinton Campaign Paid to 'Infiltrate' Trump Tower, White House Servers.
https://www.newsmax.com/politics/durham-report-spying-steele-dossier-trump/2022/02/12/id/1056594/

Newsmax. Former DNI Ratcliffe Expects More Indictments From Durham Probe. https://www.newsmax.com/newsfront/intelligence-director-ratcliffe-russia-clinton/2022/02/14/id/1056768/

Newsmax. Nunes to Newsmax: Durham Probe Will Bring 'More' Indictments Against Clinton Campaign.
https://www.newsmax.com/newsmax-tv/johndurham-hillaryclinton-campaign-2016/2022/02/14/id/1056802/

Newsmax. Probe: Hillary Lawyer Used Purported Russian Cellphone Data to Implicate Trump.
https://www.newsmax.com/politics/durham-clinton-attorney-russian-cell-phones/2022/02/15/id/1056870/

Newsmax. Trump: Clinton Campaign's Actions 'Would Have Been Punishable by Death' in Past. https://www.newsmax.com/newsfront/donaldtrump-hillaryclinton-russia-durham/2022/02/13/id/1056618/

Newsmax. White House Won't Answer Questions on Durham Report. https://www.newsmax.com/politics/durham-report/2022/02/14/id/1056812/

WSJ. A Strange Defense of Spying on Trump. https://www.wsj.com/articles/a-strange-defense-of-spying-on-donald-trump-rodney-joffe-russia-clinton-john-durham-11644965327

WSJ. Hillary Clinton's Other Dossier. https://www.wsj.com/articles/hillary-clintons-other-dossier-11644852226

WSJ. Monitoring of Trump Internet Traffic Sparks New Dispute in Durham Probe. https://www.wsj.com/articles/monitoring-of-trump-internet-traffic-sparks-new-dispute-in-durham-probe-11644970503

Trump Really Was Spied On:

Newsmax. Lesley Stahl Slammed for Unearthed Trump Interview After Durham Report. https://www.newsmax.com/newsfront/durham-report-trump-mainstream-media/2022/02/14/id/1056800/

Newsmax. Trump: 'Zero' Media Coverage of Hillary Clinton Spying Scandal. https://www.newsmax.com/newsfront/trump-clinton-spying-news-outlets/2022/02/14/id/1056738/

WSJ. Trump Really Was Spied On. https://www.wsj.com/articles/donald-trump-really-was-spied-on-2016-clinton-campaign-john-durham-court-filing-11644878973

WSJ. Who Are Those 'Techies' Who Spied on Trump? https://www.wsj.com/articles/who-are-those-techies-who-spied-on-trump-clinton-2016-election-durham-data-fusion-gps-joffe-11645139606

WSJ. Who WSJ Opinion: Durham's New Revelations About Spying on Trump. https://www.wsj.com/video/series/opinion-review-and-outlook/wsj-opinion-durham-new-revelations-about-spying-on-trump/80D76DAA-2328-4829-9852-72823D154A82

Americans Want Hillary Investigated:

Just the News. Fast growing number of Democrats want Hillary Clinton investigated for her role in Russiagate. https://justthenews.com/accountability/russia-and-ukraine-scandals/fast-growing-number-democrats-want-hillary-clinton

Newsmax. TIPP Poll: Two-Thirds of Dems Say Hillary Clinton Should Be Investigated. https://www.newsmax.com/newsfront/poll-clinton-investigate-durham/2022/02/15/id/1056876/

Sussman Trial and Verdict:

Just the News. Clinton campaign counsel testifies he didn't trust FBI, as Sussmann defense floats mistrial motion. https://justthenews.com/accountability/russia-and-ukraine-scandals/legal-scholar-turley-downplays-sussmann-lawyers-mistrial

Just the News. FBI witness in Sussmann trial says Trump-Alfa Bank allegation was 'far-reaching,' not objective. https://justthenews.com/accountability/russia-and-ukraine-scandals/second-day-sussmann-trial-opening-statements-witness

Just the News. Top 5 revelations from trial of ex-Clinton campaign lawyer Michael Sussmann. https://justthenews.com/accountability/russia-and-ukraine-scandals/top-5-revelations-trial-ex-clinton-campaign-lawyer

Newsmax. Clinton Campaign Lawyer Sussmann Seeks Durham Charges Dismissed. https://www.newsmax.com/newsfront/clintonlawyersussmann-courtfiling-durham/2022/02/17/id/1057310/

Newsmax. Durham 'Disappointed'; Thanks Jury, Team for 'Seeking Truth, Justice'. https://www.newsmax.com/newsfront/john-durham-michael-sussmann-special-counsel-verdict/2022/05/31/id/1072286/

Newsmax. Judge Rejects Michael Sussmann's Motion to Strike Info From Durham Filing. https://www.newsmax.com/newsfront/michael-sussmann-john-durham-motion-indictment/2022/03/11/id/1060741/

Newsmax. Rep. Mace to Newsmax: Durham Didn't Get Fair Shot on Sussmann. https://www.newsmax.com/newsmax-tv/nancy-mace-durham-sussman-hillary-clinton/2022/05/31/id/1072302/

Newsmax. Sussmann Acquittal Gives Dems Immunity From Corruption Charges. https://www.newsmax.com/morris/acquittal-doj-venues/2022/06/01/id/1072382/

Newsmax. Trump Slams 'Corrupt' Legal System After Sussmann's 'Not Guilty' Verdict. https://www.newsmax.com/newsfront/donald-trump-michael-sussmann-trial-durham/2022/05/31/id/1072322/

Miscellaneous:

Just the News. Donald Trump defends financial documents after accounting firm says statements 'not reliable'. https://justthenews.com/politics-policy/all-things-trump/donald-trump-defends-financial-documents-after-accounting-firm

Nunes talks Trump social platform with launch days away on 'JUST THE NEWS – NOT NOISE'.

https://justthenews.com/tv/watch-live-nunes-talks-trump-social-platform-launch-days-away-just-news-not-noise

Just the News. Trump applauds RNC censure of renegade Reps. Cheney, Kinzinger. https://justthenews.com/politics-policy/all-things-trump/trump-applauds-rnc-censure-renegade-reps-cheney-kinzinger

Just the News. Trump raised $51 million in last half of 2021, enters new year with $122 million. https://justthenews.com/politics-policy/all-things-trump/trump-raised-51-million-last-half-2021-enters-new-year-122-million

WSJ. Judge Orders Trump to Testify in New York Civil-Fraud Probe. https://www.wsj.com/articles/trump-family-new-york-attorney-general-face-off-over-civil-subpoenas-11645122253

Chapter Fifteen
March 2022

Trump Endorsements:

Newsmax. Trump Touts Success of All 33 Texas Candidates He Endorsed. https://www.newsmax.com/newsfront/trump-texas-endorse/2022/03/02/id/1059231/

NYT. Takeaways From the Texas Primary Elections. https://www.nytimes.com/2022/03/02/us/politics/texas-primary-takeaways.html

Wisconsin Voting Fraud:

Just the News. Wisconsin special counsel bombshell: 91 nursing homes had 95-100% voter turnout in 2020. https://justthenews.com/politics-policy/elections/wisconsin-special-counsel-report-2020-election-91-nursing-homes-had-95

Mo Brooks:

Just the News. Trump un-endorses Mo Brooks in Alabama Senate primary. https://justthenews.com/politics-policy/all-things-trump/trump-un-endorses-mo-brooks-alabama-senate-primary

Insider. Mo Brooks says Trump asked him to 'immediately' remove Biden from office and illegally hold a new presidential election (via Yahoo!). https://news.yahoo.com/mo-brooks-says-trump-asked-190608347.html

Insider. Trump rescinds his endorsement of Rep. Mo Brooks, saying he 'went woke' on the 2020 election. https://www.businessinsider.com/trump-pulls-his-endorsement-of-mo-brooks-says-he-went-woke-2022-3

Trump Fights Back with Statements

Insider. Trump calls Rep. Mo Brooks 'disappointing' and says he may back someone else in the Alabama Senate race. https://www.businessinsider.com/trump-mo-brooks-endorsement-disappointing-alabama-senate-2022-3

Chapter Sixteen
April 2022

Manhattan Criminal and Civil Probes:

ABC News. Manhattan DA insists Trump criminal probe remains active. https://abcnews.go.com/US/manhattan-da-insists-trump-criminal-probe-remains-active/story?id=83935329

ABC News. NY Attorney General files motion to hold Trump in contempt for ignoring subpoena. https://abcnews.go.com/US/ny-attorney-general-files-motion-hold-trump-contempt/story?id=83936230

Just the News. Trump pays $110k fine in NY AG's James case against company, must submit paperwork to end contempt. https://justthenews.com/government/courts-law/trump-pays-110k-fine-ny-ags-james-case-against-company-must-submit-paperwork

Newsmax. NY Judge Agrees to Lift Trump Contempt If He Pays $110,000 Fine. https://www.newsmax.com/politics/trump-contempt-new-york/2022/05/11/id/1069424/

Fred Upton/ Yes Impeachment Votes:

Axios. GOP Rep. John Katko, who voted to impeach Trump, won't seek re-election. https://www.axios.com/john-katko-retirement-2022-election-house-a24897ab-9efa-491e-a1ae-11b10f9364fb.html

CNN. Another one of the 'Trump 10' heads for the exits. https://www.cnn.com/2022/01/14/politics/republican-john-katko-gop-retiring-reelection/index.html

Just the News. GOP Rep. Fred Upton, who voted to impeach Trump, will not seek reelection. https://justthenews.com/politics-policy/health/gop-rep-fred-upton-who-voted-impeach-trump-will-not-seek-reelection

Red State. Republican Who Impeached Trump Learns a Hard Lesson About His New Friends. https://redstate.com/bonchie/2022/08/01/republican-who-impeached-trump-learns-a-hard-lesson-about-his-new-friends-n605168

WaPo. Fred Upton calls it quits, leaving a much different House (via MSM). https://www.msn.com/en-us/news/politics/fred-upton-calls-it-quits-leaving-a-much-different-house/ar-AAVTTCz

WaPo. What happened to the 10 House Republicans who voted to impeach Trump?
https://www.washingtonpost.com/politics/2022/03/01/what-happened-10-house-republicans-who-voted-impeach-trump/

Appendix Two
Additional Books by the Author

The author of this book (Gary F. Zeolla) is also the author of many additional books and is the translator of the *Analytical-Literal Translation of the Bible* (ALT). These books are available in paperback, hardback, and eBook formats: Kindle, Acrobat Reader, and ePUB (for iPad, Nook, etc.).

These books are available from Amazon (www.Amazon.com) and Lulu Publishing (www.lulu.com) and other online bookstores. Ordering and further details on all of these books can be found on the author's personal website: www.Zeolla.org.

Politics Books

Joe Biden's Failing Presidency

On the day Biden was inaugurated, he took over the @POTUS account on Twitter and began tweeting profusely. This five-book series reproduces Biden's tweets for the first and second years of his presidency. These books also include my comments I posted on Twitter in response to his tweets. Some of my comments were added later and reflect later developments. I have also added an occasional "Extended Comment" to provide further context and commentary to some tweets.

Joe Biden Tweets During the First Year of His Failing Presidency, Volume One: Reversing Trump, while Dividing and Destroying America, January through July 2021

Biden tweets in his first year in office promoted his "Build Back Better" policies. But with them being a reversal of Trump's policies, they were often subtle attacks on Trump and his supporters and on all who believe in conservative and traditional values.

Joe Biden Tweets During the First Year of His Failing Presidency, Volume Two: Reversing Trump, while Dividing and Destroying America, August 2021 through January 2022

Biden can be very disingenuous in his tweets and his claims about his various plans and polices. He thinks they are all grand and good for the country. But in fact, it is those very plans and policies that is causing his presidency to be failing. Those plans and polices are also dividing and destroying American. Biden's early actions set the stage for more failures later in his presidency, so it is important to remember them.

Joe Biden Tweets During the Second Year of His Failing Presidency, Volume One: Promoting Sin and Death, Causing Bidenflation, and Spewing Hate and Division, January through May 2022

In 2022, Biden declared it was his "intention" to run for a second term as President. It is for that reason I continued this series through the second year of his failing presidency. Come 2024, much of the focus will be on his third and fourth years, but this series will remind voters of his failures in his first two years in office.

Joe Biden Tweets During the Second Year of His Failing Presidency, Volume Two: Promoting Sin and Death, Causing Bidenflation, and Spewing Hate and Division, June 1 through October 15, 2022

Biden promotes sin via his support of the sinful and destructive LGBTQ movement and of abortion. He promotes death by his support of abortion and via his open-door southern border policies. The latter has led to the deaths of migrants and of Americans at the hands of those illegal aliens and by the influx of illicit drugs into the USA. He spews hate and division with his lie-filled rhetoric against "MAGA Republicans" and all who believe in conservative and traditional values.

Joe Biden Tweets During the Second Year of His Failing Presidency, Volume Three: Promoting Sin and Death, Causing Bidenflation, and Spewing Hate and Division, October 16, through December 31, 2022, Plus Updates for Early 2023

This series of five books provides the definitive record of Biden's failures in his first two years as President. These failures should not be forgotten, as they laid the foundation for his continual failures in his subsequent years as President. He has been failing miserably on both domestic issues and in foreign policy. Those failures are all chronicled in these five books.

The 2020 Election, the January 6 "Insurrection," and Their Aftermath

The following five books cover every aspect of the 2020 Election, the January 6 "insurrection," and their aftermath. Starting with claims of fraud and irregularities in that election, to the tragic events of January 6, 2021 (J6; the so-called insurrection), the subsequent second impeachment of Donald J. Trump, to the public hearings of the J6 Commission in the summer and fall of 2022. Also reproduced in these books is all Trump had to say about these and related matters during this time.

Alleged Corruption, Bias, and Fraud: Allegations of the Corruption of Joe Biden, Bias of the Media and Big Tech, and Fraud in the 2020 Election

This book covers events from October 2020 to New Year's Day 2021 that are directly related to the 2020 presidential election. Those events include revelations about the alleged corruption of Joseph R. Biden via his son Hunter Biden. However, the mainstream media (MSM) and Big Tech did their best to hide that potential corruption from the American public, so that Biden could win the election. That worked, or so it was said. But allegations of voter fraud and anomalies abounded. This book investigates those claims to determine which are valid or not.

Trump's 2020 Election Tweets, Georgia Phone Call, and January 2021 Speeches: Did Trump's Claims of Election Fraud Lead to the Capitol Building Uprising?

This book reproduces all that Donald J. Trump said publicly from Election Day 2020 to the end of his presidency related to the 2020 presidential election. Many of Trump's claims about fraud or irregularities in the 2020 election are disputed. This does not necessarily mean they are false. With my comments, I mention which grievances are valid and which are not. But whether valid or not, Trump's claims of election fraud were said to have led to an insurrection in Washington DC on January 6, 2021. Reading this book will help the reader to decide if in fact Trump's comments led to that tragic event.

Tragic Ending to Donald J. Trump's Great Presidency: Capitol Building Uprising Leads to Impeachment 2.0, as Media and Big Tech Bias and Claims of Election Fraud Continues

Democrats claim the events of January 6, 2021 (J6) were "a deadly insurrection incited by Donald J. Trump." But this book demonstrates that J6, though tragic, was not deadly (with one exception), it was not an insurrection, and it was not incited by then President Trump. This book also updates issues covered in a previous book by the author related to the bias of the mainstream media (MSM) and of Big Tech and problems with the 2020 election.

Trump Fights Back with Statements: Against the Lies of Joe Biden, Attacks from Dems, and the Bias of the Media, of Big Tech, and of the J6 Commission

If you enjoyed reading Trump's Tweets on Twitter until January 8, 2021 or are enjoying his Truths on Truth Social since April 29, 2022, then you should enjoy this book. It fills in the gap with all of his email Statements issued between those dates. These Statements were often Trump fighting back against the lies of President Joe Biden. They also reflect Trump fighting back against the ongoing bias of the mainstream media (MSM) and of Big Tech and against the Dem-controlled Commission (which Trump calls the "Unselect Committee") investigating the tragic events of January 6, 2021 (J6).

The Biased J6 Select Committee: The Public Hearings Were Half a Trial; This Book Gives You the Other Half

The public hearings in the summer and fall of 2022 about the tragic events of January 6, 2021 (J6) were the prosecution presenting its case against Donald J. Trump, with the American public as the jury. But he was not afforded a defense. This book provides that defense.

Do not miss how dangerous this precedent was. What if this were you? How would you like it if primetime hearings were held prosecuting you, aired on all major networks, but without you being able to present a defense on such a grand scale? But this book presents the other side, so the reader can make an informed decision about J6 and Trump's role in it.

The First Impeachment of Donald J. Trump

The first impeachment of Donald J. Trump began when he made a phone call on July 25, 2019. A complaint about that phone call led to an impeachment inquiry and proceedings in the US House and a trial in the US Senate. This impeachment and trial was occurring against the backdrop of the 2020 Presidential election, which was already underway in the summer of 2019, even though the election itself was still over a year away. As will be seen, and as the title of this three-volume set implies, that election was in fact the real impetus for the impeachment.

The impeachment inquiry itself began in early September 2019 and ran up until February 5, 2020. This set will also mention additional important events that occurred during that time period. It will mostly conclude two days after the close of the Senate impeachment trial, on February 7, 2020. But several updates after that date will be included in Volume Three.

Dems Cannot Beat Trump, So They Impeach Trump: Volume One: Beginnings Through HIC Hearings (Early September Through Late November 2019)

This three-volume set covers the impeachment of Donald J. Trump that occurred over the fall of 2019 to the winter of 2020. It was yet one more attempt to oust the President from office by Democrats, who never accepted he won in 2016. A complaint about a phone call between President Trump and Ukraine President Zelensky led to an impeachment inquiry to begin in early September 2019. This Volume One covers the beginnings of the impeachment inquiry through the public hearings before the House Intelligence Committee (HIC).

Dems Cannot Beat Trump, So They Impeach Trump: Volume Two: HJC Hearings and Pre-Senate Trial Events (Mid-November 2019 to Mid-January 2020)

This second volume of this three volume set continues the discussion about the impeachment proceedings in the US House. It covers the public hearings before the House Judiciary Committee (HJC) and events that occurred up until the impeachment trial in the Senate. It also directly answers a question the author has often been asked—how can the author, as a conservative Christian, support such a "crude" person as President Donald J. Trump?

Dems Cannot Beat Trump, So They Impeach Trump: Volume Three: Senate Trial and Aftermath (Late January to Early February 2020, Updates Through October 2020)

This third volume of this three volume set covers the impeachment trial in the US Senate in January to February 2020 and its aftermath. In the trial, both sides were given an equal opportunity to present their arguments. This volume also provides updates of related issues up to just before the 2020 election. It focuses on the corruption of Joe Biden that Trump wanted investigated and which led to the impeachment inquiry.

Sexual Harassment Claims
and Political Incivility

Tearing the USA Apart: From Kavanaugh, to Incivility, to Caravans, to Violence, to the 2018 Midterm Elections, and Beyond

The United States of American is being torn apart by political differences more than any time since the 1960s and maybe since the Civil War of the 1860s. This division was amplified by political events in the summer to fall of 2018. This time period could prove to be seminal in the history of the United States. This tearing apart came to the forefront and was amplified during the confirmation proceedings for Supreme Court nominee Judge Brett Kavanaugh. This book overviews the Brett Kavanaugh confirmation proceedings in detail. It then overviews these additional major events that occurred up to the end of November 2018.

Christian Books

Analytical-Literal Translation
of the Old Testament

The Analytical-Literal Translation of the Old Testament (ALT: OT) is available in five volumes. Most Old Testaments are based on the Hebrew text. But this Old Testament is based on the Greek Septuagint (LXX). The LXX is a third century B.C. Greek translation of the Hebrew Bible. The importance of the LXX is that it was THE Bible of the early Church. The purpose of the ALT: OT is to provide a translation of the Greek Septuagint that will enable the reader to come as close to the Greek text as possible without having to be proficient in Greek.

Analytical-Literal Translation of the Old Testament (Septuagint) - Volume One - The Torah

This first volume contains the Torah (Genesis, Exodus, Leviticus, Numbers, Deuteronomy). These five books are foundational to the rest of the Bible, the Jewish and Christian religions, and God's plan of redemption.

Analytical-Literal Translation of the Old Testament (Septuagint) - Volume Two - The Historical Books

This second volume contains the Historical Books (Joshua, Judges, Ruth, 1Samuel, 2Samuel, 1Kings, 2Kings, 1Chronicles, 2Chronicles, Ezra, Nehemiah, Esther). These books present the LORD's providence in the history of the ancient Israelite nation.

Analytical-Literal Translation of the Old Testament (Septuagint) - Volume Three - The Poetic Books

This third volume contains the Poetic Books (Job, Psalms, Proverbs, Ecclesiastes, Song of Solomon).

These books contain praises to the LORD, honest expressions of personal struggles, wisdom sayings, and a romantic story.

Analytical-Literal Translation of the Old Testament (Septuagint) - Volume Four - The Prophetic Books

This fourth volume contains the Prophetic Books (Isaiah, Jeremiah, Lamentations, Ezekiel, Daniel, Hosea, Joel, Amos, Obadiah, Jonah, Micah, Nahum, Habakkuk, Zephaniah, Haggai, Zechariah, Malachi).

In these books, the LORD, speaking through His prophets, denounces Israel, Judah, and surrounding nations for their sins. These warnings are applicable to us today, as the USA and other nations are now engaging in similar sins. But there is also much uplifting material in these books, with the prophets expressing strong faith in the LORD in the face of hardships.

Analytical-Literal Translation of the Old Testament (Septuagint): Volume Five, Apocryphal/ Deuterocanonical Books

This fifth and final volume of the ALT: OT contains the "extra" books found in Roman Catholic and Eastern Orthodox Bibles as compared to Jewish and Protestant Bibles. There is much debate on whether these books are inspired by God or not. Only by reading them in a literal translation can you make a decision on this controversial issue. These books were written from 200 B. C. to 50 A.D. Therefore, whether inspired or not, they provide insight into Jewish history and thought shortly before and during the time of New Testament events and thus provide important background to the New Testament.

Analytical-Literal Translation of the New Testament

Analytical-Literal Translation of the New Testament: Third Edition (ALT3)

ALT3 is the only New Testament that is a literal translation of the second edition of the Byzantine Majority Greek Text, brings out nuances of the Greek text, and includes study aids within the text. It promotes understanding of what the New Testament writers originally wrote. No other English translation gets as close to the original text as the ALT. It is truly the ideal version for the serious student of the Bible.

Analytical-Literal Translation of the New Testament: Devotional Version (ALTD)

The main difference between ALTD and ALT3 is that in the ALTD the "analytical" information is footnoted, while in ALT3 such information is included within brackets within the text. That makes the information readily available, but it makes the text awkward to read and to quote from. By putting this information in footnotes, ALTD is a much easier to read and to quote from version.

Additional ALT Books

Analytical-Literal Translation of the Apostolic Fathers: Volume Seven of the ALT (ALT: APF)

This final volume of the ALT contains the writings of Church leaders of the late first to early second centuries (c. 80-150 AD). Some of these books were seriously considered for inclusion in the canon of the New Testament. They were ultimately rejected for the canon, but all of these books were popular in the early centuries of the Church. They provide insight into the mindset of the early Church immediately after the apostles and give background to the New Testament.

Companion Volume to the ALT

This volume provides aids in understanding the translations seen in the *Analytical-Literal Translation of the New Testament* (ALT). It includes a glossary for important words in the ALT, an-eight part "Grammatical Renderings" section to explain the unique translations in the ALT, along with other background information to the ALT.

Complete Concordance to the ALT

This volume indexes every occurrence of most words in the *Analytical-Literal Translation of the New Testament*. Only minor words are omitted, like: the, a, of, etc. Sufficient context is provided for the reader to recognize the verse or to get the gist of it.

How Were the Books of the Bible Chosen?

Christians claim the Bible is the Word of God, that it is the final authority in all matters relating to Christian faith and practice, and that it is absolutely reliable in all that it teaches. But to put such confidence in the Bible requires that the correct books are in the Bible. But is there? Why are the 66 books in the Bible in the Bible, and why were other books that could have been included not included? This three-volume set answers these and many related questions.

Why Are These Books in the Bible and Not Others? Volume One – A Translator's Perspective on the Canon of the Old Testament

This Volume One of a three volume set studies the books included in the Old Testament (OT) and considers other books that could have been included in it but were not. Each of the 39 books in the OT are reviewed in detail, and it is explained why they were included in the OT. Then the debate about the "extra" books found in Roman Catholic and Eastern Orthodox Bibles as compared to Protestant and Jewish Bibles is addressed. Lastly, other books that some wonder why they are not included in the OT are discussed. It is explained why these books were rejected.

Why Are These Books in the Bible and Not Others? Volume Two - A Translator's Perspective on the Canon of the New Testament

In this Volume Two of a three-volume set, each of the 27 books included in the New Testament are reviewed in detail. Who wrote them and when, their theology, and other pertinent background information are discussed to explain why they were included in the New Testament. Arguments against the traditional viewpoints on these books are addressed and refuted.

Why Are These Books in the Bible and Not Others? Volume Three - The Apostolic Fathers and the New Testament Apocrypha

This Volume Three of a three volume set covers books not included in the New Testament. These books include the writings of the Apostolic Fathers, who were Church leaders and writers of the late first to mid-second centuries, along with "apocryphal" books, both orthodox and Gnostic. Among these apocryphal books are some that have received much publicity of late and from which many people derive their ideas of early Christian history.

Sex and the Bible

These three books look in-depth at what the Bible has to say on sexual types of relationships and related issues. By this is meant: dating, premarital sex, marriage, divorce, remarriage, marital sex, extramarital sex, homosexuality, transsexualism, abortion, and birth control.

All three books go through the Scriptures systematically, looking at relevant passages of Scripture in order. The passages are written out, with commentary afterwards.

The first book is an introduction to the various subjects, quoting the most relevant Scriptures and with only short commentary. The next two books are much more detailed, with many more Scripture passages quoted and much more detailed commentary.

The Bible and Sexual Relationships Issues

In this book, explanations and interpretations are provided for each quoted Bible passage to aid the reader in understanding the Scriptures. However, the emphasis is on the Scriptures themselves. This format will

376

enable the reader to draw conclusions about what the Bible as a whole has to teach on these personal and very relevant issues.

God's Sex Plan: Volume One: What the Old Testament Teaches About Human Sexuality

Does God have a sex plan? By that is meant, did God design the human race to function best by following a specific plan for how human beings are to interact sexually and to reproduce? What happens when this plan is followed, and when it is not followed? Are different varieties of sexual behaviors just as legitimate as God's original sex plan?

God's Sex Plan: Volume Two: What the New Testament Teaches About Human Sexuality

Many issues are discussed in this set that are related to sex, including but not limited to: monogamy, marital sex, polygamy, incest, homosexuality, premarital sex (fornication), extramarital sex (adultery), celibacy, transsexualism, reproduction, infertility, contraception, abortion, sexual harassment and assault, masturbation, pornography, gender roles, and school and other mass shootings (yes, those are related to this topic).

Bible Study

The LORD Has It Under Control: What the Bible Teaches About the Sovereignty of God

This book is for the person struggling in life and for the person struggling with how God sovereignly works in people's lives. It goes through the Bible more or less in order. Along the way, I relate examples of how I believe the sovereignty of God has been operating in my life, in hopes that my experiences will help the reader to apply the principles to your life. It also addresses the question of the relationship of God's sovereignty to the human will or volition.

Scripture Workbook: For Personal Bible Study and Teaching the Bible: Second Edition

This book contains forty individual "Scripture Studies." It is divided into two volumes. Volume I covers the essential doctrines of the Christian faith. It is these doctrines that separate the true Christian faith from cultic and other deviations. Volume II of this book then covers controversial theologies, cults, and ethics.

Scripture Workbook: For Personal Bible Study and Teaching the Bible: Edition 1.1

This book contains twenty-two individual "Scripture Studies." Each study focuses on one general area of study. These studies enable individuals to do in-depth, topical studies of the Bible. They are also invaluable to the Bible study teacher preparing lessons for Sunday School or a home Bible study.

Bible Versions and Translation

Differences Between Bible Versions: Third Edition

Why do Bible versions differ? Why does the same verse read differently in different versions? Why do some versions contain words, phrases, and even entire verses that other versions omit? Which Bible versions are the most reliable? These and many other questions are answered in this book. Forty versions of the Bible are compared and evaluated.

New World Translation: A Reliable Bible Version? Edition 2.1

The NWT is the Bible of Jehovah's Witnesses. This review evaluates the NWT by looking at select passages from Paul's Epistle to the Ephesians. The standards I use are the same standards that I use in my book *Differences Between Bible Versions*. Simply put, does the translation faithfully and accurately render the Greek text into English?

Health and Fitness Books

Nutrition and the Bible

God-given Foods Eating Plan: For Lifelong Health, Optimization of Hormones, Improved Athletic Performance

The approach of this book is to study different foods and food groups, with a chapter devoted to each major classification of foods.

Trump Fights Back with Statements

First the Biblical evidence is considered, then the modern-day scientific research is reviewed. Foods are then classified as "God-given foods" and "non-God-given foods." The main point will be a healthy eating plan is composed of a variety of God-given foods and avoids non-God-given foods.

Creationist Diet: Nutrition and God-given Foods According to the Bible

This book has been superseded by the following book, but it is still available.

What did God give to human beings for food? What does the Bible teach about diet and nutrition? How do the Biblical teachings on foods compare to scientific research on nutrition and degenerative disease like heart disease, cancer, and stroke? These and other questions are addressed in this book.

Creationist Diet: Second Edition; A Comprehensive Guide to Bible and Science Based Nutrition

This Second Edition is 2-1/2 times as long and presents a different perspective on diet than the First Edition. The First Edition mostly advocated a vegan diet, while this Second Edition also advocates for a diet that includes animal foods. However, and this is very important, those animal foods are to be what are called "old-fashioned" meats, dairy, and eggs, not the "factory farm" products that most people eat. What is meant by these two terms and the incredible difference between them is explained in this book. In addition, this book covers a wide range of diet related topics to help the reader to understand how to live a healthier lifestyle according to God's design.

Powerlifting and Back Pain

Starting and Progressing in Powerlifting: A Comprehensive Guide to the World's Strongest Sport

This 350-page book is geared towards the beginner to intermediate powerlifter, along with the person just thinking about getting into the sport. This book presents sound training, competition, dietary, and supplement advice to aid the reader in starting and progressing in the sport of powerlifting. It will also help the reader to wade through the maze of federations, divisions, and supportive gear now found in powerlifting.

Overcoming Back Pain: A Mind-body Solution (Second Edition)

I powerlifted in college, but back pain forced me to stop lifting. Eventually, the back pain worsened to the point where I was crippled by it for six years. I tried various traditional and alternative treatments, but all to no avail. But then by utilizing mind-body techniques I was able to completely overcome the back pain, so much so that I was able to start powerlifting again.

Appendix Three
The Author's Websites, Newsletters, and Social Sites

This appendix provides details on my websites, newsletters, and social sites.

Zeolla.org
www.Zeolla.org

Zeolla.org is the personal website of Gary F. Zeolla. He is the author of Christian, fitness, and politics books, websites, and newsletters and is the translator of the *Analytical-Literal Translation of the Bible*. He has a B.S. in Nutrition Science (Penn State; 1983) and attended Denver Seminary (1988-90). He is also a powerlifter, holding fifteen all-time world records and over a hundred federation records.

This website provides links to all of my writings, along with information about my Christian faith, powerlifting, and other personal details. A detailed autobiography is also available on the site.

Biblical and Constitutional Politics
www.Zeolla.org/Politics

This website presents political articles and commentary from a conservative Christian and politically conservative perspective.

"Conservative Christian" includes the belief that the Bible is God-breathed and fully reliable in all that it teaches, including about politics.

"Politically conservative" refers to the belief in limited government, separation of powers, traditional values, personal and national security, capitalism, freedom and liberty, and most of all, an adherence to the Constitution of the United States, following an originalist interpretation thereof. Currently available on the website are over 200 webpages and thirteen books.

Darkness to Light
www.Zeolla.org/Christian

Darkness to Light ministry is dedicated to explaining and defending the Christian faith. Currently available on the website are over 1,600 webpages, over twenty books and eBooks, and a free email newsletter. In these materials, a wide range of topics are covered, including: theology, apologetics, cults, ethics, Bible versions, and much more, so you are sure to find something of interest.

The name for the ministry is taken from the following verse:
"...to open their eyes [in order] to turn [them] back from **darkness to light** and [from] the authority of Satan to God, [in order for] them to receive forgiveness of sins and an inheritance among the ones having been sanctified by faith in Me" (Acts 26:18).

The words "darkness" and "light" have a wide range of meanings when used metaphorically in Scripture, but basically, "darkness" refers to falsehood and unrighteousness while "light" refers to truth and righteousness. People turn from darkness to light when they come to believe the teachings of the Bible and live in accordance with them.

Fitness for One and All
www.Zeolla.org/Fitness

I have a B.S. in Nutrition Science (Penn State; 1983). I competed very successfully in powerlifting in my late teens to early twenties (1978-85), again in my 40s (2003-09), then again in my 50s (2015-2021). But health problems forced me to stop competing each time. Now in my 60s, I am attempting a third comeback.

With all I have been through, dealt with, and accomplished, it is now my passion to help others achieve their health, fitness, and performance goals. To that end, I set up Fitness for One and All website.

Currently available on the website are over 600 webpages, hundreds of weightlifting videos, five books and eBooks, and a free email newsletter. These materials are directed towards a wide range of people, including beginning fitness enthusiasts, athletes, powerlifters, and those dealing with health problems. The name "Fitness for One and All" reflects this diversity of covered topics.

Social Sites

Facebook: www.Facebook.com/GZeolla

Gab: https://gab.com/GZeolla

Gettr: https://gettr.com/user/GZeolla

Truth Social: https://truthsocial.com/@GZeolla

Twitter: https://twitter.com/GZeolla

I am sure the reader has heard of the first and last of these sites, but you might not have heard of the other three. That is because they are newer sites that were developed by conservatives in reaction to the other two "shadow banning" conservatives.

I might have been so shadow banned of late, though I am not sure. I just know there have been many times I have posted comments on Facebook or Twitter that I thought would bring a significant reaction, but nothing, no response whatsoever. But even if I haven't already, I am sure to be so in the future, as those sites crack down on conservative speech.

That is why I set up accounts on Gab, Gettr, and Truth Social, to be sure I have a place to voice my opinions. These sites promise not to censor people's comments, beyond what is required by law.

Note also, I rarely post to Twitter due to its 280-character limit, except when responding to Biden's tweets. If the reader hasn't figured it out by now, I'm not good at being concise in my writings. But by being so exhaustive, I thoroughly cover every topic I address. And if the reader peruses all of my writings on a given subject, you will be well-versed on the topic at hand.

That said, Truth Social has a 500-character limit, Gettr a 777-character limit, and Gab a 2,000 character limit, all of which I find a bit restrictive. Only Facebook has no such limits, so I mostly post to it.

On these social pages, I post about new items being posted on any of my four websites: my personal website, my Christian website, my fitness website, and my politics website. I also post personal updates, such as about my powerlifting.

On my social pages, I ignore all comments and replies that utilize "foul" or indecent language. That means, if you reply to one of my posts using such language, I will not even read your comments, let alone respond to them. I also will not respond to *ad hominem* (personal) attacks.

Simply put, if you cannot respond to the substance of my post in a civil manner, without resorting to name-calling, personal attacks, or foul language, you will not get a response. And if my post is a link to one of my articles or books, then read that item before responding. If you do not, I will just refer you back to it, and that will be that.

Contacting the Author

The translator can be contacted by using the email link on any of my four websites. Click on the "Contact Information" link near the bottom of any page of any site. But my preceding remarks about social media responses apply to emailed comments as well.

Reviews

It would be appreciated if the reader would write a review of this book on Amazon and/ or wherever you purchased it. Such reviews are a benefit to others who might be thinking of purchasing this book, and it is a help to me to know what readers like and do not like about this book. It would also be helpful if you would mention this book on whatever social media sites you participate in. Many thanks in advance for doing so.

Made in the USA
Monee, IL
08 August 2024

63476864R00213